REACTION AND REFORM IN NEW JERSEY

EDITED BY
MICHAEL P. RICCARDS

PREFACE BY
GEORGE E. HALL

HALL INSTITUTE OF PUBLIC POLICY – NEW JERSEY
2007

A publication in the series: New Jersey 2020

CONTRIBUTORS

Michel M. Bitritto, PhD
Assistant Director of Innovation Management Enterprise Development Center, New Jersey Institute of Technology. This report was prepared for the New Jersey Commission on Science and Technology, 2006.

Joel C. Cantor, ScD
Director, Center for State Health Policy; Professor of the Department of Public Policy, Rutgers-The State University of New Jersey.

Mary Ellen Cook, MPP
Research Analyst, Rutgers Center for State Health Policy, Rutgers-The State University of New Jersey.

Ronald Chen, Esq.
Public Advocate, State of New Jersey and former Associate Dean for Academic Affairs at the Rutgers University Law School.

Sasha Corchado
Project Manager—New Jersey at the Regional Plan Association.

Thomas G. Dallessio
Executive Director, Leadership New Jersey and former Vice President and New Jersey Director at the Regional Plan Association.

Hon. Bob Franks
This economic study was conducted by Deloitte Consulting LLP. The article was contributed by the Hon. Franks, the current President, HealthCare Institute of New Jersey and former U.S. Representative from New Jersey.

Paula A. Franzese, JD
Peter W. Rodino Professor of Law, Seton Hall University School of Law and Chair of the New Jersey State Ethics Commission.

George E. Hall
Founder of the Hall Institute of Public Policy–New Jersey and majority shareholder of The Clinton Group, Inc., New York, New York.

Christopher Jones
Vice President for Research at the Regional Plan Association.

Richard A. Lee
Director of Communications of the Hall Institute of Public Policy–New Jersey, and former Deputy Director of Communications for Governor James McGreevey and Acting Governor Richard Codey. He is a PhD candidate in Media Studies at Rutgers University, New Brunswick, New Jersey.

Lovie E. B. Lilly, Ed.D.
Principal, Columbia High School, Maplewood-South Orange Public Schools.

Donald B. Louria, MD
Professor and Chairman Emeritus of the Department of Preventive Medicine, University of Medicine and Dentistry of New Jersey, Newark, New Jersey.

Robert Lucky, PhD
AT&T Bell Labs, 1961–1992, Executive Director, Communications Sciences Research Division and Telcordia Technologies, 1992–2002, Corporate Vice President, Applied Research.

Hon. Daniel J. O'Hern, Sr.
Retired Associate Justice, Supreme Court of New Jersey and Special Ethics Counsel to Governor Codey.

Alexis Perrotta
Senior Policy Analyst at the Regional Plan Association.

Salvatore Pizzuro, Ed.D.
A psychometrician, researcher, college professor, disability policy specialist, and advocate for children with disabilities and their families at New Jersey's Office of Administrative Law.

Michael Presutti
Independent scholar; Chief of Special Operations of Homeland Safety, nationally recognized construction expert, and syndicated newspaper columnist on construction, renovation, architecture, and emerging technology.

John Luciano Renne, PhD
Assistant Professor and Associate Director of the University of New Orleans Transportation Center in the College of Urban and Public Affairs.

Michael P. Riccards, PhD
Executive Director, Hall Institute of Public Policy—New Jersey; former Public Policy Scholar at the College Board in Washington, DC, and a college president at three institutions.

Frank Rusch, PhD
Professor of Education, School Psychology and Special Education at The Pennsylvania State University.

Lisa Uber
Doctoral Student at Rutgers University, School of Communication, Information and Library Studies; currently a Business Development Communication Consultant for Johnson & Johnson, and former Senior Project Manager at AT&T.

Thomas K. Wright
Executive Vice President at the Regional Plan Association.

TABLE OF CONTENTS

POLICY DEBATES

PREFACE

Last year, it was my personal pleasure to introduce two innovations on behalf of the Hall Institute of Public Policy. To encourage debate and discussion in the U.S. Senate race in New Jersey, we established a "virtual debate" site, which asked the candidates questions on the major issues facing our state and nation. We were impressed by the quality of the responses and the feedback we received from the public. This virtual debate was the first on-line political debate in the history of this state.

Then, the Institute published the first volume in its new series, *New Jersey 2020,* which reprinted some of the longer pieces on our website. Copies were sent to the State's elected officials, agency heads, media, and university and college libraries. Now we are printing the second such volume, titled *Reaction and Reform in New Jersey.*

This past year in New Jersey has been a major period of self-examination, criticism, and varied attempts at change, reform, and protection of the status quo. Any serious discussion of public policy needs to examine facts, assertions, data, and speculations, which we do in this book. We even look at two aspects of New Jersey life and culture that have received some attention in the last year or so.

I look forward to your responses to our continuing work and continuing commitment.

Sincerely,
GEORGE E. HALL
Founder

FOREWORD

The Hall Institute of Public Policy in New Jersey is a non-partisan, not-for-profit think tank located in Trenton, which explores the complex dimensions of policy issues that impact on that state and the nation. The Institute was founded in 2005 by George E. Hall, and it reflects his commitment to the use of knowledge to further solutions to our common challenges. Public policy is the nexus of a society's economic, social, political, and cultural developments, which in turn create priorities for the whole society.

This volume, the second in the series, *New Jersey 2020*, begins with a preface by the Institute's founder, George Hall, outlining some of the important successes and innovations of the Institute in the past year. The volume takes a broad sweep across New Jersey's current array of concerns from public policy to public perceptions.

The agenda in the last several years, especially at the state level, has focused on the issue of public ethics reform, thus this volume contains the report of the special ethics counsels to the 2005 acting governor, Richard Codey, by Retired Associate Justice of the Supreme Court Daniel J. O'Hare and Professor Paula A Franzese, Peter W. Rodino Professor of Law at Seton Hall University School of Law. It outlines many of the prescriptions that have been advanced for reforming our governmental system. Another major issue, which has preoccupied the new governor and the legislature, is tax reform. A guidebook on how one can evaluate the worth of different reform proposals was prepared by the Regional Plan Association and is included here.

One explosive state, local, and national issue is the use by various levels of government of the traditional right to eminent domain. With the US Supreme Court's controversial decision in Kilo v. City of New London, Connecticut, et. al. (2005), the whole issue of the "proper" power of government in this area has brought anguished calls for a closer examination. In the State of New Jersey, one such thoughtful analysis was done by the new Public Advocate, Ronald Chen.

Also, living in a state where transportation and economic access are so important, this volume includes the conclusions of a major work by Professor John Luciano Renne of the University of New Orleans. He examines methodologies for understanding the benefits and costs of transit-oriented development. On a more theoretical level, Lisa Uber of the Communications Department of Rutgers University looks at communication in a small community in New Jersey, and offers recommendations for resolving a seemingly intractable community conflict.

Another area of interest is research and medical care—two important and often interlocking economic industries. Robert Lucky, formerly of Bell Labs and Telcordia Technologies, expresses his deep concern that New Jersey is losing its long-standing commitment to research-driven industries, which has played such a critical role in its economic success. The HealthCare Institute of New Jersey commissioned a study by Deloitte Consulting on the status of pharmaceutical and medical technology industries. With their $27 billion impact, the entire State is dependent on their successes and future prospects. The New Jersey Commission on Science and Technology has also examined the growth of nanotechnology—a comparative newcomer with enormous potential. Lastly, in the area of medical care, this volume includes a major study conducted for the Rutgers Center for State Health Policy by Mary Ellen Cook and Joel Cantor on cardiovascular disease in the State.

Here, as in all the states, a major concern is education. Added to this volume are several selections from our extensive website, www.hallnj.org. Dr. Donald Lourie of the University of Medicine and Dentistry of New Jersey calls on schools to adopt a systems approach to teach socially-connected thinking. Independent scholar and expert on homeland security, Michael Presutti, presents a very different sort of education—a suggested treatment for criminal recidivism using hands-on, construction industry apprenticeships.

Lovie E. B. Lilly, the principal at Columbia High School in the South Orange-Maplewood system, discusses the challenges faced by recent immigrant children from Haiti, and what our schools might do to assist them. Advocates for the disabled, Sal Pizzuro and Frank Rush, address the postgraduate, statewide needs of students with disabilities.

The State has also seen the publication of two highly controversial and well-publicized memoirs from former governor James McGreevey and his wife, Dina. Richard Lee, his former deputy director of communications and long-time associate in Woodbridge, takes on the complexities of McGreevey, and compares him to the late Richard Nixon. Lee, who is now Director of Communications at the Hall Institute, raises important, larger issues related to Americans' attitudes toward their leaders. Last year also witnessed the establishment of a statewide poll to garner the names of the most famous New Jerseyans; among the names raised was long-time vocalist and actor Frank Sinatra. Here, I explore some of the contours of his long career and how America itself changed in that period.

Taken together, this volume weaves a rich tapestry of New Jersey—its interests, its challenges, its possible futures, and also its checkered past. It is also a chronicle of its reactions to the acceleration of the State's problems and of many honest attempts to reformulate our laws, customs, and, more importantly, our behavior in the twenty-first century.

MICHAEL P. RICCARDS
Trenton, NJ 2007

CHAPTER ONE

Summary Report of the Special Ethics Counsel to the Governor of the State of New Jersey

ETHICS REFORM RECOMMENDATIONS FOR THE
EXECUTIVE BRANCH OF NEW JERSEY GOVERNMENT
SPECIAL COUNSEL FOR ETHICS REVIEW AND COMPLIANCE

By

Daniel J. O'Hern, Sr.,
Retired Associate Justice,
Supreme Court of New Jersey

Professor Paula A. Franzese,
Peter W. Rodino Professor of Law,
Seton Hall University School of Law

Dedication

This report is dedicated to all those who labor in the trenches of public service. Our research, interviews, and analysis of the ethics audit responses left us with the indelible impression of firm resolve on the part of state employees to serve the public honestly and faithfully. More than anything, we must reinforce their resolve by demonstrating that every level of government supports their efforts.

Introduction

Our faith in government has been shaken. But this moment in history has given us the opportunity to chart a new course. Together, we have begun to restore faith, integrity, and hope to our government.... There is nothing more important to our democracy than the trust of the citizens. And when that trust waivers, the question is not whether we should act...but how much we can achieve.

> Acting Governor Richard J. Codey,
> *State of the State Address*
> *(January 11, 2005)*

On November 17, 2004, Acting Governor Richard J. Codey appointed us Special Ethics Counsel, charged with the responsibility of recommending ethics reforms for the Executive Branch of New Jersey's Government. We commend Governor Codey for his leadership and courage in giving us so significant a mandate, and we thank him for this opportunity to serve the State.

Although our mandate is broad, it is not all-encompassing. Our work is part of a larger mosaic of effort by public and private-sector parties. An effective system of advancing integrity in government requires a tripartite approach. The three major features recognized in most jurisdictions are: (1) the regulation of legislative and executive lobbying; (2) rules of conduct for government officials; and (3) campaign and finance practices. Our mission is limited to the second element, the rules of conduct for members of the Executive Branch of state government and its independent authorities. The other two pillars of integrity must be strengthened as well.

In pursuit of our mission to examine the rules of conduct governing state employees, we thoroughly reviewed the State's existing ethics and conflicts laws. We also conducted an extensive audit of ethics programs in the Executive Branch agencies, departments, and independent state authorities. In addition, we engaged in a comparative review of other state and federal ethics models, conducted numerous interviews, and solicited and reviewed public comment. Our research, interviews, and analysis of the ethics audit responses left us with the indelible impression of firm resolve on the part of state employees to serve the public honestly and faithfully. They deeply resent any outside influences on the performance of their duties.

More than anything, we must reinforce their resolve by demonstrating that every level of government supports those in the trenches of public service.

Our report proceeds on the simple principle that public office is a public trust. Recent scandals have shaken that trust. Yet, as Governor Codey has made clear, this unique moment in New Jersey's history has provided the opportunity to chart a new course that transcends partisanship and recaptures the promise of our great state.

The public wants and deserves assurances that it can rely on the integrity of its elected and appointed leaders. Citizens want and deserve evidence that leaders are making an ethical culture the central hub of governance. They want leaders who will guide managers at all levels to do the right thing when faced with tough decisions. They want to see less partisan politics and more public interest politics.

The report that we issue today sets forth a series of sweeping recommendations that include the creation of a newly-empowered and independent watchdog, to be known as the State Ethics Commission, significant enforcement and compliance checks, stringent penalties for transgressors, mandatory ethics training for all state officials and employees, routine ethics auditing, more stringent anti-nepotism laws, more effective post-employment restrictions, transparency in the contracting process, a zero-tolerance policy on the acceptance of gifts, and the imposition of the ethics laws upon gubernatorial transition teams. The public interest deserves no less.

Throughout, our recommendations aim to promote transparency and accountability in all aspects of government activity in order to better monitor ethical performance from top to bottom. As US Supreme Court Justice Brandeis observed, "Sunlight is said to be the best of disinfectants." (Louis Brandeis, Other People's Money 62, Nat'l Home Library Found. ed. 1933).

Moreover, experience teaches that it is not enough to impose strictures on state employees. Most ethics violations do not occur without the participation and consent of third parties. Hence, we have prepared and appended to our Full Report a Business Ethics Guide for third parties that do business with the State. We recommend that certification of compliance with its terms be required of all who do business, or hope to do business, with the State.

We are not so naive as to believe that our recommendations will change human nature. No regulation will deter a person determined to challenge the public interest and public trust. Still, formal rules that establish clear standards regarding performance and punishment are essential to communicate that transgressions will not be tolerated and that ethics is everyone's business.

Thomas Jefferson warned, "In every government on earth there is some trace of human weakness, some germ of corruption and degeneracy, which cunning will discover and wickedness insensibly open, cultivate, and improve. Every government degenerates when trusted to the rulers of the people alone. The people themselves therefore are its only safe depositories." (Thomas Jefferson, Notes on the State of Virginia in Merrill D. Peterson, ed., Library of Am., Literary Classics of the United States 1984) (1781–1782). Although our recommendations are significant, without a commitment that survives the current climate of ethics reform all that we will have succeeded in doing is putting more laws on the books. Ultimately, it is human oversight, rooted in leadership from the top and an unrelenting pledge to good government, that serves as the most effective and enduring check.

Implementing the systemic changes that we recommend can help to set the stage for a renewed partnership of government, its employees, and the public. By rebuilding the public's trust, we can, in the words of Governor Codey, "show government as a force for compassion and a beacon of hope." Restoring a sense of nobility and accountability to government service is vital to this enterprise. When public employees come to believe that they and their work are unseen or unimportant, a window of vulnerability opens. We are convinced that the recommendations in our report and the continuing leadership that this initiative represents have the potential to close or at least narrow that window and open a door back to the future, so that New Jersey can reclaim its great promise.

Summary of Principal Recommendations

1. CREATE AN ENTIRELY NEW, INDEPENDENT, AND PROACTIVE ENFORCEMENT AGENCY, CALLED THE "STATE ETHICS COMMISSION."

A. Make The State Ethics Commission An Independent Watchdog.
The new State Ethics Commission should replace the existing Executive Commission on Ethical Standards (ECES). To ensure maximum independence:
- The State Ethics Commission should be bipartisan and, ultimately, be composed entirely of seven public members;
- Commission members should serve staggered four-year terms;
- The Commission's Chair and Vice-Chair should be elected by its members to two-year terms.

Governor Codey has proposed legislation that would transform the newly-named State Ethics Commission from a nine-member body, with seven members from the Executive Branch and two public members, into a seven-member body, with three members from the Executive Branch and four public members. Not more than two of its public members would be of the same political party, and a Chair would be selected from among its public members. Several of our recommendations are embodied in that Bill. Given the strength of the Governor's commitment to ethics reform, this movement toward change should pave the way for implementation, over time, of an entirely independent body composed of seven public members, while also assuring a smooth transition toward that end.

B. Vest The State Ethics Commission With Much Greater Enforcement Powers Than Those Possessed By The Existing Executive Commission On Ethical Standards.
Presently, many of the State's ethical strictures are well-intended, but toothless. The new State Ethics Commission should be vested with vigorous enforce-

ment mechanisms, as well as with the responsibility for undertaking routine ethics audits and for implementing mandatory ethics training programs. It should have the authority to impose a broad range of significant penalties for non-compliance and ethics violations. The range of penalties should include:

- Removal from office;
- Suspension from office;
- Demotion;
- Public censure;
- Reprimand;
- Restitution of any pecuniary benefits received as a result of an ethics violation;
- Mandatory late filing fees (up to $50 per day) for failure to file required disclosure and authorization forms in a timely manner;
- Mandatory civil penalties (up to $10,000 per violation) for violations of post-employment restrictions.

Further, the Commission's jurisdiction should be expanded to include transgressors who leave state service, provided the Commission's investigation begins within two years past the date on which the alleged violation has been committed. That expanded jurisdiction would prevent state employees from escaping liability for ethical breaches simply by leaving state employ.

Finally, the Commission will have to coordinate its work closely with the Inspector General's Office, the State Auditor's Office, the State Commission of Investigation, and the Office of Government Integrity in the Attorney General's Office.

C. Require The State Ethics Commission To Conduct Mandatory Ethics Training For All State Employees.

The State Ethics Commission should be staffed with a full-time Training Officer with adequate support personnel, and charged with the responsibility of creating, coordinating, and refining comprehensive mandatory ethics training programs, both in-person and on-line. Each agency or department's Ethics Liaison Officer (ELO) should be required to coordinate with the Training Officer to facilitate the ethics training programs that the Training Officer develops.

Mandatory ethics training programs should include:

- Annual briefings and routine refresher courses on ethics and standards of conduct for all state employees and officers [References throughout this Summary to state "officer" or "employee" refer to any person holding office or employment in any state agency, i.e., any principal department, board, commission, authority, state college or university, and any other instrumentality, created by or allocated to a principal department.];
- Annual financial-integrity training for all state officers, board members of all state entities, and employees vested with procurement-related authority.

D. Enable The State Ethics Commission To Perform Regular And Systematic Ethics Audits And Monitoring For Ethics Compliance.

The State Ethics Commission should be staffed with a full-time Ethics Compliance Officer and adequate support personnel to ensure that, in each agency, all required employee disclosures are monitored for compliance, and all ethics codes and notices are distributed to and acknowledged by all employees. Duties of the Ethics Compliance Officer should include:

- Tracking compliance on matters including outside employment; business activities; gifts; financial disclosures; contacts by legislators, lobbyists, or governmental-affairs agents; procurements and contracts; and attendance at outside events.

E. Coordinate The Duties Of The State Ethics Commission With Those Of Other Agencies Charged With Fighting Fraud, Waste, And Ethical Misconduct In Government.

The Commission should routinely communicate and coordinate its efforts with those of the State Auditor, the Inspector General, the State Commission of Investigations, and the Office of Government Integrity of the Attorney General's Office. Just as there are joint task forces of state and federal agencies to fight crime or pollution, there can and should be a joint task force of the several agencies to fight fraud, waste, and ethical misconduct in government.

F. Improve Access To Ethics Advice and Information.

To improve access to ethics advice and information, we recommend that:

- A new, toll-free, confidential reporting hotline be made available to all state employees and to the general public for purposes of voicing concerns, asking questions, and making complaints;
- All financial disclosure forms be viewable on the Commission's website.

1. ENACT A UNIFORM ETHICS CODE, APPLICABLE TO ALL STATE EMPLOYEES, TO CONSOLIDATE THE STATE'S SCATTERED ETHICS LAWS INTO A SINGLE ACT.

Currently, state ethics restrictions are set forth in a multitude of separate codes and in the regulations of a myriad of diverse agencies. Uniform baseline standards of conduct should be enacted and made applicable to all state employees. Our proposed Uniform Ethics Code, appended to our Full Report, simplifies, clarifies, and modernizes the otherwise disparate governing strictures. Our recommendation requires:

- The State Ethics Commission to promulgate a single code of ethics, binding upon the Executive Branch, that adopts all applicable provisions of our proposed Uniform Ethics Code, as supplemented by relevant agency-specific strictures.

2. IMPLEMENT A PLAIN LANGUAGE ETHICS GUIDE THAT CAN BE EASILY UNDERSTOOD BY ALL STATE EMPLOYEES AND THE PUBLIC.

A Plain Language Ethics Guide should be adopted to explain clearly and plainly to all state employees and to the public the ethical standards and requirements that must be met by every state employee. We have drafted, and appended to our Full Report, a Plain Language Ethics Guide that reflects the current New Jersey Conflicts of Interest Law (Conflicts Law), N.J.S.A.52:13D-12 to Ð28.

We recommend that:
- Every state employee be required to certify that he or she has read the guide, understands it, and vows to uphold its terms. With that requirement in place, no employee will ever be able to use ignorance of the law as a viable defense to an ethics violation.

4. IMPLEMENT A BUSINESS ETHICS GUIDE THAT IS BINDING ON THIRD PARTIES THAT DO BUSINESS WITH THE STATE.

It is not enough to impose strictures on state employees. Most ethics violations do not occur without the participation and consent of third parties. Hence, we have drafted, and appended to our Full Report, a plain language Business Ethics Guide for third parties that conduct business with the State. Currently, there are no penalties for businesses that commit ethics violations.

Our recommendations require that:
- All persons who do business with the State certify, in writing, that they understand the rules of the Business Ethics Guide and that they are in compliance with those rules;
- A certification of compliance with the Business Ethics Guide be a prerequisite for the submission of any bid to do business with the state; penalties for noncompliance would include the disqualification of the bid.

5. PROVIDE LEADERSHIP FROM THE TOP.

The Governor should set the appropriate tone and lead by example and initiative, to avoid even an appearance of impropriety.

Toward that end, we recommend that:
- The Executive Director of the State Ethics Commission meet with every new Cabinet member shortly after inauguration;
- The Executive Director of the State Ethics Commission appear before the Cabinet at least once each year to remind all members of the ethics strictures.

The Governor's Code of Conduct, promulgated by an independent advisory panel pursuant to Executive Order 77 (McGreevey 2002), contains thorough and significant strictures consistent with the core premise that leadership and direction must come from the top. The Governor's Code of Conduct is appended to our Full Report.

6. CLOSE THE REVOLVING DOOR OF UNDUE INFLUENCE BY ADOPTING RIGOROUS POST-EMPLOYMENT RESTRICTIONS AND EFFECTIVE FOLLOW-UP PROCEDURES.

Presently, a general post-employment restriction prohibits a former state officer or employee, or special state officer or employee, from representing or acting on behalf of a party other than the State in connection with any matter in which the employee was substantially and directly involved during his or her state tenure. That is a lifelong restriction, but the only enforcement mechanism is a disorderly-persons penalty, which has never been imposed.

To construct laws that are stronger, realistic, and readily enforceable, we recommend:

- A new, explicit lifetime ban on all former state officers' and employees' use of confidential information;
- A general two-year post-employment restriction prohibiting a former state employee from representing an entity on any matter that he or she was substantially and directly involved in while in state service (That ban would allow highly qualified individuals to enter government service with the expectation that they will be able to continue to earn a living after they leave state employ. Consistent with the experience of other jurisdictions, after two years, former state employees are apt to be sought by new employers for their expertise, rather than for their ability to influence government officials.);
- A new one-year ban on "side-switching" to apply to designated state officers, heads, deputy heads, and assistant heads of principal departments, boards, commissions, and authorities (That ban would prohibit such an employee, for one year after leaving state service, from representing anyone on any matter before the agency in which he or she was employed. Our investigation revealed the significant concern about the appearance of impropriety that arises when a former senior official appears before his or her agency shortly after leaving government service.
- Greatly enhanced penalties for violating post-employment restrictions, applicable to former employees and their new employers; those penalties should include fines of up to $10,000 per offense.);

7. STRENGTHEN ANTI-NEPOTISM LAWS.

The legislature's 2004 enactment prohibiting certain relatives of state officials from serving in state government positions, N.J.S.A. 52:14-7.1, was a step in the right direction. Currently, however, there are no enforcement mechanisms or penalty provisions in the statute to ensure compliance. Therefore, we recommend the following:

- Make N.J.S.A. 52:14-7.1 part of the Conflicts Law, giving the State Ethics Commission the authority to impose a broad range of penalties for violations;
- Prohibit state officers and employees from participating in decisions to hire, retain, promote, or determine the salary of any member of their immediate family, any cohabitant, or person with whom the officer or employee has a dating relationship;
- Prohibit every state officer and employee from supervising or exercising authority over immediate family members, cohabitants, or persons with whom the officer or employee has a dating relationship.

Those recommended strictures are delineated in our proposed Uniform Ethics Code.

8.   IMPOSE THE ETHICS LAWS ON ADMINISTRATION TRANSITION TEAMS.

The ethical responsibilities and obligations of a newly-elected state adminis-tration begin not on a governor's inaugural day, but on the very first day that a tran-sition team is formed. Policies and operational and personnel decisions are forged during a transition. Consequently, the public trust is involved. Currently, transi-tion teams are not subject to the ethics laws applicable to other Executive Branch employees. To increase public confidence, we recommend that all full-time, paid transition team members:

- Be subject to the constraints of the ethics laws immediately upon appointment, and that their salaries and sources of income be fully disclosed;
- Be notified of the ethics and conflicts laws and receive ethics training immediately upon appointment, and that they be required to certify, in writing, that they are in compliance with those strictures, including all financial disclosure requirements.

We also recommend that the Gubernatorial Transition Act, N.J.S.A. 52:15A-1 to -5, be amended to subject full-time, paid transition team members to the Con-flicts Law.

9.   ENSURE TRANSPARENCY AND PROMOTE INTEGRITY IN THE CONTRACTING PROCESS.

With certain amendments to expand its scope, we recommend that the Karcher-Scutari Bill, S. 2194, 211th Leg. § 2 (N.J. 2004), be enacted to implement the State Commission of Investigation's (SCI) June 2004 recommendation that, once a matter has entered the procurement process, any contact related to the procurement between state employees and representatives of active or prospective state vendors be memorialized in writing, so that a public record can be maintained to ensure the transparency of such contacts. In order to close the circle of improper influences in the bidding process, we recommend that all intra-government contacts with state procurement officers also be memorialized in writing.

10. ADOPT A ZERO-TOLERANCE POLICY ON GIFTS.

In 2004, the legislature passed a law allowing Executive Branch officials to receive up to $250 total value in gifts, annually, from governmental affairs agents, thereby conflicting with current ECES guidelines. To eliminate confusion and to make the gift bar even more rigorous, we recommend:

- A new, simple, flat ban, prohibiting all Executive Branch employees from accepting any and all gifts or other things of value from any source other than the State for any matter related to their official duties. That zero-tolerance policy will establish a clear, bright-line standard that is easy to apply and helps to avoid even the appearance of impropriety.

OVERVIEW OF OUR FULL REPORT

Our Full Report consists of three chapters and a comprehensive Appendix. Chapter One provides an overview of our methodology, a history of ethics reform in New Jersey, and a comprehensive discussion of existing Executive Branch ethics programs and strictures. Chapter Two contains a detailed analysis of the results of our Ethics Audit. Chapter Three provides a detailed consideration of each of our recommendations, together with national comparisons.

Our appendices include: (1) our proposed Uniform Ethics Code; (2) our recommended Plain Language Ethics Guide; (3) our proposed Business Ethics Guide; (4) our Ethics Audit survey; (5) ethics training prototypes; and (6) various compilations of State and national data relevant to the task of ethics reform.

CONCLUSION

A fundamental principle of democracy is that a representative government must hold the public's trust. All government exists by the consent of the governed. Scandals undermine the public's trust in the integrity of government and threaten the fundamental premise of democracy.

Today in New Jersey, trust has been broken, and, as a result, the actions of political leaders now face more skeptical investigation than ever before. How do we restore trust? Unethical or improper behavior on the part of state officials or employees is the exception and not the rule; nevertheless, from time to time, we are reminded that our laws and regulations may not be adequate to the times and circumstances.

The best answer to potential ethical problems in government is honest people in a proper and ethical environment. Still, formal regulation is required. As part of a comprehensive approach, clear rules regarding performance and punishment have an important role to play. They can express the core values of an organization and set governing standards. But expression of core values and standards is not enough. Building values within an organization requires leadership.

During our review, we often asked, "What is the cornerstone of good government?" Hard-working citizens of our State, like Herbert Bashir of Irvington, said, "We need a return to concern for the public trust." Don Wisnowski, a former serviceman and resident of Little Falls, said, "At every level of government, many leaders have lost sight of the reason why they're there and of the values that this country was founded on. I'm heartsick about this, because I love our State." Bob Loughrey, proprietor of Uncle Bob's Ice Cream Shop in Cedar Grove, said, "Ethics in government means that our leaders should be doing the right thing for the people, not for themselves. We want them to do the right thing, not necessarily the popular thing."

Trust is the cornerstone of good government. By restoring public trust, we can, in the words of Governor Codey, "show government as a force for compassion and a beacon of hope." The time is now.

The Full Report, with all appendices, is available from the
Office of the Governor and available on-line at
http://www.nj.gov/ethics_report.pdf

Summary dated March 14, 2005

CHAPTER TWO

Fundamental
Property Tax Reform II
A Guide for
Evaluating Proposals
May 2006

A REGIONAL PLAN ASSOCIATION AND
LINCOLN INSTITUTE OF LAND POLICY PARTNERSHIP PROJECT

Acknowledgements

Regional Plan Association would like to thank our partner in this project, the Lincoln Institute of Land Policy, for both its financial support and intellectual contribution. We particularly appreciate the insights and guidance provided by Armando Carbonell, Senior Fellow and Cochairman of the Department of Planning and Development. We would also like to thank Paul Gottlieb, PhD, Associate Professor of Agricultural, Food and Resource Economics, Rutgers University, Cook College, for lending his expertise to this effort. Finally, RPA thanks its Property Tax Reform Steering Committee for its comments and insights.

This report was written by Christopher Jones and Alexis Perrotta with the assistance of Thomas Dallessio, Thomas Wright, and Sasha Corchado. It was designed by Jeffrey Ferzoco.

Property Tax Reform Steering Committee

Stephanie Bush Baskette
Carol Cronheim
Christopher J. Daggett
Hon. James J. Florio
Robert Goldsmith
Pamela Hersh
Susan Lederman
Joseph Maraziti
Anthony Marchetta
Eileen McGinnis
Sean Monaghan
Rebecca Perkins
Ingrid Reed

Summary

Reform Scenarios Rated by Crtieria	Reform Scenario				
	Vary by State Planning Area	Statewide Rate	Countywide Rate	Income Tax Substitution	Split Rate Taxation
Land Use and Social Equity					
Consistency with State Plan	High	Moderate	Moderate	Moderate	High
Housing Affordability	Moderate	Moderate	Moderate	High	High
Education Equity	High	Low	Low	High	Moderate
Efficiency and Fiscal Health					
Flexibility	High	Low	Moderate	Moderate	High
Fiscal Discipline	Moderate	Moderate	High	Low	Moderate
Fiscal Stability	Moderate	Moderate	Moderate	Low	Moderate
Local Autonomy	Low	Low	Moderate	High	High

Property tax reform and school spending were two of the most important issues during the 2005 gubernatorial election, and, in 2006, New Jersey elected officials are likely to consider specific legislation or constitutional amendments for reform. A widespread desire for relief from some of the highest property taxes in the nation is the driving force, but that is far from the only objective. High property tax rates are seen as damaging the economic competitiveness of the state and exacerbating inequities between property-rich and property-poor municipalities. New Jersey's heavy reliance on local property taxes also leads to perverse land use decisions by causing municipalities to shun otherwise beneficial housing development for fear of higher taxes, and compete for an overabundance of other development that brings in net fiscal benefits.

While there have been many general calls for reform, and some detailed proposals have been promoted, the debate, thus far, has lacked a fundamental framework for comparing proposals. This study attempts to fill that gap by comparing the potential impact of a range of school property tax reforms across a set of established criteria. To demonstrate the usefulness of this approach, five ideas for reform are evaluated. While these by no means exhaust the range of potential reforms, they include several prominent ideas and are sufficiently varied to demonstrate that the criteria can be used to compare very different concepts.

(Proposal 1) Vary the school property tax by state planning areas. This scenario would decrease school property taxes in places where the State Plan would encourage growth (such as planning areas 1 and 2 in urban and suburban centers), and increase taxes in the rest of the State to discourage growth there (such as in fringe, rural, and environmentally sensitive areas).

(Proposal 2) Assess all school property taxes at one statewide rate. This scenario would make all municipalities' school property tax rates identical, under the assumption that the funds would be redistributed and municipalities' spending on schools would not change.

(Proposal 3) Assess all school property taxes at a county rate, and consolidate school districts at the county level. This proposal would replace local school property taxes with a countywide tax, and consolidate all 611 school districts into 21 county-level school districts.

(Proposal 4) Substitute half the property tax with an income tax surcharge. Under this proposal, also known as NJ SMART, each resident's school property tax would be reduced by half. Municipalities would be reimbursed by the State for the decrease in property tax revenue. The State would raise the revenue for these reimbursements with a statewide surcharge on the income tax.

(Proposal 5) Split the school property tax rate into a higher land tax and a lower tax on buildings and improvements. This scenario proposes taxing land and built property at different rates, with land taxed more heavily. Taxes on built properties would decrease to create a revenue neutral-result at the municipal level.

Each of these proposals has its own set of intentions and theoretical underpinnings. Some are geared toward stopping sprawl, for example, while others are intended to create a fairer tax system or to ease the school tax burden on poorer municipalities. To gauge the full effect of each proposal, the five ideas are assessed, in both quantitative and qualitative terms, according to a set of seven public policy criteria previously outlined in an October 2005 RPA study, "Fundamental Property Tax Reform: Land Use Implications Of New Jersey's Tax Debate":

- Consistency with State Plan goals
- Consistency with affordable housing goals
- Education equity
- Flexibility
- Fiscal discipline
- Fiscal stability
- Local autonomy.

By measuring each proposal according to the criteria, the study attempts to determine how much school property taxes and other taxes would change under each proposal, how these changes would be distributed across 566 municipalities throughout the state, and how each proposal would change the incentives for investing in housing and other types of development, for preserving open space, and for spending on education and other local services.

While no proposal is perfect, the analysis indicates which proposals perform best across a range of objectives. Some, such as the proposals to shift to a statewide or countywide school property tax rate, would have a limited impact on improving land use and social equity without additional reforms to state grant programs. Others, including the proposal to vary taxes by State Plan category and the income tax substitution proposal, would have positive effects on affordable housing and education equity criteria but mixed effects on efficiency and fiscal health. The split rate taxation proposal receives the highest marks across criteria, however it would require a dramatic restructuring of the way property is taxed, and the long term effects are difficult to test.

When each proposal is examined closely, it is clear that the details of implementation – which are not discussed at length in this report – would have a large effect on the proposals' impacts on the state. Political viability is another important measure, which this study does not directly address. The study concludes with a recommendation to incorporate this or a similar framework into the legislative process that will select and enact comprehensive reforms.

I. Introduction

In 2006, New Jersey saw its property tax debate enter a more decisive phase. The new Governor Jon Corzine, delivered a sobering budget message that addressed the State's immediate fiscal crisis. While the tough choices in this budget were the legislature's primary focus for the next few months, there was little question that property tax reform was the next major issue on the minds of the Governor, legislators, and local officials throughout the state. The Governor himself confirmed this with one of the closing points in his budget address: "In fact, as soon as we close out the difficult debates of the budget season, we must move expeditiously to address the most pressing issue on the public's mind: fundamental property tax reform."

But what does fundamental reform mean, and how do we know it will achieve the many ambitious expectations that have been raised, including tax relief, greater fairness, fiscal responsibility, and a stronger economy? There is no shortage of proposals for fixing the property tax system, and more will undoubtedly be made as the debate continues. Groups, such as the Coalition for the Public Good, have done an admirable job of educating citizens on the issues, identifying goals, and pushing for true reform. But there is still no agreed-upon framework for evaluating numerous and dissimilar proposals.

During the previous two years, Regional Plan Association and the Lincoln Institute of Land Policy attempted to fill this void through a series of reports and roundtables. This report was the third in a series. The first, "Fiscal Policies and Smart Growth: The Case of the Somerset Regional Center" by Henry A. Coleman and Paul D. Gottlieb, examined the potential for various types of property tax reform to support New Jersey's Smart Growth policies by examining their potential impact on the goals for a new multi-municipal suburban center in Somerset County. The second, "Fundamental Property Tax Reform: Land Use Implications Of New Jersey's Tax Debate" (October 2005), described the findings of a series of roundtables on land use and property tax reform, and provided a set of criteria by which to assess a broader range of ideas.

This report takes the next step by demonstrating how the criteria described in the October report can be used to evaluate detailed proposals for reforming the school property tax system. Five proposals are assessed using both quantitative benchmarks and rational judgments. The proposals focus on school property taxes only, however each proposal could be applied to other municipal or county taxes. The five proposals by no means exhaust the potential ways of improving the tax system, nor were they selected because they are necessarily superior to other ideas. Rather, they represent a wide range of approaches that test the utility of using the criteria and readily available data. They do, however, reflect one particular objective of this project: demonstrating the potential for property tax reform to improve land use decision-making – along with the more commonly recognized goals of tax relief and social equity. Two of the five reforms – varying taxes by State Plan category and adopting a split rate system that would tax land more than buildings and other improvements – explicitly make land use reform a primary goal. The others – substituting local property taxes with income taxes, a statewide property tax, or countywide taxes – would, theoretically, have a strong land use impact as well.

There is a widely recognized connection between local property taxes and land use. New Jersey's heavy reliance on local property taxes results in wide discrepancies in the resources available to different municipalities, and, ultimately, to rising property taxes that hurt lower- and fixed-income households. Heavy reliance on locally-collected property taxes also creates competition among municipalities for development that brings with it fiscal benefits. This situation often leads to perverse land use decisions, including limitations on residential land uses that restrict the supply of housing. This property tax effect is exacerbated by a highly fragmented governance structure of 21 counties, 566 municipalities, 611 school districts, and over 400 local authorities and fire districts. This structure not only impedes rational land use planning and development, it also keeps the cost of providing public services higher than if some of these services were consolidated or provided cooperatively.

What the Report Does and Does Not Address

Many concepts have been proposed to make the property tax system fairer, less burdensome, and more efficient. The analysis demonstrates the probable outcomes of several of these concepts in more concrete terms by showing how the distribution of taxes would change among different types of localities, and how these changes would affect the incentives of different actors, from homeowners to developers to local officials.

To demonstrate these effects, the analysis assumes that each of the proposals is "revenue-neutral." That is, that the total revenues generated by the proposals are the same as the total revenues generated under the current system. Therefore, the report does not consider the impact of spending reductions that could reduce the burden of taxes overall. All of these proposals could work in combination with measures to limit spending. However, measuring those impacts would also require specifying what type of spending would be cut. For example, a cap on the rate of growth in property taxes without any substitute revenue source would trigger spending reductions that are difficult to identify in advance, since each locality would determine where and how to address the revenue restrictions. Changes in incentives that influence where families move and how aggressively localities seek new commercial and residential development will depend on what measures are taken. Even a revenue neutral-approach, however, can impact both revenues and spending over the long run. Some are likely to be more economically efficient or lead to greater fiscal discipline, which are examined in the report and could increase economic growth or provide services at a lower cost.

The report also does not consider reforms of the ways properties are assessed or collections are made, or other administrative reforms that could greatly impact the fairness and effectiveness of the system. These are important issues, but are beyond the scope of this project, which focuses on policy rather than administration.

Finally, the analysis assumes that current federal and state grant programs to localities will remain unchanged. It is important to recognize how important these grants are to local revenues, even though New Jersey relies more heavily on local property taxes than almost any state in the country. For example, about 40% of local school funding comes from state grant programs. To some extent, this mitigates disparities between wealthy and poor school districts, but it also creates a complex combination of grant programs that affect the overall equity and efficiency of school expenditures and outcomes. Ultimately, any reform of local school property taxes needs to consider what complementary changes are needed in state grants to localities, as well.

II. Criteria for Evaluating Reform Proposals

How are citizens, or public officials for that matter, to weigh very different reform ideas with complex, far-reaching implications? Regional Plan Association and Lincoln Institute's October 2005 report on Fundamental Property Tax Reform identified criteria for determining how well reform proposals would meet a diverse set of public goals, from education equity to the land use objectives embodied in the New Jersey State Development and Redevelopment Plan. Some of these criteria tend to be relatively compatible with each other, while others have a natural tension. For example, the goal of maximizing local autonomy is at odds with the goal of achieving greater equity in education funding and outcomes.

Clearly, no proposal can meet all goals equally well, and the function of the political process is to weigh the trade-offs to reflect public priorities. To do this well, both citizens and the public officials who represent them need the best possible information on what those trade-offs actually represent – in dollars and cents, in who will be most affected, and in how they are likely to shape the physical, social, and economic landscape of New Jersey. Measuring these impacts is limited by imperfect data and the complicated process of sorting out how the behavior of homeowners, developers, municipal officials, and others would change under different assumptions. However, both quantitative measures and reasoned judgments can help to piece together a picture of how the State would change under different proposals.

This report uses a combination of economic theory and available property tax, census, and land use data to evaluate how well five hypothetical property tax reforms would affect each of the eight criteria. The same methodology could be used to assess any number of proposals. While far from definitive, these evaluation tools are a means for making apples-to-apples comparisons of how different reforms would answer the following questions:

- How much would school property taxes and other taxes change?
- How would these changes be distributed across municipalities throughout the state?
- How would these reforms change the incentives for investing in housing and other types of development, for preserving open space, and for spending on education and other local services?

The following describes the specific indicators that were used to assess each criterion. They are organized into two categories: Land Use and Social Equity, and Efficiency and Fiscal Health. The first includes three policy objectives – consistency with State Plan goals, promotion of affordable housing, and attainment of education equity – that have tangible outcomes such as land developed, number of housing units, and education spending per pupil. The second category includes four criteria – flexibility, fiscal discipline, fiscal stability, and local autonomy – that are difficult to quantify, but are, nonetheless, important policy goals. One criterion identified in the first report—economic efficiency—was eliminated as a separate goal. In examining how to measure this criterion, it became clear that it overlaps with several of the others. For example, consistency with the State Plan promotes economic efficiency by promoting the use of existing infrastructure and other resources. To some extent, local autonomy can also promote the efficient allocation of tax dollars by allowing people to choose among places with different bundles of services and costs. Far from de-emphasizing the importance of economic efficiency and growth, this underscores the centrality of these objectives. In the long run, states that make efficient use of land and tax dollars, provide an adequate supply of housing, and have fiscal policies that can adapt to changing economic conditions will experience stronger economic growth. However, the criteria may not fully capture short-run impacts on economic growth, such as the effect of a changing mix of taxes on competition with other states.

In evaluating the criteria, it is assumed that the outcomes are determined by three policy levers that are primarily under local control—zoning, tax rates, and services. Because the proposals are revenue-neutral, it is assumed that each would provide the same level of service as the status quo. Tax rates can change considerably under these proposals and are quantified to the extent possible. It is assumed that, all other things being equal, development will be attracted to places with the lowest tax rates. Finally, zoning and other land use regulations are likely to be affected by the changes the proposals make to incentives for localities. These incentives are evaluated by examining the internal logic of the proposal and established theory on how these types of policies are likely to change behavior.

Land Use and Social Equity

1.   Consistency with State Plan Goals is a clear objective that is not necessarily easy to measure. With the State Development and Redevelopment Plan, New Jersey has a very specific map for testing how well property tax reforms would improve land use. As the title of this criterion implies, it captures the degree to which policies encourage growth in urban areas, suburban centers, and other areas designated by the state plan for growth, and discourage growth in areas designated as environmentally sensitive and agricultural. However, judging the impacts of tax reforms requires analysis of how they would change both incentives and actual development behavior. In this report, two benchmarks are used to evaluate these impacts:

- Policies that increase incentives for redevelopment and decrease incentives for greenfield development, both among and within municipalities, were ranked highly for this criterion.
- Proposals also rank high for this criterion if tax rates decline in municipalities that are primarily urban or suburban, both overall and in relation to rates in places that are primarily rural or undeveloped. Since many places cannot be cleanly defined in this way, it is not a definitive measure of how incentives would change.

2.   Consistency with affordable housing goals measures the extent to which policies create incentives or remove barriers to build housing statewide for low, moderate, and middle-income households. There are no definitive benchmarks for measuring this criterion, but there are several indicators that can be used to infer which policies would result in the construction of more affordable housing units:

- Policies that minimize taxes on new development, while not favoring any particular type or price of housing, are ranked highly because they are expected to produce more housing at all income levels.
- Reforms that reduce tax rates in higher-density locations, which are more often near transit and downtowns, are more likely to result in multi-family housing that would include units at different price ranges, and are, therefore, ranked highly.

3.   Education equity measures the extent to which revenues are increased, or tax rates are reduced with no change in revenues, in Abbott districts and other low-income municipalities. This factor does not address adequacy or equity in spending, much less predict education outcomes. But it does measure the degree to which school property tax reform reduces disparities in the revenue capacity of high-income and low-income municipalities. It also reduces fiscal stress on low-income districts and makes it more likely that they will attract mixed-income residents, both of which could help improve education outcomes. The benchmarks used for this criterion are straightforward comparisons of how rates and revenues change for municipalities at different income levels:

- Reforms that reduce rates or increase revenues in Abbott districts, relative to non-Abbott districts, rank higher for education equity.
- Similarly, reforms that reduce rates or increase revenues for other low-income districts also rank higher.

Efficiency and Fiscal Health

4.   Flexibility measures how well a tax works across different types of places and economic environments. For example, a tax that gets most of its revenue from new growth (e.g., tax increment financing) will work well in places that are growing rapidly but not in places that are declining, while one that uses existing sources of revenue to subsidize additional growth (e.g., economic development incentives) can be inefficient and inequitable in places that are already growing. To get a rough approximation of how well reform proposals meet this criterion, two benchmark are used:

- Reforms that allow tax rates to be adjusted to adapt to different circumstances are judged to be more flexible than those that do not.
- Proposals that bias tax rates in a counterproductive direction—higher in declining or stagnant municipalities and lower in growing places—are judged to be less flexible.

5.   Fiscal discipline measures how well a reform improves incentives for local governments to operate efficiently and hold down the costs that lead to higher property taxes. Since local school taxes are linked to budgets that require voter approval, there is currently a strong incentive to hold down costs. However, this incentive varies considerably depending on factors such as the mix of commercial and residential property, the amount and form of state aid, and spending mandated by the state and federal governments. Incentives could be strengthened either by creating a stronger link between the responsibility for taxing and spending, by state caps on revenue or spending, or by linking state aid to efficiency measures. While it is difficult to generate quantitative benchmarks, the proposals can be qualitatively assessed for how they affect this criterion:

- Proposals are ranked more highly to the degree that they either align local tax burdens with local spending authority or create stronger incentives for operational efficiencies through state aid programs and formulas.

6.   Fiscal stability measures the extent to which different proposals would provide a stable source of revenue through economic cycles, and allow rates to be adjusted to meet changing needs. Since revenues from property taxes are relatively stable compared to revenues based income, sales, and some other taxes, proposals that replace property taxes with other sources of revenues can be expected to perform poorly by this criterion. To measure fiscal stability, the following benchmark is evaluated:

- Proposals that shift the tax burden to less stable sources of revenue are ranked less highly.

7. Local autonomy reflects the long-held "value" that municipalities should control their own fiscal, service, and land use authority to the greatest extent possible. Reforms will only affect local autonomy to the degree that they restrict municipal powers to raise revenue or determine spending. Measuring this criterion is less about quantifying impacts than it is about examining the structure of the proposal. Therefore, proposals are evaluated according to the following guideline:

- Proposals are ranked highly to the degree that they preserve municipal authority over taxing and spending. In particular, authority over spending is the key variable for proposals that are revenue-neutral for the State as a whole.

III. Methodology for Selecting and Analyzing Reform Proposals

In the debate around property taxes in New Jersey there is, usually, at least one issue on which everyone agrees: property taxes should be lower. Lowering property taxes necessarily requires taking a look at what services they fund and what alternatives are available for delivering these services, either through greater efficiencies or different sources of revenues. This question inevitably revolves around how to fund public elementary and secondary education. The total bill for local school property taxes in all municipalities in 2004 was $10.183 billion, representing 55% of all property taxes. That number can only be lowered by (1) decreasing expenditures at the school district level and passing on the savings, or (2) decreasing local school property tax rates and finding a new revenue source to replace those funds.

The reform proposals analyzed in this report focus on school taxes, in part because they represent the majority of property tax spending, and in part because the trade-offs can be more clearly delineated by zeroing in on this single purpose. However, each proposal could also be applied to other municipal or county taxes. The effects on non-school taxes are likely to be similar but not identical to those of school taxes. General municipal and county tax rates are likely to vary differently than school taxes, and thus could end up with different rankings for the criteria used than those given for school taxes.

This report examines five school property tax reform proposals:

(Proposal 1) Vary the property tax by state planning areas;
(Proposal 2) Collect all property taxes at one statewide rate;
(Proposal 3) Collect all property taxes at a county rate, and consolidate school districts at the county level;
(Proposal 4) Substitute half the property tax with an income tax surcharge;

(Proposal 5) Split the property tax rate into a higher land tax and a lower tax on buildings and improvements.

There are many other options the State may choose, and many variations of each of these five proposals. These five were chosen to capture a range of revenue-neutral proposals and differentiate between the two ways in which property taxes affect land use, equity, and other considerations. The distinction is between those effects that result from the incentives and disincentives that flow from taxing property (as opposed to income, consumer sales, or other sources of revenue), and those that would result from any local tax. In other words, some of the impacts attributed to property taxes would also result from a local income or sales tax, simply because of the incentives they create for municipalities to maximize their tax base and limit anything that adds to costs.

Of these five proposals, one would shift taxation dramatically from property to income. Another would still collect the same amount of property taxes, but eliminate the effect of local fragmentation by collecting revenue at one uniform rate across the state. A third would enact a form of regional taxation through county-wide taxes, and, thus, mitigate the effect of local fragmentation. The proposal to vary taxes by State Planning areas would go even further by systematically reducing rates in areas where growth is favored by the State Plan. The remaining proposal would shift each household's burden away from the value of buildings and other built improvements and toward land value.

These five scenarios were specifically designed to be revenue-neutral. Changes to expenditures can be included as part of any property tax reform proposal, and spending should be analyzed as a separate issue. This report, instead, develops scenarios that change the basic structure of how local school property taxes are collected in the State. With spending separated out, it is possible to compare the effect of these proposals on various categories of municipalities and residents.

While these proposals can demonstrate a wide variety of impacts that property tax reform may have on the State and localities, some important issues are out of the scope of this analysis. These include how each proposal compares with the current package of property tax rebates and refunds available, and whether and how the proposals would change the existing rebate package. These issues are addressed, to some extent, in the analysis of the Income Tax Substitution proposal, but they are not addressed in the others. In reality, there would likely be an overhaul of the rebate package and state aid in addition to reform. Savings from eliminating some of the rebates might be used to makeup funding gaps in a new system, while other rebates (for example for seniors and veterans) might be unchanged.

Also out of this report's scope are variations on each proposal. For example, instead of the specific scenarios described in this report, the State could enact a statewide or countywide property tax rate to fund part (not all) of the school costs, impose an income tax surcharge that would substitute for more or less than the 50% of the property tax levy suggested in this scenario, or undertake a complete switch to a land tax instead of having land taxes fund 75% of school needs as suggested in this report's scenario. Exclusion of these issues and options only indicates the limited scope of this analysis and does not reflect their importance to finding a lasting solution for the State.

One of the primary analytic tools used measures changes in property taxes for each municipality for each of the five proposals, and then analyzes how these changes were distributed among municipalities categorized by several indicators—size, density, growth, wealth, income, State Plan classification, and Abbott designation. Each of these is associated with one or more criteria, and provides an indication of how tax burdens, spending, and land use would be likely to shift with a change in tax laws. Because of data limitations and the nature of the criteria, this method is more useful for judging some criteria and some reform proposals than others. Also, some outcomes, such as changes in zoning and land use regulations, are not captured by this method. Therefore, the evaluations also include other measures and qualitative judgments based on established theory. Much of the theoretical and empirical work on this topic is discussed by Coleman and Gottlieb in the first report in this series.

Definitions of Categories

Many of the tables in this analysis use categories of population growth, density, and urbanization. For simplicity, shorthand is used in the text. These are the definitions of these categories.

Population Growth
Tables 3, 7, 12, 18 & 22

Population growth is considered from 1990 to 2004, as reported by the US Census, and is categorized as follows:

- Declining or stagnating population = population declined or didn't change
- Slowly growing = just over 0 to 7% growth
- Moderately growing = just over 7% to 18% growth
- Quickly growing = Over 18% growth in population

Population Density
Tables 1, 5, 10, 16 & 19

Population density data is from the US Census in 2004, and is categorized as follows:

- Very low density = fewer than 1,000 people per square mile
- Low density = 1,000 to 5,000 people per square mile
- Medium density = 5,001 to 10,000 people per square mile
- High density = 10,001 to 20,000 people per square mile
- Very high density = more than 20,000 people per square mile

Urbanization
Tables 1-4, 9, 15 & 20

To quantify each proposal's consistency with the State Plan, municipalities were divided into three categories using data from the state showing the number of acres each municipality has in each State Plan planning area:

- Urban and suburban = those 283 municipalities where more than 75% of the land is categorized by the State Plan under planning areas 1 and 2
- Rural = rural and environmentally sensitive, or those 197 municipalities where more than 75% of the acres are planning areas 3 and higher
- Mixed = the remaining 86 municipalities that cannot be categorized as primarily urban or rural

Tax Rates

Throughout the report, tax rates are shown as dollar amounts per $100 of equalized assessed value.

Technical Note
Tables 4-7 & 9-12

While there were 566 municipalities in 2004, two of them are not counted in parts of the analysis because they had $0 school property taxes: Lower Alloways Creek Township in Salem County (population 1,900) and Pine Valley Borough in Camden County (population 22). These two municipalities were excluded from parts of the statewide tax and countywide tax analysis since they do not have a school property tax rate, and that fact would not change under these scenarios.

IV. Proposal #1: Vary the Property Tax by State Planning Areas

This proposal would explicitly tie property tax reform to implementation of the New Jersey State Development and Redevelopment Plan, a goal that has been articulated by a number of commissions, legislators, and policy experts over the last two decades. For example, the State and Local Expenditure and Revenue Policy (SLERP) Commission issued a report in 1988 that anticipated the first State Plan, and recommended a statewide system of differential taxes on new construction to support the land use objectives of the forthcoming plan. The report also recommended reducing property taxes by increasing income and sales taxes, instituting a circuit breaker that stops any person from paying too much in combined taxes, consolidating services on a variety of regional levels to lower overall expenditures, and many other proposals. Ten years after the SLERP report, a property tax commission convened by then-Governor Christine Todd Whitman made some of the same recommendations, including calling for supporting the State Plan's use by municipalities, counties, and state agencies as a means of holding down property taxes.

The appeal of this idea, which would decrease taxes in places where the State Plan would encourage growth relative to areas where it would discourage growth, is that it would simultaneously address two related policy objectives of "smart growth" advocates. In theory, it should back up the goals of the State Plan with financial incentives for its implementation, and lessen the incentives for fiscal zoning that cause school districts and municipalities to seek tax-generating development while shunning most kinds of residential development.

There are a number of different ways that this concept could be implemented. The SLERP Commission recommended a tier-graduated tax that applied to new structures only, and had a sunset provision for specific structures. The logic was that there was no need to provide development incentives or disincentives for structures that had already been built, and that this limited change would cause minimum disruption to the existing system. Other approaches could have differential rates for existing and new properties, but limit those rates to certain property-types, such as commercial. The tier-graduated tax could be implemented by decreasing rates in some areas and increasing them in others, or it could be implemented without any rate increases by using state revenues to reimburse districts that had decreased rates.

The scenario described in this report uses a simple two-tiered rate structure on all property. While this may not be the ideal approach, it is the clearest way to demonstrate the advantages and disadvantages. This rate structure could be done in a revenue-neutral fashion by decreasing property taxes in planning areas 1 and 2 (suburban and metropolitan areas) by the same total amount as property taxes are increased in planning areas 3 and higher (fringe, rural, and environmentally sensitive areas). Under this proposal, the state would collect property taxes from all localities and refund municipalities the same amount that they currently spend. The burden of paying for schools would not shift away from property taxes per se, but rather shift from property taxes in places where growth is encouraged to places where growth is discouraged. This approach would require the State to adjust rates and reimbursements annually, and take into account the changing needs of each district. Thus, it would ideally be combined with a comprehensive reform of education spending across school districts. A less sweeping approach could limit the State's role to setting a uniform rate reduction in areas designated for growth, and reimbursing these areas with either state revenues or a corresponding rate increase on property taxes in planning areas 3 and higher. School districts would still be responsible for setting their own budgets and rates, but would take into account the rebate or surcharge determined by the State.

Because municipalities and school districts often contain multiple planning areas, it is not always possible to characterize which municipalities would benefit most. Some single properties, in fact, encompass more than one planning area Therefore, it is not possible to analyze the overall quantitative outcomes of this proposal, such as how much property tax rates might change in each school district.

To attempt to understand what some quantitative outcomes might be, municipalities were divided into three categories: (a) primarily urban and suburban, or those 283 municipalities where more than 75% of the land is categorized by the State Plan under planning areas 1 and 2; (b) rural and environmentally sensitive, or those 197 municipalities where more than 75% of the acres are planning areas 3 and higher; and (c) the remaining 86 municipalities that cannot be categorized as primarily urban or rural. The following discussion describes how each of these groupings would be affected, and what the implications would be for the seven criteria described in Section II.

Land Use and Social Equity

Consistency with State Plan goals: HIGH

This proposal is designed to implement State Plan principles, making local taxes vary according to state planning designations. As such, there is nearly a perfect alignment between the goals of the plan and the incentives built into this proposal. The magnitude of the effect would depend on how widely the rates are made to vary.

Consistency with affordable housing goals: MODERATE

The net effects on total housing production are difficult to determine, because housing would be more expensive to build in some locations and less expensive in others. However, there would be a greater likelihood building multi-family housing that would serve a wider range of income levels and family types. Table 1 shows that most of the densest municipalities can be categorized as urban, while most of the sparsely populated municipalities are considered rural. Following that, this proposal would decrease property taxes the most in dense areas, which are more likely to be appropriate for multi-family housing. This reduction should spur an increase in housing supply in these areas, especially the supply of smaller units, and help to balance housing prices statewide and increase overall affordability.

Education equity: HIGH

Since most students and residents live in planning areas 1 and 2, this proposal would lower their reliance on local property taxes for school funding. Also, as in Table 2, at least 26 of the 31 Abbott districts are in primarily urban areas that would benefit from lower school property taxes. Although this proposal, by itself, does not guarantee that the distribution of education spending will change, it reduces fiscal stress and increases the ability to attract new residents and wealth in poorer districts, both of which could positively affect education spending and outcomes. The larger state role in school financing also increases the likelihood of more comprehensive measures to reduce education funding disparities.

Efficiency and Fiscal Health

Flexibility: HIGH

By adjusting rates to lean towards areas that have traditionally exhibited slow growth, this tool differentiates between places with differing economic environments. Table 3 shows that most of the quickly growing areas are made up of primarily planning areas 3 and higher. Under this proposal, these fringe suburbs and rural areas would have relatively higher local school property taxes than those areas that are more urban and growing more slowly. Also, since rates would need to be adjusted annually, there is an opportunity to calibrate them to changing economic circumstances.

Fiscal Discipline: MODERATE

The overall impact on fiscal discipline will depend on how revenues are reallocated to municipalities. Initially, a reallocation at current spending levels would have little effect. Over time, however, the state will need to determine how much taxes will rise, and how they will be allocated. Simple formulas based on past spending and changes in the numbers of students would have little impact on current spending restraints. Formulas that left school districts with the primary responsibility for determining service costs would loosen cost constraints under this system, while those that set spending limits or provided incentives for specific efficiency measures could reduce costs.

Fiscal Stability: MODERATE

On average, there would be little change in the sensitivity of municipal fiscal conditions to changes in economic conditions if this proposal were implemented. Local revenues will still be drawn primarily from property taxes, which tend to be a relatively stable revenue source. There might be some slight effect on particular municipalities, because of how the state adjust rates from year to year, but no statewide impact.

Local autonomy: LOW

While the amount and use of expenditures would not, theoretically, change under this proposal, the ability of municipalities to set their own property tax rates would be compromised. Also, there would be a greater likelihood of a stronger state role in determining local education spending levels, if the municipalities were playing a larger role in determining revenue sources.

Summary

Overall, varying taxes by state planning areas would tend to strongly support land use and social equity goals and have mixed results for efficiency and fiscal health. The precise impacts would depend, to a large degree, on how the proposal is structured, how much rates are made to vary, and how the State redistributes revenues. Clearly, the proposal would raise issues of fairness and generate opposition from places that would see rates increased. To some degree, this opposition could be reduced with more limited proposals, such as ones that only vary rates for new construction, or ones that combine variations in rates with across-the-board reductions in property taxes.

Share of Municipalities categorized by State Planning Area ...	Table ❶ ...by Population Density Category						Table ❷ ...by Abbott Status		Table ❸ ...by Population Growth Category					Total Mun.
	Very Low Density	Low Density	Medium Density	High Density	Very High Density	Total	Non-Abbott Districts	Abbott Districts	Declining or stagnant population	Slowly Growing	Moderately Growing	Quickly Growing	Total	
Mixed	31%	62%	6%	1%	0%	100%	16%	10%	7%	24%	23%	45%	100%	86
Urban & Suburban	4%	59%	25%	10%	3%	100%	48%	84%	23%	31%	30%	15%	100%	283
Rural	75%	25%	1%	0%	0%	100%	36%	6%	22%	17%	24%	37%	100%	197
Total	33%	48%	13%	5%	1%	100%	100%	100%	20%	25%	27%	27%	100%	566
Municipalities	184	270	76	28	8	566	535	31	116	144	152	154	566	

V. Proposal #2:
Collect All School Property Taxes at One Statewide Rate

Variations on a statewide property tax have been implemented with varying degrees of success in achieving fiscal discipline and education equity. Some states, such as New Hampshire and Massachusetts, fund education with a statewide property tax in addition to local property taxes. Others exercise state-level control over local property taxes.

A statewide tax rate is generally intended to meet two objectives—to make taxes more equitable among property-rich and property-poor municipalities, and to remove the incentives that cause the "ratables chase". In theory, by making all school districts' tax rates identical, districts with low property values would not have to set higher rates to provide for education expenses. And, since the state would be collecting the revenue and redistributing it to the districts, municipalities would not be inclined to court only low-cost, high tax revenue development - such as commercial and retail development- while eschewing multi-family housing or other residential development that leads to higher costs and forces towns to increase tax rates. As a hypothetical example, if no town in New Jersey gained a single net taxpayer, and only one town had increased school costs, the whole state would have a miniscule increase in tax rates to cover that increased cost. The incentives that now force mayors to favor strip malls over housing and parks would, theoretically, be largely removed.

A statewide property tax could take a variety of forms, such as the State collecting some share of local school property taxes and redistributing those resources, the State applying its own rate to some share of local property, or other varieties. For this report, the simplest scenario was chosen: all property in the State would be subject to the same school property tax rate, and the State would refund municipalities so that they receive the same amount for schools as they do now. The revenue-neutral, statewide school property tax rate would be $1.083. If this rate were applied to all property, the State would collect $10.183 billion, the same amount now collected from all municipalities' school property taxes.

Under this proposal, some municipalities would experience an increase in school property taxes, while others would experience a decrease. In total, there would be 5.1 million residents whose households would experience a decrease in property taxes, and 3.6 million residents who would see an increase.

As with the proposal to vary taxes by State Plan area, the method for redistributing taxes to school districts after the initial year would have a substantial impact on criteria such as education equity and local autonomy. The analysis below shows the impact for the initial year and assumes that future years would be determined by the state, either using a formula pegged to the initial year or by some standard of educational need.

Land Use and Social Equity

Consistency with State Plan goals: MODERATE

Of the 195 municipalities identified as primarily rural, most (137) would experience a decrease in property taxes. Of the 283 urban and suburban municipalities, a slightly lower share (171) would experience a decrease in property taxes. In total, municipalities in mostly rural planning areas would be net contributors to the State, with an increase in property taxes amounting to about $154 million, while urban and suburban municipalities would experience a net decrease in property taxes of about $73 million. The difference would be made up by the 86 municipalities that could not be categorized as primarily urban or rural.

Another way to examine the land use impacts is to look at the number of acres in primarily urban and primarily rural areas, and determine the changes in taxes. As with the rest of the land use analysis, the results are unclear. More acres of both rural and urban municipalities would have lower school property taxes than under the status quo system, but the differences are minor and made up by those places that cannot be categories, as rural or urban. Those municipalities represent nearly half the acres in the state. While property tax rates could change considerably in individual municipalities, this would not necessarily change the pattern or overall taxes by state planning area, which suggests that there would be limited change in the incentives that uniform tax rates would have on developers. However, the fiscal incentives for towns to use zoning to either chase or shun development would be greatly reduced. This situation would likely lead towns to give greater priority to goals articulated in the State Plan, including protecting open space in rural areas and attracting commercial and residential development to urban and suburban centers.

Consistency with affordable housing goals: MODERATE

The affect on affordable housing is unclear with a mix of both positive and negative affects. Overall housing production would likely increase, since municipalities would have less incentive to use restrictive zoning to keep out residential development, which increases school costs. However, this proposal would lower tax rates in many lower-density municipalities and increase it in most higher-density areas that are most likely to build multi-family housing (see Table 5). Notably, 25 of the 36 densest municipalities would experience a school property tax increase, including the eight densest municipalities in the state: Guttenberg, Union City, West New York, Hoboken, and East Newark in Hudson County; Cliffside Park Borough in Bergen; Passaic City; and Irvington Township in Essex. Property tax increases in these dense areas would damage the prospect for multi-family housing in the State overall, thereby working against affordable housing state policies.

Education equity: LOW

In addition to raising rates for the densest municipalities, this proposal would raise rates for the poorest. To elucidate the effect, the wealthiest and poorest municipalities are identified. Of the poorest 103 municipalities – that is, those municipalities with a median household income that is more than 20% lower than the state median – 45 would experience a decrease in school property taxes due to a switch in the statewide rate, while the remaining 59 poor municipalities, representing just under 2 million residents, would experience an increase in property taxes. On the other end of the spectrum, of the 107 municipalities with a median household income that is 50% or more higher than the statewide median, 56 would experience a decrease in school property taxes, and the remaining 51 would experience an increase. These results indicate that increased property taxes would disproportionately affect poorer areas, while decreased property taxes would benefit wealthier areas. The net effect paints a clearer picture: while the effect on each municipality may differ, the poorest municipalities, as a whole, would contribute $355 million more per year in school property taxes, while the wealthiest municipalities would contribute only $40 million more per year. This imbalance is due, in large part, to decreases in some of the wealthier areas and increases in many of the poorest. Consistently, of the 31 Abbott districts, 29 would experience an increase in property tax rates.

Efficiency and Fiscal Health

Flexibility: LOW

With a single uniform rate, there is no opportunity to calibrate tax rates for places with varying economic environments. It would not appear to be biased toward either growing or declining municipalities. Table 7 shows that there is no discernible pattern between rate of growth and whether the statewide rate causes an increase or decrease in the municipal rate.

Fiscal discipline: MODERATE

As with the proposal to vary taxes by State Plan area, the overall impact of a statewide property tax on fiscal discipline will depend on how revenues are reallocated to municipalities. Initially, a reallocation at current spending levels would have little effect. Over time, however, the State will need to determine how much taxes will rise and how they will be allocated. Simple formulas based on past spending and changes in the numbers of students would have little impact on current spending restraints. Formulas that left school districts with the primary responsibility for determining service costs would loosen cost constraints under this system, while those that set spending limits or provided incentives for specific efficiency measures could reduce costs.

Fiscal stability: MODERATE

Since there would be no statewide shift from property taxes to less stable revenue sources, there should be little impact on overall fiscal stability. Municipal revenues would still come primarily from taxes on property. Only the entity establishing the rates and collecting the taxes would change.

Local autonomy: LOW

As with the proposal to vary rates by State Plan area, the ability of municipalities to set their own property tax rates would be compromised. Also, there would be a greater likelihood of a stronger state role in determining local education spending levels, if municipalities are playing a larger role in determining revenue sources.

Summary

This proposal ranks either Moderate or Low for all seven criteria. Its main attribute is its effect in reducing the incentives for local fiscal zoning, but its actual impact on tax rates is either negligible or harmful to most criteria. However, the analysis is skewed by the fact that state education grants, spurred by Abbott and other court decisions, have already reduced many of the disparities that this tax might address. In effect, general state revenues are doing much of what a statewide property tax could do. A statewide property tax might still have merit, but only in the context of a comprehensive reform of all sources of education revenue, including state grants

Table 4 — Affect of Statewide Tax Rate on Municipalities… by Planning Area Category

% change in equalized school property tax rate due to statewide rate

	Mixed	Urban & Suburban	Rural	Total
-25% or more	10%	51%	39%	100%
-10% to -24.9%	20%	39%	41%	100%
0% to -9.9%	16%	57%	27%	100%
+ up to 10%	10%	56%	34%	100%
+10.1% to +25%	12%	71%	18%	100%
More than 25%	18%	52%	30%	100%
Total	15%	50%	35%	100%
Municipalities	86	283	195	564

Table 5 — …by Population Density Category

	Very Low	Low	Med.	High	Very High	Total
-25% or more	32%	53%	13%	3%	0%	100%
-10% to -24.9%	42%	44%	15%	0%	0%	100%
0% to -9.9%	31%	47%	11%	11%	0%	100%
+ up to 10%	36%	46%	14%	4%	0%	100%
+10.1% to +25%	24%	41%	21%	12%	3%	100%
More than 25%	23%	50%	11%	10%	6%	100%
Total	32%	48%	14%	5%	1%	100%
Municipalities	183	269	76	28	8	564

Table 6 — …by Abbott Status

	Non-Abbott Districts	Abbott Districts	Total
-25% or more	99%	1%	100%
-10% to -24.9%	100%	0%	100%
0% to -9.9%	98%	2%	100%
+ up to 10%	96%	4%	100%
+10.1% to +25%	79%	21%	100%
More than 25%	84%	16%	100%
Total	95%	6%	100%
Municipalities	533	31	564

Table 7 — …by Population Growth Category

	Declining or Stagnant Population	Slowly Growing	Moderately Growing	Quickly Growing	Total	Total Mun.
-25% or more	36%	20%	20%	24%	100%	148
-10% to -24.9%	11%	27%	27%	34%	100%	154
0% to -9.9%	13%	27%	29%	31%	100%	62
+ up to 10%	18%	22%	32%	28%	100%	50
+10.1% to +25%	15%	27%	35%	24%	100%	34
More than 25%	21%	28%	30%	21%	100%	116
Total	21%	25%	27%	27%	100%	564
Municipalities	116	142	152	154		564

VI. Proposal #3: Collect All Property Taxes at a County Rate, and Consolidate School Districts at the County Level

This proposal combines two distinct elements. One is to replace local property taxes with a county property tax, and the second is to consolidate all 611 school districts into 21 county-level school districts. Table 8 shows what the countywide tax rates would need to be to collect the same revenue in school property taxes in 2004.

Like a statewide tax rate, a countywide rate is intended to remove the incentives that cause the "ratables chase." While counties may still compete among themselves, the towns within each county would not be inclined to limit development or only promote low-cost, high-tax revenue development, because the county's increased costs would not directly require increased tax revenue. A county-wide rate is akin to a simple form of regional tax sharing. The school property tax rate for the county would apply to all municipalities in that county. Counties would essentially set a rate that would allow them to support each municipality's school budget. Tax base sharing can also occur at other levels of government, such as clusters of municipalities or places within a metropolitan region. The most famous example is the Minneapolis-St. Paul Twin Cities tax sharing district, a seven-county area where each of the 187 towns contributes 40% of the growth in its commercial-industrial tax base to a regional pool. Funds from the pool are allocated to local governments according to a formula accounting for population and property value per capita. In the scenario examined for this report, the county functions as that "regional pool" and the county school property tax rate determines each town's contribution.

The second element of the proposal, to consolidate into 21 county-level school districts, has been proposed and promoted by many, notably by State Senator Bob Smith, as a way to lower school expenditures and, thereby, lower property taxes.

This element is included here to demonstrate an important concept that is often discussed when this subject is broached in New Jersey, that of regional consolidation of services. Ernest Roeck of the Rutgers Center for Government Services has examined school consolidation and school district creation in New Jersey. His analysis finds that past school district consolidation has led to per pupil expenditure decreases. He estimates that consolidating all 611 school districts into 265 all-purpose K-12 school districts would result in annual statewide savings of 8.3% of total expenditures per pupil, or about $300 million per year with additional initial administrative savings. However, for the sake of consistency with other proposals examined in this report, this proposal is assumed to be revenue-neutral. That is, while school districts are consolidated, it is assumed for this proposal that school expenditures remain the same as they are now.

The tax rates for each county in this scenario are shown in Table 8. These rates would replace the separate school property tax rates now paid at the municipal level. Under this proposal, 323 municipalities (about 55% of the population) would experience a decrease in school property taxes, while the remaining 243 would experience an increase.

Land Use and Social Equity

Consistency with State Plan goals: MODERATE

This proposal would modestly decrease property rates in many rural, lower density, and wealthier areas while modestly increasing them in many urban, higher density, and poorer areas. About 48% of the 195 municipalities categorized for this report as urban would experience an increase in property taxes, for a net increase of $114 million among those urban areas. About 42% of the rural municipalities would experience an increase in property taxes, however the total affect would be a net decrease in property taxes of about $40 million paid by those rural municipalities. While the overall magnitude of this effect may not be great, since county rates would not vary consistently with state planning designations, the net effect would be modestly inconsistent with state plan goals of encouraging growth in planning areas 1 and 2. This result would be balanced, to some degree, by a reduced propensity for fiscal zoning, at least within the boundaries of the counties,

Consistency with affordable housing goals: MODERATE

The results for this criteria are similar to the results found for a statewide property tax. While less incentive for fiscal zoning could increase housing production, other changes would be slightly negative. A majority of the municipalities with more than 10,000 people per square mile would have rate increases, while a majority of lower density municipalities would have rate decreases. The differences are not very large, however, and the change in rates are fairly evenly spread among municipalities in all density categories, indicating a modest inconsistency with state affordable housing goals. Nonetheless, 22 of the 36 densest municipalities would experience increased tax rates, including the eight densest towns in New Jersey. This is a slightly more modest outcome than the statewide tax scenario, but still reveals a negative impact on the State's affordable housing goals.

Education equity: LOW

Of the 103 poorest municipalities (defined earlier), 52 would experience decreases in property taxes, and the remaining 51 would experience increases. The net result would be an increase of $105 million paid in property taxes for these 103 poorest towns. Of the 107 wealthiest municipalities, 49 would experience decreases in property taxes, and 58 would experience increases. The net result would be an increase of $110 million paid in property taxes for these 107 wealthiest towns. The remaining 356 municipalities that fall into neither the poorest nor wealthiest categories would experience a net decrease, so that the state would collect the same amount in school property taxes as it does presently (just over $10 billion). Overall, the switch to a countywide property tax would not disproportionately affect the poorest or wealthiest communities. However, like the statewide tax, this proposal would result in a property tax rate increase for nearly all the Abbott districts. While four districts would experience a lower tax, 27 would have a tax increase.

Efficiency and Fiscal Health

Flexibility: MODERATE

A uniform countywide property tax would be somewhat more flexible than a statewide tax, since it would allow for variations in different regions of the State that may experience different market and cyclical conditions. The proposal is not likely to bias rates strongly in either direction. Table 12 demonstrates that it is just as likely for a quickly growing municipality to have a higher or lower rate under the countywide plan as it is for a moderately or slowly growing municipality.

Fiscal discipline: HIGH

Under this proposal, counties would set both the budgets and tax rates for schools throughout the county. They would have both the incentive to keep taxes low and the ability to realize administrative efficiencies through shared services, elimination of duplicative services, and economies of scale. While efficient service is by no means assured and depends on effective governance and management at the county level, the structure of this concept should create greater incentives for these types of productivity enhancements. The Roeck study cited above indicates that these savings could be substantial.

Fiscal stability: MODERATE

As with statewide property taxes, there would be no shift to less stable taxes and little effect on the stability of local revenue at different points in the business cycle.

Local autonomy: MODERATE

As with the two previous proposals that would move the power to set and collect tax rates to the state level, this proposal would compromise local autonomy by removing the ability of municipalities to set their own school property tax rates. It would also explicitly remove the local school district level of decision-making on spending, something that would be dependent on the redistribution method left unspecified in the first two proposals. However, county seats are much closer to municipalities and school districts than Trenton, resulting in this proposal having a more moderate impact on local autonomy.

Summary

Overall, this proposal performs modestly better than a statewide property tax. Its effects on fiscal zoning are more muted, but so are its negative impacts on local autonomy. It is also affected by the same redistribution that has already occurred from state grants to localities, and cannot be completely assessed without also considering comprehensive reform in education finance. Its high ranking in fiscal discipline results not from the reforms on the revenue side, but from its explicit attention to service delivery.

Table
6

County-Wide School Property Tax Rate Necessary to Support a Revenue Neutral Scenario

Atlantic	$0.959
Bergen	$1.053
Burlington	$1.527
Camden	$1.649
Cape May	$0.339
Cumberland	$0.965
Essex	$1.082
Gloucester	$1.506
Hudson	$0.779
Hunterdon	$1.371
Mercer	$1.263
Middlesex	$1.286
Monmouth	$1.049
Morris	$1.083
Ocean	$0.748
Passaic	$1.077
Salem	$1.375
Somerset	$1.105
Sussex	$1.391
Union	$1.071
Warren	$1.217

Affect of Countywide Tax Rate on Municipalities...		Table 9 ...by Planning Area Category				Table 10 ...by Population Density Category						Table 11 ...by Abbott Status			Table 12 ...by Growth Category					Total Mun.
		Mixed	Urban & Suburban	Rural	Total	Very Low	Low	Med.	High	Very High	Total	Non-Abbott Districts	Abbott Districts	Total	Declining or Stagnant Population	Slowly Growing	Moderately Growing	Quickly Growing	Total	
% change in equalized school property tax rate due to countywide tax rate	-25% or more	10%	51%	39%	100%	32%	53%	13%	3%	0%	100%	99%	1%	100%	36%	20%	20%	24%	100%	148
	-10% to -24.9%	20%	39%	41%	100%	42%	44%	15%	0%	0%	100%	100%	0%	100%	11%	27%	27%	34%	100%	154
	0% to -9.9%	16%	57%	27%	100%	31%	47%	11%	11%	0%	100%	98%	2%	100%	13%	27%	29%	31%	100%	62
	+ up to 10%	10%	56%	34%	100%	36%	46%	14%	4%	0%	100%	96%	4%	100%	18%	22%	32%	28%	100%	50
	+10.1% to +25%	12%	71%	18%	100%	24%	41%	21%	12%	3%	100%	79%	21%	100%	15%	27%	35%	24%	100%	34
	More than 25%	18%	52%	30%	100%	23%	50%	11%	10%	6%	100%	84%	16%	100%	21%	28%	30%	21%	100%	116
	Total	15%	50%	35%	100%	32%	48%	14%	5%	1%	100%	95%	6%	100%	21%	25%	27%	27%	100%	564
Municipalities		86	283	195	564	183	269	76	28	8	564	533	31	564	116	142	152	154	564	

VII. Proposal #4: Substitute Half the School Property Tax with an Income Tax Surcharge

The income tax substitution proposal would refund half of school property taxes with an increase to the income tax. The idea has been promoted by Assemblyman Louis Manzo, and was proposed in legislation known as the NJ SMART (New Jersey Save Money and Reform Taxes) Act, sponsored by Manzo, Assemblyman John McKeon, and Senator Joseph Doria in May 2005. Proponents of the proposal expect that it would decrease inequities by switching half the property tax burden to a more progressive tax, and would mitigate the "ratables chase," because a town's higher costs or need for more tax revenue would not necessarily be directly passed on to residents.

Under this proposal, each resident's school property tax would be reduced by half. Municipalities would be reimbursed by the State for the decrease in property tax revenue. The State would raise the revenue for these reimbursements with a statewide surcharge on the income tax. Presently, New Jersey income tax payers fall into six income tax brackets, shown in Table 13. The surcharge would be a uniform percentage of each taxpayer's adjusted gross income tax liability. In this way, each taxpayer's income tax would increase by the same rate to raise the funds necessary to repay municipalities for their school property tax decreases. The rate would be determined annually, and it would be set to raise only enough revenue to pay for 50% of each household's school property taxes.

Two groups of income tax payers would be exempted from this uniform rate: those earning $30,000 or less would not pay the surcharge, and the surcharge for those earning $500,000 or more would be based on income taxes as if they had been paid at 6.37%.

All residents' school property taxes added up to $10.183 billion in 2004. Assemblyman Manzo estimates, however, that NJ SMART would not apply to this entire amount, and would affect only the 2.89 million tenants and homeowners who are full-time residents. These residents pay $6.457 billion in school property taxes per year. Under this proposal, these residents would be refunded by the State for half that amount, or $3.228 billion.

The NJ SMART bill would mostly eliminate the major property tax mitigation program now administered by the State: the FAIR program, formerly known as the Homestead Rebate and NJ SAVER programs. Under this proposal, residents over 65 would be eligible for the greater of either the NJ SMART plan (half their property taxes) or the FAIR rebate. Other property tax rebate programs, such as those protecting veterans and seniors, would be kept in place. General Fund savings from eliminating most of the Homestead Rebate and NJ SAVER programs, and from reduced school property tax deductions, would help to offset the total income tax surcharge needed to refund municipalities for half their school property taxes.

This is the only reform proposal considered in this report that includes a net decrease to property taxes and a new revenue source. Which source to use can be debated. The proponents of this proposal assert that the income tax is the best source, because it is based on a progressive structure; others may advocate for an extension of the sales and use tax on services, or other resources. In addition, the prospect of a new resource raises the issue of constitutional dedication, which is not addressed in this report. Constitutional dedication would require revenue collected from the new source, such as the income tax surcharge, to be used only for a given purpose, such as reimbursing municipalities for reduced property tax collections. Some argue that constitutional dedication is the only way to ensure that revenues end up where they are intended, while others argue that it unduly restricts the State from managing its budget each year, and does not allow enough flexibility to handle future fiscal needs. This debate would likely surface if any reform proposal were considered that requires a new revenue source to make up for a net decrease in property taxes.

This proposal would shift half of school property taxes to a state income tax surcharge. For 2004, the income tax surcharge needed to refund half the property taxes to each municipality was estimated at 25.36%. For example, the homeowner who pays $1,173 in income tax and $3,000 in school property taxes would be refunded $1,500 (half of the school property taxes) and would have to pay a surcharge of $297 (25.36% of income taxes). That household's net savings would be $1,203. While it is not possible to determine exactly how many net winners and losers – or "recipients" and "donors" – would result from implementing this proposal, it is possible to make some generalizations based on the overall wealth and tax levies of municipalities.

Tables 14a and 14b show the general impact of the plan on 566 municipalities, categorized by median income and size of school property tax levy per household. The places in green have a low median income, and the blue ones have higher incomes. The amount collected from the income tax surcharge on the green municipalities would be relatively low, and on the blue would be relatively high. The amount the municipality receives back is dependent on the size of its school property tax levy, shown on the left. Those five municipalities in dark green, representing 8,000 households, would receive the most back in property taxes relative to the income tax surcharge paid by their residents. Those 39,000 households in the 10 municipalities shown in dark blue would have the highest income tax increases, while their municipalities would receive the least back to recoup school property tax revenue.

These are generalizations meant to reveal any patterns in the impact of the plan, and they are restricted by the lack of complete data. Taking the top left green box as an example, not all residents in those nine municipalities earn under $30,000, rather those municipalities have a median household income of $0 to $30,000. Some residents in those nine towns would likely be considered "donors" under this plan, because they earn more, and the income tax surcharge would generate more from them than they had been paying in school property taxes. In addition, some of the residents in the far right column, earning $110,001 and more, would have an income tax adjustment in their favor due to the revision to the half millionaire's tax proposed in the NJ SMART bill. Nonetheless, Tables 14a and 14b show that residents in most of the towns with the largest increases in income taxes would also have the largest decreases in property taxes. In addition, the very extreme "donors" and "recipients" – those in dark green and dark blue – represent less than 1% of municipalities and 1.3% of households. These figures indicate that only a very small number of residents would be overly favored (by low income tax surcharges and high property tax refunds to their municipalities) or burdened (by high income tax surcharges and low property tax refunds to their municipalities) by this plan.

Land Use and Social Equity

Consistency with State Plan goals: MODERATE

This proposal would not necessarily work for or against the State Plan. In most places, decreases in property taxes are likely to be roughly balanced with increases in income taxes, and, as shown in Table 15, municipalities of both high and low median incomes and large and small school property tax levies are evenly distributed among State Plan areas. Incentives for fiscal zoning would be reduced, but far from eliminated, with the revenue needed from school property taxes cut in half.

Consistency with affordable housing goals: HIGH

Affordable housing goals would be supported in two ways. Lower property taxes would lower the cost of owning a home or rental property and likely lead to more housing development. Also, dense places would be much more likely to be the largest beneficiaries of the plan, while sparsely settled places would likely experience smaller property tax decreases and larger income tax increases (Table 16 shows the "recipient" to "donor" ratio increasing with population density). Assuming this plan leads to more multi-family, mixed-income housing, it would, thereby, reinforce the goals of the State's affordable housing policy. This proposal's proponents also claim that it would increase the housing purchasing power of residents simply by lowering their overall tax bill. This is likely to be true to some extent, although the largest property tax decreases are likely to go to those with the highest incomes.

Education equity: HIGH

The proposal would address education equity in general by decreasing the reliance on local property taxes for school funding, and by obtaining a greater share of the sources of school funding from higher income households and a lower share from lower income households. Tables 14a-b show that the municipalities with higher tax levies tend to also have wealthier residents, indicating that, in addition to being socially equitable, this redistribution may be geographically fair: that is, the additional income tax surcharge burden is spread fairly evenly across places that experience a commensurate benefit from the property tax rebate. This proposal would not, however, address the gap in school spending between wealthy and poorer districts.

Efficiency and Fiscal Health

Flexibility: MODERATE

Since municipalities would have the same ability to set rates as they do now, this proposal would have minimal effect on the flexibility of the current system. This proposal would have more benefits for municipalities with declining populations than for those with growing populations, however the magnitude of the difference is not very large.

Fiscal discipline: LOW

Localities would still largely determine the size and content of their school budgets, but would have half of their property taxes reimbursed by the State. This situation would create a disincentive to hold down costs, since half of any spending increase would be "free money" from the perspective of the school district. However, the State could compensate for this disincentive in various ways, such as by specifying limits on what could be reimbursed.

Fiscal stability: LOW

Since, during recessions, income tends to fall more quickly than property values, this proposal would introduce an additional element of instability into the State's revenues. Revenue shortfalls in down times would either have to be passed on to school districts and municipalities, or worsen the State's fiscal condition during times when budget shortfalls are of most concern.

Local autonomy: HIGH

Localities would still be able to set their own budgets and tax rates, so local autonomy would be preserved. Arguably, it would even be enhanced, at least in the short term, because school districts would have additional resources without any increases in spending mandates or fiscal responsibility. Over the long run, the tendency to lower constraints on local spending could induce the State to include more restrictions or incentives to hold down costs.

Summary

This proposal ranks relatively high on land use and social equity criteria, in large measure because it would remove half of the fiscal costs that localities incur to fund public education, and because the impacts are progressive in shifting the tax burden to wealthier taxpayers and towns. Performance on economic and fiscal criteria is mixed, with the largest issues being how it would affect local spending and the fiscal condition of the State.

Table 13

NJ Income Tax Brackets 2006			
Single		**Married filing jointly**	
Income	Income Tax	Income	Income Tax
$0 - $20,000	1.40%	$0 - $20,000	1.40%
$20,001 - $35,000	1.75%	$20,001 - $50,000	1.75%
$35,001 - $40,000	3.50%	$50,001 - $70,000	2.45%
$40,001 - $75,000	5.53%	$70,001 - $80,000	3.50%
$75,001 - $500,000	6.37%	$80,001 - $150,000	5.53%
$500,001 +	8.97%	$150,001 - $500,000	6.37%
		$500,001 +	8.97%

Table 14a

Municipality's Median Household Income, 2000

Half of School Property Tax Levy Per Household, aka Average Household Tax Refund	$0 to $30,000	$30,001 to $40,000	$40,001 to $50,000	$50,001 to $60,000	$60,001 to $70,000	$70,001 to $90,000	$90,001 to $110,000	$110,001 and higher	Total
$0 to $1000	9	32	36	10	1	2	1		91
$1001 to $1300		6	39	24	6				75
$1301 to $1600	2		22	44	8	5			81
$1601 to $1900		4	5	28	31	6		1	75
$1901 to $2200		1	1	10	28	12	2		54
$2201 to $2500			2	6	18	26	1		53
$2501 to $3000	1	1	1	2	5	31	10	2	53
$3000 to $3500				1	1	13	17	6	38
$3501 to $5000			1	1		8	17	9	36
over $5000		2	2	1	1			4	10
Total	12	46	109	127	99	103	48	22	566

Table 14b

Municipality's Median Household Income, 2000

Half of School Property Tax Levy Per Household, aka Average Household Tax Refund	$0 to $30,000	$30,001 to $40,000	$40,001 to $50,000	$50,001 to $60,000	$60,001 to $70,000	$70,001 to $90,000	$90,001 to $110,000	$110,001 and higher	Total
$0 to $1000	10%	35%	40%	11%	1%	2%	1%	0%	100%
$1001 to $1300	0%	8%	52%	32%	8%	0%	0%	0%	100%
$1301 to $1600	3%	0%	27%	54%	10%	6%	0%	0%	100%
$1601 to $1900	0%	5%	7%	37%	41%	8%	0%	1%	100%
$1901 to $2200	0%	2%	2%	19%	52%	22%	4%	0%	100%
$2201 to $2500	0%	0%	4%	11%	34%	49%	2%	0%	100%
$2501 to $3000	2%	2%	2%	4%	9%	59%	19%	4%	100%
$3000 to $3500	0%	0%	0%	3%	3%	34%	45%	16%	100%
$3501 to $5000	0%	0%	3%	3%	0%	22%	47%	25%	100%
More than $5000	0%	20%	20%	10%	10%	0%	0%	40%	100%
Total	2%	8%	19%	22%	18%	18%	9%	4%	100%

Table 15

Effect of Income Tax Substitution Plan by State Planning Area Category

State Planning Area Category	Likely Outcome of Income Tax Substitution Plan. (See Table 14a)		Green : Blue Ratio
	Municipalities which are likely to include residents who pay less through the surcharge than their municipalities receive back	Municipalities which are likely to include residents who will pay more through income tax surcharges than their municipalities will receive back	
Mixed	20	66	0.3
Urban & Suburban	92	191	0.5
Rural	66	131	0.5
Total	178	388	0.5

Table 16

Effect of Income Tax Substitution Plan by Population Density Category

Population Density Category	Likely Outcome of Income Tax Substitution Plan. (See Table 14a)		Green : Blue Ratio
	Municipalities which are likely to include residents who pay less through the surcharge than their municipalities receive back	Municipalities which are likely to include residents who will pay more through income tax surcharges than their municipalities will receive back	
Very low density	47	137	0.3
Low density	70	200	0.4
Medium density	31	45	0.7
High density	23	5	4.6
Very high density	7	1	7.0
Total	178	388	0.5

Under the Income Tax Substitution Plan, which municipalities are likely to include residents who will pay more through income tax surcharges than their municipalities will receive back (blue) and which are likely to include residents who pay less through the surcharge than their municipalities receive back (green)?

Table 17a

		\$0 to \$30,000	\$30,001 to \$40,000	\$40,001 to \$50,000	\$50,001 to \$60,000	\$60,001 to \$70,000	\$70,001 to \$90,000	\$90,001 to \$110,000	\$110,001 and higher	Total
						Municipality's Median Household Income, 2000				
Half of Municipality's Local School Property Taxes, or the amount that would be refunded under this plan	up to \$2 million	6	20	39	41	15	13	1	2	137
	2 to 4 million	3	7	24	19	19	13	4	4	93
	4 to 6 million		2	17	17	18	17	5	2	78
	6 to 8 million		3	8	12	7	12	7	4	53
	8 to 10 million		3	9	9	7	9	6	4	47
	10 to 20 million	1	7	9	20	15	18	15	2	87
	20 to 30 million		3	3	4	7	12	6	3	38
	30 to 50 million	2	1		5	8	8	4	1	29
	over 50 million					3	1			4
Total		12	46	109	127	99	103	48	22	566

Green Pop. 3,194,189	Blue Pop. 3,812,779
Dk. Green Pop. 1,279,100	Dk. Blue Pop. 59,366

Table 17b

School Property Tax Refund by Median Income

		\$0 to \$30,000	\$30,001 to \$40,000	\$40,001 to \$50,000	\$50,001 to \$60,000	\$60,001 to \$70,000	\$70,001 to \$90,000	\$90,001 to \$110,000	\$110,001 and higher	Total	Total
						Municipality's Median Household Income, 2000					
Half of Municipality's Local School Property Taxes, or the amount that would be refunded under this plan	up to \$2 million	4%	15%	29%	30%	11%	10%	1%	2%	100%	137
	2 to 4 million	3%	8%	26%	20%	20%	14%	4%	4%	100%	93
	4 to 6 million	0%	3%	22%	22%	23%	22%	6%	3%	100%	78
	6 to 8 million	0%	6%	15%	23%	13%	23%	13%	8%	100%	53
	8 to 10 million	0%	6%	19%	19%	15%	19%	13%	9%	100%	47
	10 to 20 million	1%	8%	10%	23%	17%	21%	17%	2%	100%	87
	20 to 30 million	0%	8%	8%	11%	18%	32%	16%	8%	100%	38
	30 to 50 million	7%	3%	0%	17%	28%	28%	14%	3%	100%	29
	over 50 million	0%	0%	0%	0%	75%	25%	0%	0%	100%	4
Total		12	46	109	127	99	103	48	22		566

Table 18

Likely Outcome of Income Tax Substitution Plan. (See Table 14a)			
Effect of Income Tax Substitution Plan by Population Growth Category		Municipalities which are likely to include residents who pay less through the surcharge than their municipalities receive back	Municipalities which are likely to include residents who will pay more through income tax surcharges than their municipalities will receive back	Green : Blue Donor Ratio
Population Growth, 1990 to 2004	Declining or stagnant population	63	53	1.2
	Slowly growing	37	107	0.3
	Moderately growing	46	106	0.4
	Quickly growing	32	122	0.3
	Total	178	388	0.5

VIII. PROPOSAL #5: SPLIT THE SCHOOL PROPERTY TAX RATE INTO A HIGHER LAND TAX AND A LOWER PROPERTY TAX

Split rate taxation has been promoted for over 100 years as a method to free the real estate market from restrictions on development, while raising revenue for public use. The current system taxes the combined values of land and buildings, and, by doing so, places an incentive on the real estate market to minimize development. Property owners are essentially penalized for building to the maximum capacity of a lot because those improvements lead to higher taxes; the bigger the building the more taxes are paid. A tax on land without consideration of the value of improvements or building, on the other hand, is considered to be more neutral in its effect.

The premise of this approach is that increases in the value of a site are generally attributable to public investment in its surroundings, and, therefore, are logically more subject to public recapture, whereas improvements on the site can be ascribed to the owner's efforts and investments. In theory, switching to a heavier land tax and a lighter tax on improvements will promote larger buildings in appropriate locations, maximize development capacity, prevent land banking and derelict areas, and promote rehabilitation and redevelopment. Development would be more likely to occur in areas near existing infrastructure, where land values are highest.

Under this proposal, land and structures would be taxed at different rates, with land taxed more heavily. Taxes on built property would decrease to create a revenue-neutral result at the municipal level. The scenario examined for this report puts three quarters of the school tax burden on the land tax and one quarter on the property tax. For example, in West Caldwell Township in Essex County, the land is valued at about $391 million and the improvements at about $721 million. The state-equalized value of land is $630 million. West Caldwell's current school property tax rate, which is based on both land and property value, is $1.11, and raises about $20 million. Under this scenario, 75% of the $20 million would be raised from a land tax, and 25% would be raised from a property tax. To accomplish that, the land tax would need to be $2.38 and the property tax would be $0.43. The immediate effect is clear: if a landowner were to invest $100,000 in improvements for his property – for example, by adding an apartment – that landowner would only have to pay an increase of $430 in local school property taxes, instead of $1,113 under the current structure.

This scenario was constructed to demonstrate how land can be taxed differently from built property with no change to the revenues or expenditures of municipalities. The shift in tax rates would, theoretically, encourage infill and higher density development in places with lower land costs.

Land Use and Social Equity

Consistency with State Plan goals: HIGH

Were the state, or even all the municipalities in a county or sub-county region, to switch to split rate taxation, it is likely that demand would increase for new housing and commercial development. This pressure would, theoretically, be strongest in places with the highest zoning envelopes, such as infill lots in Newark, Paterson, and other cities. The tax system would direct growth toward smaller lots with higher density zoning, and make other areas less attractive from a tax perspective, such as large lots in rural and outer suburban, single family residential areas. Although the higher land taxes in greenfield areas might induce more landowners to try to subdivide their properties for development, there would likely be less demand to develop this property. This conclusion is supported by academic research, including findings from a study by Jan Brueckner. Using a model that predicts development, he found that increasing the proportion of the tax on land and decreasing the proportion result in higher density and less sprawl at the metropolitan scale. The result would be consistent with State Plan goals, leading to more development in urban and suburban centers and less in rural areas.

Consistency with affordable housing goals: HIGH

Split rate taxation would likely lead to an increase in housing overall, and specifically an increase in higher density housing and infill residential development in cities. Most importantly, it would increase incentives to develop more housing, since taxes on new development would be reduced. Also, although Table 19 shows no clear pattern in how taxes would change based on the density of the municipality, there is a consistent body of literature to support the conclusion that higher density and more multi-family housing are a likely result.

Education equity: MODERATE

Consistently, this plan would have a modestly positive effect on education equity. All of the Abbott districts are in municipalities that would benefit from the proposal to some degree, although most are not in the category of those municipalities that would benefit the most.

Efficiency and Fiscal Health

Flexibility: HIGH

Municipalities would have the same ability to change rates as they do now. However, by being able to change the rates on either land or improvements, it should be easier for tax revenues to adjust to changes in the economy without changing rates that would inhibit new development. Table 22 shows no clear pattern of the plan's affect on municipalities categorized by population growth.

Fiscal Discipline: MODERATE

This proposal should have no effect on fiscal discipline. There is no change in who is taxed and who has responsibility for setting tax rates and school budgets. It simply reforms how property is taxed.

Fiscal stability: MODERATE

There would be no shift to less stable taxes and little effect on the stability of local revenue at different points in the business cycle.

Local autonomy: HIGH

More than most of the other proposals, split rate taxation would preserve the fiscal autonomy of local governments. The proposal would not change the total amount of local collections or the level of government where taxes are collected or tax rates are decided, and there would be no incentive, beyond what already exists, for the State to impose spending mandates or constraints.

Summary

This proposal ranks relatively high on both sets of criteria—land use and social equity as well as efficiency and fiscal health. However, it also faces some of the greatest implementation barriers. Its benefits are difficult to grasp intuitively, and there are few actual models of places that have implemented this form of taxation. There are also the technical difficulties of revaluing property accurately and the political hurdles of increasing taxes for some classes of property holders.

Effect of Countywide Tax Rate on Municipalities...	Table 19 ...by Planning Area Category				Table 20 ...by Population Density Category						Table 21 ...by Abbott Status			Table 22 ...by Population Growth Category					Total Mun.
If $100,000 of improvements are added, how much less will the owner pay under the Split Tax plan than under status quo?	Mixed	Urban & Suburban	Rural	Total	Very Low	Low	Med.	High	Very High	Total	Non-Abbott Districts	Abbott Districts	Total	Declining or Stagnant Population	Slowly Growing	Moderately Growing	Quickly Growing	Total	
Save $1,000 +	10%	54%	37%	100%	34%	53%	12%	1%	0%	100%	99%	1%	100%	46%	16%	15%	23%	100%	93
$800 to $999	17%	37%	46%	100%	44%	45%	10%	1%	0%	100%	99%	1%	100%	14%	18%	27%	42%	100%	130
$600 to $799	16%	47%	36%	100%	37%	40%	16%	6%	1%	100%	95%	5%	100%	17%	29%	29%	26%	100%	154
$400 to $599	19%	65%	16%	100%	19%	50%	18%	10%	3%	100%	86%	14%	100%	11%	36%	32%	21%	100%	121
$200 to $399	7%	77%	17%	100%	3%	60%	13%	13%	10%	100%	87%	13%	100%	10%	20%	53%	17%	100%	30
$1 to $199	17%	33%	50%	100%	37%	57%	3%	3%	0%	100%	100%	0%	100%	33%	33%	10%	23%	100%	30
Pay $0 or more under SPLIT plan	0%	0%	100%	100%	50%	50%	0%	0%	0%	100%	100%	0%	100%	38%	25%	13%	25%	100%	8
Total	15%	50%	35%	100%	32%	48%	14%	5%	1%	100%	95%	5%	100%	20%	25%	27%	27%	100%	566
Municipalities	86	283	197	566	185	269	76	28	8	566	535	31	566	116	144	152	154	566	

IX. Conclusion

The ranking of each proposal by criteria provides an indication of which reforms would be best suited to different goals. Table 23 summarizes the findings for the five criteria by ranking each criterion Low, Moderate, or High. These broad categories capture the general direction of change. In some cases, the analysis indicates a clear shift in incentives and probable outcomes, while, in others, the effects are clouded by data limitations or ambiguities that are difficult to test. However, the results allow us to characterize which proposals are likely to have the greatest potential to meet multiple objectives.

One important characteristic that the results do not show is political viability. This was a deliberate choice in framing the criteria, since one objective of the exercise is to encourage both citizens and public officials to consider novel concepts and politically difficult choices. However, some discussion of implementation hurdles is needed for any of these ideas to receive serious discussion. The following conclusions, therefore, incorporate both the analysis of the criteria and the political context for implementation.

Somewhat surprisingly, the two proposals that do the least to improve land use and social equity are the two proposals that shift property taxes from the local level to the state or county level by instituting uniform rates at these higher jurisdictional levels. In theory, these should have lowered rates in poorer, more urban areas, increased incentives to comply with the State Plan, and reduced inequities in tax burdens. However, the results were generally either neutral or negative on these criteria. These outcomes appear to result from two factors. One is that state grant programs already mitigate the inequities of the tax system to some extent by providing more aid to poorer school districts. The second is that wealthier districts can and do choose to tax themselves to produce superior schools. With a wealthier population and better schools to start with, higher tax rates may seem less burdensome and result in a better product than in poorer districts. If this is the case, then shifting the tax burden upward to the state or county could still be effective, but it would have to involve a comprehensive reform of grant programs and some differentiation of rates by type of place.

Varying taxes by State Plan category provides a much stronger realignment of incentives, because it consciously redirects the tax burden toward places where development is to be minimized. This shift favors urban and poorer districts and results in positive effects for land use, affordable housing, and education equity criteria. Rankings on Efficiency and Fiscal Health criteria are mixed. The one low ranking—local autonomy—indicates that this proposal would face difficult political hurdles. The "losing" municipalities would be clear from the start and could be expected to vociferously oppose this reform.

The Income Tax Substitution proposal also generates positive housing and social equity effects, but for different reasons. By shifting the tax burden from property to income taxes, it lowers effective property tax rates across the board and increases incentives for new development. The additional income tax burden would be felt most strongly in wealthier towns, so it would encourage greater equity as well. It also has mixed rankings for Efficiency and Fiscal Health criteria. Its political difficulties would stem less from its impact on local autonomy, since school districts would retain budget control while not having to raise as much in local taxes, than from resistance to any increase in income taxes. The main policy concerns are that it would increase the instability of the State's tax base and weaken spending constraints on school districts. Also, further research is warranted in how changes in both income and property tax rates would affect competitiveness with other states.

Split Rate Taxation receives High or Moderate rankings for all criteria. It strongly encourages affordable housing by lowering the effective tax rate for new development and provides greater efficiency and flexibility without negative impacts on the other criteria. However, its main impediment is that it would be difficult to implement, even leaving aside any political considerations. It would require a dramatic restructuring of how property is taxed and would require local as well as state action to implement. There are also a limited number of empirical test cases that can be examined for impacts. This reform may deserve serious attention, but is unlikely to be the sole vehicle for reforming New Jersey's tax system.

Developing a Research and Action Agenda

The twin purposes of this report are to assess several proposed ideas for reforming property taxes and to suggest a common framework and methodology for comparing other proposals. As with most research projects, the analysis in this report both provides new information and raises additional questions. There are several ways in which the research could be refined or expanded. A regression or correlation analysis could determine more precisely which relationships are statistically significant. The effects of the proposals on economic growth or property values could also be modeled with sufficient information and specification of other relevant variables. There are also an infinite number of variations in the types or details of reform proposals that could be tested. An obvious expansion of this research would be to look at the impact of proposals for reforming the non-school portion of local property taxes.

The results of this analysis also lead to the conclusion that a combination of reforms may be most effective for addressing multiple objectives. None of the proposals is clearly superior on all criteria, and there may be ways of combining elements of different ideas to produce optimum results. For example, combining the income tax substitution proposal with some form of either variation by State Plan area or split rate taxation could address some of the shortcomings of each concept.

Given the urgency for property tax reform in New Jersey, there is a limit to how much additional research can be performed before reform proposals will be considered and adopted. However, using this framework can help narrow the list of viable proposals, target additional research, and provide a common base of comparison for different reforms. In coming months, a few ideas are likely to emerge as the leading contenders for property tax reform. A refined version of this framework, or a similar model that allows for apples-to-apples comparisons across a broad range of indicators, should be incorporated into the legislative process that will select and enact comprehensive reforms.

Table 23

Reform Scenarios Rated by Criteria	Reform Scenario				
	Vary by State Planning Area	Statewide Rate	Countywide Rate	Income Tax Substitution	Split Rate Taxation
Land Use and Social Equity					
Consistency with State Plan	High	Moderate	Moderate	Moderate	High
Housing Affordability	Moderate	Moderate	Moderate	High	High
Education Equity	High	Low	Low	High	Moderate
Efficiency and Fiscal Health					
Flexibility	High	Low	Moderate	Moderate	High
Fiscal Discipline	Moderate	Moderate	High	Low	Moderate
Fiscal Stability	Moderate	Moderate	Moderate	Low	Moderate
Local Autonomy	Low	Low	Moderate	High	High

CHAPTER THREE

Reforming the Use of Eminent Domain for Private Redevelopment in New Jersey

By
Ronald Chen

EXECUTIVE SUMMARY

Eminent domain is one of the most awesome powers that Americans have entrusted to their government. When this power is invoked, citizens lose their homes and businesses. More importantly, they can also lose their place in their communities, and their sense of comfort, stability, and security.

It is, therefore, crucial that the laws governing the use of eminent domain ensure a just and transparent process in which the rights of tenants and property owners are fully protected, and eminent domain is used rarely and only in very specific circumstances. These stipulations are particularly important in situations where eminent domain is used for private redevelopment, because, in these cases, the opportunities for misuse, abuse, and injustice are often even greater.

Unfortunately, in New Jersey, the current laws governing the use of eminent domain for private redevelopment do not adequately protect the rights of tenants and property owners. These current laws:

- Allow for the use of eminent domain in areas that do not meet the constitutional requirement of a "blighted area";
- Require little meaningful notice to affected tenants and property owners;
- Offer few opportunities for real public participation;
- Provide little meaningful opportunity to appeal the designation of "blight" to an impartial third party;
- Allow for vague redevelopment plans that are not developed in conjunction with the community and can be unlimited in their duration;
- Permit compensation for taken property that is so low that it does not allow a homeowner to ever own a home in their town again;
- Do not require sufficient relocation planning;

- Are governed by ethics rules not strong enough to engender confidence in the redevelopment process.

The system for using eminent domain for private redevelopment in New Jersey needs to be reformed.

After conducting extensive research and fact finding, the Department of the Public Advocate has arrived at a set of clear principles that we believe must guide such reforms. Each of these principles is supported by a series of policy recommendations that the Public Advocate believes are necessary to uphold those principles. Key reform recommendations contained in this report include the following:

- Revise the statutory criteria for designating an area as "blighted," which triggers the ability to use eminent domain: These statutory criteria must provide real limitations on the ability to use eminent domain for private redevelopment, as the Constitution requires. For example, under current law an area can be deemed blighted if it is found to be "not fully productive," which could apply to virtually any property. Such broad criteria must be removed. Other criteria, such as property that is "underutilized," are too vague, particularly when applied to residential property. The revised criteria for designating an area as blighted should be as objective as possible, and must be based on an assessment of the current state of an area, not its potential future use. As a means of making the criteria more objective and specific, the legislature should consider making certain criteria applicable only to commercial properties.
- Promote rehabilitation: The criteria used to designate an area "in need of rehabilitation," should be expanded. This change would allow municipalities to retain the powers and benefits that come from designating an area as blighted (or "in need of redevelopment"), but without gaining the power to use eminent domain.
- Require meaningful notice to residents: All tenants and property owners in a proposed redevelopment area should receive notice via certified or regular mail at least 60 days prior to the public hearing, indicating that their municipality is considering designating their properties as part of a "blighted area." Such notice should make explicitly clear that a consequence of this designation is that their properties can be taken using eminent domain.
- Offer property owners a meaningful opportunity to appeal the blight designation: The hearing to determine the blight designation should be recorded, testimony should be provided under oath, and affected citizens should have the opportunity to bring their own witnesses. The window of opportunity for appealing the blight designation should be expanded to at least 120 days. And if the matter ends up in court, the municipality should be required to present "clear and convincing evidence" that the area has been properly designated as blighted, thus putting the burden of proof on the municipality.
- Create more specific, comprehensive, and community-driven redevelopment plans: A fully-noticed community meeting should be an early requirement of

the redevelopment planning process, and all meetings about the development of the plan should be public with recorded meeting minutes. The plan itself should be required to provide more detail, including more specific time-frames, a detailed relocation plan, an assessment of the impact on affordable housing, and specific justification as to why it is absolutely necessary to acquire each property.

- Add protections to help ensure that eminent domain is used as a last resort: Property owners should be offered the chance to rehabilitate or redevelop their own properties in accordance with the goals of the redevelopment plan, where feasible.

- Protect the rights of tenants: Tenants should be given adequate notice and provided opportunities to participate in the redevelopment process, just like property owners. Detailed relocation plans should be required to address the concerns of displaced tenants. Low-income, displaced tenants should also receive up to five years of rental assistance if comparable and affordable replacement apartments are not available within the municipality. Finally, redevelopment should trigger an obligation to complete a municipal, affordable housing plan, which will increase the availability of affordable apartments and homes.

- Require that homeowners are compensated with at least the "replacement value" of their home: Replacement value should be defined as enough to buy a home of similar size and quality within the municipality under comparable conditions. Tenants and property owners should also be offered first right of refusal for comparably sized homes in the new development, where applicable. Finally, relocation assistance levels should be increased.

- Strengthen ethics rules for the redevelopment process: Enact pay-to-play reforms that apply to all local redevelopment projects and contractors, including consultants hired as part of the project. Redevelopment contracts should be required to be competitively procured. Government officials, and those working on their behalf, should not be allowed to receive direct financial benefit from a redevelopment project with which they are involved.

Reforming the Use of Eminent Domain for Private Redevelopment in New Jersey

Eminent domain is the power of government to take private property for public use. Land taken by eminent domain is used for public purposes such as schools, parks, and roads. In almost all states, including New Jersey, eminent domain can also be used, under certain circumstances, to take private property and transfer it to another private party for the purpose of redevelopment.

Eminent domain is one of the most awesome powers that Americans have entrusted to their government. When this power is invoked, citizens lose their homes and their businesses. More importantly, they can also lose their place in their communities their sense of comfort, stability, and security.

The greater the power entrusted to government officials the more safeguards that should exist to ensure that it is used with care and discretion. It is, therefore, crucial that the laws governing the use of eminent domain ensure a just and transparent process in which the rights of tenants and property owners are fully protected and eminent domain is used rarely and only in very specific circumstances. Such restraints are particularly important in situations where eminent domain is used for private redevelopment, because, in these cases, the opportunities for misuse, abuse, and injustice are often even greater.

Some contend that eminent domain should never be used for the purpose of redevelopment. In reaction to the US Supreme Court's recent *Kelo* decision, affirming the constitutionality of using eminent domain for redevelopment, many states have been moved to restrict this power.[1] South Dakota, for example, recently outlawed the use of eminent domain for private redevelopment under any circumstances. The Department of the Public Advocate believes, however, that redevelopment of truly blighted areas is a legitimate public purpose that serves the greater good by helping revitalize communities and create more opportunities for residents. The power to use eminent domain for private redevelopment is specifically enshrined in New Jersey's constitution. Moreover, it would be a mistake to draw simple parallels between New Jersey and other states, such as South Dakota, on this issue, because of New Jersey's unique need for redevelopment.

New Jersey is the most densely populated state in America.[2] New Jersey also has some of the most aggressive land preservation and smart growth policies in the nation, with large areas such as the Highlands and Pinelands protected from overdevelopment, and a range of programs designed to channel growth into cities and towns that have already been developed. As a result, the prosperity of New Jersey's communities is more reliant on redevelopment than perhaps any state in the nation. Good community redevelopment projects can be particularly important to low- and moderate-income families in need of increased opportunities. Redevelopment almost always requires public-private partnerships that leverage tax dollars and bring private investment into our communities. And when used appropriately, eminent domain can be an important tool in making redevelopment possible in blighted areas.

Imagine a New Jersey town in need of revitalization, with a broadly supported plan to redevelop a truly blighted area. Imagine, further, that a property owner in an area crucial to that redevelopment plan is refusing to sell his or her property for any reasonable offer. Perhaps it is an absentee landlord who has let his or her building fall into disrepair and has little invested in the community. Or perhaps the property is home to an abandoned building with contaminated soil, and the owner will not sell because he or she does not want to pay to clean up the land. In rare circumstances, eminent domain can be necessary as a last resort to advance redevelopment projects, provided that the rights of tenants and property owners are protected.

Unfortunately, in New Jersey the current laws do not adequately protect the rights of tenants and property owners. The system for using eminent domain for private redevelopment in New Jersey needs to be reformed.

Scope of Work

When the new Department of the Public Advocate opened on March 27, 2006, Public Advocate Ronald Chen announced that its first major initiative would be to examine the use of eminent domain for private redevelopment in New Jersey. This examination has included extensive research and fact finding (detailed below). While some of this research will continue beyond this report and will help to further illuminate this issue, our considerable research and fact finding to date leaves little doubt that immediate reforms are necessary.

What follows are a set of principles for reform that the Public Advocate believes must be adhered to in order to protect the rights of tenants and property owners. These principles are accompanied by recommended policy reforms that are necessary to uphold the principles. Please note that the scope of this investigation and these reform recommendations are limited to the use of eminent domain for private redevelopment and are not intended to apply to the use of eminent domain for other public purposes.

Much of the recent debate nationwide on eminent domain has been fueled by the 2005 US Supreme Court case *Kelo v. City of New London*. In *Kelo*, the Court ruled that, under the Federal Constitution, it is permissible to use the power of eminent domain for private redevelopment, even if an area is not blighted. But the *Kelo* decision specifically notes that states may adopt further restrictions on eminent domain for private redevelopment. The New Jersey State Constitution does just that, allowing eminent domain for private redevelopment only in blighted areas. Thus, the taking that was upheld in the *Kelo* case would not be permissible under the New Jersey Constitution. New Jersey's right to restrict the use of eminent domain for private redevelopment in blighted areas was upheld by the US Supreme Court more than 50 years ago.

The Department of the Public Advocate will continue to gather data and conduct additional research on the use of eminent domain for private redevelopment subsequent to this report. As we continue to gain perspective on this important issue, we will keep the public informed of the Department's views, and will not foreclose other means provided to our Department under the statute to ensure that the rights of tenants and property owners are protected.

Research for This Report

In preparing this report, the Public Advocate and his staff conducted extensive meetings with a range of interested parties, including:

- Government officials, including legislators, mayors, planners, and commissioners and staff from various state agencies;
- State and national experts on eminent domain, planning, economic development, and property rights;
- A wide range of interest groups representing environmentalists, housing

advocates, transportation advocates, smart growth advocates, small and medium businesses, large businesses, small developers, large developers, community developers, apartment owners, real estate agents, planners, tenants, homeowners, and, most importantly, a diverse range of local communities impacted by eminent domain.

The Public Advocate and his staff also visited some communities impacted by the use of eminent domain for private redevelopment. Sites we visited included redevelopment areas in Camden, Long Branch, Lodi, and Collingswood. The Department also conducted numerous interviews with both government officials and individual citizens in these communities.

In addition, the Department received extensive information and feedback via letters, emails, and phone calls from individual homeowners, tenants, business owners, religious leaders, and other private citizens whose communities have been impacted by eminent domain.

The Department also gathered as much data as possible on redevelopment and the use of eminent domain for redevelopment. Unfortunately, the data that exists in New Jersey is quite limited. With the help of the Department of Community Affairs, we were able to compile some basic data on redevelopment projects that have been started since mid-2003. In addition, we relied on interest groups, national experts, and community residents to provide us with additional data and anecdotal information about how eminent domain is used in New Jersey for redevelopment.

Finally, the Department conducted extensive legal and policy research relating to eminent domain for redevelopment in New Jersey and in other states.

Current Laws and Regulations Governing the Use of Eminent Domain for Private Redevelopment in New Jersey

Before discussing eminent domain reforms, it is useful to understand the current laws governing eminent domain and private redevelopment in New Jersey.

The New Jersey Constitution authorizes the use of eminent domain for private redevelopment, stating that "(t)he clearance, replanning, development or redevelopment of blighted areas shall be a public purpose and public use, for which private property may be taken or acquired."[3] In 1949, the legislature authored statutes to govern this redevelopment process. These statutes have been updated several times, most recently in 2002. It is from this legal framework that redevelopment in New Jersey is governed.

Designating an Area as Blighted

To use eminent domain for private redevelopment in New Jersey, a municipality must first find that an area is "blighted," as required by the constitution. The legislature has established that, for the purposes of using eminent domain for private redevelopment, any one of the following seven criteria would make an area blighted:

a. The generality of buildings are substandard, unsafe, unsanitary, dilapidated, or obsolescent, or possess any of such characteristics, or are so lacking in light, air, or space, as to be conducive to unwholesome living or working conditions.

b. The discontinuance of the use of buildings previously used for commercial, manufacturing, or industrial purposes; the abandonment of such buildings; or the same being allowed to fall into so great a state of disrepair as to be untenantable.

c. Land that is owned by the municipality, the county, a local housing authority, redevelopment agency, or redevelopment entity, or unimproved vacant land that has remained so for a period of 10 years prior to adoption of the resolution, and that, by reason of its location, remoteness, lack of means of access to developed sections or portions of the municipality, topography, or nature of the soil, is not likely to be developed through the instrumentality of private capital.

d. Areas with buildings or improvements, which, by reason of dilapidation, obsolescence, overcrowding, faulty arrangement or design, lack of ventilation, light and sanitary facilities, excessive land coverage, deleterious land use or obsolete layout, or any combination of these or other factors, are detrimental to the safety, health, morals, or welfare of the community.

e. A growing lack or total lack of proper utilization of areas caused by the condition of the title, diverse ownership of the real property therein, or other conditions, resulting in a stagnant or not fully productive condition of land potentially useful and valuable for contributing to and serving the public health, safety, and welfare.

f. Areas, in excess of five contiguous acres, whereon buildings or improvements have been destroyed, consumed by fire, demolished, or altered by the action of storm, fire, cyclone, tornado, earthquake, or other casualty in such a way that the aggregate assessed value of the area has been materially depreciated.

[g. *Criterion (g) only applies to the use of tax abatements and specifically indicates that it is not a basis for a blight declaration for eminent domain purposes.*]

h. The designation of the delineated area is consistent with smart growth planning principles adopted pursuant to law or regulation.[4]

To begin redevelopment, the governing body, typically the town council, adopts a resolution directing the planning board to conduct a preliminary investigation assessing whether or not an area meets one of these seven criteria of blight. During this investigation, the planning board sends notices to all property owners in the proposed redevelopment area notifying them of a public hearing on the blight designation. This notice, however, does not need to specify that this blight designation could mean that a person's home could be taken using eminent domain. The notice also does not need to be sent to tenants, and must only be sent 10 days in advance of the hearing. This hearing represents the only required public hearing before the designation of blight.

Once the planning board has completed its research, it submits its report back to the town council. This report includes a map outlining the boundaries of the area, and an analysis describing whether or not the area meets the statutory criteria for a blighted area. After receiving the planning board's recommendation, the town council may pass a resolution designating the area as blighted.

This resolution must be sent to the Department of Community Affairs (DCA) for review. DCA's review, however, is not to determine whether the blight designation was appropriate, but only to assess the smart growth implications of designating the redevelopment area. If the proposed redevelopment is in an area designated for growth,

DCA's approval is automatic upon receipt of the resolution.[5] If not, DCA's review must be completed within 30 days, or the blight designation automatically takes effect. Once DCA approval is granted, the blight designation is official. There is no time limit as to how long the blight designation can last.

Within 10 days of the blight determination, the governing body must serve notice to residents who filed written objections at the planning board's public hearing. Those who did not file written objections are not required to receive notice of the blight designation. After the resolution is passed, property owners have only a 45-day window to appeal the blight designation in court. If no appeals have been filed with the court after 45 days, the governing body may begin taking action to acquire or condemn any property in the redevelopment area.

Writing the Redevelopment Plan

After designating the area "blighted" (the statute uses the term "in need of redevelopment"), the governing body directs the planning board, the redevelopment agency, or governing body itself to prepare the redevelopment plan. The redevelopment plan must contain several elements, including:

- The relationship of the redevelopment plan to the municipal, county, and state land use plans;
- The proposed land uses and building requirements in the redevelopment area; "adequate provisions" for the temporary and permanent relocation of citizens within the redevelopment area;
- Identification of any property in the redevelopment area that is proposed to be acquired.

The redevelopment plan is currently not required to include elements such as specific justifications as to why properties need to be acquired, timeframes for redevelopment, or an assessment of the impact on affordable housing in the municipality.

Once the plan is complete, the governing body approves the plan by ordinance, which requires a public hearing. The governing body may alter any recommendations in the proposed redevelopment plan, so long as it has a majority vote.

The governing body can select a redeveloper at any point in this process. The redeveloper is often chosen early in the process, so it can assist with the drafting of the redevelopment plan. The town may also select multiple redevelopers.

Implementing the Redevelopment Plan and Using Eminent Domain

After the redevelopment plan has been adopted, the governing body designates a redevelopment entity, which is the public body responsible for implementing the redevelopment plan and is granted all the redevelopment powers authorized by state law. These powers include the ability to issue bonds, grant tax abatements, install or construct streets and utilities, and condemn homes using the power of eminent domain. The redevelopment entity can be the governing body, a separate redevelopment agency, the local housing authority, or a county improvement authority. There may also be more than one redevelopment entity for a given redevelopment area.

The redevelopment entity has the power to condemn any property in the redevelopment area. Before taking a property, the redevelopment entity must only prove to a court that the property owner was unwilling to sell. Sufficient proof of the property owner's unwillingness to sell is his or her rejection of a single written offer that is no less than the appraised value of the house, as appraised by the governing body's appraiser.

Once the court authorizes the taking, a panel of three commissioners is appointed to determine the appropriate compensation for the property owner. The commissioners hold hearings at which a list of similar sales can be introduced as evidence, and then issue a ruling on the appropriate compensation. The property owner can appeal the decision by the commissioners and demand a jury trial for that appeal.

Once the issue of compensation is settled, the property can be taken. The property owner will also receive from the governing body compensation for applicable costs, such as moving, business discontinuance, or temporary rental expenses.

Recommended Reforms

After undertaking the extensive research described earlier in this report, the Department of the Public Advocate has arrived at a set of clear principles that we believe must guide any efforts to reform the current laws governing the use of eminent domain for private redevelopment. These principles are based, in part, on what we believe are just, fair, and appropriate policies to serve the public interest, and, in part, on the state and federal constitutional rights that the Public Advocate believes are not adequately protected under the current laws governing eminent domain.

Listed below each of these principles are policy reforms that the Public Advocate believes are necessary to uphold these principles. The policy recommendations are not exhaustive, but each represents an important step toward protecting the rights of tenants and property owners.

The Criteria for Designating an Area "Blighted"

Principle: The statutory criteria for designating an area as "in need of redevelopment" must be consistent with the constitutional requirement that an area be "blighted," and must provide meaningful limitations on the use of eminent domain for redevelopment.

The New Jersey Constitution provides that the "clearance, replanning, development or redevelopment of blighted areas shall be a public purpose and public use, for which private property may be taken or acquired." The term "blighted area" is a constitutional limitation on the power of the State to use eminent domain for private redevelopment.

Although the constitution does not further define "blighted area," the term had a widely accepted definition when applied to land redevelopment in 1947, at the time the constitution was enacted. In 1949, the legislature first attempted to define the term, outlining criteria for determining whether an area was blighted. In subsequent years, the legislature has continued to expand those criteria.

The 1949 Blighted Area Act defined "blight" as an area in which there exists, "to a large extent," one of four criteria.[6] In 1951, the Legislature reworded the first four criteria, and added a fifth criterion.[7] In 1986, a sixth category of blight was added.[8]

In 1992, the legislature enacted the Local Redevelopment and Housing Law (LRHL). The LRHL made some modifications to criteria (a) through (d) and to criterion (f).[9] The most noteworthy difference in the LRHL, however, is the substantial change made to criterion (e).

Prior to 1992, blight could be found if the conditions of the land made it both "stagnant and unproductive." But, in 1992, the Legislature effectively made the stagnancy requirement meaningless by replacing that language with a provision that an area could meet the requirements of blight if the conditions or use of the land were either "stagnant or not fully productive."

As a result, a mere finding that land is "not fully productive" now empowers a governing body to use eminent domain. Not only does this criterion go well beyond any reasonable definition of blight, but this language also puts virtually no limitation on the finding of blight, given that any property could plausibly be more productive (e.g., add one more floor to any building or one more housing unit to any development).

The 1992 legislation also makes an important language change by deleting the word "blight" from the beginning of the statute, burying the word deep within the statute, and deeming that blight exists when an area is determined to be "in need of redevelopment." While such a change in wording may have little legal importance, it has helped change the perception of what this designation means. Clearly, "in need of redevelopment" could describe almost any older neighborhood or business district in a way that "blight" could not.

Finally, in 2003, the Legislature enacted a seventh criterion for establishing that an area is blighted. Under the new section (h), an area is in need of redevelopment, and thus blighted, if "the designation of the delineated area is consistent with smart growth planning principles adopted pursuant to law or regulation."[10]

Thus, over the course of some 40 years, the legislature shifted from four narrowly drawn definitions of blight to seven broad definitions of blight. In doing so, the legislature's interpretation of the constitution's "blighted area" clause has expanded to the point where it provides virtually no limitation on taking private property for redevelopment, in apparent violation of the constitutional intent to limit this power (*see attached Appendix for additional legal analysis*).

If the legislature revised the blight criteria to make them more specific, objective, and limiting, it would reconcile the statutory language with the constitutional requirements and prevent the use of eminent domain in areas that are by no reasonable definition blighted. Such revised criteria would also facilitate a more meaningful judicial review of the initial blight designation, and help create more certainty for all parties involved in the redevelopment process.

Policy Recommendations

- Revise the statutory criteria for blight so that they provide real limitations on the ability of a governing body to designate an area as blighted. For example, as discussed above, criterion (e), stating that land that is "not fully productive" can be considered blighted, removes almost any meaningful limitation on the blight designation. Similarly, criterion (h), stating that an area consistent with smart growth principles meets the definition of blighted, essentially means that all of State Planning Areas 1 and 2 and designated centers are blighted. Criterion (h) should be removed.
- Restrict the statutory criteria for blight so that, as best as possible, they describe objective conditions, and eliminate criteria that are so vague as to be nearly impossible to subject to meaningful third party review. For example, criterion (e) notes that blight stems from "a growing lack or total lack of proper utilization." "Proper utilization" is a highly subjective term, particularly when applied to residential properties.
- Revise the statutory language to ensure that the determination of blight is based on an assessment of the current state of the property and is independent of any potential or future use of the property. For example, criterion (e) describes "land potentially useful and valuable for contributing to and serving the public health, safety and welfare." This criterion assesses the property relative to its potential or future use, and not based solely on its current condition. Therefore, such language should be removed.
- Consider applying different criteria to residential and commercial properties. Certain criteria are easier to assess and can be applied more objectively when used to evaluate a commercial entity rather than a person's home.
- State explicitly in the statute that a designation of blight must be based on the

functionality of an area, and not simply on its appearance. For example, a safe, well-functioning residential neighborhood is not blighted simply because the front lawns have no grass or the homes are unattractive in the opinion of the governing body.

- Establish in the statute some criteria for including smaller non-blighted areas within a larger area that is designated as blighted. For example, the statute could state that a certain percentage of an area must be blighted for the entire area to be designated as blighted.

Principle: Efforts to "rehabilitate communities should be prioritized and promoted so that municipalities can take advantage of tools to revitalize their communities without the threat of eminent domain."

Some argue that restricting the statutory criteria for blight will hurt New Jersey's communities by restricting their access to the many benefits and powers aside from eminent domain that come from designating an area as blighted or "in need of redevelopment." The Department of the Public Advocate shares this concern, but does not believe the answer is to allow the nearly unimpeded use of eminent domain—the criteria for blight must be restricted to be consistent with constitutional requirements and to protect the rights of tenants and property owners. However, designating an area "in need of rehabilitation" provides a municipality with the same powers and benefits as declaring an area "in need of redevelopment," with the exception of the power of eminent domain and the power to grant long-term tax abatements. Therefore, the effort to rehabilitate communities should be promoted.

Policy Recommendations

- Expand the criteria needed to designate an area "in need of rehabilitation." The Legislature may want to move language removed from the blight criteria for purposes of declaring an area "in need of redevelopment" to the statutory criteria for declaring an area "in need of rehabilitation."
- Require that, before designating an area "in need of redevelopment," the governing body must first establish that the goals of redevelopment could not be met in a fiscally prudent manner by designating the area "in need of rehabilitation."

Principle: Eminent domain for private redevelopment must not have the intent or the effect of causing protected classes of residents to permanently relocate involuntarily outside the municipality.

It is the opinion of the Department of the Public Advocate that redevelopment that systematically forces protected classes to relocate outside the municipality would violate protections provided by both our state and federal constitutions. Protected classes include racial, ethnic, and cultural minorities. Redevelopment should also not have the effect of systematically relocating low-income populations outside of the municipality.

Policy Recommendations

- Explicitly state in the statute that the income or racial, ethnic and cultural backgrounds of neighborhood residents cannot be considered in designating an area as blighted.
- Improve the process of declaring an area as blighted to ensure more meaningful public participation by all tenants and property owners, including protected classes (described in more detail below).

The Process for Designating an Area as Blighted

Principle: The process by which a municipality declares an area as blighted must be transparent and fully noticed, and must provide a meaningful opportunity for affected persons to participate early in the process.

Current laws governing the process by which an area is designated as blighted are insufficient to ensure meaningful public participation. While many municipalities do voluntarily engage in an open, transparent, and participatory redevelopment process, there are currently no adequate requirements to ensure that all municipalities engage in such a process. A number of citizens, for example, reported to the Department that they were never made fully aware that being designated an area "in need of redevelopment" meant their homes could be taken through the use of eminent domain, until long after the designation had already occurred. This lack of effective and early communication with affected citizens often leads to prolonged legal battles well into the redevelopment process, which is a bad outcome for all parties involved.

Policy Recommendations

- Require that notice of public hearings on the proposed blight designation be sent not only to property owners within the redevelopment area, but also to tenants and those living within 200 feet of the redevelopment area.
- Require that notice to tenants and property owners be sent via certified and regular mail.
- Require that such notice be written in plain language and clearly indicate that a possible consequence of such a designation is that their property can be taken using eminent domain.
- Require that such notice use the constitutional terminology "blighted" rather than the more euphemistic statutory language "in need of redevelopment."
- Require that such notice be provided at least 60 days in advance of the hearing, rather than the current 10-day requirement. This change will allow property owners and tenants time to prepare for the hearing so that they can build a record against the designation if they choose.
- Require that such notice be advertised on the municipal website, if one exists.

- Require that such notice inform property owners as to the specific criteria under which the area has been found to be blighted.
- Guarantee affected tenants and property owners the ability to access relevant documents, such as the preliminary investigation report, in advance of the hearing so that they can understand the case that the governing body is making. A hard copy of such documents should be available for inspection at the municipal building and public library. Such documents should also be available electronically, where feasible.

Principle: A proceeding to declare an area blighted must be an impartial fact-based inquiry that focuses, at a minimum, on the statutory criteria for a blighted area; the record adduced in such a proceeding must be sufficiently developed to be capable of meaningful review.

Because of the serious implications of the blight designation, the proceeding to establish that an area is blighted must be thorough and well-documented. Citizens have reported that some of these proceedings have been cursory formalities, rather than serious discussions about the validity of the blight designation. In other instances, citizens have made credible claims that they were misled about the implications of the blight designation for their properties and the future of their communities. Such insufficient proceedings do little to contribute to the public discourse about these important policy choices, and serve to undermine the entire redevelopment process.

Policy Recommendations

- Mandate that public hearings on the blight designation be recorded, and require that transcripts be made available to the public.
- Require that testimony at the public hearings regarding the blight designation be given under oath.
- Guarantee the right of citizens impacted by the potential blight designation to bring their own witnesses and submit written questions to be asked of the municipality's witnesses.
- Require that the governing body pass an ordinance to declare an area as blighted, rather than simply passing a resolution as is required under current law. In comparison to a resolution, an ordinance requires more notice and transparency, and requires a public hearing.
- Require that the record of blight determination, including the contents of the preliminary investigation report, document that a large enough percentage of the individual properties within the redevelopment area exhibit conditions of blight so as to meet the statutory standard (presuming the legislature adopts such a standard).

Principle: Property owners must have a meaningful opportunity to appeal the designation of their properties as blighted to an impartial third party.

To protect the rights of property owners, it is crucial that they have a meaningful opportunity to appeal the blight designation to a third party that does not have any interest in the redevelopment project. The Department of the Public Advocate does not believe that the creation or expansion of a state-level bureaucracy is an efficient or effective means of providing this third-party appeal. The Department believes the judiciary is a more appropriate mechanism, but only if a heightened burden of proof is required of the municipality, and if affected citizens have a realistic opportunity to initiate such an appeal. Historically, courts have given great deference to municipal declarations of blight, meaning that property owners challenging the designation bore the burden of proving that the blight designation was incorrect.

Policy Recommendations

* Increase the burden of proof on the governing body to defend the blight designation in court. The governing body should be required to present "clear and convincing evidence" that an area has been properly designated as blighted, as opposed to the burden being on the property owners to prove that the blight designation was improper.
* Require that notice be sent to all tenants and property owners in the re-development area once the governing body has accepted the planning board's recommendation and passed a resolution designating an area as blighted. Currently, notice is only required to be sent to those who filed written objections to the designation of blight. Such notice should inform citizens that they have a right to an appeal, and should provide the relevant deadlines for filing that appeal.
* Extend the 45-day window in which property owners can dispute the blight designation to at least 120 days in order to provide a more realistic opportunity to contest the designation.

The Process of Creating a Redevelopment Plan

Principle: Community members must have meaningful opportunities to participate in the redevelopment planning process.

Redevelopment should be about revitalizing a community. The redevelopment planning process should reflect that priority by making community members a direct and integral part of the process.

Policy Recommendations

* Require at least one community meeting at an early stage in the redevelopment planning process. Citizens in and near the redevelopment area should receive notice of this meeting in the same manner in which notice is provided

for the original blight designation. Such hearings should be community discussions about desired outcomes, rather than technical or procedural in nature.

• Require that when the governing body is holding its hearing on the final adoption of the redevelopment plan, tenants and property owners receive notice in the same manner in which notice is provided for the original blight designation. Any citizen whose property is proposed to be acquired under the plan should be notified as to the specific criteria under which their property has been designated as blighted, or, if the property is not blighted, the reason why acquiring this property is vital for the redevelopment project.

• Require that all meetings about the redevelopment plan, at which there is a quorum of the body charged with creating the plan, be public, and that the content of those public meetings be recorded, transcribed, and made available to the public.

Principle: Redevelopment plans must be more specific and comprehensive, and must create more certainty and understanding among all parties affected by eminent domain.

The quality and specificity of redevelopment plans in New Jersey varies widely. Good plans outline clear, community-supported redevelopment objectives and provide all interested parties with a degree of certainty about the redevelopment project. The worst examples of redevelopment plans are vague and legalistic documents that essentially amount to an assertion that the town intends to plan a redevelopment project. Such vague plans leave tenants and property owners very much in the dark about the future of their homes, their businesses, and their communities. Moreover, without time limits or more specificity in the plans, the potential for redevelopment and eminent domain can hang over the heads of homeowners and businesses for years, discouraging investment and undermining their ability to sell their properties.

Redevelopment plans should not leave members of the community in such a state of uncertainty. Average citizens should be able to read a redevelopment plan and understand the direction their community is going and how the redevelopment plan will impact their apartments, homes, or businesses.

Policy Recommendations

• Require that redevelopment plans include the following elements, in addition to current statutory requirements:

  a) An explanation of how this redevelopment project will benefit the community;

  b) An outline of the scale, character and intensity of proposed redevelopment;

  c) An explanation as to why there is no other reasonable alternative to acquiring or condemning each property that is proposed to be acquired;

    d)   Timeframes for the major stages of redevelopment plan implementation, including an estimate as to when parcels will be acquired; time limits for the redevelopment project must also be included in the governing body's contract with the redeveloper;

    e)   A detailed permanent and temporary relocation plan that documents the availability of comparable replacement housing for displaced residents (under the current statutory requirements many plans only offer very vague and general assessments of the availability of temporary and permanent housing for displaced residents);

    f)   An assessment of the impact on the community's supply of affordable housing, because if, at the time the redevelopment plan is adopted, it is implausible for it to have the degree of specificity necessary to outline items (d) through (f), then the plan must be amended with these details within six months of its initial adoption;

- Mandate that amending the redevelopment plan requires the same public process as the original plan adoption, including adequate public notice, hearings, and adoption by the governing body;
- Establish a statutory time limit on the number of years that an area can be designated as blighted without full implementation of the redevelopment plan. If an area is still not redeveloped after that time limit, the municipality should have an opportunity to renew the blight designation, but it would need to go through the same public process required for the original designation, and, in addition, explain why the redevelopment plan is not complete and how it will be completed within the timeframe of the renewed blight designation.

Using Eminent Domain for Private Redevelopment

Principle: Eminent domain should be an absolute last resort, used only in truly blighted areas after every other option has been exhausted, and the inability to acquire a property is putting the community redevelopment project in jeopardy.

The designation of an area as blighted should not trigger the widespread use of eminent domain, nor is it intended to allow a developer or governing entity to acquire properties at cut-rate prices by wielding the threat of eminent domain. Eminent domain must be used only as a last resort, and only after a small number of property owners have refused all reasonable offers to sell their properties and are putting the redevelopment of a truly blighted area in jeopardy.

Policy recommendations

- Mandate that property owners be offered the chance to rehabilitate or redevelop their own properties in accordance with the goals of the redevelopment plan in instances in which such a scenario is feasible given the goals of the plan.

- Require that, when a governing body begins condemnation proceedings on a home, the notice to the property owner includes a record of the acquisition prices paid by the redeveloper for similar properties in the redevelopment area. This will increase the transparency of the process.

Compensation and Relocation for Tenants and Property Owners

Principle: When homeowners loses their homes through the use of eminent domain, they should be compensated such that they are able to afford homes of similar size and quality within their municipalities under comparable conditions.

The term "just compensation" as used in Article I, paragraph 20 of the New Jersey Constitution should be construed to "make whole" someone displaced by eminent domain for redevelopment, and, thus, should go beyond "fair market value" when necessary, and include replacement value and temporary relocation costs. It is unjust for homeowners to lose their homes through eminent domain and receive compensation too low for them to ever own homes in their towns again. And yet, under New Jersey's current redevelopment laws, such a scenario happens all too frequently.

Requiring increased compensation may have the effect of making some re-development projects in New Jersey financially untenable, and some would argue that this is reason not to require full replacement value for taken properties. The Public Advocate believes, however, that the financial viability of a redevelopment project should not rest on paying homeowners less than it would take for them to replace their current properties. Such a project would essentially financed on the backs of current homeowners, which is unjust.

Policy Recommendations

- Require that compensation for a taken home be based on the highest value among any one of the following options:
  - The fair market value of the property at the time it is designated as blighted;
  - The fair market value of the property at the time of the taking, under the new zoning proposed in the redevelopment plan;
  - The "replacement value" of the property, which is the cost of a home of similar size and quality under comparable conditions, within a reason-able distance of the current property.
- Require that the municipality or developer offer temporary rental assistance to displaced low-income tenants, if a comparable and affordable replace-ment apartment within the municipality is not available. This assistance would be enough to make the new rental costs affordable (i.e., no more than 30% of the family's gross income), after factoring in any public subsidies the tenant already receives, such as Section 8 vouchers. Such temporary rental

assistance should be provided for five years, or until the tenant moves from the apartment to which he or she was originally displaced.

- Offer existing tenants and homeowners the right of first refusal for a comparably sized apartment or property in the new development, if applicable.
- Increase the statutory maximum levels for all types of relocation assistance, which include assistance for moving expenses, temporary rent payments, and business discontinuance. In the current statute, these maximum levels are specific dollar amounts that were set decades ago; these amounts should be adjusted to current dollars and indexed to increase automatically with inflation.

Affordable Housing

Principle: Redevelopment should increase the availability of affordable housing in a municipality.

Redevelopment offers a tremendous opportunity for a municipality to improve the quality of life for its citizens, which includes expanding the availability of safe, affordable housing. With New Jersey already suffering from a severe lack of affordable housing, redevelopment and eminent domain should be tools that help increase its availability.

Policy Recommendations

- Require any municipality that designates an area in need of redevelopment to develop an affordable housing plan to submit to the Council on Affordable Housing (COAH) for certification.
- Require that all units of COAH-certified affordable housing or publicly funded housing (such as project-based Section 8 housing or housing built with state subsidies) that are demolished as part of a redevelopment project be replaced within or near the redevelopment area.

Data Collection and Public Information

Principle: State and local governments should collect and make readily available complete information on redevelopment areas and the use of eminent domain for redevelopment in New Jersey.

Policymakers and citizens alike need complete data and public information about redevelopment and the use of eminent domain to ensure that this process is transparent and to fully understand this important issue.

Policy Recommendations

- Require all municipalities to send documentation of any current or future re-development areas to the Department of Community Affairs (DCA). This documentation should include a map outlining the physical boundaries of the redevelopment area, the preliminary investigation report used to justify the designation of blight (including the criteria under which an area qualifies as blighted), the resolution declaring the area in need of redevelopment, and the redevelopment plan.
- Require all municipalities to notify DCA of any future takings for private redevelopment within two weeks of the taking, for record keeping purposes.
- Require DCA to produce an annual report, compiling information submitted by municipalities, that outlines the following information:
  - The number of redevelopment areas that currently exist in New Jersey and basic data about their features, such as size, population, and the length of time the area has been designated as blighted;
  - The number of times eminent domain has been used in each redevelopment area;
  - Data on compensation received by property owners, where available.
  The completed report should be made available to citizens upon request and on the DCA website.
- Require each municipality to provide easy access—via the Internet and in response to direct citizen requests—to information about whether a specific property is part of a blighted area.

Ethics Reforms

Principle: Ethics rules around the redevelopment process must be strength-ened to prevent perceived or actual corruption and conflicts of interest.

Perceived or actual corruption and conflicts of interest have undermined citi-zens trust in all levels of New Jersey government. Such lack of confidence is of particular concern when it comes to the use of eminent domain for private redevel-opment, because, in such instances, the power of government is so great, the power of citizens is comparatively limited, and the direct involvement of for-profit enti-ties heightens the potential for perceived or actual corruption. Until we strengthen ethics laws and increase the transparency of the redevelopment process, even the best and most ethical redevelopment projects will fall prey to public skepticism about ethical transgressions.

Policy Recommendations

- Enact pay-to-play reforms that apply to all local redevelopment projects and contractors, including consultants hired as part of the project.

- Require redeveloper contracts to be awarded through a competitive process, such as the issuance of Requests for Proposals (RFPs). A waiver for this RFP requirement could be granted to very small projects or projects in which a single property owner already owns a large percentage of the redevelopment area.
- Bar any officials working for the governing body, or consultants or lawyers working on behalf of the governing body, from participating in the redevelopment process if they have direct, personal financial interests in the redevelopment project.
- Prohibit redevelopers or any other private entity from funding the preliminary investigation report, and require that the determination of blight be based solely on a publicly funded investigation.
- Provide support to the Department of Community Affairs to expand planning grants and improve technical assistance offered to municipalities to help them navigate the redevelopment process without relying on the assistance of developers.
- Require full disclosure of public benefits provided to developers in redevelopment projects. In order to create incentives for redevelopment, governing bodies often make investments or provide incentives that benefit developers, such as paying for public infrastructure upgrades, offering density bonuses, or granting tax abatements. To ensure that the redevelopment process is transparent, such benefits should be publicly disclosed in a single document.

Appendix:
Legal Analysis of Limitations on Use of Eminent Domain

I. The Power of Eminent Domain

The notion that an essential aspect of individual freedom is the right to enjoy one's property—and especially one's home—is one with obvious and deeply felt resonance. Indeed, the Third, Fourth, and Fifth Amendments in the federal Bill of Rights all deal in one way or another with the guarantee that one may be secure in one's own home against government intrusion. And Article I, paragraph 1 of the New Jersey Constitution provides that "[a]ll persons are by nature free and independent, and have certain natural and unalienable rights, among which are those of . . . acquiring, possessing, and protecting property. . . . "

On the other hand, in common law legal systems there has long existed a power of the State to expropriate private property without the owner's consent. In 1795, Justice William Patterson, who had been a member of the constitutional convention, described eminent domain as the "despotic power," but nevertheless recognized that such authority was an essential element of government.[1] The New Jersey State Supreme Court noted long ago that "[t]he power of eminent domain is a high sovereign power that has been allotted to the legislative branch of the government since the Magna Carta." *Abbott v. Beth Israel Cemetery Assn*, 13 N.J. 528,

543 (1953). The 1947 New Jersey Constitution "continued the legislative authority to provide for the exercise of the sovereign power of eminent domain, restricted only by the pertinent clauses of that Constitution." *Id.*

Traditionally, the power of eminent domain has been used to acquire real property, when necessary for the completion of a public project such as a road or public building, and when the owner of the required property is unwilling to negotiate a price for its sale. Its more recent and controversial application, however, has been in the context in which a government entity ostensibly exercises its power to expropriate the property of one private person, and then delivers that property to another private party for the purpose of privately sponsored redevelopment, albeit with the hope that such redevelopment will improve conditions for the public as a whole. Although the recent case of *Kelo v. City of New London*[2] has focused public awareness on the use of eminent domain to acquire property for private redevelopment, it was by no means the first judicial decision to approve the practice. Indeed, use of eminent domain for private redevelopment was found constitutional by the United States Supreme Court over fifty years ago,[3] and, as a matter of history, the mechanism of using eminent domain for private redevelopment of slums or blighted areas was well established in the early twentieth century.

In response to *Kelo*, there has been an understandable, adverse reaction to the use of eminent domain for private redevelopment. Some contend that eminent domain should never be used for the purpose of private redevelopment. South Dakota, for example, recently effectively banned use of eminent domain for private development.[4] While, of course, any state legislature is free to adopt such a position as an affirmative policy for its own citizens, a complete ban on eminent domain for redevelopment would be a departure from New Jersey's legal and social history.

As indicated more fully below, in the opinion of the Public Advocate: (1) the term "blighted area" as used in our constitution provides a substantive limitation on the power of the legislature or its delegates to exercise eminent domain for redevelopment; (2) the term "blighted area" is informed by not only the facial text but also the prevailing usage of the term, and can be given a judicially manageable interpretation by the courts; and (3) some aspects of the 1992 Local Redevelopment and Housing Law extend beyond what any reasonable interpretation of "blighted area" would allow.

II. The "Blighted Area" Limitation on Eminent Domain for Redevelopment

As the New Jersey Supreme Court observed, "[i]t has been held that constitutions do not give, but merely place limitations upon, the power of eminent domain which otherwise would be without limitation." *Abbott*, 13 N.J. at 543. Among the most fundamental of rights arising from the constitutions of both the United States and the State of New Jersey are the right to be free from deprivation of property without due process of law;[5] the right of acquiring, possessing, and protecting property;[6] and the right to be free from government appropriation of private property unless for a "public use" and with "just compensation."[7]

With respect to eminent domain generally, the New Jersey constitution states:

Private property shall not be taken for public use without just compensation. Individuals or private corporations shall not be authorized to take private property for public use without just compensation first made to the owners. N.J. CONST. Art. I, ¶ 20.

But after first defining the use of eminent domain generally, the 1947 Constitution then addresses government condemnation of property specifically for private redevelopment:

The clearance, replanning, development or redevelopment of *blighted areas* shall be a public purpose and public use, for which private property may be taken or acquired. Municipal, public or *private corporations* may be authorized by law to undertake such clearance, replanning, development or redevelopment (emphasis added) . N.J. CONST. Art. VIII, § III, ¶ 1.

Thus, while making clear that eminent domain can be used for private redevelopment, the New Jersey Constitution also places strict limits on such use. Specifically, the constitution first requires a finding that the area in which eminent domain is sought to be used for private redevelopment is a "blighted area," a term that the constitution does not expressly define. *See, e.g., Forbes v. Bd. of Trustees of South Orange Tp.*, 312 N.J. Super. 519, 528 (App. Div. 1998)(holding that "blighted area" determination is constitutionally-mandated precondition for taking property for purposes of private redevelopment). Article VIII's "blighted area" clause thus places a substantive limitation on Article I's takings clause by restricting the government's eminent domain power when the condemnation is specifically for private redevelopment purposes.

Although, pursuant to *Kelo*, the federal constitution does not limit use of eminent domain for redevelopment to blighted areas, *Kelo* itself reaffirmed a basic principle of federalism:

We emphasize that nothing in our opinion precludes any State from placing further restrictions on its exercise of the takings power. Indeed, many States already impose "public use" requirements that are stricter than the federal baseline. Some of these requirements have been established as a matter of state constitutional law, while others are expressed in state eminent domain statutes that carefully limit the grounds upon which takings may be exercised.

See id. at 2668 (noting that "[u]nder California law, for instance, a city may only take land for economic development purposes in blighted areas."). Such a state-imposed limitation is precisely what New Jersey (and several other states) enacted in the 1947 constitution, by making clear that private redevelopment only satisfies Article I's "public use" clause if the area in question is "blighted."

That the constitutional framers intended to impose a blight requirement upon the legislature's power to authorize use of eminent domain is also clear from the record of the 1947 convention proceedings. Prior to the adoption of the proposal that became Article VII, § III, ¶1,[8] a member of the Montclair Planning Board proposed that the framers adopt more open-ended language that would have given the legislature the full power to determine the boundaries of redevelopment of any area. The text of that proposal stated:

> The acquisition of real property for development or redevelopment of *any area* (emphasis added) in accordance with a plan duly adopted in a manner prescribed by the Legislature, whether the uses to which such area is to be devoted be public or private uses or both, is hereby declared to be a public use. The Legislature shall make laws governing acquisition, use and disposal of such property by an agency of the State or a political subdivision thereof. The Legislature may authorize the organization of corporations or authorities to undertake such development or redevelopment of any part thereof and may authorize municipalities to exempt their improvements from taxation, in whole or in part, for a limited period of time, under condition as to special public regulations to be specified by law or by contract between any such corporation or authority and the municipality, provided that during the period of such tax exemption the profits of the corporation and the dividends paid by it shall be limited by law. PROCEEDINGS OF THE NEW JERSEY CONSTITUTIONAL CONVENTION OF 1947, Vol. III, at 544.

One of the delegates noted that, because the proposal did not provide guidelines for determining whether an area needed redevelopment, it could "lead to a great deal of possible abuse." Id. at 545-546. In response, the proponent of the amendment stated, "I think that any enabling law the Legislature might pass would *undoubtedly restrict* the right of these towns in certain definite neighborhoods. We feel that that would be a detail the Legislature *should place in the laws and that it should not be restricted in the Constitution.* (emphasis added)" Id. at 546. The framers did not adopt this proposal. Instead of giving the Legislature unfettered discretion to define when eminent domain may be used for redevelopment purposes, the framers affirmatively placed a "blighted area" requirement in the constitution precisely to restrict the use of eminent domain for private redevelopment. Thus, the framers inclusion of the "blighted area" clause in the New Jersey Constitution provides additional support for the proposition that the clause was intended to limit the ability of the legislature to broadly define the scope of the takings power in the private redevelopment arena.

The 1947 Constitution did not expressly define the term "blighted area." Nevertheless, examination of both the facial meaning of those words, and the meaning attached to them in common usage at the time of the 1947 Convention, is instructive. The earliest use of the term "blight" for real estate purposes was by University of Chicago sociologists. Starting in the 1920s, they applied the term previously used in the plant disease field to describe changes to society that did not meet the definition of a slum. *See* Wendell E. Pritchett, The *"Public Menace" of Blight: Urban Renewal and the Private Uses of Eminent Domain*, 21 YALE L. & POL'Y REV. 1, 16 (2003). According to the Chicago school, a blighted area was one comprised of properties in a state of decline. *See, e.g.*, Homer Hoyt, ONE HUNDRED YEARS OF LAND VALUES IN CHICAGO 364 (1936). *See also* Ernest Burgess, *The Growth of the City: An Introduction to a Research Project*, in THE CITY 47 (Robert E. Park et al. eds., 1925) (arguing that a blighted area is marked by a "speeding up of the junking process in the area of deterioration"); Pritchett, The *"Public Menace" of Blight*, at 16-17 ("Blight arose around the central business district, in areas that were formerly residential. As cities expanded, these areas became mixed use districts, with industry and commerce. The formerly attractive housing was divided into smaller units for the poor, and 'parasitic and transitory services' such as flophouses proliferated.")(citing Roderick D. McKenzie, *The Ecological Approach to the Study of the Human Community*, in THE CITY 76 (Ernest Burgess et al. eds., 1925)).

Other scholars and planners echoed the "blight" definition first employed by the Chicago sociologists. See, e.g., Edith Elmer Wood, SLUMS AND BLIGHTED AREAS IN THE UNITED STATES 3 (1935)("A blighted residential area is one on the down grade, which has not reached the slum stage.");[9] PRESIDENT"S CONFERENCE ON HOME BUILDING AND HOME OWNERSHIP, 3 SLUMS, LARGE SCALE HOUSING AND DECENTRALIZATION 41 (John M. Gries & James Ford eds., 1932)("A blighted area is an area where, due either to the lack of a vitalizing factor or to the presence of a devitalizing factor, the life of the area has been sapped."); Walker, URBAN BLIGHT, at 6 ("Old buildings are neglected and new ones are not erected and the whole section becomes *stale* and unprofitable. In other words, blight is a condition where it is not profitable to make or maintain improvements. (emphasis added)") *id.* at 7 ("Instead of being improved in an appropriate manner, buildings are allowed to rot and let out to the most economically helpless of the city's inhabitants."); *id.* at 17 ("[A]ll the visible manifestations of blight appear. Structures become shabby and obsolete. The entire district takes on a down-at-the-heel appearance. The exodus of the more prosperous groups is accelerated. Rents fall. Poorer classes move in. The poverty of the tenants contributes further to the general air of shabbiness. The realty owner becomes less and less inclined or able to make repairs. . . . At length the worst sections become slums with high disease and high crime rates."); C. Louis Knight, *Blighted Areas and Their Affects Upon Land Utilization*, in THE ANNALS OF THE AMERICAN ACADEMY 134 (1930) ("We may define the term 'bighted area,' therefore, as any area in which *economic development has been considerably retarded* (emphasis added), as compared with the economic development in the larger area, of which the area under consideration is a part.")

Crucial to the historical understanding of blight was that the current condition of the area in question was one of deterioration, decay, and stagnation. See Walker, URBAN BLIGHT, at 4 ("Practically the one point on which all writers seem in agreements is that a blighted area is one which is deteriorating, and this is the point most emphasized in the . . . definitions."); CLARENCE ARTHUR PERRY, THE REBUILDING OF BLIGHTED AREAS: A STUDY OF THE NEIGHBOR-HOOD UNIT IN REPLANNING AND PLOT ASSEMBLAGE 8 (1933) ("Blight [is] an insidious malady that attacks urban residential districts. It appears first as a barely noticeable deterioration and then progresses gradually through many stages toward a final condition known as the slum."); NATIONAL ASSOCIATION OF HOUSING OFFICIALS, HOUSING OFFICIALS YEARBOOK 1936, at 241 (The association defines "[b]lighted [a]rea as "[a]n area in which deteriorating forces have obviously reduced economic and social values to such a degree that widespread rehabilitation is necessary to forestall the development of an actual slum condition."); JAMES FORD, SLUMS AND HOUSING 11 (1936)("Any area of deteriorated housing in which there is a poor upkeep of houses and premises is a blighted district and a potential slum.").[10]

Courts, too, have long echoed the notion that blight was predicated on a present, stagnant condition of the land. *See, e.g., Berman v. Parker*, 348 U.S. 26, 35 (1954)(stating that "blight" refers to an area "possessed of a congenital disease" and containing a "cycle of decay," and that blight removal is intended to eliminate conditions such as the lack of adequate streets and alleys, the absence of recreational areas, the lack of parks, and the presence of outmoded street patterns); *Levin v. Tp. Committee of Tp. of Bridgewater*, 57 N.J. 506, 538 (1971)(stating that a blighted area refers to a situation where "potentially useful land reaches a stage of stagnation and unproductiveness through one or more causes"); *id.* at 540 (noting that "removing the decadent effect of blight" can "take the difference between continued stagnation and decline and a resurgence of healthy growth")(quoting *Wilson v. City of Long Branch*, 27 N.J. 360, 370 (1958).

A constitutional understanding of the term "blighted area" can also be derived from statements made by delegates to the 1947 constitutional convention. The language that became the "blighted area" clause in the constitution was sponsored by Delegate Jane Barus, who introduced an amendment to Committee Proposal No. 5-1. Ms. Barus's amendment, which was approved without change and which ultimately became Article VIII, § III, ¶ 1 of the Constitution, stated:

Amend page 3, Section I, by adding a new paragraph 7 to read as follows:

7. The clearance, replanning, development or redevelopment of blighted areas shall be a public purpose and public use, for which private property may be taken or acquired. Municipal, public or private corporations may be authorized by law to undertake such clearance, replanning, development or redevelopment, and improvements made for these purposes and uses, or for any of them, may be exempted from taxation, in whole or in part, for a limited period of time during which the profits of and dividends payable by any private corporation enjoying such tax exemption shall be limited by law. The conditions of use, ownership, management and control of such improvements shall be regulated by law. PROCEEDINGS

OF THE NEW JERSEY CONSTITUTIONAL CONVENTION OF 1947, Vol. II, at 1245.

In support of her amendment, Ms. Barus stated:

The older cities in the State, in common with most older cities everywhere, I imagine, have been facing an increasingly difficult situation as the years advance. Certain sections of those cities have fallen in value, and have became what is known as "blighted" or "depressed" areas. This has happened, sometimes, because the population has shifted from one part of the town to another, or one section has become overcrowded. Sometimes it has happened because the district has turned to business instead of residential, or partly to business; and sometimes simply because the buildings themselves, although they were originally good and may have been fine homes, have become so outdated and obsolescent that they are no longer desirable, and hence, no longer profitable.

These depressed areas go steadily down hill. The original occupants move away, the rents fall, landlords lose income and they make up for it by taking in more families per house. It's impossible to keep the properties in good condition, the houses deteriorate more and more, and what was once a good section of town is on the way to becoming a slum. PROCEEDINGS OF THE NEW JERSEY CONSTITUTIONAL CONVENTION OF 1947, Vol. I, at 742.

See also id. at 743 (Ms. Barus stating that a "blighted area" cannot turn the tide of deterioration). The constitutional delegates approved Ms. Barus's "blighted area" proposal, *id.* at 745. Thus, although they did not adopt a specific textual definition of "blighted area," the framers of the 1947 New Jersey Constitution were in agreement with scholars and urban planners that blight, when applied to land redevelopment, necessarily included a current characteristic of decay and deterioration.

III. Portions of the 1992 Local Redevelopment and Housing Law Exceed the Constitutional Meaning of "Blighted Area"

In a series of laws enacted over the last 50-plus years the legislature has attempted to define the crucial, limiting, constitutional term "blighted area." As explained in the Public Advocate's Report, *Reforming the Use of Eminent Domain for Private Redevelopment in New Jersey* (hereinafter *"Reforming the Use of Eminent Domain"*), it is the opinion of the Public Advocate that the most recent legislative enactments have far exceeded the constitutional understanding of "blighted area," raising concerns that eminent domain is being used for private redevelopment in an unconstitutional fashion.

The 1992 Local Redevelopment and Housing Law (hereinafter "LRHL"), the broadest legislative attempt to define "blighted area," listed six criteria permitting

private redevelopment via eminent domain. A 2003 amendment to the LRHL added a seventh "blighted area" criterion. *See Reforming the Use of Eminent Domain*
at 11-12. Each of these seven criteria must satisfy the constitutional understanding
of "blighted area" in order to pass muster.[11] The most constitutionally problematic
of the criteria is (e), which permits a blight finding simply if a lack of "proper utilization leads to the area being not fully productive." *See* N.J.S.A. § 40A:12A-5.e.
Criterion (h), addressed to smart growth planning, is also beyond the constitutional
understanding of blight. Applying the analysis from Sections I and II above to
criteria (e) and (h) leads to the conclusion that the LRHL exceeds constitutional
bounds.[12]

A. Criterion (h) is Facially Unconstitutional

Under LRHL criterion (h), an area is blighted if "[t]he designation of the delineated area is consistent with smart growth planning principles adopted pursuant
to law or regulation." N.J.S.A. § 40A:12A-5.h. This criterion violates the constitutional limitation.

Smart growth speaks to future change and alternative uses for land. By
comparison, as discussed above, the term "blighted area" historically and constitutionally focuses on the present state of the land and not possible future uses for
the land. Indeed, the word "blighted," by plain meaning, implies that the deleterious condition has already occurred. Thus, there is no logical relation between an
area designated for smart growth and a blighted area; on its face, criterion (h)
exceeds constitutional bounds. Whether an area's current use is consistent with
smart growth planning principles simply has nothing at all to do with determining
whether the area is presently in a blighted condition.

If eminent domain can be used for areas that are targets of smart growth, then
numerous non-blighted areas would be at risk. The reference to smart growth areas
in criterion (h) *de facto* categorizes all State Planning Areas 1 and 2—which include
both metropolitan and suburban areas—as "blighted areas." See N.J.S.A. §13:1D-
144. While there may certainly be smart growth areas that are also blighted, there
can also be smart growth areas that in no way qualify as blighted areas; thus, to
categorically designate all smart growth areas as blighted exceeds constitutional
limits. An area could meet none of the traditional requirements of a "blighted area,"
but, because it fell within a swath targeted for smart growth, it would be deemed
blighted. The potential for abuse is apparent, and the Constitutional limitation must
be enforced.

B . Criterion (e) Violates the Constitution's "Blighted Area" Requirement

1. Criterion (e) Ignores the Present Condition of the Land, an Integral Part of Defining a "Blighted Area"

From 1951 to 1992, the precursor to the LRHL's criterion (e) permitted a finding of blight for a delineated area where there was [a] growing or total lack of prop-

er utilization of areas caused by the condition of the title, diverse ownership of the real property therein and other conditions, resulting in a *stagnant and unproductive* (emphasis added) condition of land potentially useful and valuable for contributing to and serving the public health, safety and welfare. Blighted Area Act of 1951, *codified at* N.J.S.A. § 40:55-21.1.e, *repealed by* P.L. 1992, c.79, § 59.

As the Public Advocate's Report makes clear, the LRHL made a significant and constitutionally unsupportable change in this definition of "blighted area." *See Reforming the Use of Eminent Domain* at 12-13. The LRHL replaced the long-standing criterion of "stagnant and unproductive condition" with the standard of "stagnant or not *fully productive* (emphasis added) condition." N.J.S.A. § 40A: 12A-5.e. (emphasis added). Unlike the substitution of "area in need of redevelopment" for the term "blighted area," the change in criterion (e) from *and* to *or* is important for purposes of constitutional compliance. But see *Forbes*, 312 N.J.Super., at 526-527 (claiming that "paragraph (e) of N.J.S.A. 40A:12A-5 ... made virtually no change in its N.J.S.A. 40:55-21.1 counterpart," which was constitutional).

Under the current criterion (e), stagnancy is no longer a requirement, in direct contravention of the deep-rooted understanding and definition of blight as discussed above. Furthermore, an area need not be "unproductive," either. Instead, under criterion (e), an area can be deemed blighted if it simply is "not fully productive," which, by definition, must focus on alternative, future uses of the land. As discussed above, however, blight, by definition, requires an examination of the current condition of the land and a present finding of deterioration and stagnation.

Additionally, the term "not fully productive" implies that there can be non-deteriorated areas that fall within its ambit. For instance, Drumthwacket, the Governor's official residence, is a "stately home" that is "one of the most fabled and elegant of America's executive residences," *see* http://www.drumthwacket.org/history.html, yet the property could also be considered "not fully productive," because a hotel or apartment house catering to hundreds, for instance, would be a more productive use of the property.

This "not fully productive" usage, thus, directly contradicts *"the one point* on which all writers seem in agreement (emphasis added) . . . that a blighted area is one which is deteriorating...." WALKER, URBAN BLIGHT, at 4.

Thus, this shift from an examination of whether the current state of the land is deteriorated to consideration of some alternative, prospective use does not comport with the constitutional understanding of "blighted area" and, therefore, violates N.J. CONST. Art. VIII, § III, ¶ 1. Simply put, if the criterion only requires that an area be "not fully productive," then eminent domain can be used to seize non-blighted areas, in direct violation of the limitation the New Jersey Constitution places on eminent domain for private redevelopment purposes.

A clear example of how the LRHL's removal of the stagnancy requirement from criterion (e) can lead to the taking of non-blighted areas, and thus violate the State Constitution, can be seen in the recent United States Supreme Court case *Kelo v. City of New London*. In that case, as part of a larger redevelopment project, the city of New London, Connecticut sought to take the specific homes in question to "support the adjacent state park, by providing parking or retail services for visitors, or to support the nearby marina." *Kelo*, 125 S.Ct. at 2659. The Court noted that *"[t]here is no allegation that any of these properties* [within the area designated for redevelopment via eminent domain] *is blighted* (emphasis added) or otherwise in poor condition; rather, they were condemned only because they happen to be located in the development area." *Id.* at 2660. The Court described an area that hardly could be considered stagnant, as it found that many of the properties in question had undergone "extensive improvements" and that some were being used as "investment properties." *Id.* Thus, the question was whether an area that all acknowledged was in no way blighted could nonetheless be seized for private redevelopment to create a "small urban village" with a hotel, restaurants, shopping, and other commercial uses. *Id.* at 2659. Certainly, by comparison to the use envisioned, the residential area in question was "not fully productive." The Supreme Court upheld New London's proposed taking as appropriate under the federal "public use" doctrine. *Id.* at 2668 (The Court approved the taking because "[t]his Court's authority, however, extends only to determining whether the City's proposed condemnations are for a 'public use' within the meaning of the Fifth Amendment to the Federal Constitution.").

Similarly, under criterion (e) of the LRHL, an area of well-maintained homes could be seized for private redevelopment, because there is a more economically valuable use of the land. Such a scenario was permissible in Connecticut, because, unlike New Jersey, that State does not have a constitutional "blighted area" limitation, so the *Kelo* scenario was only analyzed under the Federal Constitution. *Id.* at 2656 ("The question presented is whether the city's proposed disposition of this property qualifies as a 'public use' within the meaning of the Takings Clause of the Fifth Amendment to the Constitution."). The exact opposite, however, should be true in New Jersey, because the state constitution imposes a clear limitation on such takings by requiring that they first meet the "blighted area" test. *See Kelo* at 2668 (holding that a State can have stricter requirements than the federal "public use" doctrine by enacting constitutional prohibitions that "plac[e] further restrictions on [a state's] exercise of the takings power").[13] By removing any consideration of what condition the land currently is in, and, instead, imposing a test of what the land could be, the LRHL's criterion (e) can lead to unconstitutional takings. There is simply no constitutional support for criterion (e)'s premise that a blight finding can be made based only on a forward-looking approach without any consideration of the current conditions of land use.

The New Jersey courts have long-recognized that stagnancy, i.e., the present use of the land, is integral to a finding of blight. *See Levin*, 57 N.J. at 540 (The governing principle of state law was that "[s]oundly planned redevelopment [of blighted areas] [would] make the difference between continued stagnation and decline and a resurgence of healthy growth."). *Cf. Spruce Manor Enterprises v. Borough of Bellmawr*, 315 N.J.Super. 286, 294 (Super. Ct. 1998)("Before [a declaration of blight can occur], there must be evidence that the characteristics of the complex lead to unwholesome living conditions or are detrimental to the safety, health, morals or welfare of the community.")(invalidating "area in need of redevelopment" finding made on basis of criterion (a) and (d)).[14]

Other state courts have similarly focused on the current use of the area and not the possible, imaginable uses when determining whether a "blighted area" finding is appropriate. For instance, as the California Supreme Court made clear, a "determination of blight [should] be made—not on the basis of potential alternative use of the proposed area—but on the basis of the area's existing use. *Sweetwater Valley Civic Ass'n v. City of National City*, 555 P.2d 1099, 1103-04 (Cal. 1976). *See also Redevelopment Agency v. Hayes*, 266 P.2d 105, 127 (Cal. App. 1954) (The ruling holds that eminent domain powers "never can be used just because the public agency considers that it can make a better use or planning of an area than its present use or plan."); id. at 116 (It further holds that "[o]ne man's land cannot be seized by the Government and sold to another man merely in order that the purchaser may build upon it a better house or a house which better meets the Government's idea of what is appropriate or well-designed."). *But see Tierney v. Planned Industrial Expansion Authority*, 742 S.W.2d 146, 151 (Mo. 1987) (Here, the court approved "the concept of 'economic underutilization' as a basis for condemnation" for urban redevelopment purposes.).[15]

In addition, from a historical standpoint, an area would not be considered blighted by scholars and urban planners, if it were merely not being utilized in the most economically productive manner, yet criterion (e) would permit a blight finding under such circumstances. *See, e.g.*, WALKER, URBAN BLIGHT, at 4 ("[T]he mere fact that taxes received from a section of the community are less than the governmental expenditures made in that section is no proof of blight. Otherwise many counties of every state and many states of the Union could be characterized as blighted."); *id.* (Walker affirms that attempts to define "blighted area" as one that is not economically self-supporting or that "has become an economic liability to the community" are "entirely on the wrong track.").

2. The Legislative History of Various Statutory Interpretations of "Blighted Area" Indicates that Criterion (e) Is Beyond the Constitutional Meaning of "Blighted Area."

The legislative history of both the LRHL and its predecessor statutes provide strong support for the conclusion that criterion (e) exceeds the constitutional boundaries of Article VIII, § III, ¶ 1. According to the statement attached to the 1951 Blighted Area Act, the subsection (e) declaration of blight was added as an amendment to the 1949 law for the following purpose: "to make uniform the definition of 'blighted area' as given in the act which this bill amends, in the Local Housing Authorities Law (P.L. 1949, c. 300), and in the Redevelopment Agencies Law." (P.L. 1949, c. 306).

Rev. Stat. Cum. Supp. § 40:55-21.1 (1951). The New Jersey Supreme Court has ruled that subsection (e) in the 1951 Blighted Area Act was "undoubtedly based" on the "legislative determination[s]" in the Local Housing Authorities Law of 1949 and the Redevelopment Agencies Law of 1949. *See Levin*, 57 N.J. at 510-511. Both of those statutes define "blighted area." The findings in both of those statutes call into question the constitutionality of the current definition of "blighted area" in criterion (e).

The Local Housing Authorities Law, L. 1949, c. 300, *codified* at N.J.S.A. § 55:14A-31, *repealed* by P.L. 1992, c.79, § 59, contained the following relevant legislative determination:

> It is hereby found and declared (a) that there exist in many communities within this State blighted areas (as herein defined) or areas in the process of becoming blighted; (b) that such areas impair economic values and tax revenues; that such areas cause an increase in and spread of disease and crime and constitute a menace to the health, safety, morals and welfare of the residents of the State, that these conditions necessitate excessive and disproportionate expenditures of public funds for crime prevention and punishment, public health and safety, fire and accident protection, and other public services and facilities; (c) that the clearance, replanning and preparation for rebuilding of these areas, and the prevention or the reduction of blight and its causes, are public uses and purposes for which money may be spent and private property acquired and area governmental functions of State concern; (d) that there are also *certain areas* where the condition of the title, the diverse ownership of the land to be assembled, the street or lot layouts, or other conditions prevent a proper development of the land, and that it is in the public interest that such areas, *as well as blighted areas*, be acquired by eminent domain and made available for sound and wholesome development in accordance with a redevelopment plan, and that the exercise of the power of eminent domain and the financing of the acquisition and preparation of land by a public agency for such redevelopment is likewise a public use and purpose (emphasis added). . . . L. 1949, c.300, ¶ 1.

The legislative determination thus distinguished "blighted areas" from "certain areas where the condition of the title, the diverse ownership of the land to be assembled, the street or lot layouts, or other conditions prevent a proper development of the land." *Id.* Importantly, the "certain areas" that were distinguished by the Local Housing Authorities Law were those areas contained in the Act's "blighted area" definition (e), since repealed, which stated:

> The term 'blighted area' is defined to be that portion of a municipality which by reason of, or because of, any of the conditions hereinafter enumerated is found and determined as provided by law to be a social or economic liability to such municipality: A growing or total lack of *proper utilization* of areas caused by the *condition of the title, diverse ownership of the real property therein and other conditions*, resulting in a stagnant and unproductive condition of land potentially useful and valuable for contributing to and serving the public health, safety and welfare (emphasis added). N.J.S.A. 40:55C-3(e), *repealed by* P.L. 1992, c.79, § 59.

The definition is repeated verbatim in the 1951 Blighted Area Act, which is consistent with the stated goal of wanting a uniform definition of "blighted area." The understanding of blight in the Local Housing Authorities Law thus informs the understanding in the Blighted Areas Act. At the time definition (e) was added to the 1951 Blighted Areas Act it was admittedly beyond the constitutional understanding of "blighted areas," because it was addressed to "certain areas" that were specifically not blighted areas. Thus, even prior to the LRHL, subsection (e)'s definition of blight did not conform with constitutional standards. Because, as noted above, LRHL criterion (e) simply expanded for the worse the already questionable 1951 Blighted Areas Act definition (e), criterion (e) in the current law is constitutionally deficient.

Additionally, the legislative history of the LRHL itself supports the conclusion that criterion (e) is unconstitutional. In January 1987, a New Jersey commission recommended abolishing the Local Housing Authorities Law, the Redevelopment Agencies Law, and the Blighted Areas Act, and consolidating their principles "into a single Local Housing and Redevelopment Law in Title 40A of the Revised Statutes." State of New Jersey County and Municipal Government Study Commission, *Local Redevelopment in New Jersey: Structuring a New Partnership xiii* (1987). The commission's report became the basis for the 1992 LRHL. See Senate Community Affairs Committee Statement to Assembly Bill No. 1138 (1992) ("This bill, entitled the 'Local Redevelopment and Housing Law,' revises, consolidates and clarifies the various statutes related to the exercise of redevelopment and housing powers by local governments into a modern and comprehensive statute. The revision was recommended by the County and Municipal Government Study Commission in its report, *Local Redevelopment in New Jersey.*"). In recommending changes to the determination of whether an area is blighted, the commission stated:

> The concept of a 'blighted area' has changed considerably since the term was introduced in earlier redevelopment statutes. Over the past three decades, *the focus of public action* with respect to redevelopment has *shifted* from the elimination of 'unsanitary,' congested and unsafe slums, to the rehabilitation and conservation of declining neighborhoods, and to the enhancement and improvement of underutilized commercial and industrial areas. It is evident that the concept of a 'blighted area' is no longer relevant and, in fact, carries an unnecessarily [sic] negative connotation. In some cases, *this can represent a political constraint in municipalities that are considering the redevelopment of parts of their communities* (emphasis added). State of New Jersey County and Municipal Government Study Commission, *Local Redevelopment in New Jersey: Structuring a New Partnership* 58 (1987).

The Commission then recommended that "a new local housing and redevelopment law allow municipalities to designate an area as either being an 'area in need of redevelopment' or an 'area in need of rehabilitation.'" *Id.* The Committee suggested that "[t]he definition of an area in need of redevelopment should be *adapted from* the current definition of a blighted area, *broadening it* to include the *under-utilization of existing commercial and industrial properties in the community.*" *Id.* The legislature followed the commission's recommendation by defining a "blighted area" based on the underutilization of the land.[16]

The constitutional term "blighted area" and its concomitant limitation on the use of eminent domain for private redevelopment is not a fluid and evolving concept tied to shifts in the "focus of public action" and the desires of "municipalities that are considering the redevelopment of parts of their communities."[17] Nor is the constitutional meaning of "blighted area" one that can be adapted and broadened beyond "the current definition." To the contrary, as discussed above, the "blighted area" clause was intended and understood as a fixed limitation on the legislature's power. By expanding the "current definition of a blighted area," the LRHL criterion (e) exceeds constitutional bounds.

3. The Expansive Scope of Criterion (e) is Unique Among the States

The conclusion that the LRHL's criterion (e) is unconstitutional is bolstered by the fact that no other state gives local government as expansive an authority as contained in criterion (e). All 50 states, the District of Columbia, Guam, Puerto Rico, and the Virgin Islands have redevelopment statutes defining "blighted areas." Only eight of these statutes would permit a blight finding based on the economic use of the land.[18] Of these few statutes, none contains language as permissive as New Jersey's LRHL criterion (e).

Four of the eight jurisdictions permitting such "economic use" takings also require a stagnancy finding—as New Jersey did prior to the enactment of the LRHL—if the blight determination is sought based on economic use.[19] Of the remaining four jurisdictions that do not require stagnancy, and, thus, would permit sole consideration of future use and not present condition in making an "economic use" blight finding,[20] just two jurisdictions—New Jersey and New York—have a constitutional "blighted area" clause. See N.Y. CONST. Art. XVI, § 6.

As compared to New York, New Jersey's constitutional "blighted area" clause is far more restrictive. As discussed above, New Jersey's constitution permits the use of eminent domain for private redevelopment only if a "blighted area" determination is first made. The New York Constitution permits takings for private development under far broader circumstances, because it does not impose a "blighted area" requirement. Rather, New York authorizes the use of eminent domain for redeveloping "economically unproductive, blighted or deteriorated areas." N.Y. CONST. Art. XVI, § 6. Whereas New Jersey's constitution mandates that blight be found before private redevelopment can proceed via eminent domain, New York's constitution permits such takings for areas that are, for instance, simply "deteriorated." *Id.*

Yet, although New Jersey's constitution is far more restrictive than the New York counterpart, New Jersey's redevelopment statute is far more permissive than New York's statute in allowing takings without a traditional blight finding. New York's redevelopment statute permits redevelopment to "prevent further deterioration" (*see* N.Y. GEN. MUN. LAW §970-c(a)(ii)), which necessarily implies that some deterioration must have already occurred before eminent domain power can be used for private redevelopment, in contrast to the LRHL's criterion (e). Additionally, New York's statute requires a finding that an area is "economically unproductive" (*see id.*), which also implies a notion of stagnation and present condition evaluation, whereas the LRHL's "not fully productive" standard just suggests a more profitable alternative use.[21]

Finally, as a practical matter, even if the LRHL's criterion (e) somehow satisfies constitutional norms, reliance on that criterion alone to support the use of eminent domain for private redevelopment may place New Jersey in an anomalous position.[22] *Cf.* Colin Gordon, *Blighting The Way: Urban Renewal, Economic Development, And The Elusive Definition Of Blight*, 31 FORDHAM URB. L.J. 305, 314 (2004) Gordon argues that language in redevelopment statutes that "graft[ed] economic considerations, such as underutilization of land," onto the traditional notion of blight constituted an "almost complete debasement and deregulation of 'blight' as a guiding designation for urban renewal and redevelopment.").

References

1. *Kelo. v. City of New London*, Connecticut, et al., 125 S. Ct. 2655 (2005).
2. U.S. Census Bureau, Census 2000 Summary File 1: GCT-PH1-R. Population, Housing Units, Area, and Density (geographies ranked by total population): 2000.
3. New Jersey Constitution, Art. 8, § 3, ¶1.
4. N.J.S.A. § 40A:12A-5.
5. DCA has interpreted the statute to mean that any redevelopment in State Planning areas 1 and 2 or designated centers does not require DCA review.
6. The 1949 statute provides that "the term 'blighted area' shall mean an area in any municipality wherein there exists to a large extent:
   a) Buildings and structures on the property are unfit, unsanitary and unsafe for human use and habitation by reason of age, physical deterioration, dilapidation or obsolescence;
   b) Buildings and structures which are so situated and used as to have therein more inhabitants than can be fitly and safely housed;
   c) Buildings and structures which have economically deteriorated and where there is a disproportion between the cost of municipal services rendered to the area as compared with the tax revenue derived therefrom; or
   d) A prevalence of factors conducive to ill health, transmission of disease, infant mortality, juvenile delinquency, crime and poverty.
7. The 1951 statute provides that "the term blighted area shall mean an area in any municipality where there exists any of the conditions hereinafter enumerated:

a) The generality of buildings used as dwellings or the dwelling accommodations therein are substandard, unsafe, unsanitary, dilapidated, or obsolescent, or possess any of such characteristics, or are so lacking in light, air or space, as to be conducive to unwholesome living;

b) The discontinuance of the use of buildings previously used for manufacturing or industrial purposes, the abandonment of such buildings or the same being allowed to fall into so great a state of disrepair as to be untenantable;

c) Unimproved vacant land, which has remained so for a period of ten years prior to the determination hereinafter referred to, and which land by reason of its location, or remoteness from developed sections or portions of such municipality, or lack of means of access to such other parts thereof, or topography, or nature of the soil, is not likely to be developed through the instrumentality of private capital;

d) Areas (including slum areas) with buildings or improvements which by reason of dilapidation, obsolescence, overcrowding, faulty arrangement or design, lack of ventilation, light and sanitary facilities, excessive land coverage, deleterious land use or obsolete layout, or any combination of these or other factors, are detrimental to the safety, health, morals, or welfare of the community;

e) A growing lack of proper utilization of areas caused by the condition of the title, diverse ownership of the real property therein and other conditions, resulting in a stagnant and unproductive condition of land potentially useful and valuable for contributing to and serving the public health, safety and welfare.

8. The 1986 statute added the following language:

(f) Areas, in excess of 10 contiguous acres, whereon buildings or improvements have been destroyed, consumed by fire, demolished or altered by the action of storm, fire, cyclone, tornado, earthquake or other casualty in such a way that the aggregate assessed value of the area has been materially depreciated.

Footnotes
For the Appendix:
Legal Analysis of Limitations on Use of Eminent Domain

1. Van Horne's Lessee v. Dorrance, 2 U.S. 304, 311 (1795).
2. 125 S. Ct. 2655 (2005).
3. *Berman v. Parker*, 348 U.S. 26 (1954) (permitting use of eminent domain for private redevelopment of slums and blighted areas). See also *Hawaii Housing Authority* v. Midkiff, 467 U.S. 229 (1984) (holding that a state statute that permitted condemnation of property and its redistri-

bution to alleviate the concentrated property ownership of the state was a legitimate public purpose and a rational power by the state legislature).

4. 2006 S.D. H.B. 1080 (forbidding transfer of property taken by eminent domain to a private entity for seven years, unless a resale offer was made to original owner).

5. U.S. CONST., amend. xiv.

6. N.J. CONST. Art. I, ¶ 1.

7. U.S. CONST., amend. v; N.J. CONST. Art. I, ¶ 20.

8. *See infra* pages vii-viii.

9. Historically, a slum was defined as: a residential area with an extreme condition of blight. The slum is relatively easy to locate and define. There seems to be a general agreement that it is an area in which the housing is so unfit as to constitute a menace to the health and morals of the community, and that the slum is essentially of social significance.

Mabel L. Walker, URBAN BLIGHT AND SLUMS 3 (1938). *See also* NATIONAL ASSOCIATION OF HOUSING OFFICIALS, HOUSING OFFICIALS YEARBOOK 1936, at 243 ("Slum—an area in which predominate dwellings that either because of dilapidation, obsolescence, overcrowding, poor arrangement or design, lack of ventilation, light or sanitary facilities, or a combination of these factors, are detrimental to the safety, health, morals and comfort of the inhabitants thereof."); Walker at 3 ("A slum district is defined as an area or neighborhood, the buildings in which are used predominantly, though not necessarily exclusively, for habitation and residence and in which, owing to the age, design and character of the buildings, the inadequacy of open spaces in proportion to built-upon spaces or the poor distribution of open and built-upon spaces, the existing plan and arrangement of lots and streets and utilities, the types of business or industries which have invaded or surround the district, or other causes and factors, the physical conditions are not conducive to the physical and moral health of the inhabitants and residents, and present difficulties and handicaps to the attainment of sanitary hygienic and moral standards, which difficulties and handicaps may be removed or lessened by the replanning and rebuilding of the area or neighborhood.")(quoting Model City Charter of the National Municipal League); *id.* ("The term 'slum' means any area where dwellings predominate which by reason of dilapidation, overcrowding, faulty arrangement or design, lack of ventilation, light or sanitation facilities, or any combination of these factors, are detrimental to safety, health, or morals.")(quoting United States Housing Act of 1937, 42 U.S.C. § 1437 *et seq.*, known as Wagner-Steagall bill).

It should be noted that a slum was not always a blighted area; the two concepts could be distinct. A slum, as long as it was an economically productive area (e.g., landlords profiting precisely because of overcrowding) would not be classified as being in a blighted condition as that term was historically understood. *See, e.g.*, PRESIDENT"S CONFER-

ENCE ON HOME BUILDING AND HOME OWNERSHIP, 3 SLUMS, LARGE SCALE HOUSING AND DECENTRALIZATION 2 (John M. Gries & James Ford eds., 1932 (The report notes that in some circumstances "a slum has become economically profitable because of the high rents that can be obtained for improper use, and is no longer blighted according to the definition."). WALKER, URBAN BLIGHT, at 6 ("A blighted area is generally unprofitable, but the opposite may be true of certain slums," noting that because slums tend to be overcrowded, they are therefore profitable). As a leading scholar commented in explaining the difference between a "blighted area" and a "slum," "the term 'blight' is used in an economic sense, while the designation 'slum' is essentially of social significance," such that a blighted area is one that has deteriorated from an economic standpoint and, therefore, becomes less profitable to the city, the general public, and the owners of its real estate. Depreciation has set in and the area is rapidly becoming a liability rather than an asset. Its characteristics are changing and its future is indefinite. When "blight" has progressed far enough to seriously affect social conditions, such as health, morality and standards of living, then the "slum" stage is reached and the section becomes not only uneconomic but also socially undesirable. Walker, URBAN BLIGHT, AT 5, 6 (quoting Regional Plan Association, Information Bulletin No. 16).

10. *See also* Walker at 5 (quoting National Municipal League, Model City Charter (1937)): "A blighted area is defined as an area in which, owing to the obsolescent condition and character of the buildings therein, the existing division or arrangement of lots and ownerships and street and other open spaces, the mixed character and uses of the buildings, and other factors and causes, values have depreciated with consequent decline or stagnation of development and damage and loss to community prosperity and taxable values, and where a restoration of the economic vigor of the area and of its attainable contribution to the economic strength and prosperity of the community may require a replanning of the area, and, for the accomplishment of such replanning, a concentration or redistribution of ownership or developmental control is requisite."

11. Technically speaking, the LRHL criteria refer to an "area in need of redevelopment" and not the constitutional term "blighted area." Despite this attempt to eliminate the constitutional language, case law and the LRHL itself make clear that the seven criteria must comport with the constitutional "blighted area" clause. *See Forbes*, 312 N.J.Super., at 529 (Because the "[d]efinitional standards were not changed in any material respect" between the 1992 LRHL and the 1951 Blighted Area Act, an area cannot qualify as area in need of redevelopment, unless "it meets exactly the same standards of blight required by the Blighted Area Act."); *id.* ("The word 'blight' may have been left out of the LRHL but the concept and long-standing definition of blight remain firmly fixed therein . . . [Thus] [t]he area must be found to be blighted in confor-

mance with the same standards as theretofore even though we no longer call it a blighted area but rather an area in need of redevelopment."). *See also* N.J.S.A. § 40A:12A-6.c ("An area determined to be in need of redevelopment pursuant to this section shall be deemed to be a "blighted area for the purposes of Article VIII, Section III, paragraph 1 of the Constitution. If an area is determined to be a redevelopment area and a redevelopment plan is adopted for that area in accordance with the provisions of this act, the municipality is authorized to utilize all those powers provided in section 8 of P.L. 1992, c.79 (C.40A: 12A-8)"); N.J.S.A. § 40A:12A-3 ("'Redevelopment area' or 'area in need of redevelopment' means an area determined to be in need of redevelopment pursuant to sections 5 and 6 of P.L.1992, c. 79 (C.40A: 12A-5 and 40A:12A-6) or determined heretofore to be a 'blighted area' pursuant to P.L.1949, c. 187 (C.40:55-21.1 et seq.) repealed by this act, both determinations as made pursuant to the authority of Article VIII, Section III, paragraph 1 of the Constitution.").

Thus, each redevelopment criterion of the LRHL must satisfy the constitutional "blighted area" requirement before it can legally be sustained. The term "area in need of redevelopment" is simply a semantics change that cannot obscure constitutional considerations applicable to the "blighted area" clause. *See, e.g., Concerned Citizens of Princeton, Inc. v. Mayor and Council of Borough of Princeton,* 370 N.J.Super. 429, 456 (App. Div. 2004) (The opinion concludes that this "change in verbiage [from "blight" to "in need of redevelopment"] was 'cosmetic only' since the definitional standards for such a designation remained virtually unchanged.")(quoting *Forbes,* 312 N.J. Super, at 528-529).

12. This section of the Appendix is only intended to provide legal support for the report's conclusion that criteria (e) and (h) are unconstitutional. This section is not in any way intended to imply that other criteria are therefore constitutional as a full analysis of the remaining criteria is beyond the scope of the Appendix. It should be noted, however, that LRHL criteria (a)-(d) may withstand constitutional scrutiny, even though criteria (a) and (d) are more analogous to the traditional definition of a "slum," which can be distinct from a "blighted area" as discussed above, see supra note 1. This distinction may be because criteria (a)-(d) are very similar to the criteria (a)-(d) in the 1951 Blighted Area Act that were found by the State Supreme Court to be constitutional. In sustaining the statutory definition of blight in the 1951 Blighted Area Act, the *Wilson* Court in 1958 stated:

Manifestly, the grant of power [accorded by the constitution] contemplated development and implementation by the Legislature. Definition of blight was the ordinary and expected incident of the exercise of that power, and no reasonable argument can be made that the connotation ascribed to it overreaches the public purpose sought to be promoted by the constitution.

Wilson, 27 N.J. at, 381-82. *See also Forbes*, 312 N.J.Super, at 528-529
  (Forbes states that "[t]he 1951 statutory definition, moreover, clearly
  constituted and came to constitute a community consensus and expressed a common understanding of what is meant by blight subject to
  public remediation.")(citing, *Wilson*, 27 N.J., at 370)). The *Forbes* Court
  noted the similarities between criteria (a)-(d) in the 1951 Act and
  the LRHL:

The only change made by paragraph (a) of the 1992 Act in its 1951 counterpart was the elimination of the reference to dwellings and the addition of
  unwholesome working as well as living conditions, making clear that the
  described conditions were not to be limited to residential properties only.
  The only change made by paragraph (b), which addresses discontinuance of use, was the addition of commercial as well as manufacturing or
  industrial purposes to which the property had originally been put. The
  only change made by paragraph (c) was the addition of public lands. The
  only change made by paragraph (d), one of the provisions at the heart of
  this controversy, was the elimination of the parenthetical reference to
  "slum areas."

Id. at 526. It should also be noted that *Wilson's* approval of criterion (e) in the
  1951 Blighted Area Act is of no import to the constitutionality of criterion (e) in the LRHL, given the radical changes to the 1951 version of
  criterion (e) made by the LRHL.

13. A *Kelo*-type taking of property for private redevelopment purposes without a
  prior finding of blight should not be permissible in New Jersey, precisely
  because New Jersey has the heightened constitutional protections that
  Kelo acknowledges would impose limitations on the eminent domain
  power. Yet, as it currently stands, criterion (e) vitiates the "blighted area"
  clause's restriction on takings for private redevelopment.

14. Nonetheless, the New Jersey Courts have not adequately addressed the constitutionality of the LRHL's criterion (e). Since passage of the LRHL in
  1992, the only reported New Jersey court decision that analyzes criterion
  (e) from a constitutional perspective is Forbes, in which the only discussion states in full that, "[m]oreover, paragraph (e) of N.J.S.A. 40A:12A-
  5, here implicated as well, also made virtually no change in its N.J.S.A.
  40:55-21.1 counterpart." *Forbes*, 312 N.J. Super. 526-527. Moreover,
  even though the Forbes Court seemingly found criterion (e) constitutional, upon application of that criterion, the court noted the ample evidence
  that the area in question was truly a "blighted area" as that should properly be understood for purposes of the New Jersey Constitution:

There was certainly substantial evidence that the Village's central business
  district as a whole was becoming stagnant, deteriorated, obsolescent, and
  that its economic vitality was seriously declining.

Forbes, 312 N.J. Super., at 530 (Forbes cites evidence of "unproductive and
  inaccessible rear areas of commercial properties" and "functionally
  obsolescent structures.").

15. It is unclear why the Missouri Court discussed "economic underutilization" as a basis for upholding a "blighted area" designation, because that concept does not appear to be a criterion for making a "blighted area" determination under Missouri's redevelopment statute. See MO. ANN. STAT. § 100.310(2) ("'Blighted area' [means] an area which, by reason of the predominance of defective or inadequate street layout, insanitary or unsafe conditions, deterioration of site improvements, improper subdivision or obsolete platting, or the existence of conditions which endanger life or property by fire and other causes, or any combination of such factors, retards the provision of housing accommodations or constitutes an economic or social liability or a menace to the public health, safety, morals or welfare in its present condition and use."). *See also* MO. ANN. STAT. § 99.020 (3)("'Blighted' shall mean any area where dwellings predominate which, by reason of dilapidation, overcrowding, lack of ventilation, light or sanitary facilities or any combination of these factors are detrimental to safety, health and morals.").

    Missouri's constitution does contain a "blighted area" clause similar to New Jersey's:

    Laws may be enacted, and any city or county operating under a constitutional charter may enact ordinances, providing for the clearance, replanning, reconstruction, redevelopment and rehabilitation of blighted, substandard or insanitary areas, and for recreational and other facilities incidental or appurtenant thereto, and for taking or permitting the taking, by eminent domain, of property for such purposes, and when so taken the fee simple title to the property shall vest in the owner, who may sell or otherwise dispose of the property subject to such restrictions as may be deemed in the public interest. MO. CONST Art. VI, § 21.

16. The new criterion (e), however, exceeds even the commission's recommendation, because it does not limit the underutilization-based definition of "blighted areas" to commercial and industrial properties. There is simply nothing in criterion (e) that would exclude private redevelopment of residential properties, such as the Drumthwacket example discussed above. While the New Jersey Constitution does not distinguish between commercial and non-commercial blight, case law does provide support for the contention that criterion (e) should not be used, at the very least, to support a taking of a residential area for private redevelopment. Discussing the predecessor to LRHL criterion (e), the Supreme Court in *Levin* noted that:

    > Sensibly, then it must be said that the Legislature intended by means of (e) to encourage the proper and sound growth of suburban and rural land, *particularly open areas* which because of the conditions described therein were stagnant and unproductive but which, in the judgment of the municipal authorities, were potentially useful and valuable.

    Levin, 57 N.J. at 515 (emphasis added); id. at 537-538 (finding that in enacting subsection (e) of the Blighted Area Act, the legislature "declared that where parcels of *vacant land* are characterized by lack of proper utilization, . . . the area is blighted")(emphasis added). *See also Forbes*, 312 N.J. Super. at 259 (stating that "concept of blight also embraced the total unproductivity of *unimproved vacant land*")(emphasis added); *id.* at 259-60 (noting that commercial blight "embraced . . . all the adverse physical conditions of property that individually or in combination impeded its reasonable productivity and resulted in its negative impact upon the general welfare and economic well-being of the community").

17. Were "blighted area" simply a statutory construct, then the legislature would certainly be free to amend the definition to fit shifts in public perception and municipal needs. However, as is clear in New Jersey, "blighted area" is a constitutional limitation, which any statutory interpretations cannot ignore or exceed.

18. "Economic use of the land" includes arrested economic development, stagnant and/or unproductive character of the land, loss of population, and improvement in value of land by placement of development. *See* Hudson Hayes Luce, *The Meaning of Blight: A Survey of Statutory and Case Law*, 35 REAL PROP. PROB. & TR. J. 389, 396. (2000) As of 2000, 10 of the 54 jurisdictions would have permitted a blight finding based on the economic use of the land. *See id.*, at 401. Since that time, the District of Columbia, Indiana, and Massachusetts have eliminated this criterion, and Minnesota has added the criterion, leaving eight jurisdictions that permit a "blighted area" determination to be based on economic use of the land. Missouri is not considered by the Department to be a jurisdiction that statutorily authorizes a blight finding based on economic use of the land, because the permission for such taking in that state appears to be based only on case law. *See supra* note 15.

19. These jurisdictions are Delaware, Minnesota, Nevada, and Oregon.
    In Delaware:
    'Blighted area' means that portion of a municipality or community which is found and determined to be a social or economic liability to such municipality or community because of any of the following conditions. . . A growing or total lack of proper utilization of areas caused by the condition of the title, diverse ownership of the real property therein, tax or special assessment delinquency exceeding the fair value of the land, or the existence of conditions which endanger life or property by fire or other causes and other conditions, *stagnant and unproductive* (emphasis added) condition of land potentially useful and valuable for contributing to and serving the public health, safety and welfare. DEL. CODE ANN. tit. 31, § 4501 (3)(e).
    In Nevada:
    [e]xcept as otherwise provided [if the subject of the redevelopment is an eligible railroad or facilities related to an eligible railroad], 'blighted area'

means an area which is characterized by at least four of the following factors . . . A growing or total lack of proper utilization of some parts of the area, resulting in a stagnant and unproductive (emphasis added) condition of land which is potentially useful and valuable for contributing to the public health, safety and welfare. NEV. REV. STAT. § 279.388.1(h).

In Oregon:

'Blighted areas' means areas that, by reason of deterioration, faulty planning, inadequate or improper facilities, deleterious land use or the existence of unsafe structures, or any combination of these factors, are detrimental to the safety, health or welfare of the community. A blighted area is characterized by the existence of one or more of the following conditions . . . A growing or total lack of proper utilization of areas, *resulting in a stagnant and unproductive* (emphasis added) condition of land potentially useful and valuable for contributing to the public health, safety and welfare. OR. REV. STAT. § 457.010 (1)(h).

In Minnesota:

A redevelopment project may include any work or undertaking to acquire open or undeveloped land determined to be blighted by virtue of the following conditions: a combination of these or other conditions which have prevented normal development of the land by private enterprise and *have resulted in a stagnant and unproductive* (emphasis added) condition of land potentially useful and valuable for contributing to the public health, safety, and welfare. Acquisition of such land shall be a redevelopment project only if a redevelopment plan has been adopted which provides for the elimination of these conditions, thereby making the land useful and valuable for contributing to the public health, safety, and welfare and the acquisition of the land is necessary to carry out the redevelopment plan. MINN. STAT. ANN. § 469.028 Subd.3(3).

20. In addition to New Jersey, these jurisdictions are New York, Oklahoma and Virginia. In New York:

'Blighted area means an area within a municipality in which one or more of the following conditions exist (ii) a predominance of economically unproductive lands, buildings or structures, the redevelopment of which is needed to prevent further deterioration which would jeopardize the economic well being of the people. N.Y. GEN. MUN. LAW §970-c(a)(ii).

In Oklahoma, there are multiple eminent domain statutes, the broadest of which states that:

'Blighted area' shall mean an area in which there are properties, buildings, or improvements, whether occupied or vacant, whether residential or nonresidential, which by reason of . . . arrested economic development . . . any one or combination of such conditions which substantially impair or arrest the sound growth of municipalities, or constitutes an economic or social liability, or which endangers life or property by fire or other causes, or is conducive to ill health, transmission of disease, mortality, juvenile delinquency, or crime and by reason thereof, is detrimental to the public health, safety, morals or welfare. OKLA. STAT. ANN. tit. 11, §38-101 (8).

As compared to the LRHL's "not fully productive" standard, Oklahoma's "arrested economic development criterion appears in plain meaning to be much more restrictive. Further, while not having been directly addressed by the Oklahoma courts, the Oklahoma term suggests some finding of traditional blight criteria, such as stagnation or deterioration, before a taking would be permissible on this ground. *See City of Midwest City v. House of Realty, Inc.*, 100 P.3d 678, 686 (Okla. 2004) The ruling notes that there is "a distinction between removal of blight and economic redevelopment. The former is the public purpose that constitutionally justifies the subsequent sale of the property for private use. [Here,] efforts at redevelopment are best understood in the context of how the Legislature has linked the removal of blight with economic development."). Additionally, Oklahoma does not have a constitutional limitation requiring a "blighted area" finding before eminent domain can be used for private redevelopment. *Id.* at 683 n.6.

In Virginia, "'[b]lighted area' means any area within the borders of a development project area which impairs economic values and tax revenues." VA. CODE ANN. § 58.1-3245.

21. While the distinction may not be capable of precise quantification, there is some difference between "unproductive" and "fully productive." That New Jersey had an "unproductive" standard in criterion (e) for over 40 years, until the LRHL rejected it for the "not fully productive" measure, is proof alone that there is some difference between the two terms and ample reason to believe, given the constitutional deficiencies in LRHL criterion (e), that "unproductive" is a more restrictive measure.

22. The LRHL permits seizure if only one of the seven criteria for use of eminent domain is satisfied. See N.J.S.A. § 40A:12-5. Courts nationwide, however, have loathed approving takings for private redevelopment if the sole ground is economic use of the area. *See* Luce, *The Meaning of Blight*, at 464 ("[F]or states in which [redevelopment authorities have attempted to base a finding of blight on the economic use of land], if this is the sole factor (or one of only two factors) cited, the courts tend not to find blight."); *id.* at 468 (Luce states that "[o]nly the Missouri courts have found blight where economic use was the sole factor."). Although the article was published in 2000, at this point, to the best of the Department's knowledge, Missouri courts remain the only ones to have approved what are essentially non-blighted takings. As noted above, Missouri's redevelopment statute does not have an "economic use" criterion, but the state constitution does have a "blighted area" clause. *See supra* note 15.

CHAPTER FOUR

Transit-Oriented Development: Measuring Benefits, Analyzing Trends, and Evaluating Policy in New Jersey

By
John Luciano Renne

New Jersey is a leader in smart growth and Transit-Oriented Development (TOD) policy. According to the Office of Smart Growth website, the State traces its policies to 1934 when Governor Harry A. Moore appointed a temporary planning board and the first state planning act was passed. (*A chronology of planning policy can be found at: http://www.nj.gov/dca/osg/smart/chronology.shtml*). Contemporary policies for growth management have stemmed from the 1970s, when Governor Brendan Byrne established the Governor's Office of Policy and Planning, and, from 1986, when Governor Thomas Kean signed into law the State Planning Act creating the State Planning Commission and the Office of State Planning (renamed the Office of Smart Growth in 2002).

Table 1 describes some of the key smart growth policies in New Jersey. New Jersey has provided incentives for expanded employer-based commuting alternatives, the preservation of rural lands, and the transfer of development rights (TDRs). The process for a State Plan and the State Planning Commission has been unique to New Jersey. Policies in the Garden State have sought to gain "cross acceptance" (similar to "consistency" in Florida). Cross acceptance is a process whereby municipalities, counties, and the State reconcile goals and objectives within the plan. The State Plan must address land use, housing, economic development, transportation, natural resource conservation, agricultural retention, recreation, redevelopment, historic preservation, intergovernmental coordination, and public facilities and services. The State Planning Commission is an intergovernmental body, including members from the public, that oversees the plan through monthly meetings to guide the New Jersey planning process.

A number of other policies and initiatives have been tied into the State's planning process. The Brownfield Redevelopment Task Force is a state intra-agency group that has assisted counties and local governments in redeveloping brownfields, which has helped achieve the smart growth goal of redevelopment. The State's Municipal Planning and Zoning law has mandated that municipalities establish a policy statement about how their local plans relate to the State Plan, the county master plan, and the plans of surrounding local governments. It also has required that any development exceeding 150 acres or 500 dwelling units must notify the State Planning Commission and hold a public meeting.

A New Jersey Supreme Court decision led to the Fair Housing Act of 1985, which required each of the 566 municipalities in New Jersey to develop a "fair share" of low and moderate income housing opportunities. As a result, the Council on Affordable Housing (COAH) was established to define housing needs, to set criteria for municipalities to address affordable housing, and to guide the planning process. Over the years, the definitions and methods have been debated and have yielded two subsequent Supreme Court decisions. According to attorney Chanin French in an article in the American Planning Association's *Practicing Planner*:

> The three cases comprising the *Mt. Laurel* doctrine articulate New Jersey's strong commitment both to reversing longstanding trends of exclusionary zoning and codified NIMBYism and to providing a realistic inventory of affordable housing for its low- to moderate-income residents. Granted, the *Mt. Laurel* cases have not solved New Jersey's affordable housing shortage and, in condoning "Regional Contribution Agreements," the courts have allowed municipalities and developers to 'buy out' of their obligations by paying other municipalities like Camden and Newark to make up the difference, resulting in the stigmatization of the state's inner cities. (French 2004).

The Department of Transportation Act, enacted in 1992, mandated that the New Jersey Department of Transportation consult with the Office of Smart Growth in coordinating transportation infrastructure with statewide land use planning. In 2002, under Executive Order of Governor James McGreevey, the Smart Growth Policy Council was established to ensure that all state agencies incorporate smart growth principles into their functional plans and regulations. It also sought to advance smart growth planning via legislation and administrative changes in transportation, new schools, and brownfields.

Finally, the New Jersey Transit Village Initiative is comprised of an intrastate agency task force that promotes TOD. Currently, 16 Transit Villages have been designated across the State. Participating municipalities have received special funding, expedited state development approvals, and technical expertise. The next part of this paper provides an in-depth discussion and analysis of the Transit Village Initiative.

Table 1: New Jersey's Smart Growth Policies
Source: (McGreevey 2002; New Jersey Department of
Community Affairs 2005; New Jersey Department of Transportation 2005;
US Environmental Protection Agency 2005)

Policy/Program	Description
Provide Incentives to Expand Commute Alternatives	The New Jersey Department of Transportation developed the Smart Moves for Business (SMFB) program to reduce traffic congestion and increase commuter choice. The SMFB provides participating companies tax credits and funds for programs to increase employee commute options, such as carpooling, tele-commuting, and flex hours.
Open Space Preservation/Transfer of Development Rights (TDRs)	New Jersey uses tax money to purchase and preserve open space. In March 2004, the State became the first state in the nation to authorize TDRs on a statewide level to allow mu-nicipalities to transfer development rights from rural areas to urban locations.
State Plan/State Planning Commission	Established in 1986, the State Plan includes goals and objec-tives for growth management. The plan results from a process of "cross acceptance" where the public works with municipal, county, and state government to establish a vision for the future of New Jersey. The purpose of the State Plan is to *"Coordinate planning activities and establish statewide planning objectives in the following areas: land use, housing, economic development, transportation, natural resource conservation, agriculture and farmland retention, recreation, urban and suburban redevelop-ment, historic preservation, public facilities and services, and intergovernmental coordination."* (N.J.S.A. 52:18A-200(f)). The State Planning Commission consists of members from state, county, and local government and the public. The commission oversees the State Plan and meets monthly to guide the statewide planning process.
New Jersey Brownfield Redevelopment Task Force	Created in 1998, this group assists municipalities and counties in using brownfield redevelopment to help implement smart growth strategies and in initiating an inventory of marketable brownfield sites for prospective developers with the support of an interstate agency team of representatives.
State Rules for Municipal Planning and Zoning	Municipal master plans must include a policy statement that describes the relationships between the local plan and the State Plan, master plans of surrounding municipalities, the county master plan, and the applicable solid waste management plan. All applicants for development that exceeds 150 acres or 500 dwelling units must serve notice of a public hearing to the State Planning Commission.

Department of Transportation Act	The Department of Transportation must consult with the Office of Smart Growth in preparing the State Transportation Plan in order to meet the transportation needs of various urban areas statewide and to better coordinate with land use planning.
Fair Housing Act/Council on Affordable Housing	Based on a State Supreme Count decision know as Mount Laurel, the Fair Housing Act of 1985 established a constitutional obligation for each of the 566 municipalities in the state to establish a realistic opportunity for the provision of fair share low- and moderate-income housing obligations, generally through land use and zoning powers. The Council on Affordable Housing was created to: (1) define housing regions, (2) estimate low- and moderate-income housing needs, (3) set criteria and guidelines for municipalities to determine and address their own fair share numbers, and then (4) review and approve housing elements/fair share plans and regional contribution agreements (RCAs) for municipalities. As a quasi-judicial organization, COAH can also impose resource restraints and consider motions regarding housing plans.
Smart Growth Policy Council	By Executive Order under Governor McGreevey (January 31, 2002), the Smart Growth Policy Council is charged with ensuring that state agencies incorporate the principles of smart growth and the State Plan into their functional plans and regulations. This council is to recommend legislative and administrative changes to advance smart growth and to ensure that state funding, including transportation and school infrastructure, is consistent with the State Plan and smart growth principles. It seeks to coordinate and consolidate redevelopment initiatives, especially those involving brownfields, and to review water resource capacity in the State to reduce conflicts between development and the protection of water and natural resources.
New Jersey Transit Village Initiative	The Transit Village Initiative is a program that seeks to revitalize and grow selected communities with transit as an anchor. Although the Transit Village Initiative is staffed and directed by the New Jersey Department of Transportation (NJDOT), a task force of nine state agencies meets regularly to facilitate TOD. Within each agency at least one person is appointed as the Transit Village representative. Each municipality also has a contact person who works directly with this representative, in addition to working with the Transit Village coordinator at NJDOT. The benefit of being a Transit Village is that this designation not only gives these municipalities priority for state grants, but also allows for the municipalities to have direct contact with the representatives at these agencies. This is often helpful in getting some development approvals expedited.

Conclusion

In summary, this section presents smart growth policies and TOD trends in New Jersey, and the larger study examines Maryland, Florida, Oregon, and California. Although each state differs in its approach, these five have shown a commitment at the state policy level to encourage a better coordination of land use and transportation planning in the promotion of smart growth, unlike most other states.

New Jersey, Oregon, and California have been the leaders in promoting state-level TOD policy. It is my opinion that this state leadership will be instrumental for regions, counties, and localities to follow suit. The system in New Jersey, which designates Transit Villages, has rewarded localities for "doing it right." With the state's assistance, these municipalities can continue to build upon their successes. Based on personal experience, the Transit Village Initiative has gained popular support in state government, local governments, and the private sector (more on the Transit Village Initiative is discussed in the next chapter). Also, New Jersey Transit's Transit-Friendly Communities Program (TFCP) provided grants for planning assistance to promote TOD at a number of rail stations. The TFCP pre-dated the Transit Village Initiative and was instrumental in getting municipalities to consider the benefits of TOD.

Similar to TFCP, the State of California also has rewarded local governments for promoting smart growth and TOD through the Community Based Transportation Planning grant program, although most people interviewed felt that not enough money was put into TOD to make a difference. Victoria Eisen, a transportation and land use planning consultant who formerly worked for the Association of Bay Area Governments, best summarized the relationship between local and state government with respect to TOD:

> Ultimately local governments have land use statutory power, so the only thing the State can do is to use its dollars as carrots to reward local jurisdictions that have done it right. You cannot do a controlled experiment to see if it would have happened or not, so rewarding is the only way to do it. (Eisen 2004).

Her statement applies not only to California but also to all states. The Growth Management Study Commission encouraged Florida to consider a system where TODs would be designated and then rewarded with state funding and regulatory exemptions.

Data presented in this section on TODs support the need for more smart growth policies. Over the past 30 years, mostly in the absence of supportive state policies, TODs have emerged in regions around the United States. Trends show that shares of transit, walking, and bicycling to work have grown or remained stable at levels much higher than regional averages. While auto-dependence has engulfed America, these TODs, for the most part, remain pockets where multiple modes still serve the journey-to-work. This phenomenon is also reflected in vehicle ownership. Lower rates of households in TODs own two or more vehicles compared to the regional averages.

While the data presented here supports the claims for smart growth policies, I do not claim that the commuting and vehicle ownership patterns are a result of these policies. Cause and effect is best determined through field research by talking to policy makers and locals responsible for building TODs. This approach is used in the following observations on New Jersey. Many of the policies discussed were enacted in the mid- to late-1990s, and their impacts would not appear as early as the 2000 census. Some of the policies were even enacted post-2000. The intent was to show that TODs demonstrate positive outcomes and state policy can encourage more development of this type in the future.

Transit Villages in New Jersey

Transit-oriented development in New Jersey is an old concept that has been revived under new circumstances. Originally, commuter-rail suburbs were built along a vast rail network serving New York City and Philadelphia. This lifestyle enabled people to escape living in the city while still accessing employment. New Jersey has become the most urbanized state in America and one of the wealthiest (in terms of income per capita). Its strategic location on the Northeast Corridor, between New York City and Philadelphia, has produced a strong job base for the State; however, New Jersey is not entirely reliant upon these two metropolises. Many employment opportunities within the State have emerged. New York, Philadelphia, Trenton, Newark, and Jersey City, all traditional employment centers, have been well-served by rail infrastructure. In New Jersey, massive suburbanization and sprawl have resulted in deplorable traffic congestion. TODs (otherwise known in New Jersey as Transit Villages) have offered residents another escape, but, this time, they have been returning from suburbia to traditional historic downtowns.

The State has promoted TOD through the New Jersey Transit Village Initiative since 1999, and there are now 16 designated Transit Villages. Each Transit Village municipality works directly with the state government to promote compact, mixed-use housing and economic development around its station. This chapter provides an overview of the New Jersey Transit Village Initiative and presents data from a recent evaluation to assess the outcomes of the program. The assessment of the Transit Village Initiative was funded by a grant to the Alan M. Voorhees Transportation Center by the New Jersey Department of Transportation. I was the Project Manger and co-principal investigator for this study along with Assistant Research Professor Jan Wells, who served as the Principal Investigator.

Research methods examining the Initiative included interviews with local and state representatives and private developers. Public perception was gauged through household mail surveys. Some of the mail survey questions, investigating opinions on urban development and housing, were repeated from a statewide telephone poll, also conducted as part of this research. Data from this New Jersey case study will facilitate answers for all three research questions; however, emphasis is placed on data pertaining to the third question, the extent to which market forces and state policy encourage compact and affordable housing in TODs. A detailed description of the research methods and a presentation of results are preceded by an overview of the New Jersey Transit Village Initiative.

Overview of the New Jersey Transit Village Initiative

Established by Governor Christine Todd Whitman in 1999, the New Jersey Transit Village Initiative is an interagency state program that promotes TOD. A Transit Village is synonymous with a TOD and defined as the area within a half-mile of a designated transit station. The NJDOT is responsibilities include staffing and directing the program and managing a task force consisting of multiple state agencies that govern the Initiative. The Transit Village Initiative Task Force includes representatives from the following agencies: New Jersey Transit, the Department of Environmental Protection (DEP), the New Jersey Redevelopment Authority (NJRA), the Department of Community Affairs (DCA) (including representatives from the Office of Smart Growth and Main Street New Jersey), the Economic Development Authority, the Housing and Mortgage Finance Agency (HMFA), the Commerce and Economic Growth Commission, and the New Jersey Council on the Arts.

Members of the task force work directly with representatives from the local governments. Often, developers need approval from various state agencies to carry out certain activities, such as site remediation from the DEP or traffic impact studies from the NJDOT. Task force representatives, as well as the Transit Village coordinator from the NJDOT, coordinate with local officials to expedite the development application approval process. Other benefits of being a Transit Village include receiving preferential consideration for state grants and receiving technical assistance on planning and development issues. Each year, representatives from Transit Villages are invited to a forum where experts help local planners and officials overcome TOD obstacles. Also, local Transit Village contacts are encouraged to call upon task force members for assistance. This "direct line" between the state and local government makes the Transit Village Initiative unique when compared to other TOD programs in the United States.

Criteria for Becoming a Transit Village

For Transit Village designation, a municipality must have met specified criteria supporting TOD when applying to the State. Applications are accepted during defined periods as dictated by the task force in conjunction with the governor's office. According to the NJDOT, local governments interested in becoming Transit Villages must commit in writing to growth in housing, jobs, and population. They must have a train, ferry, or major bus station, and meet a number of smart growth criteria, including an "adopted land-use strategy for achieving compact, transit-supportive, mixed-use development within walking distance of transit. This can be in the form of a redevelopment plan, zoning ordinance, master plan or overlay zone." (New Jersey Department of Transportation 2005, website). Other criteria include having vacant land near the station and a pedestrian and bicycling-friendly urban environment.

Overview of Research Methods
to Assess the Transit Village Initiative

To assess the Transit Village Initiative, the NJDOT provided a research grant to the Alan M. Voorhees Transportation Center (VTC) at Rutgers University to study the first seven designated Transit Villages, including: Morristown, Pleasantville, Rahway, Riverside, Rutherford, South Amboy, and South Orange. Metuchen was designated a new Transit Village while the study was underway and was selected with South Orange and South Amboy for local household surveys. Upon completion of the study in October 2003, the State announced six new Transit Villages: Belmar, Bloomfield, Bound Brook, Collingswood, Cranford, and Matawan. In February 2005, the State announced the addition of New Brunswick and Journal Square in Jersey City as the fifteenth and sixteenth Transit Villages.

Research into the New Jersey Transit Village Initiative began with a general TOD literature review. Next, a demographic comparison of the Transit Village area to the municipality as a whole was conducted. Data from the 2000 US census was gathered, and block groups were chosen to represent the half-mile Transit Village area. Interviews were then held with each of the state agency task force members and local officials from the Transit Villages. Private developers with building experience in the villages were also interviewed. We then created questions that the Eagleton Institute of Politics administered in a statewide telephone poll in April 2003 gauging opinions on urban development and support for housing. We also created extensive follow-up household mail surveys, which Eagleton conducted in Metuchen, South Amboy, and South Orange. The questionnaire asked the same questions as the statewide phone poll and additional questions to gauge perceptions of recent town improvements related to the Transit Village Initiative. Finally, attendance at seven Transit Village task force meetings (held quarterly), where state policy decisions were made, supplemented two years of research.

Transit Village Evaluation

The VTC assessment of the New Jersey Transit Village Initiative took place from September 2002 to October 2003. An economic impact evaluation followed and extended our work to August 2004. This section summarizes the Transit Village Initiative evaluation, and relates it to my question—To *what extent does government policy promote compact and affordable housing in New Jersey's Transit Villages?*

Demographic Analysis

This section describes the data collected, and then presents selected results related to housing, population, race/ethnicity, household economics, commuting, and vehicle ownership.

Methods for Data Collection

To extract data, we developed a protocol that included the identification of all 2000 census block groups surrounding transit stations in Morristown, Pleasantville, Rahway, Riverside, South Amboy, and South Orange. These were chosen because they were the first group of Transit Villages designated in New Jersey. Block groups that had more than 50% of their land area located within a half-mile radius of the station center were chosen to represent the Transit Village. Table 2 shows census variables that were compared between the municipality and the Transit Village. Table 3 shows variables developed with date from New Jersey Transit about each station and data from the New Jersey Department of Education about each municipality. These variables provide data for a comparison of travel behavior, vehicle ownership, and socioeconomics in the Transit Villages compared to the municipalities.

Table 2: Census Variables Collected
Source: Wells and Renne 2003

Variable	Variable
Total Population	Percentage of Single Family Homes
Total Land Area	Percentage of Units Built before 1940
Percentage of School-aged Children	Percentage of Crowded Units
Percentage 62 Years or Older	Homeownership Rate
Percentage White, Non-Hispanic	Median House Value
Percentage Black	For-Sale Unit Vacancy Rate
Percentage Asian	Median Gross Rent
Percentage Hispanic	Rental Vacancy Rent
Percentage Foreign Born	Median Gross Rent as Percent of Income
Percentage of Households with Married Couples	Percentage of Households with No Vehicles
Percentage of Households with Female Single Parents	Percentage of Households with Three or More Vehicles
Percentage of Households with Single Persons	Percentage of Workers Using Public Transportation
Median Family Income in 1999	Percentage of Workers Walking to Work
Poverty Rate	Median Travel Time to Work
Unemployment Rate	

Table 3: Data Collected from New Jersey Transit and the New Jersey Department of Education
Source: Wells and Renne 2003

Station Area Variables from New Jersey Transit	Municipal Level Data from the New Jersey Department of Education
Number of Train Departures (weekday towards New York City)	State Aid (2002-2003)
2002 Average Rail Weekday Ridership	Expenditure Per Student
Total Intercity Bus Routes	
Number of Weekday Bus Departures	
Number of Connecting Shuttle Services	
Number of Ferry Departures	
Total Number of Commuter Parking Spaces	
Percentage Owned by Municipality	
Percentage Owned by NJ Transit	
Utilization Rate	
Monthly Fees	
Number of Bicycle Spaces	

Selected Results - Housing

Demographic analysis found a higher percentage of multifamily dwellings in the Transit Villages compared to the average for the respective municipalities in the following towns: Morristown, Rahway, Rutherford, South Amboy, and South Orange (as shown in Table 4). This was not the case for Pleasantville and Riverside, which are located in southern New Jersey, a less densely populated part of the State. Pleasantville's Transit Village contains a major bus transfer station (many passengers pass through Pleasantville on their way to and from Atlantic City), and Riverside is home to the new South Jersey River Line (light rail), which opened in 2004.

The Transit Villages of Morristown, Rahway, South Amboy, and South Orange showed higher housing density compared to the average for their respective municipalities (as shown in Table 4). Conversely, Rutherford's Transit Village housing density was considerably lower than the town average. *Due to unusual circumstances, half of the Transit Village area in Rutherford lies in another municipality (East Rutherford) and is not formally designated as a Transit Village. Therefore, the data presented here only accounts for the designated area in Rutherford.* Transforming these parcels to high-density residential is currently underway.

As reported in Table 5, homeownership rates were lower in the Transit Villages of Morristown, Rahway, Rutherford, South Amboy, and South Orange, than respective town averages. Analysis of housing-affordability data proved inconclusive. At the census block level, median rents are reported in ranges, making a comparison with the municipalities virtually impossible. Analysis did show that these Transit Villages exhibit a diverse housing stock, which includes both affordable and premium-priced housing in close proximity to the train stations.

Table 4: Housing Supply Characteristics in the New Jersey Transit Villages
Source: U.S. Census 2000; Wells and Renne 2003

Town	Percentage of Multifamily Homes within Transit Village	Percentage of Multifamily Homes within Municipality	Housing Density Within Transit Village (units per gross acre of land area)	Housing Density Within Municipality (units per gross acres of land area)
Morristown	78.4%	63.5%	5.3	4.0
Pleasantville	31.5%	36.0%	1.4	1.9
Rahway	53.5%	39.1%	5.5	4.1
Riverside	29.2%	29.1%	3.2	3.2
Rutherford	67.9%	44.6%	2.6	4.0
South Amboy	40.4%	35.8%	3.0	3.1
South Orange	42.1%	30.5%	3.7	3.1

Note: The percentage of multifamily housing in Transit Villages versus municipalities was statistically independent at the 95% level based on both a paired samples test and a nonparametric Wilcoxon signed rank test. Housing density between the Transit Villages and the municipalities was not statistically independent.

Table 5: Homeownership Rates and Median Gross Rent in the New Jersey Transit Villages
Source: U.S. Census 2000; Wells and Renne 2003

Town	Homeownership Rate within Transit Village	Homeownership Rate within Municipality	Median Gross Rent within Transit Village[1]	Median Gross Rent within Municipality
Morristown	24.6%	39.5%	$775-$1,128	$914
Pleasantville	63.3%	56.3%	$495-$574	$715
Rahway	47.7%	62.7%	$469-$928	$732
Riverside	66.0%	67.7%	$584-$807	$670
Rutherford	43.7%	65.5%	$709-$928	$832
South Amboy	59.4%	64.2%	$435-$888	$767
South Orange	59.7%	72.1%	$275-$1,900	$879

[1] Data available only for individual block groups, therefore the range is reported.
Note: The homeownership rate in Transit Villages versus municipalities was statistically independent at the 95% level based on a paired samples t test and 90% based on a nonparametric Wilcoxon signed rank test. Because median gross rent was reported in ranges for the Transit Villages, statistical tests for independence were not performed.

Selected Results Population, Race/Ethnicity, and Household Economics

Higher population diversity was found in the Transit Villages compared to the municipalities. Table 6 shows that in every case, except for South Orange, a smaller percentage of white, non-Hispanics resided in the Transit Villages compared to the municipalities as a whole. A higher percentage of foreign-born residents lived in every Transit Village, except South Amboy.

Other demographics also indicated Transit Villages were more demographically diverse than municipalities. In Riverside and South Amboy, for example, the percentage of married couple households was higher in the Transit Village than the average for its respective municipality. With the exceptions of Rutherford and South Orange, the percentage of school-aged children was higher in the Transit Villages. Rutherford and South Orange were also the only two towns where the percentage of residents aged 62 years or older was higher in the Transit Villages compared to the towns average.

Table 6: Racial/Ethnic and Foreign Born Compositionof the Transit Villages
Source: U.S. Census 2000; Wells and Renne 2003.

Town	Percentage of White, Non-Hispanics within Transit Village	Percentage of White, Non-Hispanics within Municipality	Percentage of Foreign-born within Transit Village	Percentage of Foreign-born within Municipality
Morristown	40.6%	50.7%	42.1%	32.4%
Pleasantville	15.9%	17.9%	15.8%	12.9%
Rahway	38.7%	53.2%	19.6%	17.2%
Riverside	87.0%	88.1%	10.9%	10.2%
Rutherford	64.6%	75.6%	27.7%	20.1%
South Amboy	88.8%	90.0%	8.7%	9.0%
South Orange	62.6%	58.2%	20.0%	16.9%

Note: The percentage of white, non-Hispanics in Transit Villages versus municipalities was statistically independent at the 90% level based on both a paired samples t test and a nonparametric Wilcoxon signed rank test. The percentage of foreign born in Transit Villages versus municipalities was statistically independent at the 95% level based on both a paired samples t test and a nonparametric Wilcoxon signed rank test.

Because median family income varies by block group, comparison was difficult. However, the poverty rates were higher in all Transit Villages, except South Amboy. Unemployment rates were also higher in all Transit Villages, with the exceptions of Morristown and Riverside.

Selected Results – Commuting and Vehicle Ownership

This study found that residents of these seven Transit Villages tended to own fewer vehicles and take the train to work more often than the towns as a whole. Table 7 shows that the percentage of workers commuting on transit and the percentage of households without vehicles were greater in each of the Transit Villages than the averages for their respective municipalities.

Table 7: Vehicle Ownership and Transit Commuting to Work
Source: U.S. Census 2000; Wells and Renne 2003

Town	Percentage of Workers Commuting on Transit within Transit Village	Percentage of Workers Commuting on Transit within Municipality	Percentage of Households without Vehicles within Transit Village	Percentage of Households without Vehicles within Municipality
Morristown	7.3%	6.3%	23.2%	15.5%
Pleasantville	19.9%	14.2%	27.0%	20.9%
Rahway	14.3%	9.4%	15.4%	11.7%
Riverside	1.8%	1.5%	10.2%	10.4%
Rutherford	22.0%	16.9%	16.3%	10.0%
South Amboy	7.5%	5.9%	12.8%	11.9%
South Orange	23.1%	21.2%	15.8%	11.5%

Note: The percentages of transit commuter households without vehicles in Transit Villages versus municipalities were statistically independent at the 95% level based on both a paired samples t test and a nonparametric Wilcoxon signed rank test.

Summary of Demographics

Demographic analysis confirms some of our previous findings such as higher percentages of renters and higher shares of transit, walking, and cycling work in Transit Villages. Our report to the NJDOT concluded, "Transit Villages in New Jersey feature a younger population, more racial and ethnic diversity, more immigrants, lower household economics . . . more rental housing, higher vacancy rates, and exhibited better transit habits—fewer cars, higher use of trains and buses, and more residents walking to work." (Wells and Renne 2003, p. 5).

Stakeholder Interviews

From October 2002 to March 2003, Professor Jan Wells and I interviewed a number of stakeholders, including task force members, private developers, and local officials in each of the Transit Villages. This section summarizes these interviews relating to state policy on compact and affordable housing in New Jersey's Transit Villages.

Methods for Data Collection

Each designated municipality selects a city employee to serve as its Transit Village contact person. In October and November 2002, Jan Wells and I conducted in-person interviews with the Transit Village contacts, and other local officials in Morristown, Pleasantville, Rahway, Riverside, Rutherford, South Amboy, and South Orange. Each interview was informal and lasted for approximately one hour. Determining the municipality's view on the usefulness of the Transit Village Initiative was our goal. Each interviewee was asked to describe the level of support the program provided. We inquired whether they had received grants from participating state agencies or specific technical assistance from Task Force members. We asked whether the designation had stimulated developers interests in their Transit Villages, and if the initiative was producing any noticeable outcomes.

Interviews were also conducted with task force representatives from the eight state agencies between November and December 2002. (Because of a personnel transition, an interview was never conducted with the New Jersey Council on the Arts after several attempts to interview the newly appointed Transit Village contact failed.) These interviews were also conducted in person and lasted approximately one hour each. During these interviews we asked questions about each agency's involvement in the Transit Villages. The Transit Village Initiative's goal includes providing municipalities preference for state grants. We asked if their agency had a system for ranking the Transit Village municipalities above others that were applying for assistance. (See http://policy.rutgers.edu:16080/vtc/tod/tod_projects.html for grant maps of each Transit Village.) We also asked for the representatives general opinions on the Transit Village Initiative's progress and for examples illustrating successes and challenges.

Developers were the last group interviewed. Meetings with four development companies that had built or were in the process of building in Transit Villages took place in March 2003. These interviews lasted approximately a half hour to one hour, and included both in-person and telephone interviews.

The following sections summarize the municipal, state, and developer interviews. Overall, our style was informal yet professional to ensure that the interviewees felt comfortable confiding what was considered to be sensitive information. Building rapport with the developers was essential due to their reluctance to divulge information. Following the model used in municipal and state interviews, we employed an informal style allowing natural conversation progression, addressing our main questions regarding the Transit Village Initiative including successes and short-comings.

Municipal Interviews

In the municipal interviews, it became clear that the Transit Village designation was not the sole reason transit-focused development was occurring. Each of the local representatives noted that the designation had resulted in benefits, but those benefits were virtually impossible to quantify. Those at the municipalities who were not directly involved with the Transit Village Initiative reported confusion about the local Transit Village contact's role and the benefits of the program. An interviewee in South Orange revealed "a lack of understanding on the local level of what the Transit Village gives us. The town's engineer has gotten and used grants, but I have no idea what else is available. I recommend the State should do a training demonstration to all people in the town to educate about the Transit Village benefits." (Adam-Shippy 2002).

South Orange is located along a corridor that in 1996 became a direct line to Manhattan (NJ Transit's Midtown Direct). We learned that "property values started skyrocketing once people had a direct ride to Manhattan." (Adam-Shippy 2002). This may have been a factor that generated plans for several new development projects within the Transit Village, including 115 units on the site of a former supermarket and 100 rental units above ground-floor retail. In addition, the development company, LCOR, had recently completed 200 rental units in the Gaslight Commons development across from the train station.

A number of public works projects had recently been completed or were under construction in the South Orange Transit Village, including train station and historic fire station renovations, as well as traffic calming and pedestrian improvements. Furthermore, a major arts center was being built next to the train station. Since 1991, South Orange had been designated as part of the Main Street New Jersey program and had worked within the municipal government on façade improvements, a farmers market, local festivals, and the creation of several retail stores below the train station. Our interviewee in South Orange reported that the town had received a jitney from NJ Transit as part of the initiative, and matching funds from the Transit Village program to start a second bus route. She noted that the jitney helped provide local shuttle service to the train station for those who lived beyond walking distance. "The intent is to alleviate the parking crunch at the station and to reduce the need for more parking." (Adam-Shippy 2002).

NJ Transit also gave Rahway a bus, similar to the one in South Orange. According to local planner and Transit Village representative Lenore Slothower, there were a number of transit-oriented redevelopment projects underway in the downtown. "We are completing one of the first mixed-use libraries in the country, with office space on the upper level that will hopefully be rented out as doctors' offices" (Slothower 2002). When we met with representatives in Rahway, the town had just been designated as a Transit Village, thus Slothower could not yet report any major benefits. In several follow-ups since the initial conversations, she discussed increasing developer interest attributed to the Transit Village status. Rahway's downtown redevelopment zone declaration assisted in its Transit Village designation. The progressive mayor James Kennedy placed downtown redevelopment at the top of his agenda. Not long before the designation, NJ Transit and the City of Rahway spent over $13 million demolishing buildings and renovating the train station area, including the creation of a new plaza. The city was actively improving public space and encouraging developers to build luxury units. "The Mayor's vision is to bring people to live in the downtown first, and then retail will naturally improve." (Slothower 2002).

In South Amboy, City Administrator Stan Marcinczyk reported that the DCA awarded the town a Smart Growth grant to conduct a comprehensive revitalization and redevelopment plan. (Marcinczyk 2002). He also reported that NJ Transit was funding $7.7 million for the reconstruction of an intermodal transit plaza. When asked how important the Transit Village designation was in clinching these and other grants, Marcinczyk could not give a specific answer, although he felt it played a significant role in securing public money that facilitated the "rebirth" of a blue-collar town. One example was Lighthouse Bay, a new project built on the waterfront that caters to higher-income earners, which is inconsistent with South Amboy's history. The town had identified a surplus of space within its school system; consequently, Marcinczyk welcomed new families and their children into South Amboy and its schools. Marcinczyk verbalized the hope that the new children would help raise school test scores. Unfortunately, newer and older residents have not gotten along well, as reported by *The Star-Ledger* in an article titled "A Tiny City's Great Divide," which found that the new housing development has struggled with social cohesion despite efforts to promote smart growth and TOD. (Slutsky 2004).

Eric Maurer, the business administrator of Morristown, said he felt the Transit Village designation had helped the town win grants. He reported receiving seven grants since the designation. (Maurer 2002). This was especially helpful since the town had a moratorium on development during the construction of a sewer plant from 1984 to 1992. Maurer reported that the extraordinarily long moratorium had squelched developers' interests. Chancery Square, a downtown project with 131 rental units, was the first development in 30 years. The Transit Village designation, along with new direct train service to Manhattan, helped revitalize Morristown. Because of these changes developers were more interested in Morristown. As a result, NJ Transit was in the process of negotiating its first joint-development project to turn its commuter parking lot into a transit-oriented, mixed-use project.

Interviews with Thomas Bellucci and Robin Reenstra-Bryant, borough administrator and director of the Downtown Partnership in Rutherford, respectively, revealed a lack of understanding about the Initiative. Bellucci's inexperience as borough administrator may have been the reason for his lack of knowledge about the Transit Village initiative. He said, "Rutherford has a local bus service tied to the train schedule. The bus was given to us through the Transit Village program but it is not really reliable. The service is important and vital to the town, and we have multiple back-ups for the bus." (Bellucci 2002).

Rutherford's appointment by NJ Transit to the Transit-Friendly Communities Program (this was the only Transit Village in the Transit-Friendly Communities Program) qualified the town for planning assistance for TOD in its downtown. (The NJ Transit's Transit-Friendly Communities program began as a federal demonstration project that provided money for planning support to promote TOD. The planners at NJ Transit responsible for the program were also members of the Transit Village Initiative Task Force.) Reenstra-Bryant reported on the Downtown

Partnership sponsoring a façade improvement program, and on a number of special events attracting people into the Transit Village. (Reenstra-Bryant 2002). Bellucci informed us of a grant from NJDOT to improve sidewalks and street lighting and to create new bicycle racks at the train station. Both interviewees felt the designation was important to Rutherford. The downtown commercial vacancy rate was at an all time low, and within a five-minute walk of the train station were 28 restaurants. Also, a new transit-oriented residential project, Boiling Springs, was under review. It would be one of the first new residential projects near the train station. Moreover, the "downtown area has been revitalized over the past year with the Upstairs/ Downtown live-work program financed by HMFA money." (Bellucci 2002).

Southern New Jersey Transit Villages, Pleasantville and Riverside, differed from their northern counterparts. In both places, officials had encountered difficulties in spurring development, yet both were optimistic that being a Transit Village was a step in the right direction. Gary La Venia, town administrator of Riverside, said, "Transit Village designation has led to minor improvements thus far, mostly streetscape improvements, but there is hope that the Watchcase tower site will be redeveloped next to the new station." (LaVenia 2002). The Watchcase site was a historic factory that suffered from land contamination; however, several developers were looking into the cleanup and residential conversion. La Venia informed us that the DEP and the NJ Economic Development Authority, both members of the Transit Village task force, were about to fund a feasibility study assessing remediation. Overall, he felt there was a lot of hope along the River Line corridor that towns would be redeveloped. Housing affordability and easily accessible employment centers in both Trenton and Philadelphia were strengths. La Venia felt the Transit Village designation, which elevated prospects for Riverside's redevelopment, gave the town an edge over other towns along the line.

Like Riverside, Pleasantville also was aggressively promoting downtown redevelopment. Stuart Wiser, the city planner, reported, "Transit Village designation has been a planning tool that has helped focus revitalization efforts in the city as well as getting 'brownie points' for state grant applications. . . . Has it helped? Probably. Has it influenced thinking? Definitely!" (Wiser 2002). Wiser's sentiments seemed to be shared across the Transit Villages.

The interviewees in the Transit Villages were all impressed with the technical assistance provided by task force members. In many instances, local planners and/ or officials would contact Monica Etz, the Transit Village coordinator at NJDOT, to ask assistance in helping to overcome development obstacles. Etz and other members of the task force would help troubleshoot problems to find solutions. This often entailed site visits to review specific problems.

Municipal interviews revealed that the Transit Villages were in towns with strong leadership. This finding was confirmed in a recent Transit Cooperative Research Program report that included a short case study on TOD in New Jersey. (Cervero et al. 2004). In each of the Transit Villages, a "strong" mayor or municipal official championed the town's redevelopment. For example, Rahway's mayor, Kennedy, has worked for over a decade trying to clean up the city's image. Mayor O'Leary of South Amboy has been diligently working to do the same. These municipalities have sought numerous downtown revitalization efforts, including the Transit Village designation. Pleasantville, for example, has participated in endeavors such as the Urban Enterprise Zone, the Urban Coordinating Council, and the Neighborhood Preservation Program. Each of these designations created more state and federal resources for igniting development. Virtually every Transit Village had multiple local organizations responsible for different economic development aspects, such as business improvement districts, Main Street programs, and designated redevelopment zones.

Despite a general resistance to new housing throughout New Jersey (due to the fear that additional school children might lead to higher property taxes for existing residents), the Transit Villages all have promoted new housing within the half-mile radius of the stations. Morristown, Rahway, Rutherford, South Amboy, and South Orange all had new compact housing developments either under construction or in the approval process. Interviews with Riverside and Pleasantville also revealed support for compact housing, but these towns were working to attract initial developers to the Transit Village. Land ownership proved a major obstacles for some Transit Villages trying to pursue compact housing. Most parcels were small and independently owned, obstructing the construction of apartments or town homes, which required larger sites. Land must be secured before projects are considered viable, and, in most instances, towns leave this responsibility in the hands of the private sector. In some cases, a proactive approach was taken. Using a redevelopment zone, Rahway had exercised the power of eminent domain to acquire land from owners not willing to sell. Another issue was brownfields. Since some of the Transit Villages, including Rahway, South Amboy, and Riverside, were characterized by abandoned and former industrial sites, redevelopment was contingent upon contamination clean-up support. Slothower said the DEP expedited a site approval in Rahway's Transit Village. Pleasantville and Riverside were also exerting their Transit Village status to leverage state clean-up funds.

Interviews proved the towns supported compact housing near their transit stations, but plans mostly neglected affordable housing. The years of economic stagnation that each town experienced contributed to its desire for luxury housing. Each Transit Village was eager to attract wealth. Moreover, one- and two-bedroom units made the housing unattractive to families with children. Towns were happy to receive the tax influx from new development but did not want the financial burden of more school-age children. (This is because New Jersey public schools are funded through property taxes.) South Amboy was the only exception. It had built single-family housing and extended a welcome to new school children because its schools had extra capacity. Its actions were not entirely altruistic. South Amboy's new development was also targeted to higher-income earners, and it hoped the new students would boost the schools test scores. (School districts receive aid from the government based on standardized test scores administered each year.) South Amboy ranked low in comparison to other public school districts in New Jersey.

All of the interviewees expressed the view that luxury housing would help revitalize the downtown. When asked about the need for affordable housing, most responded that they had plenty of it, and the towns needed more high-income housing. New luxury apartments at Gaslight Commons in South Orange ranged from $1,500 - $2,000 per month for a one- or two-bedroom apartment in 2003. Rents were much higher than existing rentals, but most of the Transit Villages were targeting a new demographic profile—young professionals without kids. Jeff Jotz, who works with Slothower in Rahway, commented that in five years the town hoped to become "a new Hoboken." Hoboken is a New Jersey city directly across the Hudson River from Manhattan that has gone through massive gentrification over the past 10 years, and consequently has attracted Manhattan-priced rents. Clearly, the municipalities were looking at the Transit Village designation as a way to promote higher-class lifestyles and economic improvement in their towns.

In summary, the municipal interviews revealed in every Transit Village that local officials were supportive of compact housing but resistant to affordable housing. They also felt that the Transit Village designation was important in attracting developers. Local officials were uncertain whether the Transit Village Initiative was the reason they had been awarded grants, but they suspected that it contributed to the strength of their grant proposals. While the exact value of the Transit Village status was undetermined, all agreed it supported a new pro-TOD mindset.

State Agency Interviews and Quarterly Task Force Meetings

Interviews with members of the State's Transit Village task force also aimed to determine the Initiative's outcomes and effectiveness. Initially, Jan Wells and I held personal interviews with each representative of the task force during November and December 2002. After the initial meeting, we regularly attended Transit Village task force quarterly meetings at NJDOT's headquarters. These meetings allowed us to watch the group grow and change over an extended period (from fall 2002 to summer 2004). This section summarizes initial interviews, and draws from the seven task force meetings we attended while researching the Transit Village Initiative. Direct quotes are not presented, because the meetings content was confidential. We were guests invited to listen (and sometimes provide input) at the task force meetings, but we had promised to keep confidential the details of task force meetings and personal interviews with the task force members.

Like the municipal interviews, the initial meetings with the state task force representatives revealed confusion about the investments and outcomes of the Transit Village Initiative. Respondents reported that financial support had led to some success with redevelopment, but it was impossible to quantify. When asked if the State tracked grants issued in the Transit Villages, the information provided was incomplete. Monica Etz, the Transit Village coordinator, provided us with a database of grants, but advised that more needed to be done in the future to track the various state agency investments. (The results, after much work to get both state and municipal input, were the Transit Village grant maps, which can be found at http://policy.rutgers.edu:16080/vtc/tod/tod_projects.html.) The problem stemmed from inconsistencies among the tracking methods each agency used (if it tracked its investments at all). Consolidating these records into one database proved challenging. In some cases records were never found.

Interviews revealed that the first few years of the initiative were disorganized (from 1999 to 2001), as the former task force coordinator from the NJDOT was unable to hold regular meetings. Moreover, the meetings held over the first couple years were spent developing the criteria for designating future Transit Villages. The State had chosen the first five Transit Villages (Morristown, Pleasantville, Rutherford, South Amboy, and South Orange) upon launching the program in 1999, but provided little financial or technical support for the first couple of years. Meanwhile, the Task Force decided upon a focus for the program. Most grants were periodically awarded to Transit Villages on an ad hoc basis. It was not until the announcement of subsequent Transit Villages, including the six designated in October 2003, that each town was awarded a $100,000 grant with the designation.

Interviewees revealed that expedited development approval for municipalities was a major Transit Village benefit. Many members said the task force's regular meetings encouraged teamwork and collaboration with colleagues at different agencies. This benefited local governments. For example, some villages received Smart Growth Planning Grants from the DCA, environmental approvals from the DEP, and funding for parking structures from NJ Transit or NJDOT.

Interviews revealed that strong support from the governor's office for smart growth and TOD created a political atmosphere that drew accolades. On the other hand, nothing related to the Transit Village Initiative has been institutionalized into state legislation. There have not been any laws like those in California that would embed the Transit Village Initiative for the long-term future. Over the past few years, Transit Villages have become increasingly popular. State representatives stated that more and more local municipalities have become interested in achieving designation.

During the quarterly task force meetings that we attended, members continually discussed each town's development progress. The group worked together figuring out which state funding sources could be used to fund various projects in the villages. When the time came to designate new Transit Villages, the task force received numerous applications. Every state representative read over each application, ranked the candidates based on the established criteria, and candidly discussed the applicants prospects with the rest of the task force until a consensus was reached. The rejected municipalities were sent letters that explained the task force's rationale and invited them to consider reapplying in the future, after resolving specific issues.

Interviews with Developers

The last group of interviews was held with developers who had built or were in the process of building in several of the Transit Villages, including Morristown, Metuchen, Rahway, South Amboy, and South Orange. These interviews confirmed findings from the municipal interviews (for all places except South Amboy) that the towns were targeting childless professionals who wanted to live in more compact, downtown environments, especially in locations with good transportation connections. The developers were building luxury housing, mostly with one- and two-bedroom plans. They reported that their typical buyer was either single or married and without children. They viewed this housing as transitional, for buyers who wanted easy accessibility to jobs in New York City.

Transportation connections were important for the developers. In an interview with the Baker Development Company in South Amboy, one person noted that while the rail station was the basis for the designation as a Transit Village, the town chose their site because it had access to rail, highways, and Manhattan ferry service, in addition to waterfront views. "People have purchased because of the train, both for work and for cultural reasons" the interviewee said. "The primary benefit is to have access to Manhattan in a reasonable amount of time. Residents now have this with both the train and the ferry." (Baker Development Corporation 2003).

A developer who had recently constructed a project in Metuchen and was planning one for Rahway noted that his biggest obstacle was acquiring enough land to make the development work. At the time, he was in the process of negotiating with 13 separate land owners to secure a two-acre site. "Currently we have about half of the parcels but this process makes development very difficult," he said. "The good news about Transit Villages is that approvals are easy, but there are more complicated site issues, such as parking, land acquisition, and brownfields." (Schwartz 2003).

Anthony Marchetta of LCOR, another developer who had recently constructed a project in South Orange, said he fought for parking reductions on his site because of being in a Transit Village. The town compromised and permitted 1.8 parking spaces per unit instead of the standard 2.0 spaces. He noted that, because of the development's proximity to the train station, fewer households had second cars. He said that over 65% of his renters commuted to work via train, and even at 1.8 parking spaces per unit the lot was underutilized because the average vehicle ownership was only 1.35 cars per unit. He felt 1.2 spaces per unit would have been appropriate.

The relationship between the Transit Village task force and developers was indirect. Interviewees did not reveal any direct contact with the Transit Village task force other than giving guest lectures on recent successful developments. As we found in the municipal and state interviews, developers noted that the municipality was able to use its status as a Transit Village to expedite approvals. This was a huge advantage to developers, because quicker approvals enable higher profits. (This relationship between approvals and profits is due to the "time value of money." Because developers borrow money for construction, the longer it takes to get an approval, the more developers have to pay in interest costs.) In one instance, the NJDOT allowed a parking exception along a state road next to a new development in Metuchen. As found during the municipal interviews, the DEP also tended to expedite remediation approvals. One developer stated that problematic state government bureaucracy persisted despite the Transit Village status. The developer was frustrated that the NJDOT took a long time to approve a traffic-impact study on a nearby intersection.

In summary, the municipal, state, and developer interviews revealed that cooperation between the state and local governments enabled the Transit Villages to use
their status to facilitate redevelopment. The Transit Village criteria, mandating that
towns must have a commitment to population growth and housing in a compact,
transit-supportive manner, enticed some developers ready to build new apartment
units and town homes. New developments targeted luxury consumers without
children. The towns and developers had no desire to build affordable housing, as
each town expressed having an abundance of it. While the Transit Village Initiative promotes affordable housing in its mandate, the state representatives could not
enforce the construction of new, lower-cost housing. During the application process to become a Transit Village, task force members checked to see if towns were
certified by COAH, although COAH certification did not seem to be a determining
factor in approving granting or rejecting the town as a Transit Village. (Transit Village status is a voluntary state designation that indicates the town has met its "fair
share" of affordable housing, as defined by COAH. As of January 1, 2004, COAH
released new guidelines governing the provision of affordable housing across the
State. There are no specific provisions for including affordable housing in Transit
Villages, but the Transit Village task force maintains that this is an important goal
toward which they are working.)

Public Opinion: Results from the Statewide and Household Surveys

In April 2003, the Eagleton Institute of Politics administered a statewide
telephone poll on development, housing, and transportation in New Jersey. Jan
Wells and I wrote eight transportation-related questions, and Eagleton added 10
demographic questions that had been used in past statewide surveys. The results of
the survey yielded a sample of 802 respondents from randomly dialed telephone
numbers across the State of New Jersey. In order to produce a random sample, the
interviewer questioned the youngest male age 18 or older from each household. If
no male was available with whom to speak, the interviewer asked for the oldest
female (age 18 or older). Results presented below have been weighted based on
gender and education to accurately represent the State of New Jersey as a whole.

Local household mail surveys were conducted in Metuchen, South Amboy, and
South Orange. The questionnaire consisted of 37 questions written by Jan Wells and
me and administered by Eagleton in July and August 2003. Eagleton researchers
used a residential directory and randomly selected 1,500 households in each town.
They matched residential addresses with census blocks, more than 50% of which
were located within a half-mile train station radius. They sent 1,000 packets to randomly selected households. They also randomly selected and mailed questionnaires
to 500 households in the municipality outside of the Transit Village area.

The overall response rate of the household surveys was 40%. The response
rate was 48% in Metuchen, 31% in South Amboy, and 40% in South Orange. These
rates are based on the original 1,500 sent to households within each town (see Table
8). For the household survey, each address received a packet that included a cover

letter explaining the purpose of the questionnaire, instructions about how to fill out the questionnaire, the questionnaire itself, and a return envelope with postage paid. Residents were also asked to return a separate postcard (postage paid) that tracked each address. This allowed for the complete anonymity of the responses while tracking each address response. A postcard was sent to every address a week later reminding them to complete the survey, and a second full mailing was sent to each address that did not respond within three weeks.

Table 8: Survey Response Rates
Source: Renne and Wells 2003

Survey	Responses	Within Transit Village (1,000 sent)	Outside Transit Village (500 sent)
Statewide Poll	802 respondents	-	-
Household	40% overall (1,783)	1,155	628
Metuchen	48% (716)	489	227
South Amboy	31% (461)	275	186
South Orange	40% (606)	391	215

Table 9 shows the household survey respondents, compared to the demographics for each town as a whole. In Metuchen, respondents were less likely to be young (17–29), male, Asian and African American, and low-income earners. They were more likely to be over 30, female, white, and from households with earnings over $100,000. A similar pattern was noticed in South Amboy, except respondents were slightly less likely to come from households earning more than $100,000. In South Orange, respondents were more likely to be over the age of 30, more likely to be white, and from households earning more than $100,000. Overall, the survey under represents young households and nonwhite residents.

Table 9: Characteristics of Household Survey Respondents and Residents of Each Municipality

Variable	Metuchen Census, year 2000	Metuchen Survey year 2003	South Amboy Census, year 2000	South Amboy Survey, year 2003	South Orange Census, year 2000	South Orange Survey, year 2003
17 – 29	12.0%	4.1%	15.1	4.3%	22.8%	4.9%
30 – 49	34.2%	40.7%	34.7%	41.9%	29.8%	44.5%
50 – 74	25.2%	43.3%	20.5%	41.5%	20.6%	38.9%
75 and Over	7.0%	11.9%	6.7%	12.3%	5.9%	11.8%
Male	48.5%	45.6%	47.4%	39.6%	48.0%	48.2%
Female	51.5%	54.4%	52.6%	60.4%	52.0%	51.8%
Asian	7.3%	6.1%	0.6%	0.8%	3.5%	3.6%
Black	4.7%	3.0%	1.1%	0.6%	31.3%	19.9%
White	84.6%	86.8%	90.0%	95.9%	58.2%	73.1%
Percentage of Households Earning Less than $20,000	9.3%	4.3%	17.9%	14.8%	12.0%	4.0%
Percentage of Households Earning More than $100,000	34.7%	41.3%	12.9%	11.2%	42.6%	55.5%

Note: Data from the US census were collected in 2000 and data from the survey were collected in 2003. This makes for an uneven comparison, especially for household earnings.

Statewide Poll Results

Three questions from the statewide poll are useful in examining resident support for new housing and redevelopment in downtown areas, as well as transit's value when choosing a home location. The questions asked were:

How important is it that the state actively encourage growth and development in existing downtown areas and commercial centers in New Jersey very important, somewhat important, not too important, not at all important?

Do you favor or oppose new housing construction in the downtown area or commercial center of your town?

Thinking back to when you moved to your current home, was the availability of public transportation a major reason, minor reason, or not a reason why you chose this location?

Results showed that 84% of respondents felt that it was either "very important" or "somewhat important" that the State actively encourage growth and development in existing downtown areas and commercial centers, with 55% reporting that it was "very important." (see Table 10).

Table 10: New Jersey Public Opinion of the State's Role in Promoting Growth and Development in Existing Downtown Areas and Commercial Centers
Source: Renne and Wells 2003

Very Important – 55%
Somewhat Important – 29%
Not too Important – 8%
Not at all Important – 6%
Don't Know/Refused – 2%

n = 802

A reported 49% supported housing in their downtown, while 41% opposed it (4% responded that there was no downtown area or commercial center, 2% responded that it "depends," and 4% had no opinion). When looking at results by race, it became clear that African Americans were greater advocates of new housing construction (as shown in Table 11).

Table 11: Percent in Favor of Housing Construction within the Downtown or Commercial Center of the Respondent's Town, by Race and Ethnicity
Source: Renne and Wells 2003

Black – 78%
Hispanic – 52%
White – 44 %

n = 802

To determine whether a person could be classified as a smart growth supporter, we decided respondents needed to feel it was at least somewhat important for the State to actively encourage downtown and/or commercial-center growth and development. In addition, they had to support new housing in the downtown or commercial centers of their towns. Table 12 reports that those living in the more urbanized areas were more in favor of smart growth.

Table 12: Support for Smart Growth based on Community Type
Source: Renne and Wells 2003

	Percent Supporting Smart Growth
Major Urban Centers	63%
Other Urban Areas	59%
Older Towns and Suburbs	47%
Rural Areas	40%
Growing Suburbs and Towns (located at the edge of rural areas)	35%

Other characteristics were important in determining support for smart growth as well. Table 13 shows that over half of African Americans, transit users, Democrats, and households with children support smart growth, while less than half of whites, Hispanics, non-transit users, Republicans, and households without children were in favor of it.

Table 13: Comparison of Characteristics of Support for Smart Growth

Characteristic (Smart Growth Supporter)	Percentage in Favor of Smart Growth	Characteristic	Percentage in Favor of Smart Growth
African American	70%	White	41%
		Hispanic	46%
Transit User (at least once a month)	56%	Non-Transit User (less than once a month or never)	40%
Democrat	56%	Republican	38%
Households with Children	54%	Households without Children	39%

Again, with respect to the availability of transit in selecting home location, results varied by race and ethnicity, with Hispanics and African Americans showing greater concern (as shown in Table 13). Twenty-three percent of all respondents considered transit accessibility when choosing their homes (12% said it was a major factor, and 11 percent reported it was a minor factor).

Table 14: Percent of Respondents who Reported the Availability of Public Transportation as a Major Reason in Choosing the Location of their Current Home, by Race and Ethnicity
Source: Renne and Wells 2003

Black – 19% Hispanic – 27% White – 9% n = 802

Results of Statewide Logistic Regression

In evaluating reasons why respondents supported or opposed new housing in their town's downtown or commercial centers, I conducted a logistic regression for those who responded either "favor" or "oppose" to this question. I used the following variables in the analysis: number of years in current home (0 = more than 5 years, 1 = less than 5 years); the importance of transit when they chose their current home location (0 = it was not a reason, 1 = it was a reason); live within walking distance to a train station (0 = no, 1 = yes); use transit at least once a month (0 = no, 1 = yes); children in household (0 = no, 1 = yes); live within an urban center (0 = no, 1 = yes); Hispanic (0 = no, 1 = yes); African American (0 = no, 1 = yes); feels it is somewhat or very important that the State actively encourage growth and development in downtown or commercial centers (0 = no, 1 = yes). Table 15 shows a bivariate analysis (one-way analysis of variance tests) with five of nine variables that have F-values that are statistically significant at $p<.01$. Furthermore, seven of nine have F-values that are statistically significant at $p<.05$.

Table 15: Bivariate Correlates of Support for New Housing (State Poll)
(One-Way Analysis of Variance tests)

Correlate	Mean Square	F-Value	Sig.
Number of years in current home (0 = more than 5 years, 1 = less than 5 years)	Between groups = .009 Within groups = .238	0.038	p = .85
Importance of transit when they chose their current home location (0 = it was not a reason, 1 = it was a reason),	Between groups = .975 Within groups = .178	5.493	p< .02
Live within walking distance to a train station (0 = no, 1 = yes)	Between groups = .866 Within groups =.212	4.088	p < .05
Use transit at least once a month (0 = no, 1 = yes)	Between groups = 4.317 Within groups = .202	21.356	p < .01

Correlate	Mean Square	F-Value	Sig.
Children in household (0 = no, 1 = yes)	Between groups = 1.751 Within groups = .239	7.328	p < .01
Live within an urban center (0 = no, 1 = yes)	Between groups = 3.879 Within groups = .162	23.908	p < .01
Hispanic (0 = no, 1 = yes)	Between groups = .013 Within groups = .069	0.188	p = .67
African American (0 = no, 1 = yes)	Between groups = 3.580 Within groups = .119	30.179	p < .01
Feels it is somewhat or very important that the State actively encourage growth and development in downtown or commercial centers (0 = no, 1 = yes)	Between groups = 4.750 Within groups = .123	38.746	p < .01

Support for housing is statistically correlated at the 95% level with the following variables: the importance of transit when the respondent chose home location; whether the respondent lived within walking distance to a train station; whether the respondent used transit at least once a month; the presence of children in the household; whether the respondent is from an urban center; whether the respondent is African American; and whether the respondent felt it was at least somewhat important for the State to actively encourage growth and development in downtown areas.

Because bivariate correlations do not show direction (i.e. we cannot predict who favors or opposes new housing), a multivariate logistic regression analysis was conducted. The regression used support for new housing in the downtown or commercial centers of the respondents' towns (favor or oppose) as the dependent variable. As shown in Table 5.12, five of the nine variables were statistically significant at the 95% level (p<.05). Odds ratios (Exp(B)) explain the significant variables magnitude. Those who use transit at least once a month were 1.8 times more likely to support new downtown housing. Similarly, households with children were 1.4 times more likely to favor new downtown housing. Those living in an urban center, African Americans, and people who felt that it was at least somewhat important for the State to encourage growth and development in existing downtown and commercial centers were respectively 1.74, 2.81, and 3.63 times more likely to support new housing in the downtown or commercial center of their town. The model accurately predicted 76.3% who favored new housing, and it predicted 63.9% correct overall. (A separate analysis in the larger study consists of a similar logistic regression analysis with only significant variables. The "hhildren in household" variable was eliminated because it turned up as insignificant upon running the data.)

This model shows a strong link among growth, housing, and transportation in New Jersey. These findings suggest the State should consider designating Transit Villages in places such as Newark, Jersey City, Trenton, and Camden, because their residents reflect the types of demographics most likely to support new housing and smart growth. The February 2005 decision by the Transit Village Initiative designating New Brunswick and Journal Square in Jersey City supports this finding.

Table 16: Multivariate Logistic Regression Analysis of Correlates of Support for New Housing in the Downtown (State Poll)

Correlate	B-value	Std. Error	Sig.	Exp (B)
Number of years in current home (0 = more than 5 years, 1 = less than 5 years)	-0.113	0.170	$p = .50$	0.89
Importance of transit when they chose their current home location (0 = it was not a reason, 1 = it was a reason),	-0.002	0.206	$p = .99$	1.00
Live within walking distance to a train station (0 = no, 1 = yes)	0.320	0.184	$p = .08$	1.38
Use transit at least once a month (0 = no, 1 = yes)	0.5865	0.193	$p < .01$	1.80
Children in household (0 = no, 1 = yes)	0.336	0.170	$p < 0.05$	1.40
Live within an urban center (0 = no, 1 = yes)	0.554	0.234	$p < 0.02$	1.74
Hispanic (0 = no, 1 = yes)	-0.204	0.335	$p = .54$	0.82
African American (0 = no, 1 = yes)	1.032	0.280	$p < .01$	2.81
Feels it is somewhat or very important that the State actively encourage growth and development in downtown or commercial centers (0 = no, 1 = yes)	1.289	0.246	$p < .01$	3.63
Constant	-1.469	0.258	$p < .01$	0.23

Summary statistics: Goodness-of-Fit Chi-square 92.8, $p < .01$. Pseudo R-square: Cox and Snell 0.123, Nagelkerke 0.165. Percentage Classified Correct (cut value 0.5): Favor Housing – 76.3 %, Oppose Housing – 48.6 % Overall – 63.9 %

Selected Results of the Household Surveys in Metuchen, South Amboy, and South Orange

Surveys were sent to residents inside and outside the half-mile Transit Village area, but the results reported are for the full, town because the towns are so small and differences were not discovered between the Transit Village and non-Transit Village samples. Because our survey methodology over-sampled the Transit Village area, results were weighted.

Before viewing household survey results, it is useful to look closer at each town's demographics. Table 17 shows that Metuchen, South Amboy, and South Orange have some commonalities and differences. All three towns are relatively small (less than three square miles). South Orange was the most populated, dense, and had the smallest white, non-Hispanic population in 2000. It was also the richest and had the highest share of commuters using transit. South Amboy had the largest white, non-Hispanic population, and the highest female, single-parent household percentage. It was the poorest of the three and had the lowest share of workers using transit. Metuchen had the highest percentage of married couple households, the highest home ownership rate, and the most single-family detached homes. It also had the lowest poverty rate.

Results of the household surveys show that support was slightly higher in the Transit Villages for the State to actively encourage downtown and commercial center growth and development, compared to the statewide average (as shown in Table 18). Support was particularly high in South Orange, where over 70% of the residents felt that it was "very important." Table 19 shows that new housing support was similar across South Amboy and South Orange, compared to the state average. However, Metuchen's support was more than 50% lower. Metuchen's built-out nature of single-family homes and recent completion of two compact townhouse developments in the downtown may have contributed to its opposition to new housing. (In Metuchen, South Amboy, and South Orange, the train station is in the downtown.)

Table 17: Demographics of Metuchen, South Amboy, and South Orange
Source: US Census, 2000

	Metuchen	South Amboy	South Orange
Population	12, 840	7,913	16,964
Land Area (square miles)	2.7	1.6	2.9
Population Density (persons per square mile)	4,756	4,946	5,850
Race/Ethnicity			
Hispanic	4%	7%	5%
Black	5%	1%	31%
Asian	7%	0%	3%
White, Non-Hispanic	82%	90%	58%
Foreign Born	14%	9%	17%
Households			
Single Person Household	11%	26%	25%
Married Couple Household	82%	49%	55%
Female, Single Parent Household	6%	14%	10%
Median Family Income (1999)	$85,022	$62,029	$107,641
Poverty Rate	4%	7%	5%
Housing			
Single Family, Detached	73%	64%	70%
Homeownership Rate	81%	64%	72%
Percent of Workers Using Transit	17%	6%	21%
Percent of Workers Using the Train	16%	4%	17%

Table 18: Public Opinion of the State's Role in Promoting Growth and Development in Existing Downtown Areas and Commercial Centers
Source: Renne and Wells 2003

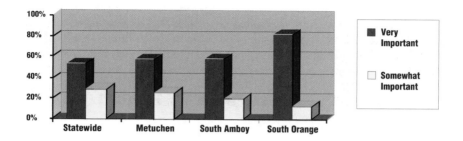

Table 19: Support for Housing within the Downtown or Commercial Center of the Respondents Town
Source: Renne and Wells 2003

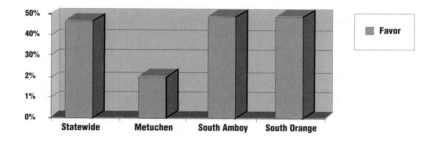

The household survey reported that the Transit Villages' quality-of-life was higher than the state average (Table 20). Metuchen had the highest rating with over 60% of respondents rating their town an excellent place to live. Although South Amboy had the lowest rating compared to the other Transit Villages, improvement over the past three years there was high, as shown in Tables 21–24. The figures showed the majority of residents across all Transit Villages reported the downtowns had improved or stayed the same with respect to downtown attractiveness, walkability, safety, and options for restaurants.

In order to test if improvements in downtown attractiveness, walkability, safety, options for restaurants, and entertainment and shopping options were part of the same scale (see questions Q7–Q12 in Appendix 4), Chronbach's Alpha was used. The overall Chronbach's Alpha was 0.792 (0.777 in Metuchen, 0.855 in South Amboy, and 0.784 in South Orange). Chronbach's Alpha ranges from 0 to 1.0, and normally a score of = 0.7 is considered good, and = 0.8 is considered excellent evidence of a single scale. This finding suggests that these questions constitute a single scale of downtown improvement. Therefore, it is legitimate to add up the scores of each question to form one improvement variable, which ranges from 6 to 30. A dichotomous variable was created to show if the respondent felt the town had improved or gotten worse. A score less than 18 represents improvement, while a score above 18 represents a worsening environment compared to three years ago. The mean score across all respondents was 15.4 with a standard deviation of 3.4, and 86.4% of the respondents had a rating lower than 18. This data cannot conclude that improvements were a direct result of the Transit Village Initiative, but it is evident that public perceptions express improvement in downtown attractiveness and Transit Village amenities over the past three years.

Table 20: Rating of the Town as a Place to Live
Source: Renne and Wells 2003

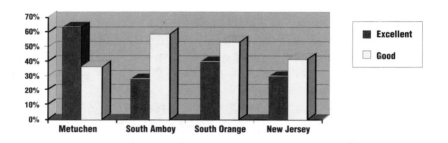

Table 21: Do You Feel the Downtown is More or Less Attractive Now Compared to Three Years Ago?
Source: Renne and Wells 2003

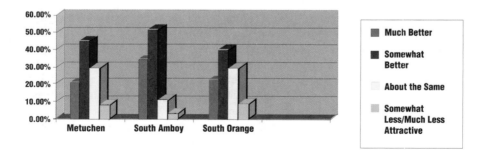

Table 22: Is It More or Less Pleasant to Walk around the Downtown Now Compared to Three Years Ago?
Source: Renne and Wells 2003

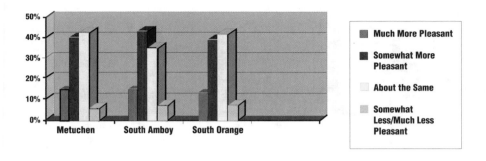

Table 23: Does the Downtown Seem More or Less Safe Now Compared to Three Years Ago?
Source: Renne and Wells 2003

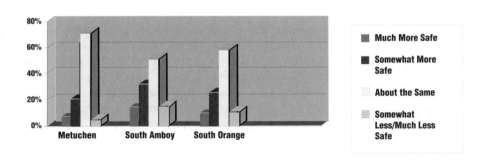

Table 24: Does the Downtown Offer Better or Worse Restaurant Options Now Compared to Three Years Ago?
Source: Renne and Wells 2003

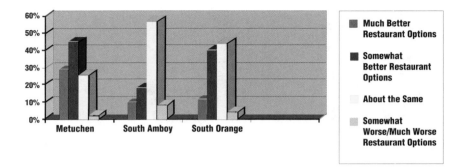

Results of Local Household Logistic Regression

This section discusses the logistic regression results examining why respondents in Metuchen, South Amboy, and South Orange favor or oppose new housing in the downtown Transit Village area. I used the following variables in this analysis: whether the respondent feels it is somewhat or very important that the State actively encourage growth and development in downtown or commercial centers (0 = no, 1 = yes) –SGSI; rating of the town as a place to live (0 = poor or fair, 1 = good or excellent) – *Rating*; scale of improvement over the past three years (0 = feels the town has gotten worse, 1 = feels the town has improved) – *Change*; if the respondent lives in a multifamily building (0 = no, 1 = yes) – *Multifamily*; whether children (under 18) are present in the household (0 = no, 1 = yes) – *Kids*; number of vehicles available for regular use (0 = 2 or more cars, 1 = less than 2 cars) – *Cars*; use transit at least once a month (0 = no, 1 = yes) – Transit; employment status (0 = not employed, 1 = employed) – *Job*; renter or homeowner status (0 = homeowner, 1 = renter or other) – *Rent*; number of years in current home (0 = more than 5 years, 1 = less than 5 years) – *Residence*; age (0 = over 30, 1 = under 30) Age; sex (0 = male, 1 = female) – *Sex*; lives in South Orange (0 = no, 1 = yes) – *South Orange*; lives in Metuchen (0 = no, 1 = yes) – *Metuchen*; lives inside Transit Village designated area (0 = no, 1 = yes) – *Village*; and the importance of transit when they chose their current home location (0 = it was not a reason, 1 = it was a reason) – *Imptransit*. These variables were chosen based on other studies as well as a local understanding of reasons that people would support downtown housing.

Table 25 shows bivariate correlations (one way Analysis of Variance tests) with 10 of 16 variables having F-values that are statistically significant at p < .01. The variables SGSI, *Change, Multifamily*, and *Metuchen* were significant at p < .01. The odds ratios report that those who felt it was either somewhat or very important for the State to encourage growth and development in downtown or commercial centers were 2.43 times more likely to favor new housing in the Transit Village. Those who perceived positive change in the downtown over the past three years were also more than twice as likely to favor new housing. Residents of multifamily buildings were 1.73 times more likely to favor new housing. Conversely, Metuchen residents were likely to oppose new housing in the Transit Village area (as discussed earlier). Other variables, such as *Rating, Transit,* and *Residence* were significant for determining who supports new housing, but at a lower level of confidence. Overall, the model correctly predicted about two-thirds of the cases (66.5%).

Table 25: Bivariate Correlates of Support for New Housing (Local Survey) (One way Analysis of Variance tests)

Correlate	Mean Square	F-Value	Sig.
Feels it is somewhat or very important that the State actively encourage growth and development in downtown or commercial centers (0 = no, 1 = yes)	Between groups = 4.288 Within groups = .103	41.834	p < .01
Rating of the town as a place to live (0 = poor or fair, 1 = good or excellent)	Between groups = .197 Within group = .056	3.501	p < .10
Scale of improvement over the past three years (0 = feels the town has gotten worse, 1 = feels the town has improved)	Between groups = 2.895 Within groups =.115	25.237	p < .01
Lives in a multifamily building (0 = no, 1 = yes)	Between groups = 7.368 Within groups = .198	37.301	p < .01
Children in household (0 = no, 1 = yes)	Between groups = .865 Within groups = .237	3.649	p <.10
Number of vehicles available for regular use (0 = 2 or more cars, 1 = less than 2 cars)	Between groups = 1.498 Within groups = .222	6.744	p < .01
Use transit at least once a month (0 = no, 1 = yes)	Between groups = 2.384 Within groups = .244	9.753	p < .01
Employment status (0 = not employed, 1 = employed)	Between groups = 1.335 Within groups = .197	6.780	p < .01
Renter or homeowner status (0 = homeowner, 1 = renter or other)	Between groups = 4.541 Within groups = .126	36.136	p < .01
Number of years in current home (0 = more than 5 years, 1 = less than 5 years)	Between groups = 4.287 Within groups = .188	22.861	p < .01
Age (0 = over 30, 1 = under 30)	Between groups = .202 Within groups = .043	4.696	p < .05

Correlate	Mean Square	F-Value	Sig.
Sex (0 = male, 1 = female)	Between groups = .171 Within groups = .248	0.691	p = .41
Lives in South Amboy (0 = no, 1 = yes)	Between groups = 8.997 Within groups = .218	41.180	p < .01
Lives in South Orange (0 = no, 1 = yes)	Between groups = 28.355 Within groups = .225	126.094	p < .01
Lives inside Transit Village designated area (0 = no, 1 = yes)	Between groups = .060 Within groups = .227	0.266	p = .61
Importance of transit when they chose their current home location (0 = it was not a reason, 1 = it was a reason)	Between groups = .068 Within groups = .249	0.271	p = .60

References

Adam-Shippy, Nancy. 2002. "Personal Interview, Director of Main State South Orange." South Orange, New Jersey.

Baker Development Corporation. 2003. "Personal Telephone Interview." New Brunswick, New Jersey.

Bellucci. 2002. "Personal Interview, Borough Administrator, Rutherford." Rutherford, New Jersey.

Cervero, Robert, GB Arrington, Janet Smith-Heimer, Robert Dunphy, Steven Murphy, Christopher Ferrell, Natasha Goguts, Yu-Hsin Tsai, John Boroski, Ron Golem, Paul Peninger, Erik Nakajima, Ener Chui, Mel Meyers, Shannon McKay, and Nicole Witenstein. 2004. *Transit Oriented Development in America: Experiences, Challenges, and Prospects*. Washington, DC: National Academy Press.

Eisen, Victoria. 2004. "Personal Communication, 19 November."

French, Chanin. 2004. "New Jersey Court Requires Good Faith Negotiations Prior to Bringing Mt. Laurel Litigation." *Practicing Planner* 2.

LaVenia, Gary. 2002. "Personal Interview, Town Administrator, Riverside." Riverside, New Jersey.

Marcinczyk, Stan. 2002. "Personal Interview, City Administration, City of South Amboy." South Amboy, New Jersey.

Maurer, Eric. 2002. "Personal Interview, Business Administrator, Morristown." Morristown, New Jersey.

Reenstra-Bryant, Robin. 2002. "Personal Interview, Director of the Rutherford Downtown Partnership, 24 October." Rutherford, New Jersey.

Renne, John Luciano. 2005. Transit-Oriented Development: Measuring Benefits, Analyzing Trends, and Evaluating Policy. Rutgers University Ph.D. dissertation, 2005.

Schwartz, Joel. 2003. "Personal Interview." Princeton, New Jersey.

Slothower, Lenore. 2002. "Personal Interview, Planning Director, City of Rahway." Rahway, New Jersey.

Slutsky, Irina. 2004. "A Tiny City's Great Divide." in *The Star-Ledger*. New Jersey.

Wells, Jan S., and John L. Renne. 2003. *Demographics of the New Jersey Transit Villages*. New Brunswick, New Jersey: Alan M. Voorhees Transportation Center, Edward J. Bloustein School of Planning and Public Policy.

Wiser, Stuart. 2002. "Personal Interview, City Planner, Pleasantville." Pleasantville, New Jersey.

CHAPTER FIVE

Intractable Conflict in the Holly City: Framing, Identity, and Opportunities

By
Lisa A Uber

Abstract

This essay examines an intractable conflict surrounding the proposed sale and development of the Holly Farm property in Millville, New Jersey, and whether there may be a resolution to the conflict that embraces the expressed interests and concerns of involved parties. I first present an overview of the conflict and provide examples supporting my analysis of the situation. Next, steps are offered for reducing the intractable nature of the conflict, and potentially resolving the controversy. The approach I employ is that of an illustrative case study aiming to shift the discussion away from purely legal or land rights issues, towards the exploration of alternate frames through which the nature of the conflict may be understood differently. I argue that there is more at stake here than simply deciding whether or not to sell or develop the Holly Farm property (and to whom to sell it), and that consideration of identity, meaning, and knowledge in the process of framing may assist the parties to develop more tractable resolutions than those publicly discussed in the conflict.

It is with respect and consideration for Millville, its residents, and other stakeholders that I have approached this investigation, discussion, and analysis of the Holly Farm conflict, and how it may be understood and informed by research in the areas of communication, public policy, and organizational studies. While the essay makes reference to and discusses positions understood to exist in the Holly Farm conflict, I have purposely avoided focusing on the two extreme decision choices (develop the Holly Ridge adult community or preserve the property entirely) in an effort to explore alternative frames. I wish to thank representatives from the city of Millville as well as the environmental stakeholders for their time and courtesy in providing access to the public documents that shaped my understanding of the different perspectives in the conflict.

> *"Would you tell me, please, which way I ought to go from here?"*
> *"That depends a good deal on where you want to get to, said the Cat."*
> *(Lewis Carroll, 1960)*

Introduction

The Southern New Jersey city of Millville is located in Cumberland County. Known as *The Holly City of America*, Millville enjoys an interesting history related to glass production, farming, holly trees, and beautiful natural resources. Founded in the early nineteenth century, the city experienced an economic downturn in the 1980s when much of the industry and jobs left the area. Currently, plans are underway for economic revitalization that seeks to balance Millville's historic uniqueness and natural resources with modern construction, technology, new services, and the promise of job growth. Much of the proposed development is expected to bring new residents and services to the city.

That Millville refers to itself as *The Holly City* suggests a continuing interest in the past and present relationships between the city and the holly plant. From my review of publicly available documentation, I believe that the holly plant represents a civic sense of historic uniqueness and pride that is shared by all residents, including those in favor of developing the land for housing and entertainment purposes, as well as those seeking to preserve the land. The Holly Farm property has a contentious history, with issues ranging from watershed development and road expansion to waste disposal, power plant construction, and ecological preservation. After the Holly Farm was no longer operated as a business, the farm and surrounding land were sold and changed ownership several times before becoming the property of the utility company Conectiv. Once again being offered for sale, several bids were received for the property. Initially the highest bid was from the development corporation Millville 1350, LLC, however, at the time this essay was written, New Jersey's Green Acres Program had offered the highest bid for the property. Available public sources showed that these were the two primary parties interested in the land purchase. Several environmental groups and citizens contested the initial development plans submitted by Millville 1350. Legal judgments were made in favor of these groups. The developer subsequently revised and resubmitted plans to the City of Millville, and it is these plans that are discussed and presented in the publicly available documentation. As of the initial writing of this essay in late 2004, no further legal action had been taken, however, since that time, the environmental groups and citizens have sought the assistance of the court to halt the proposed sale and development. As of early 2007 the property remained undeveloped and had not been sold. Stakeholders in the conflict include Conectiv; Green Acres; Millville 1350; various state and federal environmental groups and experts; professionals and experts in the areas of policy, law, and planning; Millville City officials; local residents; and citizens from other areas. The documentation did not show that any neutral parties (such as mediators or facilitators) had been involved. The primary opposition to the sale of the Holly Farm and surrounding land has been from environmental groups and citizens, stating that the property contains endangered species and is environmentally sensitive.

What is the past, present, and future identity of Millville, and how might an understanding of identity affect individual and collective approaches to the conflict? What information exists, how is it utilized (and by whom) in the conflict, and what emerges as knowledge? How is knowledge produced and managed, and is there shared knowledge? How is information manipulated or captured by parties for their own use? What roles do science, experts, and professionals contribute to the situation? The following section presents research relevant to these questions and the conflict. Informed by research, the essay seeks to demonstrate different ways of approaching knowledge, identity, and decision making, and how an understanding of each may contribute to conflict management or resolution.

Methods

Documentation on the conflict was gathered via telephone and e-mail discussions, internet websites, and paper records. Individuals representing the City of Millville as well as the environmental stakeholder groups were contacted in an effort to locate publicly available information about the conflict. The documentation examined included the following: economic analysis from the consulting firm Gabel Associates dated December 1, 2003; transcript of public hearing dated August 16, 2004; community impact report from Master Consulting for Millville 1350; testimonies of Millville Planning Director Kim Warker and environmental advocate Jane Morton Galetto dated December 1, 2003; summary document of December 1, 2003 hearing prepared by the city; clippings and online stories from local and regional newspapers, including opinion and editorial articles; Millville 1350 model for environmental planning statement; final planning board review document dated August 16, 2004; key points document from the city; various documents detailing legal actions opposing or supporting the proposed sale and development; press statements from stakeholders; and letters to city and state officials from private citizens, local government officials, and legal, scientific, and environmental agencies. The documentation was reviewed for themes related specifically to knowledge, identity, meaning, and communication.

Background and literature review

One theme that emerged in reviewing the documentation, especially the transcripts and letters, was how the role of experts figured into the conflict, and whether it was the citizens or the process that determined requirements for who could be viewed as an expert. In the August 2004 public meeting, citizens were announced and declared to be experts, however it was unclear from review of the transcript how a person might qualify to be counted as an expert. On the topic of experts, held beliefs, and what counts as science, Polanyi (1953) suggests that determining who is an expert may not be a simple process based wholly upon what we already view as science, rather it should include mutually agreed upon scientific beliefs or local knowledge. It was unclear to what extent local knowledge contributed to the process of decision making in the Holly Farm conflict. However, stakeholders in the dispute appeared to view the role of scientific experts as being important to guide decision making.

The construction of knowledge, meaning, and identity are perhaps, then, of equal importance. Baumard (2001) explains that "human beings acquire knowledge through their engagement in the creation and organization of their own experiences" (p. 59), and suggests that there are two dimensions of knowledge: (1) cognitive, related to paradigms, mental models, and representations, and (2) technical, related to know-how and expertise applied to a specific context. He contends that it is through the process of social interaction that knowledge, identity, and meaning are constructed.

One example of a specific context in which social interaction occurred in the Holly Farm conflict was observed in the transcript of the August 16, 2004 public hearing. The transcript presented a textual record of each person's turn speaking during the meeting. Mokros (2003) explains "initial turns in talk in conversation are representative of a type of context where framing definitions may be productively examined and compared. This assumes that individuals differ in the framing definitions they bring to any engagement. This then also means that the definition of the situation is continuously relevant and a potential focus for negotiation during the course of interaction" (p. 14). Following this thinking, what counts as knowledge (and to whom) is understood as being negotiated and framed through the process of communication. Mokros highlights the significance of "turns in talk" in the communication process, and how these can affect the definition of a situation.

In the example of the public hearing, the transcript detailed a specific order for turns in talk. The City of Millville, speakers supporting the developer, and experts were the first to be granted speaking turns in the hearing. Following them, anyone who had opposing views or objections to the matter discussed was given a turn to talk. Non-expert citizens were the last to appear on the agenda. Only one person spoke at a time and held the floor. Once he or she was finished speaking, the next person got the floor and began to speak. The transcript noted that time ran out in the meeting, and it appears that, because of this, some individuals were not granted turns to talk.

Related to group decision processes and public forums, Hirokawa and Poole (1996) explain that the "order in which group members take up issues can have important effects on outcome," and that even a routine procedure such a straw poll can empirically influence aggregate outcomes" (p. 245). One may consider what would have counted as knowledge and what the outcome of the hearing might have been if the order of speaking turns had been constructed differently (e.g., opposing parties were granted the initial turns in talk, followed by those supporting the matter). With an interest in exploring situations for possibilities of different sequences or contexts, such as the turns in talk examples discussed above, the concept of "framing" is introduced.

Miller (2000) proposes models of societal processes whereby framing may occur. He explains that scholars "invoke the concept of 'framing' in reference to the perceptual lenses, worldviews or underlying assumptions that guide communal interpretation and definition of particular issues" (p. 211). One of the models he focuses on uses the construct of narrative:

The use of narratives emphasizes the importance of meaning in the framing process as a counter to the traditional emphasis of science on getting the facts straight. People tell stories to attach meaning to events going on around them, to fit their observations to their values, and to relate that meaning to particular contexts of social behavior or action. Narratives are, in other words, a way of making sense of the world, or relating the way one sees things happening with the kinds of happenings one would like to see." (Miller, 2000, p. 218).

In the case of the Holly Farm conflict, a majority of the information appears in narrative form from all stakeholders, even when presenting scientific data. Drawing upon the idea of narratives and frames, something that may preserve the meaningfulness of the individual stakeholder narratives would be to create a collective or shared narrative document. This document might serve as a shared knowledge resource for all stakeholders, even those in disagreement, so long as their views and narratives have been accurately represented in the shared narrative document. The construction of this shared knowledge document may then be useful for furthering understandings amongst stakeholders or in the process of decision making.

To assist with the construction of knowledge in environmental conflicts, Özesmi and Özesmi (2003) propose a cognitive mapping approach based on the knowledge of both experts and local citizens (p. 43). Cognitive maps are qualitative models that can describe how a given system operates. "The map is based on defined variables and the causal relationships between these variables." (Özesmi & Özesmi, 2003, p. 44). The maps can provide both knowledge and narrative, because they are able to contextualize the information captured. Modeling knowledge and information in an explicit or visible manner can prove useful in considering four types of problems: (1) understanding human behavior and how human actions can affect an ecosystem, (2) developing an understanding of ecosystems where detailed scientific data are lacking, but local knowledge of people adapted to an ecosystem is available, (3) building a tool to help mitigate and provide insight to environmental conflicts that involve many parties, and have no easy solutions or right answers, and (4) providing a basis for ecosystem management where public involvement is desired or mandated by law. (Özesmi & Özesmi, 2003, pp. 43–44).

A different type of mapping approach for mitigating environmental conflict disputes is suggested by Brody, Highfield, Arlikatti, Bierling, and Ismailova (2004) through the use of process and technology. The authors note that "intractable conflicts can be costly, time-consuming, and reduce the likelihood that policies aimed at sustainable development will be implemented." (Brody, et al., 2004, p. 11). To address these issues from a perspective that considers the conflict "within the context of larger ecological and human management systems," they propose the use of "Geographic Information Systems (GIS) to map potentially competing environmental values." (Brody, et al., 2004, p. 12). The use of this tool may assist by providing scientifically valid and objective data related to contentious environmental areas, and highlighting areas that may be opportunities or risks associated with development. The use of GIS mapping has been shown to help alleviate conflict of interest between groups, if they can at least agree on data and its representative categorizations. Although this method may not be appropriate for all conflict situations, it may prove useful in situations resistant to other attempts for resolution by providing empirical data as a starting point that stakeholders can agree upon as valid and factual.

In the process of collecting data and information during a conflict, participants should be sensitive to and seek to reduce potential biases that their own values, goals, or interests can bring to the process. Certainly, these biases do not simply go away (nor should they), and they are important to the construction of identity, meaning, and point of view, however, based on my review of the documentation, these matters were confused to such an extent that it is difficult to discern facts from opinions or characterizations. For example, I reviewed at least three documents containing different numbers describing the same physical entity known as the Holly Farm property. Other documents showed similar inconsistencies, such as the percentage of land available for development in the City of Millville. It was unclear which of these documents, if any, represented information that was accurate or factual. How can decision makers function effectively or make informed decisions when operating on information that is inconsistent?

Decision scientist James March (1994) explains that "decisions are framed by beliefs that define the problem to be addressed, the information that must be collected, and the dimensions that must be evaluated. Decision makers adopt paradigms to tell themselves what perspective to take on a problem, what questions should be asked, and what technologies should be used to ask the questions. Such frames focus attention and simplify the analysis" (p. 14). The choice of reference frames then influences whether citizens experience disagreement or controversy. Disagreements are "disputes in which parties are able to resolve the questions at the heart of their disputes by examining the facts of the situation." (Schön & Rein, 1994, p. 3). Controversies are disputes that are "immune to resolution by appeal to the facts." (Schön & Rein, 1994, p. 4). Although the difference between disagreement and controversy seems clear in these definitions, during a conflict it may not be so clear. For example, what gets presented as a fact could mask a controversy, and controversies may contain facts. Why should we be concerned about these differences? Schön and Rein (1994) contend that:

> Sustained policy contention can undermine public learning, because any attempt to conduct public inquiry into policy issues requires a minimally coherent, more or less consensual framework within which the results of policy initiatives an be evaluated and the findings of investigations can be interpreted. When policy controversies are enduring and invulnerable to evidence, what tends to result is institutionalized political contention, leading either to stalemate or to pendulum swings from one extreme position to another, as one side or another comes to political power. This may not be so bad if the policy situation is one that benefits from neglect or inaction, or if many contending actors happen to interact in such a way as to produce a happy policy outcome. But inaction is as

likely to be harmful as helpful, and happy accidents do not often result from contention (pp. 8–9).

Given these concerns, how might one best approach working with frames, narrative, and decision making in the context of an intractable conflict? Schön and Rein (1994) propose that "human beings can reflect on and learn about the game of policy making even as they play it, and, more specifically, that they are capable of reflecting in action on the frame conflicts that underlie controversies and account for their intractability" (p. 37). If stakeholders can be reflective in practice, they may be able to see problems and address them before they become unmanageable. Facilitators and mediators may be helpful in assisting groups to navigate the resolution of especially difficult problems that can become controversies.

Regarding the use of mediation and facilitation in environmental conflict resolution, Cohn (2002) explains that, "although not everyone uses it yet, government agencies, private-sector companies, environmental groups, landowners, and individuals are increasingly turning to environmental conflict resolution. Consensus-building techniques are used to address issues that previously were often subjected to lengthy and contentious political, legal, or public relations campaigns." (Cohn, 2002, p. 400). He suggests that the use of environmental conflict resolution "provides a forum where people can come together and help shape a project," and "when it works, can help achieve a better project with less opposition because it takes people's needs into consideration. It is a very powerful democratic force." (Cohn, 2002, p. 400).

Cohn (2002) cautions that "dispute resolution cannot replace the political process, but it can supplement it" (p. 401). It appears that the best outcomes are realized "when the costs of mediation are divided among the parties, rather than being the sole responsibility of one. And it works best when the mediator, facilitator, or other third-party convener is recognized by all parties as impartial and independent." (Cohn, 2002, p. 401). He explains that "conflict resolution is not always the chosen means of resolving environmental, land use, or natural resource issues," and it "is unlikely to work when one party feels it can win a legal, political, or public relations victory and thus sees no reason to compromise." (Cohn, 2002, p. 401).

A useful technique known as *situation appraisal* (Kepner & Tregoe, 1997) may be helpful as a first step towards resolution. The process has five steps: (1) list threats and opportunities, (2) separate and clarify concerns, (3) consider seriousness, urgency, and growth, (4) determine analysis needed, and (5) determine help needed. (Kepner & Tregoe, 1997, p. 169). Applied to the Holly Farm conflict, the situation appraisal method may serve as a useful tool for putting into practice the narrative consideration of all aspects of the controversy (i.e., economic, environmental, ecological, etc.) to document information and concerns. Once complete, stakeholders may then determine how to best frame the situation and consider the use of mediation or facilitation resources.

Discussion

The literature presents a number of practical ideas based on research for addressing conflict, approaching and framing controversies, and balancing scientific data with local knowledge and interests. This section of the essay focuses on integrating these ideas with specific issues in the Holly Farm conflict, suggesting decision-making criteria and potential frames that aim for processes and solutions that are resistant to intractability and that consider the larger systemic community involved in the conflict.

I first recommend that a narrative document be developed that represents an appraisal of the situation and knowledge as understood and conferred upon by all parties and stakeholders, especially those in disagreement. I believe that the manipulation of information and facts, whether purposeful or accidental, has helped make this conflict intractable. Creating a shared knowledge document may allow discussions to occur via a common language developed by stakeholders. A common language can serve to minimize differences in understanding information or facts. If these differences can be resolved, citizens and stakeholders may be able to recognize shared goals and have fewer politicized discussions related to decision making and conflict resolution. If controversy persists, it may be helpful to utilize a facilitator or mediator. Depending on the nature of the Holly Farm conflict, it may be eligible for assistance from the USIECR (US Institute for Environmental Conflict Resolution) or similar groups. (Dahl, 2003).

Next, consideration should be given to developing alternative frames that embrace the goals of all stakeholders in the conflict. Wade-Benzoni (1999) argues that "the current 'win-lose' versus 'win-win' debate on the relationship between economic competitiveness and environmental protection is biased toward win-lose by a narrow focus on the economic interests of a specific actor. When economic interests are broadened to include the interest of other parties, especially other parties in future generations, the opportunity to create aggregate value becomes more apparent" (p. 1393). The documentation and criteria considered by the City of Millville, planners, and developers showed a trend of using economic issues or data as the primary basis for decision making. When the city planners or developer discussed environmental issues, they appeared to use language that minimized or dismissed environmental issues, as well as the environmentalists themselves. Similar use of language was observed in documentation from environmental groups. The environmental group and citizens largely categorized the City of Millville, planners, and the developer as being only concerned with money or economic development and unconcerned with the environment.

The Holly Farm conflict is complex and is affected by a number of proposed development efforts in Millville and surrounding areas. The construction of meaning and identity, and how these relate to what counts as knowledge and beliefs, is not often explicitly expressed in the documentation, however I see this as a central issue to why this conflict has remained intractable. For example, all stakeholders, regardless of position in the conflict, expressed their views with passion and framed their statements in ways that reflected what the conflict meant to them, their families or constituents. Letters from citizens and experts showed accounts of attachment to the city, pride in the community, and connection to the history of Millville and the holly plant, along with a desire to see growth and economic prosperity. I believe that these discussions related to identity, meaning, and knowledge should be given equal attention along with the economic analyses, environmental statements, and other information that we understand as science and that we use for decision making. If attention is afforded to how identity, meaning, and knowledge affect conflict and decision making, it can help stakeholders make decisions that all parties can live with.

Knowledge is shaped by language in discourse, and can be affected by the roles and identities of individuals. For example, the documentation stated that the mayor believed that 90% of Millville was in favor of the project. This statement was presented to the public. It is unclear how this knowledge was constructed, or why a person in a position of power would make a statement without reference to related empirical data. Was there a survey conducted amongst the residents to obtain this information? I did not find evidence in the documentation to support this. One effect of this may be that citizens and stakeholders are prevented from having discussions related to factual issues at hand, and may also be unable to make informed decisions, because fact and opinion have become confused and inseparable. Another example was found on the environmental side of the conflict, where there was inconsistent information in the documentation as to whether Holly Farm is protected property, and exactly which species on the property are endangered. If these matters cannot be resolved, how can parties make decisions concerning the property? Conflicting and inconsistent information and knowledge presented as scientific facts were found to exist on all sides of the conflict. I recommend that if all parties desire to have conversations that will constructively resolve the conflict, they work to accurately represent data or facts.

I believe that there is more at stake in this situation than deciding whether or not to sell the Holly Farm property to a developer. With so much development planned for the City of Millville and surrounding areas over the next five to ten years, these issues and conflicts will continue if they are not addressed in a manner that considers all stakeholder interests. The ways in which public conflicts are handled affect how the residents view themselves, the city, local government, and professional citizens considered to be experts.

Overwhelmingly, the documentation I reviewed appeared framed as a discourse on economic data related to development of the Holly Farm property. Environmental concerns were raised, however I did not find documentation that offered anything beyond high-level assessments lacking specific detail on how risks and concerns were to be addressed. In most cases, they appeared to be ignored. Absent were any discussions of whether development should occur there or somewhere else. As I understand from the documentation, there are thousands of acres of land available for development in the city. Perhaps one might reframe the conflict and ask *where is the best place to locate Holly Ridge to minimize risk and maximize benefit for the community,* instead of asking *should we develop the Holly Farm,* simply because it is for sale. For example, the developer may purchase land that is located elsewhere and less contentious. According to the documentation, the Holly Farm property is not the only place in Millville where one could build a golf course and adult community. Perhaps in evaluating the situation from different perspectives, it may be determined that there is land that is a better fit with development goals and carries lower economic and environmental risk than the contentious Holly Farm site. If the reference frame were shifted to be about the City of Millville, or Millville within the context of Cumberland County, different solutions would emerge. Another option would be to sell the Holly Farm property to Green Acres, but develop the property as an arboretum and park focused on increasing the business of ecotourism. Environmental groups and individuals demonstrating interest and commitment could assume primary roles and responsibility for caretaking and preservation. According to the documentation, environmental groups have lobbied for years to acquire this property and protect it. Perhaps this approach could leverage this interest towards economic gain and serve to unite the community on an issue it currently appears divided on.

Exploring further a theme discussed previously, ecotourism is "travel that encompasses natural and cultural resources, while conserving and sustaining environments and local economies." (Kosko, 2004). A strategy embracing ecotourism has potential to help the local economy, create jobs, and actively involve residents in the preservation of town natural resources. For example, in 1996 the New Jersey Audubon Society estimated that birders contributed approximately $10 million annually to the local Cape May economy. (Kane, 2004). This demonstrates that a strategy embracing ecotourism may prove lucrative for a community seeking to experience economic growth. Although Millville and Cape May are different cities with different identities and opportunities, the comparison may yield interesting ideas. Perhaps tourists would be interested in seeing the endangered species said to be on the Holly Farm property. The uniqueness of the Holly Farm experience might then be promoted as part of a visit to a town that already has much to offer for tourists, such as the historic Wheaton Village and recently renovated downtown area. Millville has natural resources that one cannot find elsewhere in the same combination. I suggest that this unique aspect of the town be leveraged in a manner that minimizes destruction of environmentally sensitive lands, while at the same time maximizes economic growth and opportunity. In reviewing the documentation, I question whether developing the Holly Farm property with a sizeable adult community and golf course represents the best course of action, given the array of economic and environmental risks and concerns presented in the documentation, and suggest that alternate frames should be considered in resolving the conflict.

Although it seems that the developer made efforts to address concerns raised by various environmental groups and others opposed to the project, the analyses presented appeared incomplete and open to risk. One example is documentation calling for additional field studies and analyses of environmental, ecological, and economic risk issues to be completed before any decision is made on the sale of the property for development. The study described by the environmental consultancy Herpetological Associates in the transcript of the August 2004 public hearing was conducted sporadically over a three-month period. It focused on a few species of birds and snakes, but did not discuss plant life or non-endangered living parts of the ecosystem, or how all of these individual parts interact. In the context of an ecosystem, a snake is not simply a snake. It is both predator and prey for other species. If, for example, snakes were a food source for birds or animals, then the destruction or movement of snakes would affect the birds or animals that depend on them for survival. Similarly, if insects or reptiles that the snakes depended upon for food disappeared, this would affect the snakes. Therefore, it seems insufficient to map only a few endangered species, without mapping and achieving an understanding of other parts of the ecosystem, and how those parts interact. Development will always have an impact on species. What this impact would be is unknown, but it could be investigated and estimated by scientists. This example is not meant to suggest that development should or should not occur, rather it is intended as an example of an important level of discussion that was absent from the documentation reviewed. I offer that this absence of detail is a risk, and should be investigated prior to any decision related to the use or sale of the Holly Farm property. A complete environmental and ecological assessment should be conducted in an effort to better understand what exists, and ultimately will help stakeholders make more informed decisions.

An approach that considers Millville's identity and provides for additional economic opportunities and the housing goals of the community may be realized elsewhere, but the Holly Farm cannot. A significant concern raised in the documentation is that the development of the Holly Farm property could divide the community, put the ecosystem in jeopardy, and carry significant risk if success (as estimated in the developer's plan) is not realized. Upon review of the economic analyses provided, there appears no discussion of how to protect the success of the golf course and housing development project, or what Millville would do if the project fails. While this is not the desired outcome, and stakeholders wish for the project to be successful, they would be remiss not to consider a recovery position in the event that all does not go as planned.

It is unclear how or why a project characterized by the city as a model for environmental planning does not have the support of key environmental groups and agencies. While it may be easy to claim that the answer has to with political interests or groups of vocal citizens, I believe the situation is more complex. The fact that this disconnect exists is indicative that significant risks or alternatives have yet to be addressed. Making a decision without first properly mitigating these risks may prove costly to a town that cannot afford economic problems. If the risks and concerns present in the conflict were explored, the situation might be different.

Conclusion and recommendations

The Holly Farm provides a visible, place-based connection to Millville's historic past and possible future. The manner in which this longstanding conflict becomes resolved could unite or divide the community. Because no final decision has been reached as of this writing, I offer that there is opportunity to reflect on the situation and review options that may best consider all concerns and positions. How might this be achieved? I recommend first starting with a situation appraisal to help determine possible alternate frames of reference. Next, risk assessments could be conducted against each frame to help reach a decision based on the input of all affected parties and stakeholders. The risk assessments should consider detailed economic, environmental, and ecological analyses. Those who conduct these analyses should be neutral parties, acceptable to and agreed upon by all stakeholders in the conflict. These assessments might also be used to create a backup plan in case the development fails. Stakeholders from all areas should be involved in this process. Lastly, recognizing the controversial and intractable nature of the Holly Farm conflict, it may be useful to have a facilitator or mediator assist. The facilitator or mediator should be a neutral party, acceptable to and agreed upon by all stakeholders in the conflict.

Although housing or developments may be rebuilt or relocated, natural resources and local histories are not so flexible. It is clear from the documentation that citizens and stakeholders on all sides of the conflict have deep connections to the area. This connection should be considered along with any scientific or legal facts in the resolution of this matter, because, without the support of its citizens, a city wishing for growth and development may find itself with a difficult task. The identity of Millville and its residents is tied to historic, ecological, civic, and economic relations with the holly plant and the Holly Farm. To not consider these relationships risks further dividing a community attached to its holly heritage.

References

Baumard, P. (1999). *Tacit Knowledge in Organizations*. London: Sage Publications.

Brody, SD. Highfield, W., Arlikatti, S., Bierling, D. H., & Ismailova, R. M. (2004). Conflict on the coast: Using geographic information systems to map potential environmental disputes in Matagorda Bay, Texas. *Environmental Management. 34, (1)*, 11–25.

Carroll, L. (2000). *Alice's Adventures in Wonderland & Through the Looking Glass*. NY: Signet Classics.

Cohn, JP. (2002). Environmental conflict resolution. *BioScience. 52, (5)*, 400–404.

Kane, R. (2004). *Ecotourism and Conservation*. Retrieved December 9, 2004 from http://www.njaudubon.org/Conservation/opinions/96sum.html

Kosko, K. (2004). *Ecotourism: A Natural Alternative for Exploring New Jersey*. Retrieved December 9, 2004 from http://www.oar.noaa.gov/spotlite/archive/spot_ecotourism.html

Dahl, R. (2003). Finding Middle Ground. *Environmental Health Perspectives. 111, (12)*, 650–652.

Hirokawa, RY, & Poole, MS (1996). *Communication and Group Decision Making.* Thousand Oaks, CA: SAGE Publications, Inc.

Kepner, CH & Tregoe, BB. (1981). *The New Rational Manager: An Updated Edition For A New World.* Princeton, NJ: Princeton Research Press.

March, JG. (1994). *A Primer on Decision Making: How Decisions Happen.* New York, NY: The Free Press.

Miller, CA. (2000). The dynamics of framing environmental values and policy: Four models of societal processes. *Environmental Values, 9*, 211–233.

Mokros, HB. (2003). A constitutive approach to identity. In H. B. Mokros (Ed.), *Identity Matters: Communication-Based Explorations and Explanations.* Cresskill, NJ: Hampton Press.

Özesmai, SL & Özesmi, U. (2003). Ecological models based on people's knowledge: A multi-step fuzzy cognitive mapping approach. *Ecological Modelling. 176*, 43–64.

Polanyi, M. (1952). The stability of beliefs. *The British Journal for the Philosophy of Science, 3, (11)*. 217–232.

Schön, DA & Rein, M. (1994). Frame reflection: Toward the resolution of intractable policy controversies. New York: Basic Books.

Wade-Benzoni, KA. (1999). Thinking about the future. *American Behavioral Scientist, 42, (8)*, 1393–1405.

CHAPTER SIX

New Jersey and Research – Together No Longer?

By

Robert Lucky

In this essay, I contend that New Jersey's historical position as the leading research state in telecommunications is endangered, if it has not already been irreparably damaged. As New Jersey's high technology industry revolves around two major fields – telecommunications and pharmaceuticals – the loss of one of these two bases would be highly consequential to the State's economy and reputation.

In what follows, I examine why there is a crisis in New Jersey's research infrastructure. Inasmuch as I have been personally involved in New Jersey's telecommunications research culture for more than four decades, it is impossible for me to write dispassionately about this issue. Thus, much of this paper will recount and rely on personal experience.

I recently chaired a study of the National Academy of Engineering on the health of R&D (research and development) in telecommunications. The report, entitled "Renewing Telecommunications Research," paints a bleak picture of what has happened to telecommunications research, a past, great strength of the United States, and, of course, New Jersey. It proposes increased government funding and specific mechanisms to stimulate new research opportunities in this field.

In this position paper I do not discuss the recommendations in the National Academy report, but I will frame the problem as it relates to New Jersey. For that reason, there will be more emphasis on Bell Labs than there is in the report. Moreover, in the interest of opening debate on this issue, I try to take simplistic positions without the usual caveats and qualifiers that necessarily fill official documents, such as an Academy report. The opinions that I express are my own, and readers are welcome to enter into a dialogue.

Summary of this Paper

This paper is longer than I had originally intended. In order to get my main points across, before I lose the attention of readers, let me give the main points now:

The Lucent Bell Labs building in Holmdel, New Jersey – one of the largest office buildings in the state – is being converted to commercial office space. Fort Monmouth's Communications and Electronics Command in New Jersey is to be closed and moved to Maryland. The former RCA Sarnoff Laboratory in Princeton has been downsized and converted to a for-profit division of a West Coast company. These events illustrate the decline of telecommunications research in New Jersey.

New Jersey is the birthplace of the industrial research laboratory, and as the home of the most famous industrial lab in the world – Bell Labs – had an enviable reputation for its research, as well as the education and professionalism of its residents.

California's Silicon Valley – which New Jersey once tried to emulate – as well as its world famous university system, has now moved the center of technology and talent to the West Coast.

Bell Labs' research funding came as an allowed component of monopoly pricing of the Bell System prior to its breakup in 1984. After that, research had to be funded from the profits of an intensely competitive industry. After the dot-com crash, there was overcapacity in the network, and profits were elusive and unstable.

I argue that a competitive telecommunications industry is intrinsically incapable of supporting research. One unique characteristic of the industry is the free-rider problem, wherein competitors who do not support research can benefit from the research of others who do. Moreover, the basic product has tended to become commoditized, and commoditized industries do not historically support research.

The industry has restructured so that, now, almost all the research is done by equipment vendors, like Lucent. Consequently, funding for research is both volatile and lessened. Research conducted by equipment vendors is not done for the primary benefit of the end consumer, but rather to sell product to the service providers, such as Verizon.

As the industry has vacated research, nearly all research is now being done at universities. Some 97% of research publications are now authored by academics. As research has moved to universities, New Jersey does not have a particularly strong position relative to other states.

Government has a special role in funding telecommunications research, because of the great social benefits that ensue. States also have a role, and California has a large state initiative – the California Institute for Telecommunications and Information Technology – that manages a large, state-wide program. New Jersey has nothing equivalent, while its reputation and its talent inexorably dissipate.

Bell Labs Holmdel–Visible Symbol of the Decline of Telecom Research

A long time ago I left school with a fresh Ph.D. in electrical engineering, looking to decide among the easy-to-get offers from the great industrial research labs in the United States. The decision boiled down to two alternatives – should I go to California or New Jersey?

While I was pondering this career choice, I came across an article about New Jersey in National Geographic Magazine. The article called New Jersey "the research state," with special mentions and pictures of Bell Labs, the RCA Sarnoff Labs, and the Institute for Advanced Physics at Princeton University, among other New Jersey research institutions. Well, I thought, if New Jersey was the research state, that was where I wanted to be. That article cemented my decision.

In early 1962, I drove into the long driveway in Holmdel, New Jersey, towards the entrance of the new Bell Laboratories facility that was to be my work location. I drove underneath the three-legged water tower designed to look like a transistor and past the reflecting pond fronting the all-glass exterior of the giant laboratory. I still remember the mist rising from the pond that morning and the pride I felt as one of the first people to occupy that huge, landmark building.

Bell Laboratories Holmdel Facility

More than four decades have passed since I first entered that building, and, in that time, unimaginable changes have taken place. As a young researcher, I harbored great dreams for telecommunications, but nowhere among those dreams was the idea of a home computer or an Internet that would connect me with people and information anywhere in the world. But all of this technology would pale in comparison with the stunning revelation that one day, in my future, there would be no Bell System, and that the great building I was entering that long-ago morning would no longer exist.

Today, the Bell Laboratories facility in Holmdel is a deserted building – one that was designed to house over 6,000 employees. The property has been sold to a real estate firm, and the building, which was scheduled for demolition, will be turned into commercial office space. In a recent visit there I was filled with nostalgia and sorrow to see weeds growing up through the pavement in the nearly-empty parking lot, where once I hunted for any parking slot, no matter how far a walk from the side entrance.

For many of us who had any association with Bell Labs or with research in telecommunications, the closing of the Holmdel Labs is the symbolic end of the era of the great industrial research labs. In telecommunications, it attests to the fundamental restructuring of the industry and the shrinking industry commitment to basic research. For New Jersey, it represents a significant loss of technical jobs and a blow to the State's pride. Moreover, a scant five miles from the doomed Holmdel research facility is the Army Communications and Electronics Command at Fort Monmouth, which is also scheduled for abandonment. Between Fort Monmouth and the Holmdel facility of Bell Labs, Monmouth County will have lost about 10,000 highly technical jobs. New Jersey has been world famous for two areas of research – telecommunications and pharmaceuticals – and one of them is now endangered.

If, today, a young researcher were to choose which state – New Jersey or California – should be called the "research state," is there any doubt whatsoever what that choice would be?

The Historical Role of New Jersey in Telecommunications Research

New Jersey is considered the birthplace of the industrial research laboratory. In the early years of the last century, Thomas Edison, the "Wizard of Menlo Park," founded the country's first industrial research laboratory in West Orange, New Jersey. Although Edison is usually seen as the prototypical lone inventor, he had a staff of researchers who worked with him on a great variety of inventions. Edison is credited with over 1,000 US patents, including fundamental patents on the telegraph, the motion picture projector, the phonograph, and of course, the electric light.

Today, Edison's lab is open as a museum, and a tour there is like entering a time warp, returning to a simpler day of science. The wooden rooms are filled with glass beakers, stoppered bottles, and strange mechanisms. A chemical smell permeates the facility, and there is a strong feeling of this having been the precursor of the great industrial laboratories that would arise in the following decades.

The greatest of these industrial research labs was, without question, the Bell Telephone Laboratories, which was founded in 1925 by the Bell System. The first such lab was in New York City, downtown on West Street, where a train actually ran regularly through the second floor of the building. Before the Second World War, the main force of Bell Labs was moved to a sprawling location in Murray Hill, New Jersey. Bell Labs also built facilities in Whippany, New Jersey, and, of course, Holmdel. During the period from about 1960 to 1983, Bell Labs employed approximately 25,000 people. Most of this force was dedicated to development of systems and components for telephony, but about 1,200 engineers and scientists were engaged in very basic research, ranging from theoretical physics and chemistry to computer science.

Bell Laboratories scientists have won six Nobel Prizes, and their discoveries and inventions have changed the world. Arguably, the greatest invention of the last century was the transistor, which was conceived by Bardeen, Brattain, and Shockley at Bell Labs in 1947. Other significant inventions included the laser, the light emitting diode, and the CCD (charge-coupled device – the heart of modern digital cameras). Claude Shannon's information theory was one of the great intellectual achievements of the century, and Arno Penzias and Robert Wilson won a Nobel Prize in physics for the discovery of the radiation from the "Big Bang" that created the universe.

Among communication landmarks, Bell Labs scientist Karl Jansky first discovered radio signals from outside the earth, and began radio astronomy on a hill near the future location of the Holmdel Labs in 1933. President Dwight Eisenhower sent the first radio signals to a satellite from this same location in 1961. Coincidentally, the inventor of radio, Guglielmo Marconi, came to New Jersey in 1899, two years after he made his invention in Bologna, Italy, and transmitted the first radio signals in the United States from Atlantic Highlands to ships entering the New York harbor.

I could go on at length with the list of achievements of Bell Labs, but that is well chronicled elsewhere. It is difficult to overestimate the importance and worldwide influence of this great New Jersey institution. Bell Labs was the envy of the world, and every scientist and engineer of note crossed the doors of this lab at one time or another in their careers.

The other notable industrial research lab specializing in communications and electronics was founded by RCA Chairman David Sarnoff in 1942, occupying an expansive estate on the entrance road to Princeton. The Sarnoff Labs earned acclaim for its pioneering research on digital television and high definition television. Like Bell Labs, it has since fallen on more difficult times. After RCA became a part of General Electric, the Sarnoff Lab was donated to SRI Consulting and has since become a for-profit division of that West Coast research company, existing on government and commercial contracts to fund its work. It is now considerably smaller than it was through much of its past history.

I was fortunate to have been at Bell Labs during its "golden years" of the 1960s and 1970s. One of my lasting memories is of the second floor foyer near the steps to the cafeteria in Murray Hill. During the lunch period, this foyer was always ringed with quiet researchers intent on playing the deeply intellectual oriental game of GO. Where else would people play GO during their lunch hours?

At this time at Bell Labs there were artists-in-residence, and several well known researchers rode unicycles in the hallways. One famous mathematician had a net that could be pulled down from the ceiling of his office to catch wayward balls as he practiced his world-renown juggling skills. There was an air of scientific discovery and curiosity in the very corridors of the long building. I have always said that the best thing about the old Bell Labs was that there was a world expert in every subject of interest, and that the expert would be right down the hall.

New Jersey Tries to Create its Own Silicon Valley

Even in the 1960s, however, there was a premonition of a different kind of industrial research paradigm coming about in California. It is a little known and almost forgotten episode in New Jersey's scientific history, but there was an ultimately-abortive attempt to replicate Silicon Valley in New Jersey.

In retrospect I must credit someone at Bell Labs or elsewhere in New Jersey's scientific community with recognizing at an early time the importance of what was happening in California. A committee of research executives from New Jersey's labs was formed, and this committee hired Stanford University's dean of engineering, Fred Terman – who is generally credited with creating Silicon Valley – to help replicate his California success in New Jersey.

I remember well the exhilaration I felt listening to Fred Terman describe his vision for New Jersey at Murray Hill in the mid-1960s. Terman's thesis was that, as Stanford was the heart of California's Silicon Valley, so New Jersey needed a university to serve as its own nucleus for a similar endeavor. Alas, he opined, New Jersey did not have such a university. Although Princeton had world renown for its physics research, it was too small and too uninterested in engineering innovation and development. Terman's bold idea was that New Jersey should create a new university in the model of Stanford.

Forty years later, I can still hear in my mind Terman describing his thrilling recipe for the creation of a "Stanford" in New Jersey. Such a university, he said, needed only to have "spires of excellence." The metaphor stuck in my mind of driving across the English countryside and seeing in the distance the spire of a distant church – the only visible sign of the next town or village. In the case of a university, Terman believed that a university's reputation was not established by the size and quality of its staff, but by the few academic stars that were "seen" and known worldwide.

Terman said that New Jersey already had many such spires of excellence. There was a multitude of world famous scientists in the State, including a substantial number of Nobel Laureates. All that was needed was an educational venue in which these people could volunteer their time. The premise was that the new university would have only a graduate curriculum, taught by these local scientific and engineering celebrities.

Needless to say, this university never got started. After a year or so of enthusiastic committee meetings among the participants from New Jersey's various industries, the project imploded. My understanding is that one of the major contributors (Exxon) withdrew its support during an economic downturn, and that the domino effect collapsed the rest of the support. In any event, it would have been nearly impossible to have kept together such a coalition over the necessarily long period of heavy commitments with only the promise of vague, long-term benefits.

Even if the graduate university had been created, I do not believe that it would have succeeded, either educationally or as a nucleus for a New Jersey "Silicon Valley." It is difficult to think of an "existence proof" of a famous university without an undergraduate program. Moreover, it would have been extremely difficult to gain the reputation needed to attract top quality applicants – the *sine qua non* that separates all great universities from the pretenders. Of course, the New Jersey industries would have sent some of their employees to the new school as part of their commitment to the endeavor, but that is not quite the same thing as the competition for slots that exists at the famous graduate schools.

The proposed school would have lacked the infrastructure and culture represented by the vast alumni networks of Stanford and nearby University of California, Berkeley. In addition, those "spires of excellence" would have been drawn from the New Jersey scientific culture, which, in the 1960s, was not at all inclined to entrepreneurship. Finally, in retrospect, there is considerable argument about whether a university like Stanford is either necessary or sufficient for the establishment of a vital entrepreneurial culture. Since 1960 there have been a number of attempts all over the world to replicate Silicon Valley, and I believe that none of these pre-planned programs has been successful. The areas around Boston, Massachusetts, and Cambridge in the UK are the best examples of organically-grown entrepreneurial activity, but even they pale in statistical comparison to California's Silicon Valley.

In a later section I will offer some opinions about the venture culture in New Jersey as compared with California, but for now I want to return to the history of telecommunications and its impact on New Jersey's research community.

The End of the Monopoly

It seemed during the 1970s that the "golden years" at Bell Labs would go on forever. But hidden under the surface of the good times were two tectonic shifts that would soon change the research landscape forever. One such event was taking place in the world of technology, where the nascent Internet was only a blip on the radar, while the other was more immediately evident, and was happening in the world of policy and legality.

I was driving home from work one evening in the early 1980s, when I heard on the radio that the US Justice Department had instituted an antitrust suit against AT&T. I remember that moment, but I had no premonition at the time that anything cataclysmic would happen as a result of the suit. My thinking was conditioned by the previous AT&T consent decree in 1956 that had constrained AT&T's businesses and given away AT&T's patents. As onerous as these conditions had been, they seemed to have had little affect on research at AT&T.

In 1983, I had the unforgettable experience of taking the stand in Judge Harold H. Greene's courtroom to attempt to justify Bell Labs' research program. At that time this antitrust proceeding was the "trial of the century," and I lack the words to describe adequately the aura of tension and absolute power that existed in that courtroom. Judge Greene listened intently to me and argued a number of points over two days, but in the end gave me one of the most unusual compliments I have ever had. He said that I was the only witness "who did not have a Bell-shaped head." Nonetheless, Bell Labs was only a peripheral issue in the trial. When the Modified Final Judgment was confirmed, I commented to one of the top executives that it was significant that AT&T had been allowed to keep the name "Bell Labs," when the Bell companies were all being divested. "Don't kid yourself," the executive said, "They simply didn't care."

The implementation of the Modified Final Judgment in 1984 required that a portion of Bell Labs be used to seed the creation of a Bell Labs equivalent for the operating telephone companies – the "Baby Bells" – that had been spun off from the parent company. The new research company became known as Bellcore. It was jointly owned by the seven operating telephone companies, and as time went along it established research labs in New Jersey in Morristown, Piscataway, Red Bank, and Livingston. I use the term "research labs" advisedly for lack of a more descriptive noun, because – like Bell Labs – most of the engineers and scientists at Bellcore were not involved in research, but rather in software development, standards, and systems engineering. Of about 5,000 staff, only 300 or so were doing basic research.

The original Bell Labs research organization had to "tithe" in 1984, giving 10% of its staff to the new Bellcore, while assuring, under court order and supervision, that the sample was fair and balanced in every measurable way. As painful as this order was, because longstanding relationships were torn apart, from the standpoint of New Jersey's research infrastructure it was beneficial. More research jobs were being created in the State. Bellcore was hiring to augment its seed staff, and now there were more research labs in New Jersey locations than before.

The Rise of Competition

Prior to 1984, Bell Laboratories was funded from what was known as the license contract fee, derived from the telephone service revenues of the operating Bell companies. AT&T had a monopoly position in the telephone business, and the rates that were charged for service were overseen by the Federal Communications Commission (FCC). As long as the FCC agreed that the R&D program at Bell Labs was reasonable, the expense for Bell Labs could be added as part of the rate base to determine the charges to businesses and consumers for telephone service. In other words, a small amount of the monthly fee a customer paid on his telephone bill went to fund Bell Labs, almost a government-sanctioned taxation. In 1980, the budget for the research area (just the area that did fundamental research) was approximately $300M. If there were roughly 100 million customers in the US, then the fee charged the average consumer for research at Bell Labs would have been about 25 cents a month. From this miniscule fee had come the transistor, laser, and much of the technology that had built the best telephone system in the world. In terms of social benefit, it was a great bargain.

It is characteristic of fundamental research that it thrives on stability of funding and environment, and, prior to 1984, these attributes unquestionably existed. Even on the very eve of divestiture, in early 1984, I do not recall any sense of urgency or impending disaster in the research department. It was perhaps both easy and necessary for researchers to imagine that their jobs and charters would remain unaffected by the business headlines surrounding the antitrust trial. But for all the angst of the AT&T breakup, it was not the division of the company itself, but the emergence of competition in the industry that endangered basic research. The stability of the monopoly funding was gone; AT&T would have to fund Bell Labs from its own profits in a newly competitive environment.

AT&T executives in 1984 exuded a confidence about the company's future. After all, AT&T owned "the network." It represented an enormous total investment that had been built over the period of a century. Who could threaten such an asset? Unfortunately for AT&T, the answer proved to be a lot of companies. Two factors made this possible: the development of optical transmission and a permissive business and regulatory environment favoring the emergence of competitors.

The first major competitor to threaten AT&T's core business was MCI. In the beginning, MCI offered cut-rate service over lines that it leased from AT&T, but within only a few years optical transmission systems became so cost-effective that MCI began to build its own network. Other companies began to do the same thing, and, incredibly, in 1988 AT&T wrote off its entire, old analog network, an accounting loss of about $6.7 billion. AT&T was building its own new network just like everyone else. That irreproducible asset – the national telephone network – had turned out not to be so valuable after all.

With competition building, the price for telephony services began to decrease rapidly. Between 1984 and 2002 the average price per minute of a phone call declined from $1.20 to 25 cents. Some of this decline was undoubtedly due to technology, as optical transmission made long distance transmission nearly free, but competition also undoubtedly played a big part. At the same time, the Internet was taking off, mobile telephony was growing, and new services were proliferating. It was a heady time in the industry. Many people saw this as a triumph of divestiture, but it is impossible to know what would have happened if AT&T had not been broken up.

As the pricing of telephony plummeted, there was necessarily much more focus on the bottom line. The strange and almost unfathomable economics of the industry made the price competition quixotic. Telecommunications is essentially a service business. There is no calculable price for a telephone call, as there would be for the manufacture of a widget. I often think in the roughest terms that the price of a phone call is the payroll divided by the number of calls. This, of course, ignores capital costs and debt management and many other important factors, but it is a crude way of thinking that accentuates the difference between telecommunications and a traditional manufacturing business.

The incremental costs of adding an additional phone call are essentially zero. Moreover, the allocation of pricing between different categories of service, such as consumer and business, has always been a subject of contention. There have been learned arguments that either consumer services subsidized business or vice versa. This means that the possibilities for competitive pricing in various niches are plentiful.

One industry analyst said, "It's like the DRAM (computer memory chip) business; pricing is set by the most idiotic competitor – it's a race to the bottom." At the time of that quote, the analyst was unaware that AT&T was competing with a chimera. It was later discovered that the Worldcom (MCI) profits had been a bookkeeping sham. By the time that chicanery came to light, however, the damage had been done.

Since research was a line item on the cost side of the ledger, it might have been an early victim of the divestiture, but, instead, it was saved by the dot-com boom of the nineties. Telecom was one of the favorites as the market surged and deals went down right and left. In the midst of this boom AT&T decided in 1996 to break itself up further with its own trivestiture, creating: a services company, AT&T; an equipment company, Lucent; and a computer company, NCR. Then, in 2000, Lucent spun off a networking company, Avaya, and, in 2001, further spun off a microelectronics company, Agere.

As a result of all this corporate activity, the old Bell Labs was now split among at least five companies – Lucent, AT&T, Bellcore, Avaya, and Agere. What became lost in the process was the critical mass that made research so vibrant and effective. That world expert in physics, software, microelectronics, or whatever was no longer in easy reach down the hall. He or she was in another company with its own trade secrets and access barriers.

The largest part of the old Bell Labs was at Lucent, which retained the large campus in Murray Hill, New Jersey, and the huge modern glass building in Holmdel. Lucent featured Bell Labs technology in its advertising and continued its generous support of research. Historically, AT&T had devoted 1% of its revenue to research, and Lucent adopted that policy itself. In the good early days of Lucent, while the market surged, it was almost difficult to find imaginative ways to spend the money that was being lavished on research.

Then, in 2001 and 2002, came the dot-com crash. The NASDAQ lost 78% of its value, and the market cap losses in telecom were estimated to be about $4 trillion. The telecom industry had greatly over-invested in capacity, and huge debts hung over the industry.

Can a Competitive Telecom Industry Support Basic Research?

The turn of the millennium was the moment of truth. The euphoria of the dot-com bubble was dissipating, and the reality of the new industry was becoming apparent. It is not my purpose here to discuss in any detail the economics of the telecom industry; there are much more learned discussions elsewhere. My concern is with the impact of the restructuring of the industry on its ability to fund basic research. Before I even discuss the issues, let me answer my own question. I believe that the answer is no – the industry is no longer intrinsically capable of supporting fundamental research.

There are a number of issues here, some of which are unique to telecom and others of which are shared by any competitive industry. Let me start with the obvious – if research is to be funded from profits, then there must be profits, and those profits must be robust enough to allow funding for an activity – research – that often sinks to the bottom of the food chain. Moreover, top management must believe that there will be a return on investment (ROI) from research, and that this return will occur within the timeframe demanded or desired by investors.

My contention is that there has been a general withdrawal from industrial research across a broad sector of American industry. The era of the great industrial labs – Bell Labs, IBM, GE, RCA, GM, and so forth – is gone. But even the residue of this period is drying up. A new report by the National Science Foundation asserts that there has been a trend among leading American industries to eliminate much of their high-risk, long-range, and fundamental research. Instead, they have turned their focus to short-term results and to incremental improvements of current product lines.

In spite of AT&T's long standing commitment to basic research and to the great achievements Bell Labs has made, even here it is hard to make the case that the company has seen a significant return on its research investment. There are many examples of Bell Labs innovations that have yielded great social benefits, while failing to return any profit to the company itself. A classic example is the computer operating system software UNIX, which is in widespread use throughout the Internet. This software, as well as the computer languages C and C++, was written in the research department at Bell Labs. AT&T made several concerted attempts to turn a commercial profit on UNIX, but in all likelihood never made any profit whatsoever on its investment.

I, along with all of my peers in research and research management, am convinced that corporate America has backed off from any commitment to basic research. Nonetheless, this is a belief that is almost impossible to prove. There are no reliable statistics on research funding in industry. What is considered research in one company is development in another, and there is no metric for reporting the time frame of research or what part of that research is considered "fundamental." Instead, there is anecdotal evidence from researchers and managers everywhere. The National Science Foundation report that I mentioned previously was based on surveys of research directors.

So the difficulties in maintaining funding for basic research in telecom, are in one sense, a part of a larger tapestry in American industry. However, the situation for research in telecom is historically unusual in several ways. Perhaps most important was the overhang that Bell Labs created by its dominance of the entire field. For that reason government funding agencies had long felt that it was unnecessary to fund telecom research and, instead, spent their support on other areas, such as computer science, that were, in comparison, neglected. And, of course, because of the AT&T monopoly, there were not other significant industrial research labs devoted to telecom.

The fragility of research funding in telecom after the dot-com crash was greatly exacerbated by the volatility of the industry. Profits were elusive and moved from one part of the business to another – notably from wireline voice to wireless and data. Moreover, this was an industry new to competition and in the throes of technological revolutions and corporate mergers and acquisitions. It was not a good time to count on stable funding for research departments.

Today, there is some sense of greater stability in the industry. A series of mergers has resulted in a trend toward consolidation. People often quip that the industry is trying to undo the divestiture and recreate the Bell System. The Columbia economist Elie Noam has argued for some years that the natural state of the industry would be to have dominant players in each sector of the business, and that the primary competition would be intermodal, that is, competition among the dominant players in wireline, wireless, cable, and satellite.

Any sense of stability, however, is undermined by the underpinnings of technology driving the cost and price of telecommunications ever downward as services become commoditized. I sometimes wonder if there is any bottom to the price that can be charged for telecommunications, and then I answer my own question – it may be free. I already expect broadband Internet access to be free wherever I travel, and with Internet telephony riding on top of free broadband access, where is the profit to be made? Already today, Skype offers free voice telephony, and its usage and services are growing rapidly.

So can a bitterly competitive industry, whose basic service is tending to be free, support basic research? I think not.

The Free-Rider Problem in Telecom

As bad as the preceding business arguments are, the very nature of telecommunications argues against industrial support of research. Research in telecommunications often takes the form of a non-excludible public good, with much in common with the classic economics conundrum: how do you fund a lighthouse?

In the case of a lighthouse, any passing ships can use the services of the lighthouse, whether or not they have paid for its support. There is no viable way of excluding non-paying ships from participation in the good. I suppose there are examples, but it would seem that a private lighthouse would be a bad investment. Unfortunately, the same elements are present in telecommunications research.

Consider the paradigm for funding research in the pharmaceutical business. One pharmaceutical company can sponsor research that finds a better drug, which is differentiated by its effectiveness as compared with drugs from competitors. Perhaps it even acts against a disease for which there is no comparable drug available from competitors. Because of this differentiation, and because the composition of the drug can be protected by patents and trade secrets, the originator of the drug can charge high prices for the drug, thus recouping its research investment and enabling it to re-invest in future research programs.

Almost nothing in this example applies to the telecommunications business. In telecommunications, differentiation is usually bad, since it works against connectivity and interoperation. In telecommunications, every user must have very similar equipment so each user can exchange data with everyone else. The more users who share a telecommunications service, the more value for every user -- in other words, the more the merrier. In economic theory, this side effect of gaining value with each compatible additional entrant is known as "network effect," or "network externality."

The network effect argues strongly against individuality. Telecommunications is informally governed by international standards to which every equipment and service provider rigidly adheres. Some of these standards run to a thousand pages or more of detailed specifications that must be incorporated, while leaving only some details of actual implementation open to the design discretion of individual manufacturers. Companies with patents cannot prohibit other companies from licensing their patents at reasonable rates, because, otherwise, the subjects of their patents will not be chosen as standards, and if no one else uses the inventions, they can not either.

If research cannot be protected and cannot provide differentiation, why do it? Let someone else do it, and adopt their ideas. After the divestiture of AT&T, the new competitors all decided not to do any research. MCI had no Bell Labs equivalent and took pride in is policy of eschewing research. MCI chairman William McGowen is said to have told Congress that Bell Labs was AT&T's "expensive hobby." Nonetheless, MCI was able to take full advantage of all the technology that had been created at Bell Labs in the implementation of its own long distance network. An issue that was to become pervasive in the research infrastructure was only starting to become apparent – that of the free rider.

An example of the free rider phenomenon that was especially irritating to researchers at Bell Labs was the famous Sprint "pin drop" commercial. In slow motion it showed a pin dropping. Because Sprint's network was optical, the commercial inferred that you could hear this miniscule sound. (In point of fact, the absence of noise was because the transmission was digital.) Because of the appeal and ubiquity of this advertisement, many, if not most, in the public believed that

Sprint had created optical transmission systems. It had not – it was largely the work of Bell Labs (though Corning Glass is credited with the initial breakthrough on the fabrication of low loss fiber). But all the Bell Labs innovations in optical technology were used by everyone else, including the cable industry players.

The Service Providers Abandon Research

Starting with MCI's decision not to support research, essentially all of the service providers have abandoned research. Before 1984, all of the seven Bell Operating Companies had their own research labs. At divestiture, the agreement included the necessity for these companies to share their own equivalent of Bell Labs, which was Bellcore. All seven companies supported the Bellcore research program, which at that time had a total support of a little more than $100 million. Partly because of this shared facility, each of the operating companies dismantled its own research laboratory. There was also considerable motivation for this decision in trying to compete with new entrants who did not have the expense of funding research.

After a few years, the Baby Bells began to compete with each other. Their lawyers began to feel that having a shared facility providing software, systems engineering, and research was likely to lead to antitrust issues. For this reason, or perhaps because they had become tired of the expense, they decided to sell Bellcore to SAIC (Science Applications International Corporation). After the sale, they supported research at Bellcore on a subscription basis with declining amounts over a few years, and then withdrew completely from any research support. Like all of their service provider competitors, they believed that it was unnecessary to conduct any research. Bellcore, renamed Telcordia Technologies, was sold two years ago to a financial entity. Its research budget is now approximately half of what is was in the years after divestiture, and the majority of this funding is being obtained from the government for work on specific military applications.

Of the seven original Baby Bells, only SBC retained the vestige of a research lab – a relatively small lab in Austin, Texas, that mostly does testing and contract engineering. Then, when SBC bought AT&T and took its brand, it became the owner of the AT&T Labs, headquartered in Florham Park, New Jersey. Considering that no other service provider does research, the future of this lab would seem in jeopardy. However, indications are that, for good will alone, this lab will be secure for at least a few years.

Research by service providers has had a mixed history in terms of its return on investment. There are certainly examples where research has improved the efficiency of their operations – routing strategies and voice synthesis for automated response come to mind immediately. On the other hand, research on new applications and services seems to have had few successes. Almost all new applications have come from outside the telecom service provider community. Ideas like peer-to-peer file sharing are unlikely to occur, given the centralized control culture common to the industry.

Perhaps the most important paradigm change caused by the Internet was to enable the user at the periphery to implement new services without needing cooperation from the central network. Millions of users were thus enabled, and their combined creativity far exceeds that available to the operating telephone companies.

Quite a few years ago I gave a talk at the FCC. I have no idea what it was about, but I will never forget something that the speaker before me said. That speaker was Mitch Kapor, the originator of the software Lotus 1-2-3. Kapor said that the greatest invention of the computer industry was not the PC, but the concept of a third-party plug-in on a standard backplane bus, so that innovation could be enabled by a plethora of other manufacturers. Telecom did not have such a concept, Kapor said; everything had to be implemented by the central carriers. At the time, I thought this idea was impossible to apply to complex, centrally-controlled telephone network, but I was wrong. The Internet changed all that.

Years later, I gave a talk at the Bell Labs auditorium. I told the assembled researchers that, once, we were in control of the network, "but now we don't control the evolution of the network any longer." I waved my arms, and added, "The people out there are running things now."

The Industry Becomes Horizontally Structured

Prior to divestiture, AT&T was a vertically-integrated company, providing services while doing its own manufacturing. In the old model, the Bell System encompassed every need to furnish both network capability and services to the end user. Of course, that ended with the breakup in 1984. Since that time, the industry has become a horizontally-structured sector, with separate companies being service providers, application developers, and equipment manufacturers.

This restructuring of the industry has had a profound effect on telecommunications research. What has happened is that almost the entire research burden has fallen to the segment of the industry represented by equipment manufacturers, i.e., Lucent, Alcatel, Nortel, Cisco, and others. There are two major problems with this placement for research – the amount and volatility of funding available for research, and the beneficiary for whom the research is intended.

Obviously, with large sectors of the industry abandoning research, there is less total funding available. The service providers claim, with some justification, that they continue to pay for research in the prices that they pay for equipment, but with intense competition among the equipment vendors – not all of whom support research – it is difficult to support increased prices from those who do sponsor research. Given the stringent standards that all equipment must adhere to, significant product differentiation is hard to achieve.

Among the equipment vendors, only Lucent continues to support a relatively large research program at Lucent Bell Labs. Through difficult times it has steadfastly given 1% of its revenues to their research program. It deserves a great deal of credit for sticking with research, but as its revenue has shrunk, so has the research budget. With this year's revenue projected at about $8 billion, that 1% would mean

$80 million for research. Compare this figure with the research funding prior to divestiture, which was a little more than $300 million. It is no wonder that the Holmdel Lab had to be sold!

Not only is there less revenue from which to draw the research budget, but the volatility of revenue in the equipment vendor segment can be extreme. All of the equipment vendors compete for the capital expenditure budgets of the service providers. Depending on the service providers' fortunes, this is an amount that can vary widely. The equipment vendors have only a small number of customers, these customers have a great deal of power to influence design and pricing, and these are customers whose financial performances are well correlated. If one is having a bad year, so may others.

After the bursting of the dot-com bubble, there was over-capacity in the network. All of the service providers cut back their cap-ex budgets, and the equipment providers were left to compete for a total cap-ex pot that went from $119 billion in 2000 to $53 billion in 2003. This is hardly the kind of business that can maintain stability of funding for long-range, fundamental research.

In the old days at Bell Labs, research was devoted to making the best possible telephone service for the end user, that is, you and me. It really was akin to some kind of religion, although Judge Greene was skeptical, stating that our motives were more profit-oriented and anti-competitive. I still believe, however, that in those days researchers had almost no sense of a profit motive.

In any event, those days are gone. Now that telecom research is in the hands of the equipment vendors, like Lucent, the focus is no longer on the best service for the end user, but, instead, is completely bent to the needs and desires of the large service providers. As a simple example, I have a cell phone manufactured by LG Electronics and sold through Verizon. Was that cell phone designed with me in mind or with Verizon in mind? The answer seems obvious. In spite of the fact that there is a USB port on the camera phone, pictures that it takes cannot be downloaded directly to my PC. Instead, I must send the pictures to my PC through Verizon at a cost of 25 cents each. Similarly, all cell phones must now incorporate GPS (Global Positioning System), so that location can be obtained for 911 calls. But the GPS capability can only be accessed through a monthly subscription service, not as a stand-alone capability for the user. Obviously, Verizon and the other service providers have a lot more market clout than you or I. It is their needs that are being met, whether or not they are in the best interests of the end consumer.

The economic benefits of network externality apply to research that may be shared among all users, but the equipment providers, instead, must concentrate to whatever degree possible on differentiating their products to sell to the service providers. Research that is funded by end users should, in contrast, concentrate on standards, common technology, and shared benefits. This is why the current industry structure is flawed with respect to its research paradigm, and why government funding of research on behalf of the end user is needed.

Who Does Telecom Research Today?

In the preceding sections I have argued that the telecom industry today is incapable of supporting fundamental research in the way that it once did. So is telecom research to be completely abandoned, or can it be funded otherwise and done elsewhere?

There are people who occasionally say that perhaps telecom is no longer a field that is fruitful for research. After all, optical transmission has made enormous capacities plentiful at miniscule costs, and the Internet is so embedded in every computer and application that it would be almost unthinkable to change it in any fundamental way that would disenfranchise current equipment and applications.

But the whole history of telecom research has been one of continued breakthroughs that have benefited humanity. In recent years, the pace of research breakthroughs seems unabated. The hot topics today are centered mainly on wireless technology and networking strategies. The wireless spectrum has been opening up to almost unlimited capacity due to very sophisticated signal processing that has only recently been invented. In networking, researchers are looking to improve the security and dependability of the Internet.

Of course, the most important discoveries and inventions in the future are those that will surprise us. Some reviewers of the National Academy report on telecom have said that we should prove that there is diminished innovation in telecom because of what is happening to industry research. But that is impossible to prove. What did we not invent that we should have? The truth is that we will never know what we have missed. The only measurable event would be the transition of industry dominance from this country to another.

Today, there are as many research publications and conference presentations on telecommunications as there have been in prior decades. My own belief is that there is a lower standard of novelty and importance in these publications, but that, too, is impossible to prove. The number of papers and presentations is not determined by the expertise and funding of research, but rather by the availability of publication space and conference time. There may be some analog to Gresham's Law about bad publications filling up the space formerly occupied by "good" publications.

If there are as many publications as ever, and industry has stopped funding research, who is writing these publications? And the answer is, overwhelmingly, academics. Today the great majority of all research papers are being written at universities, a little more than half of which are outside the United States.

To put some numbers behind this phenomenon of passing the torch from industry to academia, I did a survey of the authorship of papers in the principle research journal, *IEEE Transactions on Communications*. The authorship data shows a steady decline from 1970 to 2005 in the percentage of papers written by authors from industry. In 1970, about 85% of the papers were written by industry. By the year 2004, only 7% of the papers were authored by writers in US industry. Almost all the other papers were written at universities, and slightly less than half the papers were from US universities. (A very few papers were written by government employees.)

In order to get the most recent available data, I surveyed the approximately 1,300 papers presented at the two major international communications conferences in 2005 – the IEEE International Communications Conference and the IEEE Global Communications Conference. This data was even more striking. Only a scant 3% of these papers were authored by US industry! [The approximate percentages are: US Industries – 3%, US Universities – 34%, Asia – 26%, Europe – 20%, Other Countries – 17%]

It is clear that the participation of US industry in publishing research papers is minimal. The only US industrial research labs with more than one paper were:

Qualcomm	9
Lucent	6
Telcordia	4
IBM	4
Marvell Semiconductor	3
Mitsubishi Research US	3
Motorola	2
Conextant	2

Since the breakup of the Bell System, it might be argued that new industrial research labs have taken the place of the traditional telecom companies within the research community. However, this data would suggest that only Qualcomm has contributed to the published literature in the usual venues.

In the authorship data another trend is quite evident. In the papers published in Globecom 2005 (St Louis), 459 of the 675 authors from US universities (68%) have Asian surnames. We do not know how many of these authors are US citizens, but the implications for our visa policies are clear from even the most casual perusal of the programs for these conferences. We do know that 56% of PhDs in engineering and 45% of the PhDs in computer science are being awarded in the US to foreign nationals. The bottom line of all this data is that research in communications today is being done largely by foreign national graduate students at US universities.

The question remains, however: Is it bad that almost all research in telecommunications is now being done at universities? I would argue that, while this situation is not terrible, it is far from ideal. Often, researchers at universities have little idea what problems are important. This is particularly true at the many second- and third-tier schools. Most academic authors are caught in the "publish or perish" syndrome, and are looking for mathematical problems not requiring laboratory work, large systems analyses, or purchase of any expensive equipment. Thus, the research publications get filled with an infinite number of variations of unimportant results. (For those in the field, a good example is in the thousands of papers and reports on methods for obtaining quality of service.)

This is where the influence of Bell Labs is missed. It is unnecessary for industry to dominate research publications, but it is necessary for them to lead the universities in the direction of problems with practical importance, by having enough of their own publications to establish the important issues. In my opinion, this guidance is now missing, and much of the university talent is being wasted.

Government Support of Telecommunications Research

It would seem that government has an important role in funding research in telecommunications, and that role is more important now than it has been in the past, when industry was generous in its own support of research. Moreover, the primary benefits of research in telecommunications have, in the past, flowed to the public, and, as I have argued here, that is no longer the main objective of the research being funded by the industry.

Most federal government funding has come from two agencies – NSF (National Science Foundation) and DARPA (Defense Advanced Research Projects Agency). NSF funding goes almost exclusively to universities and is guided by peer review of other academics. DARPA, on the other hand, funds both academia and industry, and takes a much more proactive role in project management to create research programs geared to more specific military needs.

In the past, DARPA has contributed greatly to the evolution of telecommunications as we know it today. It was their funding and guidance in the early 1970s that created the Internet, whose further development was passed on to NSF and subsequently privatized. DARPA also led the development of optical technology at a time before the bandwidth need of the Internet was apparent, and when industry's funding and vision were lacking. Wireless technology has also benefited greatly from DARPA funding. The CDMA technology used in many of our cellular phones today (and the choice for third generation standards worldwide) had it origins in DARPA work.

These and other DARPA contributions to telecommunications were the outgrowths of DARPA policies that were aimed at improving the commercial infrastructure, due to the growing realization that military communications would have to rely increasingly on commercial networks in the future. Today, however, there are different policies in place, and DARPA research programs must be justified by a more immediate military need.

NSF is the agency of choice when academics look to fund their research programs. Here, however, the emphasis has often been on the implementation of high speed networks connecting supercomputers for physics research. Research in communications, *per se*, has also taken a back seat to the programs devoted to computer science. Partly for these reasons, the supply of funds at NSF for telecommunications is far short of the demand from the academic community. It is said that the acceptance rate for proposals in this field is in the single digits of percentage of those submitted. In the last year, however, NSF has taken a critical look at its coverage of telecommunications research and has started a program on the future of Internet.

State funding of research also contributes to the overall support of telecommunications. The largest such program, by far, is in California, where the California Institute for Telecommunications and Information Technology (known colloquially as "Cal-IT squared") melds together a number of California universities with generous state support and complementary industrial funding to create a broad range of research projects. The program is managed from a large, new building specifically designed for this purpose at the University of California, San Diego.

A few years ago there was an attempt in New Jersey to do something similar to the California program. The plan was to put a bond issue on the ballot to fund initiatives in four areas of research pertinent to New Jersey's talent base – one of these areas was telecommunications. The promise of ample funding (on the order of $100 million) drew imaginative proposals from New Jersey's universities, most of which proposed research programs that cut across and melded together the individual programs and academic departments of these universities. For example, one such proposal promised a new building, shared by Princeton University, Rutgers University, and Stevens Institute of Technology, to do research in wireless communications. Needless to say, the idea of the bond issue stagnated somewhere and never happened.

New Jersey's Universities and Technical Culture

With the downsizing of Bell Labs, many of its leading researchers left the company to join the ranks of academia. Some, although far from a majority, stayed in New Jersey to teach at its four major research universities – Princeton, Rutgers, Stevens, and New Jersey Institute of Technology (NJIT). Even so, New Jersey does not rank among the top states for academic research in engineering and computer science.

In the *US News and World Report* ranking of the top 50 engineering graduate schools, Princeton is ranked 18th, while Rutgers is at 47th. There is no question which state has the strongest engineering graduate schools. California has Stanford, UC Berkeley, UCLA, UC San Diego, UC Santa Barbara, UC Davis, and UC Irvine all on the list, with Stanford and Berkeley at 2nd and 3rd, right behind Massachusetts Institute of Technology (MIT).

All research universities aspire to move up the *US News* list, but this is extremely difficult. For a school to move up, another must move down, and, once made, reputations are very hard to change. Moreover, the school's reputation and its resultant listing are almost self-fulfilling prophecies; the schools at the top have their choice of the best graduate students, and this infusion of talent keeps them there. Even when a university upgrades its faculty with academic stars, gifted graduate students are slow to follow.

The California schools have even taken over the preeminence in telecommunications research once so dominated by New Jersey's industrial research labs. In the 1970s, the Internet grew up mostly there, with the first node at UCLA. UC Berkeley took the UNIX software from Bell Labs, rewrote parts, and founded Sun Microsystems. Qualcomm in San Diego is probably the leading research company in wireless, and UC San Diego has greatly benefited from its nearness and the generosity of its founder, Irwin Jacobs, a famous communications theorist from MIT. As Bell Labs was winding down, some of the less famous California schools were gaining in reputation, particularly UC Santa Barbara and UC Irvine. The Cal-IT2 program is fueling a telecommunications research capability that had already become world-class.

Aided by Bell Labs refugees, Rutgers has created a program in wireless research that has considerable national reputation. Both Stevens and NJIT have also improved their faculty and programs, and, of course, Princeton remains one of the country's elite research universities. Nonetheless, the truth is that, when people think of academic research states in technology, they probably do not think of New Jersey. It would be unrealistic to think that this could be easily changed.

This leads me back to a question that I raised earlier in this paper -- what stops New Jersey from being like Silicon Valley? When I compare the two, I see some similar ingredients, but also some that are missing in New Jersey. One of the most important ingredients is the technical talent, and New Jersey had this in great supply. Even though this talent is now leaving New Jersey, much still remains. Another ingredient is the attractiveness of the State itself to sought-after people who can choose to live anywhere in the world. This is, of course, a matter of taste, but, personally, I would stack up New Jersey's appeal against almost any place, except San Francisco. All of us who live in New Jersey know that the State is a far more appealing place to live than its reputation would have outsiders believe. (This is a subject outside the scope of my argument here, but I would do something about this paradox, and the most significant thing would be to beautify, in some architecturally-imaginative way, the section of the New Jersey Turnpike near Newark Airport.)

I do not think that talent and geographic attractiveness are the issues, as much as culture and what I will call "connectedness." Historically, Bell Labs dominated the technology culture and was self-contained. There were so many engineers and scientists at Bell Labs, and its locations stretched across the State. For many of its people, there was no need for a larger, outside culture or presence, and none grew. Moreover, the culture inside Bell Labs was scientific, academic, and inquisitive, rather than intrinsically entrepreneurial. However, during the dot-com boom and immediately after, when Bell Labs downsized, many leading researchers left to start companies. In optical technology particularly, there were Bell Labs researchers omnipresent in the startup community. Once aroused, the researchers showed that they could become entrepreneurial. Although a number of these new companies were in New Jersey simply because that is where the people lived, many were in California and elsewhere.

New Jersey has lacked a robust venture capital infrastructure, and, in my opinion, it has been geographically-challenged in that there is no epicenter for technology and venture capital activity, as there is in Palo Alto and Stanford. In short, I often think that there is no "there" there, just as when I am asked where in New Jersey I live, I often resort to the exit number on the Garden State Parkway. We do not seem to have the technology "watering holes" that I see in Silicon Valley, where engineers and venture capitalists meet.

During the dot-com boom and even now, I find that graduate students at Stanford and Berkeley dream about starting companies, while those in New Jersey imagine scientific fame. The technology "air" simply feels different in the two places.

I concede that there is unfairness in my comparison. No place in the world can compare with Silicon Valley, and few come close. Only Cambridge, Massachusetts, and, to a lesser degree, Austin, Texas, have similar attributes and activities.

The Bottom Line

New Jersey had a past greatness and fame for industrial research and for tele-communications research. Much of this fame was due to Bell Labs, and, though Bell Labs still exists, it is necessarily not what it was before. All of us who were involved there are saddened by this, but I believe that there is nothing to be done to recreate the "old" Bell Labs. Indeed, most of us would agree that not only is re-creation impossible, but it might not even be desirable, inasmuch as the world has changed. The larger picture is that, though New Jersey still has the biggest share of telecommunications researchers in the world, the industry itself is no longer ca-pable of supporting them. As time goes on, that talent will migrate and dissipate.

Telecommunications research has now moved to universities, and, unfortunately, New Jersey is just another state in the world of academia. The one thing that the State could do to change New Jersey's decline from preeminence would be to implement a State initiative like that in California. The talent is here, the money is not.

CHAPTER SEVEN

Strong Medicine: New Jersey and the Pharmaceutical and Medical Technology Industry

Economic Study Conducted by Deloitte Consulting LLP for the HealthCare Institute of New Jersey

About the 2006 Survey

The HealthCare Institute of New Jersey (HINJ) commissioned the first economic impact study of the New Jersey pharmaceutical and medical technology industry in 1997. Since then, the study has served as an annual benchmark for one of the State's leading economic drivers. This is HINJ's 10th consecutive economic survey.

The 2006 survey is compiled from 25 of the leading pharmaceutical and medical technology companies that comprise HINJ's membership. The sample group, which was surveyed regarding 2005 data, includes 22 of the 23 HINJ companies that participated in the previous year's study (Mitsubishi Pharma America was not a current-year participant), and also captures data from new study participants Adams Respiratory Therapeutics, Inc., Chugai Pharma USA, and Lundbeck Research USA. The net inclusion of two additional HINJ members in this year's survey also benefited the 2005 aggregate results reported by the HINJ survey participants.

The data elements presented in this year's report remain consistent with those in the prior year's report, readily highlighting the year-to-year fluctuations in a variety of key industry metrics. Additionally, the survey includes state and local taxes paid by the HINJ member companies.

The study seeks to identify the various elements of the state of New Jersey's economy that retain the pharmaceutical and medical technology industry as a core part of its economic engine and then to quantify the economic impact of this vital industry. This study employs widely accepted economic multiplier formulas.

New Jersey's Pharmaceutical and Medical Technology Industry

Curing the State's Economic Ills

The economy of New Jersey has long thrived on the concentration of life science businesses in the State. Despite the impact of consolidation and strategic realignments, New Jersey's pharmaceutical and medical technology industry still remains a leading economic sector within the State.

In 2005, HINJ member companies had an estimated overall economic impact of more than $27 billion on New Jersey's economy. This figure is up significantly over last year's estimated, overall economic impact of $22 billion. Direct HINJ member company spending was approximately $21 billion, and economic activity resulting from the industry's presence and investment in the State resulted in almost $6 billion more.

Economic Impact of the Pharma/Med Tech Industry on New Jersey

Pharma/Med Tech Activity Area	2005 Direct Economic Impact on NJ Spending by HINJ Survey Participants (amounts in billions)	2005 Total Economic Impact on NJ Spending by HINJ Survey Participants (amounts in billions)
Payroll *	$5.679	$7.240
Benefits	$1.258	$1.258
Vendor Spending	$4.043	$7.071
Capital Spending	$2.196	$3.919
R&D	$7.540	$7.540
Charitable Donations	$0.152	0.152
Estimated $ Impact	**$20.868**	**$27.180**

Note: Multiplier effects are only calculated for the following activities and are based on the 2003 IMPLAN model: payroll, vendor spending, and capital spending.
* Direct economic impact includes pretax dollars paid to NJ residents.

The industry continues to contribute greatly to New Jersey's economy, and, as a result, many businesses in the State depend on pharmaceutical and medical technology companies for their continued growth.

Employment

In 2005, HINJ member companies participating in the survey accounted for 60,560 New Jersey-based jobs. This figure represents a slight increase from the 60,274 jobs in the prior year, as the industry in the State steadied itself after consolidation and cutbacks led to the significant employment reduction noted in the prior-year survey. Consequently, the pharmaceutical and medical technology industry continues to be one of the State's largest employers.

HINJ Employment by Function

A significant portion of HINJ member companies employment (27%) is devoted to research and development, a figure relatively unchanged from last year's study. The consistency of this figure illustrates the industry's continuing commitment to sustaining its growth by discovering new medicines and devices.

Business Function	NJ Employment Share 2005	NJ Employment Share 2004
Research	13%	15%
Clinical Development	14%	10%
Corporate Administration	26%	25%
Manufacturing/Quality Control	15%	15%
Sales & Marketing	16%	23%
Other	16%	12%

Gender Equity in the Workforce

The pharmaceutical and medical technology industry is often cited as one of the best industries for professional women. The work environment and culture in the industry actively attracts and rewards the contributions and strengths of highly-educated women. Working Mother Magazine compiles an annual 100 Best Companies for Working Mothers list, and many HINJ member companies frequently rank near the top.

In 2005, slightly more than half of the workforce in New Jersey's pharmaceutical and medical technology industry was comprised of women. This qualified and educated workforce benefits from advancement opportunities presented in this dynamic industry.

HINJ Firms' Workforce Composition, 2005	
Male – 30,216	Female – 30,340

Payroll

In 2005, New Jersey's economy benefited from the approximately $7.0 billion aggregate payroll earned by HINJ survey participants for jobs based within the State. Although the short commute attracts many residents from neighboring states, such as Pennsylvania and New York, New Jersey residents held 79% of State-based jobs. Total payroll has increased over the prior year, partially due to the modest increase in employment and annual market wage increases.

NJ Payroll for HINJ Survey Participants

2005 -- $7.0 billion   2004 -- $6.6 billion

In 2005, pharmaceutical and medical technology industry workers received competitive wages and benefits, commensurate with their educational and skill levels. The average base salary was $93,948 (a 6.7% increase over 2004), and total compensation for industry employees was approximately $115,701 (a 5.2% increase over 2004).

Labor Income & Benefits of NJ Pharmaceutical/Med Tech Firms			
	2005	**2004**	**% Change**
Average Base Salary	$93,948	$88.090	6.7%
Average Compensation	$115,701	$110,017	5.2%
Average Benefits Paid	$26,293	$24,705	6.4%

How Industry Employees Compare to Other Sectors

The following chart illustrates the pharmaceutical and medical technology industry's position near the top among other major New Jersey employment industries. With average compensation of $100,000, pharma/biotech employees benefit from the second highest annual compensation among the listed industries. This average compensation is commensurate with the high skill and education levels of pharma/biotech personnel.

Average Compensation -2004
($ in thousands)
[Source: Bureau of Labor Statistics]

Security & Commodity Brokerage – $126
Pharma/Biotech – $100
Telecom – $84
Insurance – $82
Computer & Data Processing Services – $79
Computer & Electronic Products – $67
Banking – $60
New Jersey Average – $48

Workers directly employed by the industry are also active consumers, creating spending impacts of $5.7 billion and contributing $1.6 billion of additional income to New Jersey's economy. Industry workers represent diverse communities geographically and economically, and the spending impacts are also benefiting the entire State.

(Amounts in Billions)	2005	2004
NJ-BASED PAYROLL	$7.0	$6.6
...going to NJ residents[1]	$5.7	$5.3
NJ income created from after-tax[2] spending	$1.6[a]	$1.6[b]

[1] Results of surveyed companies indicate that 79% and 80% of the NJ workforce's compensation were earned by State residents in 2005 and 2004, respectively.
[2] Effective tax rates of 33.3% for 2005 and 29.9% for 2004 were used to estimate disposable income from the industry's NJ-based payroll.
a Disposable income multiplier is from the 2003 NJ IMPLAN model.
b Disposable income multiplier is from the 2001 NJ IMPLAN model.

Industry Spending, Spin-off Jobs and Related Impacts

The pharmaceutical and medical technology industry is a significant employer within New Jersey, and contributes to the development of other employment throughout the State.

In 2005, approximately 101,500 "spin-off" jobs were created as a result of industry activity. Spending by pharmaceutical company employees supports almost 36,000 jobs. Purchases by pharmaceutical and medical technology companies of goods and services supported over 34,000 jobs, and investment in capital projects supported more than 31,000 jobs across many business sectors.

Once again, the pharmaceutical and medical technology industry topped the Alliance for Action's Annual Capital Construction Forecast, leading all other sectors of the economy in capital construction investment. Over the next two years, the industry is expected to have capital construction figures of $4.3 billion, generating more jobs and facilities in New Jersey. (source: HINJ).

Other NJ Jobs Tied to Pharma / Med Tech Activities

Household spending – 35,866
Vendor activity – 34,381
Capital projects – 31,290
Total "spin-off" 101,537

In total, HINJ member companies provided 162,093 jobs throughout New Jersey: 60,556 through direct employment and 101,537 "spin-off" jobs. In another words, for each HINJ member job, another 1.7 jobs are created in the State's economy.

Payroll Spending

Payroll spending by pharmaceutical and medical technology companies benefited New Jersey residents beyond those directly employed by the industry.

For example, in 2005, HINJ member company payroll expenses generated $5.7 billion in income for direct employees who were State residents. Expenditures resulting from this payroll figure generated $1.6 billion in income for other State residents who provided consumer goods and services.

Income to NJ Residents
($ in billions)

NJ resident employee payroll – $5.7
NJ resident household spending – $1.6
NJ spending on vendor activity – $2.3
NJ spending on capital projects – $1.7
TOTAL – $11.3

NOTE: *Multipliers are from the 2003 NJ IMPLAN model*

These income gains generated significant sales across State-based businesses, no doubt improving the income gains for their employees. It is important to note that the income gains illustrated above exclude the impact of spending in-state by HINJ member employees, who are residents of border states and commute daily.

Sales for NJ Businesses Due to Pharma/Med Tech
($ in billions)

Household spending – $4.4
Vendor activity – $7.1
Capital projects – $3.9
Total Sales from pharma/med tech – $15.4

NOTE: *Multipliers are from the 2003 NJ IMPLAN model*

The HINJ member economic impact generated $15.4 billion in NJ business sales, representing a tremendous impact on local communities, privately owned businesses, and public corporations.

Vendor-Related Spending

To support their day-to-day operations, HINJ member companies rely on a tremendous number of vendors who provide a wide array of goods and services. Vendor-related spending originating from NJ-based facilities exceeded $21 billion in 2005, of which an estimated $4 billion was spent on vendors located within the State. The $4 billion spent on NJ-based vendors resulted in an estimated $3.1 billion of additional NJ sales, for a total State impact of approximately $7.1 billion.

Vendor-Related Spending
($ in billions)

Vendor-related spending tied to NJ facilities – $21.5 billion
....portion procured from NJ suppliers – $4.0 billion
Additional NJ sales created from pharma – $3.1 billion*
Total NJ sales created from pharma – $7.1 billion

* Multiplier is from the 2003 NJ IMPLAN model.

Capital Projects

For years, the pharmaceutical and medical technology industry was singularly responsible for the State's robust capital construction forecasts. Overall capital expenditures in 2005 were $2.2 billion, a significant increase over the prior year and a positive sign of the industry's commitment to the State of New Jersey. This capital spending included construction of new facilities, as well as the renovation and maintenance of existing facilities. New construction accounted for 48% of industry capital projects. In the aggregate, HINJ member companies participating in this year's survey reported 128 facilities, located across 15 counties and 72 municipalities.

New Jersey Capital Expenditure by HINJ Members
($ in millions)

	2005	2004
New Construction	$1,058	$624
Renovation & Maintenance	$1,139	$727

Capital spending tied to NJ facilities	$2.2 billion
Additional NJ sales created from pharma	$1.7[a] billion
Total NJ sales created from pharma	$3.9 billion

[a] Multiplier is from the 2003 NJ IMPLAN model.

Research and Development

A Robust Pipeline

Research and development drives the pharmaceutical and medical technology industry. The discovery and production of breakthrough medicines and cutting-edge technologies enable HINJ member companies to do what they do best: extend and improve the quality of life.

In 2005, HINJ member companies participating in this year's survey invested $7.5 billion in research and development activity. This figure represents a 17% increase over the $6.4 billion reported by those same HINJ member companies for the prior-year period. This level of spending evidences the industry's commitment to research and development, and provides the funding to support the various projects and initiatives being worked on by the 27% of NJ-based employees devoted to research and development.

Throughout the industry, the future is primed with promise. Within pharmaceuticals, there are almost 900 products in development, and over 70 New Drug Applications (NDAs) have been submitted.

Product Studies in Year 2005	Products in Development	Studies/Trials Underway or Planned
Pre-Clinical	169	839
Phase I	215	635
Phase II	185	443
Phase III	204	830
Phase IV	110	462
NDAs Submitted	78	481
Total	961	3690

In the medical technology field, 131 new product applications, or Premarket Approvals (PMAs), are currently on file with the Food and Drug Administration by HINJ member companies. A total of 55 significant improvements to existing medical devices, known as 510(k)s, were also approved in 2005. Overall, these developments in products and technologies promote the long-term sustainability of the industry.

Medical Technology – 2005
PMA – 131
510K – 55
Total – 186

R&D Strategic Alliances

The research and development agenda of HINJ member companies works toward continued innovations and breakthroughs. To support and achieve this goal, the industry relies on strategic alliances, partnerships, and collaborations with contract manufacturers, academic institutions, and other entities.

Developing quality partnerships plays a critical role in the allocation of research and development dollars. In 2005, approximately 8% of the $7.5 billion research and development dollars was tied to strategic alliances. Of that figure, approximately 24% ($147 million) of the strategic alliance research and development spending was tied to New Jersey-based institutions and businesses further underscoring the importance of expanding the State's life sciences agenda. This trend is expected to continue, and the interaction among HINJ members and other companies sets the stage for future generations of HINJ membership and State economic growth.

HINJ Members Enter Into Strategic Alliances for

Contract Manufacturing 20%

Licensing 27%

Research Collaboration 35%

(e.g., academic collaborations)

Other 18%

Charitable Contributions - Global

Whether around the corner or around the globe, HINJ member companies are good corporate citizens and contribute generously to a host of charitable causes.

In 2005, the estimated total worldwide giving by HINJ member companies was over $4.4 billion, up from $3.5 billion in 2004. Based on the most recent data available, an estimated $152 million of this amount directly benefited New Jersey causes. The following provides a view of how member charitable activities are allocated:

Area of Contribution - Worldwide — 2005

Arts 4%

Community/Civic relations 10% (e.g., indigent drug programs)

Corporate match of employees giving 10%

Education 14%

Employee contributions to private charities through corporate campaigns 8%

Health-related 23%

Product donations 11%

Other 20%

Taxes

The HINJ member companies and their workforces contribute significantly to the tax revenue that supports many State services. For 2005, estimated total state, local, and municipal taxes paid by the HINJ member companies participating in this year's survey were estimated to be $650 million, and were comprised of the following amounts:

New Jersey State Taxes	Dollars (in millions)
New Jersey Withholding	$292.8
Income and Franchise Tax	$141.3
Corporate Business Tax	$41.7
Sales and Use Tax	$40.1
Disability and Unemployment	$8.4
Other	$1.2
New Jersey Local and Municipal Taxes	
Property Taxes	$123.6
Other	$0.3
Other	
Environmental Permits, Fees, and Licenses	$0.6

Rebates

In addition to the taxes paid by HINJ member companies and their employees, the industry also pays rebates to the State and federal government for medications used by recipients of these prescription programs. Rebates were developed in the federal Omnibus Budget Resolution Act (OBRA) 90 legislation as a mechanism that would allow governmental purchasers the same pricing available to large commercial purchasers. For programs sponsored by State government, the rate of these rebates is written into the State budget.

Based on the most recent data available, the entire industry paid the following rebates to the State of New Jersey:

Rebate Type	Dollars (in millions)
Medicare	$294.4[a]
PAAD	$132.9[b]
Senior Gold	$6.0[b]

[a] 2005 estimate. The State of New Jersey retains 50%, or $147.2 million, of this amount. The remaining 50% is remitted to the federal government. Source: Fiscal Year 2006 2007 State of New Jersey Budget at D-202.

[b] 3rd and 4th quarter 2004 plus 1st and 2nd quarter 2005. Source: Department of Health and Senior Services

The Pharmaceutical Assistance to the Aged and Disabled program (PAAD) and the Senior Gold program were started in New Jersey in 1975 and 2001, respectively. PAAD was the first ever state-sponsored drug program for seniors in the United States. (Source: HINJ).

New Jersey's Business Environment: A Healthy Dose

HINJ members often cite New Jersey as a pre-eminent location for the global pharmaceutical and medical technology industry, largely due to unique attributes, such as: a skilled, highly educated workforce; access to markets and capital; and a high concentration of life sciences companies throughout the State. As a result, New Jersey provides an environment that encourages innovation and rewards ingenuity, qualities that support the growth and development of the pharmaceutical and medical technology industry.

Twenty-one of 25 HINJ member companies that participated in this year's survey provided their assessment of the quality of life and the business environment in New Jersey. The following table summarizes the ratings from the 21 companies across a series of metrics that are critical to attracting and retaining pharmaceutical and medical technology companies to the State.

HINJ Member Quality of Life Assessment in New Jersey

Aspect of New Jersey	Excellent	Very Good	Good	Fair	Poor	Total
Tax incentives	1	4	8	6	2	21
Quality of local colleges/universities	4	4	13	0	0	21
Quality of workforce and accessibility	5	7	7	1	1	21
Availability of desirable space	1	6	9	4	1	21
Quality of life	3	8	6	4	0	21

HINJ member companies cited a positive quality of life and the availability of quality institutions and employees as favorable aspects of New Jersey. However, HINJ members continue to believe the State could do more in the way of providing State tax incentives.

Members of the HealthCare Institute of New Jersey

Adams Respiratory Therapeutics, Inc.
Altana Pharma
BD
Berlex Laboratories
Bristol-Myers Squibb Company
Chugai Pharma USA
C.R. Bard, Inc.
Daiichi Pharmaceuticals*
Eisai Inc.
GE Healthcare
Hoffmann-La Roche Inc.
INO Therapeutics, LLC
   (HINJ associate member)

Johnson & Johnson
Lundbeck Research USA
MedPointe Pharmaceuticals
Merck & Co., Inc.
Novartis Pharmaceuticals
Novo Nordisk Pharmaceuticals
Organon
Pfizer Inc.
Sankyo Pharma*
Sanofi-Aventis Pharmaceuticals
Schering-Plough Corporation
Stryker Corporation
Wyeth

* Merged on April 3, 2006, to become Daiichi Sankyo.

About Deloitte

Deloitte refers to one or more of Deloitte Touche Tohmatsu, a Swiss Verein, its member firms, and their respective subsidiaries and affiliates. Deloitte Touche Tohmatsu is an organization of member firms around the world devoted to excellence in providing professional services and advice, focused on client service through a global strategy executed locally in nearly 150 countries. With access to the deep intellectual capital of 120,000 people worldwide, Deloitte delivers services in four professional areas, audit, tax, consulting, and financial advisory services, and serves more than one-half of the world's largest companies, as well as large national enterprises, public institutions, locally important clients, and successful, fast-growing global growth companies. Services are not provided by the Deloitte Touche Tohmatsu Verein, and, for regulatory and other reasons, certain member firms do not provide services in all four professional areas.

As a Swiss Verein (association), neither Deloitte Touche Tohmatsu nor any of its member firms has any liability for each other's acts or omissions. Each of the member firms is a separate and independent legal entity operating under the names "Deloitte," "Deloitte & Touche," "Deloitte Touche Tohmatsu," or other related names.

In the US, Deloitte & Touche USA LLP is the US member firm of Deloitte Touche Tohmatsu, and services are provided by the subsidiaries of Deloitte & Touche USA LLP (Deloitte & Touche LLP, Deloitte Consulting LLP, Deloitte Financial Advisory Services LLP, Deloitte Tax LLP, and their subsidiaries), and not by Deloitte & Touche USA LLP. The subsidiaries of the US member firm are among the nation's leading professional services firms, providing audit, tax, consulting, and financial advisory services through nearly 30,000 people in more than 80 cities. Known as employers of choice for innovative human resources programs, they are dedicated to helping their clients and their people excel. For more information, please visit the US member firm's web site at www.deloitte.com/us.

CHAPTER EIGHT

Nanotechnology: Assets and Opportunities for New Jersey

By
Michel M. Bitritto

Executive Summary

The emerging fields of nanoscale science, engineering, and processing are providing the unforeseen power to understand and control the properties of many natural and human-made products at the atomic and molecular level. Much the way information technology has changed the world in the last several decades, the ability to control matter at the nano level (about 80,000 times smaller than the thickness of a human hair) will change most technology-based products of the future, and significantly impact the global economy.

According to the National Science Foundation, the market in the United States for products and services based on nanotechnology could reach over $1 trillion by 2015. Application of nanotechnology will result in revolutionizing technology-based markets as diverse as pharmaceuticals and medical devices, sensors, power generation, the environment, information technology, and data storage. Even tennis balls and cosmetics are being impacted significantly by nanotechnology. Nanotechnology is critical to New Jersey's economic growth and our ability to create new, high paying jobs across much of our industry base.

Federal and state governments and most recently the private sector have made significant investments in nanotechnology because of its potential economic impact. The Federal investment is currently about $1 billion annually, and, in his 2006 State of the Union Address, President George W. Bush called for doubling the R&D budget in areas like nanotechnology to remain globally competitive. An analysis of 33 large global corporations by Lux Research, a premier global research and advisory firm focusing on the business and economic impact of nanotechnology, estimated that $3.8 billion of corporate R&D went into nanotechnology in 2004.

Global competition among regions for research, talent, and high technology industry is occurring. The winners will be those best able to provide R&D funding, establish state of the art nanotechnology facilities, scale-up and prototype, deliver commercialization services and support, establish manufacturing capabilities, and encourage the pull-through of large corporations that will be relying on less risk adverse, entrepreneurial start-ups to develop and demonstrate the technology.

Nanotechnology is a major platform for economic growth in New Jersey, and has implications for the State's overall economic competitiveness. New Jersey possesses a strong position in key industries, including pharmaceuticals, materials, electronics, telecommunications, and energy that will need to integrate nanotechnology into their existing product mix, and develop new products based on nanotechnology to remain competitive. New Jersey has significant university assets critical to the advancement of nanotechnology and the entrepreneurial spirit required to translate science into commercial products that meet the needs of society. However, New Jersey will need to invest in its research base and infrastructure, and provide capital and commercialization support to emerging businesses to reach its potential.

With targeted and significant investments in infrastructure, programming, and entrepreneurs, New Jersey can be a hotspot for nanotechnology. Investment in universities and emerging technology businesses is critical in order to prepare the workforce and create economic growth for New Jersey.

Without a significant investment, New Jersey will fall behind.

Ensuring the Competitiveness of New Jersey Industry

New Jersey is concerned about ensuring quality job growth in the years ahead, particularly in the face of stiff global competition for knowledge-based work. Nanotechnology is an emerging technology that many view as leading the next industrial revolution. Not only will nanotechnology drive the formation of new, growth-oriented innovative companies in New Jersey, but also the advancement of nanotechnology will be critical to preserving quality jobs in industries in which New Jersey, today, holds a competitive edge. New Jersey is recognized as an international leader in many key industries where nanotechnology is expected to have a major impact. (See Appendix I)

In the area of pharmaceuticals, New Jersey is one of only five states with a large and highly specialized presence of drug and pharmaceutical companies, according to the Biotechnology Industry Organization. By 2014, Lux Research estimates that pharmaceutical companies in New Jersey and elsewhere are expected to have 23% of their sales revenues derived from incorporating nanotechnology into pharmaceutical products. Sales of nano-based delivery systems for therapeutics will lead those sales. In electronics, the American Electronics Association (AeA) notes that New Jersey is third in the nation in defense electronics. Nanotechnology is projected to revolutionize electronics, accounting for 75% of sales revenue by 2014, according to Lux Research. Advances in logic chips patterned on nanolithography, memory chips based on nanomaterials, and nanostructured chip cooling systems will be among those innovations and consistent with areas of expertise at Princeton University, Rutgers University and New Jersey Institute of Technology (NJIT).

Building on New Jersey's Focus in Nanotechnology

New Jersey has a solid standing in nanotechnology activities, with 388 patent and federal R&D grants to universities and industry from 1995 to 2005. These achievements place New Jersey sixth in the nation in patent awards, twelfth in National Science Foundation (NSF) awards, and nineteenth in National Institute of Health (NIH) awards, compared to other states.

Most near term (1-5 years) applications of nanotechnology will build on the field of nanomaterials, in which New Jersey-based industries and universities are recognized globally as "stars." These short-term, material-based opportunities can result in a range of commercial applications from stronger and lighter materials for automotive and aerospace applications to antibacterial nano-particles in wound dressings and more efficient nano-catalysts for use in energy generation.

An analysis of patent and federal R&D awards in nanotechnology by Battelle for the Mid-Atlantic Nanotechnology Alliance, a Federally funded initiative of New Jersey, Pennsylvania, and Delaware, found that in New Jersey:

- 34% of the State's nanotechnology activities are in nanomaterials, particularly in high temperature materials, nanoporous materials, and carbon nanotubes. Across the Mid-Atlantic region, New Jersey's strength in nanomaterials is reflected in 60% of the patent and federal R&D awards in the broad category of nanomaterials. Among the leaders in nanomaterials in New Jersey are Honeywell International and Exxon Mobil.

- 16% of New Jersey's awards in nanotechnology are found in nanocomposites that are made from the mixing of two or more materials to result in unique properties. For example, the distribution of small amounts of nanoparticles in some materials can significantly change electrical properties of those materials, while a nanocoating on a solid surface can impart resistance to ultraviolet rays or oxygen permeation. Among the leading institutions in this area are Rutgers University and NEI Corporation.

- In the next 5 to 15 years, it is expected that nanotechnology will be critical in the development of nanodevices and nanoelectronics for medical treatments, diagnostics, faster computers, and advanced sensors.

- 27% of the state's nanotechnology activities are found in the emerging area of nanoelectronics, particularly optoelectronics and thin films. The emerging nature of this field is reflected by the institutions leading this area, Rutgers University and Princeton University.

- 14% of the State's nanotechnology activities are found in the emerging area of nanobio applications, involving primarily biological sensors, drug targeting, and DNA-related tools. Rutgers University and Princeton University lead the state in this area.

- 9% of the state's nanotechnology activities are found in the enabling areas of nanofabrication, nanotools, and manufacturing technology, in general, led by NJIT, Rutgers University and Princeton University.

The expertise in our universities and colleges align extremely well with federal nanotechnology funding priorities. Our global reputation for excellence in material science and basic research and our proficiency in engineering and manufacturing technologies increase the opportunity for our researchers and emerging technology businesses to successfully compete for federal grants. New Jersey, however, has not made significant investments in its universities over the last 10 to 15 years. As a result, our dominance in some areas of research is in jeopardy. The availability of matching state funds can increase the likelihood of obtaining federal funds.

In the 2006 federal nanotechnology budget outlined below, over $750 million is available in grants in technology areas directly related to research currently taking place in New Jersey universities. Additionally, close to $150 million is budgeted for nanotechnology research facilities and equipment acquisitions sorely needed in New Jersey.

1. Fundamental Nanoscale Phenomena and Processes ($234 million)
2. Nanomaterials ($228 million)
3. Nanoscale Devices and Systems ($244 million)
4. Instrumentation Research, Metrology, and Standards for Nanotechnology ($71 million)
5. Nanomanufacturing ($47 million)
6. Major Research Facilities and Instrumentation Acquisitions ($148 million)
7. Societal Dimensions ($82 million)

New Jersey's Assets in Nanotechnology

New Jersey holds a leading national position in key industries like pharmaceuticals, medical devices, chemicals and materials, telecommunications, and information technology, which will ultimately pull-through the technology developed in our universities and emerging businesses to create high paying, technology-based jobs.

New Jersey has a robust base of companies actively engaged in nanotechnology R&D, with more than 50 New Jersey companies generating patents and receiving federal R&D awards in nanotechnology. Some of the New Jersey companies currently engaged in nanotechnology include Honeywell, Exxon Mobil, Lucent, Engelhard, Sarnoff, Orthodiagnostics, Salvona, Inmat, NanoOpto, NEI, Nanopac Technologies, Nanonex, Nanomedica, UHV Technologies, Tech Elan, Kulite Semiconductor, Parelec, and others.

New Jersey has world-class universities engaged in interdisciplinary nanotechnology research with over 150 faculty members, 125 post-doctoral fellows, and close to 400 graduate students.

Focus Areas Identified From Interviews and Review of Grant Awards

Universities	Materials Synthesis & Characterization						Nanoelectronics					Nano-bio			Energy Applications		
	Advanced Characterization (non-commercial)	Ceramic-based nanomaterials and nanocomposites	Carbon nanotubes	Nano0coatings	Nano-composites (non-ceramic)	Polymers and Synthetic Proteins	Electronic Materials/Thin Films	Nano-Lithography	Nano-Magnetics	Nano-Electro-Mechanical systems	Nano-optoelectronics	Biomaterials, Tissue Engineering and Regenerative Medicine	Bio-imaging & sensing	Drug discovery, development & delivery	Catalysis & Fuel Cells	Energy Storage	Solar Cells
New Jersey Institute of Technology	X		X		X		X				X		X	X	X		X
Princeton	X					X	X	X	X		X		X				
Rowan								X	X								
Rutgers		X		X	X		X		X		X	X		X		X	
Stevens Institute			X		X	X	X					X					

- **Princeton University** is the sole New Jersey university awarded a very prestigious Federal Nano Research Center Grant. It has more than 24 faculty members, 50 graduate students, and a dozen postdocs involved in nanotechnology research.

Their nanotechnology efforts span a number of centers and academic departments, including PRISM (Princeton Institute for the Science and Technology of Materials), PCCM (Princeton Center for Complex Materials), NSF-MRSEC (a National Science Foundation funded Materials Research Science Education Center), and individual departments such as Electrical Engineering, Chemistry, Physics, Mechanical and Aerospace Engineering, Chemical Engineering, and Geology, as well as the Plasma Physics Lab. Areas of concentrations and specialized/ unique expertise in nanotechnology include: bionano interface, nanofabrication/ nanoprocessing, nanostructured materials/nanotextures, nano and QC devices, nano organic and nano photonic systems, nanofluidics, self assembly, nano theory and modeling, nanoimaging and analysis, and nano infrastructure for research, prototype development, and industrial collaboration.

Princeton University has three, major, multi-user facilities for nano/micro processing and fabrication, imaging and analysis, and theory and modeling computations, representing more than $30 million in specialized equipment. New additions to the Nanoprocessing Suite will include a Laser Writer, Nanoimprinter, and High Res E-Beam writer. The multi-user facilities operate in support of over 200 academic, industry, and government lab collaborators, including Exxon, Rhodia, Sarnoff, Nanonex, NanoOpto, BioNanoMatrix, Sunstones, and Vincogen.

In addition to its extensive nanotechnology facilities, Princeton University brings a strong research focus in:

- Thin film electronics and nano over large areas, including the scaling of electronic devices to nanoscale, growth of novel materials on near-atomic scale, materials processing, and application in electronic devices, electrical properties of thin films, and microstructures of semiconductors and solid-state physics;

- Nano-imprint lithography involving applications in nano-electronics, nanomagnetics, nano-optoelectronics, semiconductors, and polymers;

- Microfluidics and other nano-related aspects of condensed matter including miniaturized automated systems for fluidic handling, flow and stability of micro and nanostructures in liquid phase, transport phenomena on free surface thin-film structures, energy flow in biomolecules, applications of microlithography to biology, and general properties of complex quantum systems;

- Ultrafast lasers including development of laser spectroscopy, atomic beam surface diffraction and reflectivity, synchrotron x-ray surface diffraction and reflectivity, and scanning probe microscopy (STM and AFM).

Rutgers University has approximately 100 faculty members, 300 graduate students, and 100 postdocs involved in nanotechnology research from eight different academic departments. Their areas of focus are in three main areas: Energy and Engineering (mostly chemical), Electronics and Sensors (assorted devices, including opto and telecom), and Bio (bio-nano, bio-Pharma, bio-materials). They have about $35 million in nano funding, which includes a recent notification that they will receive an Engineering New Jersey Research Center (ERC) grant of approximately $20 million in the area of Structured Organic composites. Four technology transfer laboratories are being planned as testing grounds for new technologies to manufacture pharmaceutical materials and bionano products. Rutgers plans to use the facilities to bring together pharmaceutical manufacturers, equipment manufacturers, instrument suppliers, and computational modeling and control specialists. Rutgers faculty will provide the research needed to integrate the various components into manufacturing platforms. The facilities will be open to large and small companies and other university researchers.

The plan consists of the following proposed laboratories:

1. Continuous Organic Macrocomposite Manufacturing
2. Organic Nanoparticle Synthesis and Processing
3. Hierarchical Synthesis of Organic Microcomposites
4. Pharmaceutical Mini-Micro Manufacturing

Rutgers University currently has about $50 million invested in equipment applicable to nano research within its academic departments and centers. There have been several faculty spinouts to date. There has been significant external collaboration with Picatinny Arsenal, Lucent, and Ft. Monmouth; Princeton, NJIT, Stevens, Rowan University, and other universities; Federal Labs; and small companies like Polymerix and Semorex. Rutgers has 12 to 15 courses per year that are predominantly modern Nano-oriented in Chemistry, Physics, Materials Science, etc.

Current focus areas in nanotechnology that stand out at Rutgers University, include:

- Synthesis of unique nanostructures, including establishing structure-properties-processing relationships in nanophase coatings and bulk materials, synthesis and processing of nanophase materials, nanostructured ceramics and polymers, and thin films;

- Interfacial science for nanoelectronics involving basic studies of surface, ultra-thin films, and interface systems for next generation transistors, high-K dielectrics, optoelectronics and molecular electronics, and technologically important electronic, photonic, organic, and biological heterostructures;

- Biomaterials involving the synthesis and characterization of biocompatible polymers for medical and dental applications, cellular bioengineering, and analysis and control of cell-biomaterial interactions, as well as applications for immune cell engineering, biomimetic materials interfaces to control cell functions, and functional induction of epithelial tissues;

- Energy applications, particularly energy storage chemistries enabled by advances in materials science;

- Quantum, condensed matter and organic electronics involving theoretical studies, such as strongly interacting electron systems, and novel magnetic states in strongly frustrated materials, theory of spin glasses, physics of quantum computation, and flux states in disordered superconductors;

- Simulation modeling involving molecular dynamics simulations, surface science diffusion in glasses, thin films, and coatings.

The New Jersey Institute of Technology has approximately two dozen faculty members, 12 graduate students, and six postdocs involved in nanotechnology research from six different academic departments (Electrical, Biomedical, Mechanical, and Chemical Engineering; Chemistry; and Physics) working collaboratively on nanotechnology with researchers from federal, corporate, and military laboratories. Their areas of focus include carbon nano tubes, nano particulates, semiconductor wires, fuel cells, nano-magnetism, nanobio, coatings, nanopharmaceuticals, and nanoenergetic materials.

NJIT has over $10 million in nano funding, has developed interdisciplinary nanotechnology courses, and holds regular seminars and nano meetings. External collaborators include Lucent, Mt. Sinai Hospital, Honeywell, Intel, Picatinny Arsenal, and others.

Focus areas of nanotechnology activity include:

- Advance Characterization applying a range of approaches, including raman spectroscopy, infrared screens, and ultra-violet characterization;

- Nanomaterials synthesis ranging from self-assembled silica and semiconductor nano-films to polymers and synthetic proteins, controlled fabrication of carbon nanotubes and wires, to nano coatings for corrosion protection films, and nano composites made of carbon nanotubes and organic semiconductors. Functionalization of carbon nanotubes by unique microwave processing technology and subsequent integration into complex structures and devices;

- Nanoparticulate process technology with applications ranging from advanced energetics to next generation pharmaceuticals with emphasis on novel coating processes for controlled production at nano-scale;

- Nanoelectronics involving a range of activities from electronic materials to nano-optoelectronics using carbon nanotubes and nano-semi-conductors, as well as wide area electronics using nano structured materials;

- Bionano involving efforts in biomaterials (stem cell differentiation research, biosynthetics processing), bioimaging and sensing, and drug delivery;

- Energy applications in catalysis and fuel cells (including bio-fuel cells) and solar cells;

- Manufacturing, scale-up technologies, and prototyping expertise, which can ultimately be a foundation for rapid prototyping at the nano level.

Stevens Institute of Technology has 25 faculty members, 22 graduate students, and eight involved in nanotechnology research from five different academic departments (Chemical, Biomedical & Materials Engineering; Chemistry & Chemical Biology; Physics & Engineering Physics; Civil, Environmental & Ocean Engineering; Mechanical Engineering). Several research centers also participate in nanotechnology, including the NJ Center for Micro-Chemical Systems, the Highly Filled Materials Institute, the Design and Manufacturing Institute, and the Center for Environmental Systems.

Stevens has $9 million in Federal grants, NJ Department of Environmental Protection (DEP) nano funding, and significant investment from the US Army Research Development and Engineering Center (ARDEC) for dual use applications. Several laboratories at Stevens support the nanotechnology research for dual use applications, including MicroChemical Lab, MicroDevice Lab, MicroParticle Characterization Lab, and Nano Imaging facility. Stevens has developed an interdisciplinary nanotechnology graduate program that spans five different academic departments. The program will soon be open to industry participants. External collaborators include Lucent, Cornell, MIT, ARDEC, Bristol=Myers Squibb (BMS), FMC Corporation (FMC), Sarnoff, University of Medicine and Dentistry of New Jersey (UMDNJ), mPHASE Technologies, etc.

Key focus areas funded at Stevens by the National Science Foundation include:

- Nanoscale processes in chem/bio-microreactors;

- Nanocomposites involving nanoparticle and structural synthesis, particularly in the use of nanoscale inclusions and surface-mediated assembly of polymers;

- Nanomaterials involving carbon nanotubes and high temperature applications;

- Micro- and Nanoelectromechanical Systems (MEMS/NEMS) devices for active structures, Radio Frequency (RF) switches, and nanomanipulators;

- Nanobio involved in sensor applications drawing on nanoelectronic and nanomaterials expertise;

- Environmental nanotechnology for pollutant treatment;

- Environmental fate, transport, and toxicological impact of organic and inorganic nanoparticles.

Rowan University has approximately eight faculty members and five graduate students involved in nanotechnology research from five different academic departments (Chemical Engineering, Chemistry, Electrical & Computer Engineering, Mechanical Engineering, Physics) working collaboratively on nanotechnology with researchers from Columbia University, Drexel University, University of Maryland-College Park, Washington University in St. Louis, India Institute of Technology in Delhi, and India Institute of Technology in New Delhi.

Rowan University has grants of more than $2.0 million through collaborations with the NSF Nanoscale Science & Engineering Center with Columbia, NSF Nanoscale Interdisciplinary Research Team with Columbia, NSF Focused Research Group with Drexel University, and Materials Science & Engineering Center with University of Maryland. Its nano-related equipment includes a scanning electron microscope (SEM) with e-beam writer 20 nm resolution, JEOL variable temperature atomic force microscope with scanning tunneling microscope, and nano-indenter External collaborators Three-One-Two, local start up.

It has developed a curriculum in Nanoelectronics.

Focused areas of activity in nanotechnology include:

• Nano-lithography involving nano stamping, patterned magnetic media, and masks for nanoimprint lithography;

• Nano-magnetics including electric transport magnetization, microwave resonance, magnetic ordering on electronic properties, and scanning property mapping techniques;

• Nanomaterials ranging from organic synthesis, synthesis of new materials by traditional and low-temperature methods molecular modeling, and novel applications of high-performance polymers.

Picatinny Arsenal's radiofrequency plasma reactor, the largest and first of its kind in North America, can produce a wide range of nano particles in sufficient quality and quantity to meet the product development and market assessment needs of commercial partners. A very significant federal investment went into this dual use facility (military and commercial uses). It has a highly trained staff, characterization equipment, and office space available for use by collaborators through the duration of joint projects. It plans to add equipment to ultimately be able to produce parts from nanocomposites.

Lucent Technologies, is the home of the New Jersey Nanotechnology Consortium (NJNC), which provides rapid and cost-effective access to nanotechnology research and development services for university researchers. The nucleus of the NJNC is the world-renowned Bell Labs nanofabrication laboratory in Murray Hill, along with the 1,000 Bell Labs scientists and researchers who are available to support the research of small nano-based businesses and university faculty. By combining fabrication capabilities of this lab with regional academic research institutions and universities, NJNC is able to carry out basic and applied nanotechnology research and help bring nanotechnology ideas from concept to commercialization.

The Lucent facility is a 20,000 square foot, $400 million, fully depreciated asset, which employs 30 full- and part-time, highly skilled staff. The ability for researchers using the facility to draw on the 1,000 Bell Lab scientists at the site in Murray Hill is as important to their success as the facility itself. At this time, the impact of Lucent's merger with Alcatel on future access of New Jersey researchers to the nanofacility is unknown.

The Mid Atlantic Nano Association (MANA) was formed in the Fall of 2004 as a unique tri-state, federally-funded initiative of New Jersey, Pennsylvania, and Delaware. MANA is focused on developing on-the-ground strategic alliances of industry and universities that can effectively position the tri-state region for leadership in nanotechnology, which will attract additional investment.

The founding members of MANA—the New Jersey Commission on Science and Technology, the Ben Franklin Technology Partners of Southeastern Pennsylvania, and the Delaware Technology Park—were successful in securing $300,000 start-up matching funds from the US Department of Commerce Economic Development Administration to create the nation's first multi-state nanotechnology initiative. Battelle's Technology Partnership Practice, a leading technology-based economic development consulting firm, was hired to assist the MANA partners.

The strategic MANA project is focused on having an impact on the region's nanotechnology development. The goal is to be able to identify opportunities for strategic alliances in nanotechnology based on competitive analysis, market potential, and availability of regional assets to accelerate commercialization and bring more federal nanotechnology research funding into New Jersey and the region. The region leads the nation in a number of areas:

The MANA region (New Jersey, Pennsylvania, and Delaware) ranks high in its ability to attract federal nanotechnology grants, demonstrating significant innovation, research, and commercial strength across the region. As the nation's first tri-state collaboration in nanotechnology, the region can have a significant competitive advantage attracting federal nanotechnology funding, since increased collaboration across disciplines and institutions is a key goal of the Federal Nanotechnology Initiative.

When the accomplishments of each of the states in the tri-state region are consolidated, the region has done very well attracting federal funding. Strategic collaborations in the future will improve on the current results:

- Second nationwide in nano-related patents
- Third in NSF nano-related grants
- Fourth in NIH nano-related grants

Nano-focused networking groups, like the Greater Garden State Nano Alliance and Strengthening the Mid-Atlantic Region for Tomorrow (SMART), are bringing together researchers, legislators, and large and small companies for discussions on nanotechnology research and market needs.

Short- and Long-Term Opportunities
For New Jersey In Nanotechnology

Areas of potential opportunity for New Jersey to grow jobs in nanotechnology are based on the State's assets, expertise, competitive advantage, and potential for commercialization. Both short-term and long-term opportunities for job growth exist, especially those that build on New Jersey's strengths in materials research and manufacturing.

New Jersey universities are recognized globally as "stars" in the field of materials research, which is the foundation of nanotechnology in everything from catalysts, composites and coatings for large, near-term (~5 year) markets like automotive and recreation to longer-term markets (10+ years) in energy, nano drug development and delivery, and bio materials. Combining the material science strengths of our universities with the market pull-through provided by New Jersey-based materials giants like BASF, Honeywell, and Engelhard and the pharmaceutical drive of companies like Johnson and Johnson, Merck, and Schering Plough provides a robust infrastructure and potential supply chain in nano based materials.

Building on New Jersey's global reputation in Advanced Materials and Manufacturing, major opportunities for the State's investment focus include:

Nano Prototyping and Manufacturing: The need to address the challenges of nanotechnology scale-up and manufacturing is critical to realizing the trillion dollar opportunity in nanotechnology. New Jersey has considerable strengths in this arena; there is little competition from other universities and significant potential for federal funding since this is a key NSF focus area for the nation. The translation of discovery to commercialization, often referred to as the "valley of death," includes the need for rapid prototyping, scale-up, and proof of concept.

Given the strength in nanomaterials found within the industrial sector in New Jersey, it is critical that there be a mechanism to move up the nano value chain and translate these nanomaterials into nano-enabled devices and products, where the major economic gains from nanotechnology will be realized. Investment in nano-prototyping and manufacturing could result in New Jersey becoming a leader in the precision and customized manufacturing processes involved in nanomanufacturing, and it could contribute to retention of 21st century manufacturing jobs, now lost to offshoring.

New Jersey possesses significant facilities to realize this nano-prototyping and manufacturing focus. The universities in New Jersey have existing facilities for nano-scale synthesis, characterization, and small-scale fabrication and processing, which provide a strong foundation for future investments. New Jersey also has specialized nano-related scale-up facilities with the presence of Picatinny's RF Plasma Reactor and the Lucent wafer facility.

The direction of rapid prototyping must be driven by market demand and be specific to application areas. No single, multi-user prototyping or manufacturing facility will meet the very different needs of the Bio-Pharma nano sector and those of optoelectronics, catalysis, energy, etc.

Bio-Nano: New Jersey has a significant advantage not only because the heart of the pharmaceutical industry is located here, but also because of our university research capacity in bio-materials and bio-pharma. Opportunities span novel nano-based drug delivery devices, including sustained or rapid release technologies and drug development with target specificity. Implants made of nano composite materials, which offer superior mechanical properties or tailored surface chemistry to reduce rejection, or release drugs are major long term opportunities.

Nano-based personal care products are currently the largest commercial applications of nanotechnology. Nano materials are being used in cosmetics and sunscreens along with anti-aging and moisturizing lotions, which are very effectively absorbed through the skin. This market is expected to grow significantly with the aging of baby boomers and increased concern over UV damage to the skin.

Other short-term (5 years) commercialization opportunities will most likely involve novel and more effective delivery of drugs currently on the market through nano-based devices and implants. New to the world, nano-drugs will have much longer lead times to commercialization. Engaging large pharma and medical device companies will be challenging, because of the large investments required to commercialize new technologies and the risks involved. Researchers and emerging small businesses will need to demonstrate their technology through prototypes, and provide animal and human data to demonstrate viability and safety before attracting many pharma companies to nano-based solutions.

The key advantage for New Jersey in nanobio is its established base of pharmaceutical and medical device companies. Tailoring unique scale-up, testing, and demonstration facilities may offer New Jersey a way to ensure that future nanobio activities can be rooted within the state and linked with clinical research activities underway at UMDNJ. While New Jersey has active research programs in bio-materials and nano-based drug delivery led by Rutgers, there is a significant need to ramp-up university strengths in this area to achieve the significant promise of nanobio. Partnering with both Pennsylvania and New York will enhance opportunities to conduct clinical trials.

Electronics and Photonics: Opportunities for displays, sensors and networks, MEMS/NEMS, data storage, and memory are significant, potentially long-term nanotechnology opportunities for New Jersey. Nano-electronics is an area to which New Jersey universities bring broad strengths and opportunities. All of the universities, from the major research universities like Princeton and Rutgers to the more focused research institutions like NJIT, Stevens Institute, and Rowan, have active programs.

However, many current opportunities are tied to telecom, so near-term markets are limited. In the long-term, New Jersey can maintain its traditional strengths and position itself for the next wave of commercial opportunities through investment. Princeton, working closely with Sarnoff, Lucent, and other emerging nano-based New Jersey companies and universities, can be at the head of the next generation of technology, which some envision as the replacement for electronics with optical technologies.

Clean Energy and the Environment including Catalysts: Major market potential in the near- and long-term includes catalysts, absorbents, batteries, fuel, and solar cells. Engelhard and BASF are leaders in nano-based catalysts for energy conversion, and New Jersey has a rich university base in materials upon which to build. Opportunities also exist for collaboration with MANA partners, especially the University of Delaware, which has one of the nation"s largest centers for energy-related research and catalysis.

With the escalating price of oil now routinely above $60 a barrel, the economic feasibility of alternative/clean energy sources rises as a clear market opportunity. Clean energy technologies—including solar power, fuel cells, microturbines, and wind power—accounted for less than $7 billion in 2000, and are forecasted to grow at more than 30% annually, reaching over $80 billion by 2010. What we can expect in the future is not one substitute for oil and natural gas, but a diversified energy future, with many technologies helping to meet our needs, including those based on nanotechnology.

In the area of alternative clean energy, New Jersey's strength is found more in its industry sector than in its university sector. At the industry level, New Jersey has a long history in petro-chemicals, and many potential industry partners exist, such as Degussa Metals Catalysts, Johnson-Matthey Fuel Cells, Headwaters NanoKinetix, Hydrocarbon Technologies (coal liquefaction), Philips Lighting, and Nano-Engineered Innovation. At the university level, New Jersey is not a leader in fuel cell or solar power research, though focused programs exist, such as the energy storage center at Rutgers, and several research teams across the state are working on solar power and fuel cells. This is an area in which New Jersey can make investments to help grow into an emerging market in collaboration with industry and its MANA partners.

Funding Opportunities for New Jersey in Nanotechnology

For New Jersey to achieve its potential in nanotechnology and grow our economic base, significant State investment in the near-term will be required.

Funds are needed to provide university researchers and small and medium sized businesses with facilities, equipment, and grant support to invent, develop, and commercialize nanobased technologies. In addition to physical facilities and equipment, investment needs to be made in student training and development of an infrastructure to enhance collaboration among researchers and corporations. Public and private funding that provides commercialization support will also be required. The areas in most need of investment are as follows:

1) Nanotechnology Multi-User Center(s) of Excellence: a collaborative, inter-university infrastructure for nano research, development, and commercialization targeted to the interests of New Jersey-based industry partners and in alignment with national priorities and Federal funding. The goals of the Center(s) go beyond basic research to economic development and job creation in New Jersey.

Funds are needed for new construction and/or renovation of existing space (clean room, laboratory, office, and public space) at one or more university locations through a competitive proposal process. No one nanotechnology facility will be able to support the range of opportunities for New Jersey described above. A "generic" facility will offer little advantage to federal funding agencies and corporate partners. The goal is to create state-of-the-art, fully equipped, multi-user nanotechnology facilities that build on university research strengths and bring value to New Jersey businesses as demonstrated by corporate investment and collaborative research.

2) A State Nano Equipment Fund: The equipment needed to support nanotechnology research in New Jersey universities and colleges will be costly, will include clean rooms, and will vary significantly based on the focus of the research. Although a laboratory researching biomaterials for improved artery stents and one developing improved composite materials for aerospace applications may share some characterization equipment, each research area will require specialized equipment that could also be available for use by emerging businesses and corporate researchers.

3) Faculty and Students: Attracting star faculty to New Jersey's universities will require sufficient funds for research, graduate students, and postdoctoral positions. High profile faculty experts can draw significant corporate and federal funding to their institutions.

4) Emerging Business Support: Angel support and venture capital is less available to New Jersey-based emerging businesses than those located in other states, such as California and Massachusetts. To keep the best and brightest in New Jersey, the State should provide some portion of the support that would be provided by a stronger in-state venture community.

Examples of possible State support:

- Commercialization grants for support at the end of a Small Business Innovation Research (SBIR) Phase 2, for scale-up, prototyping, assistance with clinical trials, etc;

- IP Fund for legal expenses to support nano patent applications and licensing university intellectual property;

- Subsidized Incubator rent and operational support for start-up companies developing nanotechnology based products;

- Business Fellowship support to include apprentice positions for graduating MBAs to work in nano-based companies for one to two years to assist in commercialization;

- Statewide Business Development/Mentoring Group, an assemblage of former corporate executives, venture capitalists, Wall Street market segment analysts, etc., who have networks into various corporations/market segments in NJ (Pharma, telelcom, etc.) and are committed to providing guidance and commercialization support to some of the State's top, emerging, nano-based technology businesses as referred through the New Jersey Commission on Science and Technology (NJCST), New Jersey Economic Development Authority (NJEDA), etc.

5) Matching Funds for Nanotechnology Research and Development at Universities and Emerging Businesses, a guarantee of matching State funds to significantly improve chances for third-party funding and increase federal grants in New Jersey.

6) Industrial Support/Angel guarantees, key, State-related entities involved in technology-based economic growth in New Jersey, such as the Office of Economic Growth, the New Jersey Commission on Science and Technology, the Economic Development Authority, the Commerce Commission, the Department of Labor, etc., which would work together to develop a portfolio of economic vehicles to incentivize investors in New Jersey companies that are commercializing nanotechnology.

Such economic vehicles might include:

• Tax credits for investors in nanotechnology-based businesses;

• An enhancement of Techniuum's angel investment guarantee for nano-technology (Techniuum is an NJ EDA initiative to attract technology companies to New Jersey.);

• Increased Net Operating Loss lifetime totals for nano businesses to $10 million;

• A state match at some predetermined level for eligible corporate investments in university research in nanotechnology;

• A relaxation in intellectual property licensing fees for nanotechnology developed within New Jersey universities but licensed to New Jersey businesses;

• A new Business Employment Incentive Program (BEIP) program for nano businesses (defined by having client contracts of a predetermined minimum revenue) that delays the need to pay payroll taxes (or places the tax revenues in a general nanofund to be used for low cost equipment loans, etc.) until a specific employee or revenue milestone is met;

• Aggressive support of immigration reform to encourage some of the best and the brightest US educated, immigrant nano scientists and engineers to remain in New Jersey.

Competitive State Investments in Nanotechnology

Funding to support research, technology development, prototyping, and commercialization is essential to reach New Jersey's potential in nanotechnology. Several other states have invested very significant funds to encourage nanotechnology economic development, particularly New York.

New York State is the national leader in the development of a statewide nanotechnology infrastructure to encourage economic development and increase high tech jobs. It has invested well over $700 million during the last five years, and received federal funding to create a nanotechnology center at the State University at Albany. The center, a research and development partnership between the University at Albany and corporations, is a model of corporate and university, state, and federal government collaboration. IBM and other New York-based businesses along with several out-of-state corporations have provided matching investments estimated to be well over a billion dollars. Honeywell has invested $5 million in Albany. Corporate researchers will share the space with faculty. New York is using the Center to lure other nano manufacturers to the region and has set its eyes on a semiconductor manufacturer.

This facility is largely an industry-driven asset with IBM, bringing major partners such as Samsung, Hitachi, and others into the center. The partners, in turn, are now bringing in their suppliers to build a supply chain cluster.

Arizona and California have each invested about $100 million in nanotechnology centers, research, and business support. The California Nanosystems Institute is a research center run jointly by UCLA and UC Santa Barbara. It was established in 2000 with $100 million from the State of California and an additional $250 million in federal research grants and industry funding. Its mission is to encourage university collaboration with industry, and enable the rapid commercialization of discoveries in nanosystems. Arizona raised $400 million through a voter initiative in 2000 that created a 0.6% sales tax increase for education. Nanotechnology, biotechnology, information technology, and manufacturing science will each receive $100 million. The 20-year initiative is estimated to provide $1 billion for infrastructure enhancement at three state universities in support of new economy jobs.

Our MANA partners, Pennsylvania and Delaware, have had little state investment to date. Ben Franklin Technology Partners of Southeastern Pennsylvania has established the Nanotechnology Institute with Drexel University and the University of Pennsylvania to focus on life science. Its mission is to focus on the transfer and commercialization of nanotechnology discoveries and knowledge to stimulate economic growth through support of multi-institutional/inter-disciplinary research and development, industry-focused R&D, entrepreneurial business development and commercialization, risk capital, workforce development, economic research, and community of interest networks. Pennsylvania approved $10.5 million in state funding in September 2000, and recently the Governor announced a desire to invest significantly in high technology leading to economic growth, including nanotechnology. Delaware has had no significant state investment in nanotechnology, but the University of Delaware is seen as a center of excellence in nano-based fuel cell technology.

A Summary of What Other States Have Invested
Additional information in Appendix IV

- **Arizona**—Arizona State University has directed approximately $100 million to nanotech activity;

- **California**—State provided $100 million for the California Nanosystems Institute;

- **Georgia**—Georgia Tech has requested $38 million for a nanotech research center;

- **Illinois**—State provided $36 million for construction of a building for the Center for Nanoscale Materials;

- **Maryland**—Governor proposed $2.5 million in operating funds for a University of Maryland nanotech research initiative;

- **Massachusetts**—State provided $5 million to the University of Massachusetts Lowell nanotech manufacturing center;

- **New York**—State has invested approximately $740 million over the past five years and has been able to leverage approximately $2.7 billion from industry partners and another $146 million from federal sources to support programs in Nanotechnology; new $435 million Institute for Nanoelectronics Discovery and Exploration (INDEX)—one of only two to be created in the nation—will be located at the Center of Excellence in Nanoelectronics at the State University at Albany; the center has attracted International Sematech, a consortium of the 12 major computer chip manufacturers, to enter into a state and industry partnership and invest $400 million over the next five years;

- **Ohio**—State has provided $22.5 million for a Wright Center of Innovation focused on nanotechnology, $4 million for a Biomedical Research and Tech Transfer Partnership award, and $5.3 million for three Wright Projects;

- **Oregon**—State has provided at least $21 million to the Oregon Nanoscience and Microtechnologies Institute;

- **Pennsylvania**—State provided $10.5 million for the Nanotechnology Institute.

Appendix I
The Impact of Nanotechnology On Current Markets[1]

Selected Product Categories	MANA Regional Position Today	2014 Sales Revenues Incorporating Nano-technology	Expected Developments
Specialty Chemicals, Materials, & Coatings	Significant Employment Strong Regional Specification	14%	Key gains in sales expected over 2005-2009 period, led by advances in coatings. Existing companies (directly or through partnerships) will dominate wide-scale introduction of nano-materials into marketplace.
Pharmaceuticals	Significant Employment Significant Regional Specialization	23%	Advance delivery of therapeutics with major impact in 2010-2014 period. Similar to biotech, Pharma outsourcing nano-research to universities and emerging companies.
Industrial Machinery	Significant Employment Not Regionally Concentrated	8%	Advanced nano-processing and other nano-tools are key areas for advancing new nanotech company formation. Nanotech tools market could exceed $2.7 B by 2014.
Industrial Electronics & Instruments	Very Large Employment Not Regionally Concentrated	75%	Logic chips patterned on nanolithography techniques, memory chips based on nanomaterials, nanostructured chip cooling systems, nanocomposite RF/EMI shielding. Key opportunity for nano-intermediates to arise in 2010-2014 period.
Paper Products Manufacturing	Very Large Employment Regionally Specialization	5%	Limited nanotech opportunity for conventional paper products—niche anti-reflective coatings and nano-particals enhanced bonding agents. Opportunity lies in creating new paper products such as papers coated with nanoscale poly-electrolytes for integrated sensor and printable electronics applications.
Medical Instruments & Equipment	Very Large Employment Regional Specialization	30%	Wide variety of nanocomposite materials, nanocoatings, nanosensors used in orthopedics, implants, and invasive instrument applications. Nanoparticle uses for enhanced imaging capabilities.
Consumer Electronics	Very Large Employment Regional Concentration	75%	Similar to Industrial Electronics & Instruments.
Automotive	Large Employment Not Regionally Concentrated	21%	Nanocomposites/nanocoatings already used today on specific vehicles. Will be applied across product lines as prices decline with volume. Assessment does not include use of carbon black in tires or impact on vehicle electronics.
Computers	Large Employment Not Regionally Concentrated	37%	New nanolithography techniques will be required to sustain the semiconductor historical price/performance curves. All-leading edge, integrated circuits introduced from 2007 onward will be patterned with these techniques. The products they power will thus be considered nano-enabled products downstream in the value chain.
Other Land-Based Transportation Equipment (e.g., military vehicles, rail cars)	Large Employment Significant Regional Concentration	25%	Nanocoatings, polymer fuel cell components, high temperature superconducting wires for motors, nano-particulate fuel additives, and nanosensors. Non-cost sensitive markets will find other uses in highly valued structural and surface applications
Battery and Fuel Cells	Significant Regional Specialization	33%	All PEM fuel cells represent nanotech applications due to the use of nanostructured catalyst materials. Batteries will eventually be impacted by super capacitor alternatives using nano-structured materials. Solar/photovoltaic cells have seen nanotech-enabled products coming to market in 2006.

[1] **Information Supplied by Lux Research**

Appendix II

What is Nanotechnology?

Nanotechnology is the science of creating and building with materials about the size of a nanometer—a human hair is 80,000 nanometers wide. Nanotech can be applied to a wide range of uses—from helping tennis balls keep their bounce to keeping soldiers safe from biohazards.

Today, there is a growing number of commercial applications based on nanotechnology, which include cosmetics and sunscreens, non-reflective eyeglass coatings, catalysts that increase energy output from fuels, and composite materials used in automotive bumpers. However, recent progress in the measurement, modeling, and ability to manipulate matter at the molecular level, atom by atom, to create large structures with fundamentally new properties and functions, will be revolutionary and change not only our most technology based industries, but also humankind's fundamental understanding of matter.

The Commercialization Model

It is expected that the introduction of nanotechnology into the marketplace will, most likely, first involve a mix of the existing product lines of major corporations and the offerings of start-up companies, often in focused niches, offering innovative tools and furthering research and development for specific new product advances.

Second, the demands of success in many important fields have changed. Scientific excellence in emerging fields like nanotechnology demand interdisciplinary collaboration and "Big Science" investments. Achieving the critical mass of capabilities and resources required to support productive R&D in these fields demands the combined efforts of multiple institutions.

A third development is the changing demands of industrial innovation, in which companies are moving away from a reliance on internal R&D and seeking broader sources for innovation across universities, other firms, and federal research labs—a phenomenon referred to as "open innovation." With open innovation the level of collaboration between universities and local industry becomes critical for advancing technology innovation in a specific area.

Appendix III

Federal Investments

The National Nanotechnology Initiative (NNI)

The National Nanotechnology Initiative is a multi-agency US Government program aimed at accelerating the discovery, development, and deployment of nanoscale science, engineering, and technology. The purpose of the initiative is to accelerate discovery and deployment of nanotechnology, expand knowledge, strengthen the economy, support national and homeland security, and enhance the quality of life for all citizens.

The vision of the NNI is a future in which the ability to understand and control matter on the nanoscale leads to a revolution in technology and industry, highlighting areas of focus for Federal funding and how they relate to opportunities for NJ.

The goals are to maintain a world-class research and development program, to facilitate technology transfer, to develop educational resources and a skilled workforce supplied with an infrastructure and tools, and to support the responsible development of nanotechnology.

The NNI budget grew from $464 million in 2001 to $1.05 billion in 2006. Eleven agencies have nano R&D budgets with most investment by National Science Foundation, Department of Defense, Department of Energy, National Institutes of Health, and National Institute for Standards and Technology.

- Fundamental Nanoscale Phenomena and Processes ($234 million)
- Nanomaterials ($228 million)
- Nanoscale Devices and Systems ($244 million)
- Instrumentation Research, Metrology, and Standards for Nanotechnology ($71 million)
- Nanomanufacturing ($47 million)
- Major Research Facilities and Instrumentation Acquisitions ($148 million)
- Societal Dimensions ($82 million)

Nanotechnology Centers-USA

Department of Energy Nanoscale Science User and R&D Centers

Five user facilities, called the Nanoscale Science Research Centers (NSRCs), are now under construction at national laboratories supported by the Department of Energy. The research facilities will focus on synthesis, processing, and fabrication of nanoscale materials. They will be co-located with existing user facilities to provide sophisticated characterization and analysis capabilities.

Specialized equipment and support staff will be available to the research community, where access will be determined by peer review of proposals. Those listed below were conceived with broad input from university and industry user communities in order to define the scope of the equipment suite within each facility. They have been reviewed by external peers and by DOE's Basic Energy Sciences Advisory Committee.

National Institute of Standards and Technology (NIST) User Centers

Considered the most technically advanced research facility of its kind in the world, the new Advanced Measurement Laboratory (AML), dedicated on June 21, 2004 at the Commerce Department's National Institute of Standards and Technology (NIST), will support some of the world's most delicate experiments in nanotechnology and measurement at the atomic level. Commerce General Counsel and Deputy Secretary Designate Theodore W. Kassinger, Sen. Paul Sarbanes (D-MD.), Rep. Chris Van Hollen (D-MD.) and Dr. John H. Marburger III, Director of the White House Office of Science and Technology Policy, were among the participants in the formal opening ceremony at the NIST campus in Gaithersburg, MD.

The $235 million, 49,843 square meter (536,507 square foot) laboratory features five separate wings—two of them buried 12 meters (39 feet) underground—with stringent environmental controls on air quality, temperature, vibration, and humidity. The new facility allows NIST to provide the sophisticated measurements and standards needed by US industry and the scientific community for key 21st century technologies such as nanotechnology, semiconductors, biotechnology, advanced materials, quantum computing, and advanced manufacturing.

NIST research efforts planned for the new facility range from improved calibrations and measurement of fundamental quantities, such as mass, length, and electrical resistance, to the development of quantum computing technology, nanoscale measurement tools, integrated microchip-level technologies for measuring individual biological molecules, and experiments in nanoscale chemistry.

The NIST Center for Neutron Research (NCNR) serves more than 1,700 scientists annually from industry, university, and government agencies. The NCNR is the only cold (i.e. low energy) neutron facility with comprehensive capability in the United States, providing tools essential to study the complex biological, polymeric, and composite materials that are at the forefront of nanomaterials research.

Appendix IV

Competitive States, Their Investments and Their Strategies[2]

[2] Some of this information provided by State Science and Technology Institute

The following is an overview of some of the largest and most recent efforts by states other than New Jersey to support and advance nanotechnology. The summary includes information about research centers that these states have funded, initiatives they have undertaken, groups created to support nanotech, and reports prepared to examine the state of nanotechnology.

Arizona

Proposition 301, a voter initiative that passed in 2000, created a 0.6% sales tax increase for the purpose of enhancing education in Arizona. A portion of this 20-year initiative, estimated at $1 billion, provides for infrastructure enhancement at the three state universities in support of new economy jobs in Arizona. At Arizona State University

(ASU), this $400 million state investment is focused on biotechnology, nanotechnology, information technology, and manufacturing science.

The initiative started in State Fiscal Year 2002. An Arizona Biodesign Institute (AzBio) was created in 2002 for the purpose of integrating new advances in biotechnology with that of nanotechnology and info-technology.

Combining the 301 initiative and ASU's commitment, the Arizona Biodesign Institute's total investment over the next five years is estimated to be $200 million ($140 million for two new buildings) and approaching $500 million over 10 years. Approximately $100 million of this investment is specifically coupled to nanotechnologies.

Additional investments in specific nanotechnology activities include Proposition 301 Materials/Nanotechnologies seed funding and equipment matches at approximately $0.5 million per year for shared user fabrication and characterization facilities at ASU (the Center for Solid State Electronics Research and the Center for Solid State Science), and upcoming seed investments in nanoelectronics and in sensing.

Arkansas

In 2005, during a visit to the Arkansas Research & Technology Park, US Senator Mark Pryor (D-Ark.) announced formation of the Arkansas Nanotech Alliance. Pryor will chair the statewide consortium, bringing together "universities, federal agencies, and private sector partners to develop, launch, and nurture nanotechnology initiatives."

He said that, in building an Arkansas nanotechnology community, some of the possibilities include:

- Establishing an information base, serving as a nanotechnology "clearinghouse" for regular news, funding updates, and user services;

- Developing inter-institutional and inter-departmental research proposals to enhance federal funding and establish Arkansas as a major nanotechnology research center;

- Linking industry to nanotechnology research performed in the state, thereby enabling technology transfer, commercialization, and economic development;

- Setting up open access research instrumentation centers for universities and industries;

- Reaching out to the nanotechnology community by co-sponsoring scientific, educational, and business meetings and conferences.

No other members of the Alliance were identified in Pryor's announcement, and the March 24, 2005 issue of the Arkansas Democrat-Gazette reported, "No federal funding is associated with the alliance - yet, Pryor said."

California

The California Nanosystems Institute (CNSI) is a research center run jointly by UCLA and UC Santa Barbara. CNSI was established in 2000 with $100 million from the State of California and an additional $250 million in federal research grants and industry funding. Its mission is to encourage university collaboration with industry and enable the rapid commercialization of discoveries in nanosystems.

Groups

Several promotion and networking groups are very active including:

- NanoBioConvergence;
- MIT-Stanford-Berkeley Nanotech Forum in Northern California;
- NanoBioNexus in San Diego;
- Northern California Nanotechnology Initiative (regional).

Reports

A Blue Ribbon Task Force on Nanotechnology issued a report titled "Thinking Big About Thinking Small: An Action Agenda for California," which urges California to act quickly or risk losing its nanotech edge to other states and nations. The report, commissioned by state controller Steve Westly and Rep. Mike Honda, proposes actions including:

- Offer a "state income tax holiday" and sales-tax exemptions to nanotech investors and firms;

- Provide matching funds to nano-research enterprises;

- Seek federal funds to bankroll in-state nanotech initiatives;

- Make it easier to license and market California-developed nano-related products;

- Retrain mid-career professionals for the nanotech industry;

- Mandate science-math instruction in K-12 schools at a minimum of one hour a day;

- Monitor possible safety and environmental hazards of nanotechnologies. A report from the California Council on Science and Technology, titled "Nanoscience and Nanotechnology: Opportunities and Challenges in California 2004," provides an analysis of numerous aspects of nanotechnology, including, among others, its economic impact; affected scientific disciplines; commercial best practices; workforce development issues and social and ethical issues. The report issues options for California's state officials and congressional delegation to maintain and enhance California's nanotechnology competitiveness.

Connecticut

In July 2005, Governor M. Jodi Rell signed Special Act 05–13 to help create higher education degree programs in nanotechnology. The law requires Connecticut's Commissioner of Higher Education, in consultation with the Office of Workforce Competitiveness, to review the inclusion of nanotechnology, molecular manufacturing, and advanced and developing technologies at institutions of higher education. A report on their findings was due to the legislature by January 1, 2006.

Georgia

Georgia Tech sought state funding of $38 million toward a new nanotechnology research center, when the Georgia Legislature went into session in January 2006. Andrew Harris, director of Government Relations, indicated in an article in the alumni newsletter that the state legislature had already allocated $7 million for planning and design of the facility, and that university officials were optimistic the governor would recommend funding the remainder of the state's $45 million share of the nanotechnology research center. He described the effort as an $80 million project, and said that Georgia Tech would raise $35 million privately.

Illinois

Illinois AtomWorks coalition was one of the earliest and best known nanobusiness initiatives in the country. It was initiated by The Illinois Coalition, a private/public partnership of the Illinois Department of Commerce, the Chicago Mayor's Office, and numerous corporate leaders. The organization serves as a clearinghouse of nanotechnology information, provides nanotechnology education, increases public awareness of nanotechnology's potential benefits, builds a community of interest for individuals and companies involved in nanotechnology, and develops networks of resources on behalf of those trying to commercialize nanotech innovations. It is currently creating an asset-inventory database of local infrastructure to support the nanotech community, establishing research and industry forums to address current issues, and building an online nanotechnology information hub. It plans to investigate the feasibility of a nanotechnology business park for the region, identify solutions to early-stage funding requirements of nanotech start-up companies, and attract national nanotechnology conferences to the region.

Illinois Research Centers

The Center for Nanoscale Materials (CNM) at Argonne National Laboratory is a joint partnership between the US Department of Energy (DOE) and the State of Illinois, as a part of DOE's Nanoscale Science Research Center program. The state provided $36 million for the CNM building. The CNM serves as a user-based center, providing tools and infrastructure for nanoscience and nanotechnology research. The CNM's mission includes supporting basic research and developing advanced instrumentation that will help generate new scientific insights and create new materials with novel properties.

The University of Illinois's Micro and Nanotechnology Laboratory (MNTL) for semiconductor, nanotechnology, and biotechnology research will grow due to an $18 million expansion project that paves the way for new bionanotechnology facilities and additional space for researchers. The money for this expansion is part of a state grant to the university that is funding construction of the Institute for Genomic Biology (IGB) and the new National Center for Supercomputing Applications (NCSA) facility. The MNTL expansion project, which was scheduled for completion in 2006, adds 45,000 square feet of space for offices, general-purpose laboratories, and a 3,000 square foot bionanotechnology laboratory.

The website of the Illinois governor's office provides links to several Illinois research centers, including:

- The Beckman Institute for Advanced Science and Technology - University of Illinois;
- Micro and Nanotechnology Laboratory - University of Illinois;
- Institute for Nanotechnology - Northwestern University;
- The James Franck Institute - University of Chicago;
- Nano-CEMMS (Center for Nanoscale Chemical-Electrical-Mechanical Manufacturing Systems), an NSF-sponsored center for nanoscale science and engineering.

Maryland

The Chesapeake Nanotech Initiative (CNI) is a collaborative effort between Maryland, Virginia, and the District of Columbia to accelerate the development of innovative products and entrepreneurial businesses in nanotechnology in the region. On May 31, 2005, Maryland Governor Robert L. Ehrlich, Jr., Virginia Governor Mark R. Warner, and District of Columbia Mayor Anthony A. Williams agreed to sign a memorandum of agreement to form CNI. The Initiative was being launched by the Maryland Department of Business & Economic Development, Virginia 's Center for Innovative Technology, and the DC Office of the Deputy Mayor for Planning and Economic Development.

CNI is raising funds from the State of Maryland, the Commonwealth of Virginia, the federal government, and other sources.

Maryland Research Centers

Governor Ehrlich's FY 2007 Science & Technology Budget calls for $2.5 Million in new operating funds for a University System of Maryland Nanotechnology research initiative to encourage joint nano-biotechnology business development in Maryland and to develop nanobio science in specific medical areas, such as drug delivery, gene therapy, medical devices, and coatings where nanotechnology has a direct application.

Massachusetts

Research Centers

In 2004, the University of Massachusetts Lowell Nanotechnology Manufacturing Center was awarded $5 million under the state's economic stimulus package and the John Adams Innovation Institute. The award went toward the creation of a statewide Center of Excellence at the Nanomanufacturing Center. The matching grant came from the economic stimulus package, which created the $20 million University Investment Fund managed by the John Adams Innovation Institute, a division of the quasi-public economic development agency called the Massachusetts Technology Collaborative. The center is seen as a test facility for nanotechnology manufacturers that might serve to take small-scale breakthroughs at a billionth of a meter from the lab to the factory.

Reports

Although Massachusetts' universities may be at the fore of nanotechnology research and development, they must continue to win on research for the state to stay competitive for federal funds, according to a recent report by the Massachusetts Technology Collaborative (MTC) and the Nano Science and Technology Institute (NSTI). Massachusetts is experiencing a surge in nanoscale technologies, according to Nanotechnology In Massachusetts. As of February 2004, close to 100 companies in the state were using or developing the technologies, half of which are within the healthcare and electronics industries. Massachusetts' venture capital community also has invested in companies using or developing nanotech. In 2003, these firms attracted more than $120 million in funding, second only to California's $480 million. The report cites nine Massachusetts universities involved in nanotech R&D, including Harvard University, the Massachusetts Institute of Technology, and the University of Massachusetts campuses. Additionally, two of the nine National Nanotechnology Initiative Centers and Networks of Excellence are located in the state.

For Massachusetts to remain competitive in nanotech R&D domestically and abroad, the report argues, the state's universities must continue producing the innovations that have made the state a leader.

Initiatives

The Massachusetts Nanotechnology Initiative is a project of the Massachusetts Technology Collaborative to foster research, new ventures, and new job creation from the Commonwealth's base of nanoscale science and engineering. The website includes information on major nanotech research centers in Massachusetts and shared use resources for researchers and entrepreneurs.

Michigan

In 2002, the state helped launch the Michigan Small Tech Association (MISTA) as a promotion and networking group. The MISTA is a community of companies, universities, and individuals involved in or supporting micro and nanotechnology development in Michigan. Its goal is to promote acceleration of the industry through research, commercialization, and the fostering of business relationships.

New York

New York has a series of programs to bolster university research and encourage the commercialization of the technology developed as a result of these programs. The state has funded a variety of nanotechnology projects through these programs; unfortunately, funding just for the nanotech projects is not available.

The Centers of Excellence Program, through Empire State Development (the state's economic development agency), supports major upgrades of research facilities and other high technology and biotechnology capital projects, allowing colleges, universities, and research institutions to secure research funding that will lead to new job creation. The program received $250 million in FY2003. One of five funded centers, the Center of Excellence in Nanoelectronics (http://www.albanynanotech.org/Programs/nanotech_centers.cfm) is focused on nanotechnology. The goal of the center, according to its website, "is to act as a world class center for pre-competitive and competitive technology deployment, quick turn-around prototyping, and workforce training and development using universal 200mm and 300mm wafer platforms. Its aim is to assemble the critical mass necessary for the creation of vertically and horizontally integrated industry-university consortia and public-private partnerships to convert long-term prospective innovations into real business opportunities and revenue-generating ventures within a technically aggressive and economically competitive technology development and deployment environment."

The Strategically Targeted Academic Research (STAR) Centers receive "financing for the design, acquisition, construction, reconstruction, rehabilitation or improvement of research and development facilities, including equipment." Of the eight STAR centers, one is focused on nanotechnology. The Nanoelectronics and Optoelectronics Research and Technology Center at the University at Albany and Rensselaer Polytechnic Institute "will serve as a fully integrated, long-term, visionary research and development resource that provides the science and technology base for future generations of integrated circuitry (IC)."

The Centers for Advanced Technology (CAT) program brings university and industry researchers together to develop new technologies and commercialize these developments. The program is designed to result in new products and processes, create new businesses, and, ultimately, high-quality, high-value jobs. Of the 15 CATs, one is focused on nanotechnology, the Center for Advanced Technology in Nanomaterials and Nanoelectronics.

Additionally, in January 2006, then-Governor Pataki and legislative leaders announced that they would allocate $80 million to support a $435 million nanotechnology center to be built in Albany. The center, the Institute for Nanoelectronics Discovery and Exploration (INDEX), will also include the Georgia Institute of Technology, Harvard University, the Massachusetts Institute of Technology, Purdue University, Rensselaer Polytechnic Institute, and Yale University. INDEX will focus on the development of nanomaterial systems; atomic-scale fabrication technologies; predictive modeling protocols for devices, subsystems and systems; power dissipation management designs; and realistic architectural integration schemes for realizing novel magnetic and molecular quantum devices. In addition to the state support, INDEX will receive direct funding from IBM.

North Carolina

In 1998 the major research universities, Duke, UNC, and NC State, formed a joint research consortium called NC Center for Nanoscale Materials. NCCNM received primary funding from the Office of Naval Research Multidisciplinary University Research Initiative. From this consortium has arisen a number of small companies, which are now strong patent producers and magnets for nanoscience SBIR grants.

Ohio

Research Centers and Projects

Ohio's Third Frontier Initiative includes grants to support large-scale, world-class research and technology development platforms designed to accelerate the pace of commercialization through the Wright Centers of Innovation. Wright Centers are collaborations among higher education institutions, nonprofit research organizations, and Ohio companies. In FY 05, the state provided $22.5 million to the Ohio State University for the Ohio Center for Multifunctional Nanomaterials and Devices, which focuses on research, development, and commercialization of nanocomposites, polymer-based biomedical devices, and polymer photonics.

The Biomedical Research and Commercialization Program has awarded $4 million since FY 02 for a Targeted Nanoparticles for Imaging Therapeutics Project at Case Western Reserve University. In addition, the state has awarded $5.3 million for three Wright Projects to support near-term commercialization projects requiring major capital acquisitions and improvements at Ohio higher education institutions and nonprofit research organizations.

Oklahoma

The Oklahoma Nanotech Initiative (ONI) is a project established in 2004, and coordinated by the State Chamber of Oklahoma and funded by the Oklahoma Center for the Advancement of Science and Technology (OCAST), Oklahoma'stechnology-based economic development agency.

ONI's main objectives include:

• Generating awareness of the emerging field of nanotechnology and educating Oklahomans about the potential impact of the industry on the state;

• Promoting Oklahoma and its resources as a valuable site for industry location;

• Serving as an information hub for the academic, financial, industrial, and business communities.

Research Centers

The University of Oklahoma's Center for Semiconductor Physics in Nanostructures (C-SPIN) announced receipt of a six-year, $7.8 million National Science Foundation grant in 2005. In a collaborative effort with the University of Arkansas, the center conducts research in semiconductor nanodevices. Its focus is on developing novel nanoferroelectric materials that will increase the limits of optical resolution, advance handheld wireless devices, and provide inexpensive memory that is fast, flexible, scalable, low-power, and nonvolatile, according to OU physics professor Matthew Johnson.

The NSF grant is supported by matching funds from OU and UA as well as the Oklahoma State Regents for Higher Education and the Arkansas state government, making the total funding close to $12 million. The OU/UA grant renews funding for C-SPIN, which previously received an award in 2000. Funding for C-SPIN also includes outreach to community high schools and grade schools, teachers and students, and national laboratories and businesses. C-SPIN provides teaching kits to area schools and laboratories as well as a number of museums in Oklahoma. One of the program's goals is to educate society on the understanding of scientific methods, experiments, logic, and research, and implications for future technological and medical developments.

Oregon

State government authorized $21 million in 2003, with an additional $7 million in the governor's subsequent FY 05 biennial budget proposal, to launch the Oregon Nanoscience and Microtechnologies Institute (ONAMI) targeted at fundamental and translational research for industrial applications, with significant support from Hewlett-Packard and other Oregon companies.

According to its website, The Oregon Nanoscience and Microtechnologies Institute is Oregon's first "Signature Research Center" for the purpose of growing research and commercialization to accelerate innovation-based economic development in Oregon and the Pacific Northwest. It is a collaboration involving Oregon's three public research universities (Oregon State University, Portland State University, University of Oregon); the Pacific Northwest National Laboratory; the state of Oregon; selected researchers from the Oregon Graduate Institute and the Oregon Health and Sciences University; and the "Silicon Forest" high technology industry cluster of Oregon and southwest Washington.

Pennsylvania

The Nanotechnology Institute (NTI) is a collaboration led by Ben Franklin Technology Partners of Southeastern Pennsylvania, Drexel University, and The University of Pennsylvania. Its mission is to focus on the transfer and commercialization of nanotechnology discoveries and knowledge to stimulate economic growth through:

- Multi-Institutional/Inter-Disciplinary Research & Development to facilitate the transfer and commercialization of discoveries and intellectual knowledge that support rapid application of nanotechnology to the life sciences sector and the creation of new enterprises around this technology;

- A Comprehensive Approach requiring the strategic alignment of six programmatic areas: Industry-Focused Research & Development, Entrepreneurial

Business Development & Commercialization, Risk Capital, Workforce Development, Economic Research, and Community of Interest Networks.

$10.5 million in state funding was approved in September 2000. According to the NTI website, "the NTI research management's stress on outcomes has resulted in a disclosure rate per research dollar of seven times that of the individual institutions."

Texas

Texas has two organizations focused on promoting nanotechnology:

• Nanotechnology Foundation of Texas (NFT) describes itself as a research initiative funded by tax-deductible donations from individuals, corporations, and foundations. The Foundation's purpose is to accelerate nanotechnology research in Texas by: providing funding to help current nanotechnology researchers expand their fields of investigation; sponsoring annual Nano Summit conferences to encourage collaboration among Texas nanotechnology researchers, and to educate both Texans and those outside the state about the research being done in Texas in order to develop broader funding sources for Texas research; and recruiting the most qualified graduate students and post-doctoral researchers into the field of nanotechnology.

• Texas Nanotechnology Initiative states, "the best general description for TNI is as a state-wide industry trade group for nanotechnology. We will act to further the interests of our members through networking, education, and communication in order to promote the steady growth of a robust nanotechnology community in Texas." The organization "is dedicated to establishing Texas as a world leader in the discovery, development, and commercialization of nanotechnology. We have organized a consortium of Texas-based universities, industry leaders, investors, and government officials in order to foster communication, collaboration, and the sharing of resources to accelerate the realization of our goal."

Virginia

To develop and promote higher education research facilities and faculty in Virginia, Gov. Mark Warner proposed $218.8 million in his fiscal year 2006-08 biennial budget proposal for investment in university R&D. In response, state institutions of higher education have pledged to match the governor's proposal with a $299 million commitment.

The funding allows for the hiring of top researchers in the fields of biomedical science, biomaterials engineering, nanotechnology, and modeling and simulation, whose presence will attract more grant-funded research to the Commonwealth, according to the governor's office. In addition to having economic benefits, the initiative invests in the search for cures for cancer, diabetes, tuberculosis, and Alzheimer and Parkinson's diseases, the governor said.

The Virginia Nanotechnology Initiative (VNI), initiated in 2002 as InanoVA, with seed funding from CIT Group and has remained a program within CIT to work with Virginia's universities, federal laboratories, state agencies, and industrial partners to promote collaborative nanotechnology research, workforce development, technology transfer, and commercialization. CIT will also play an active role in the Chesapeake Nanotechnology Initiative, but VNI will remain as a CIT program, continuing its role in advocacy, collaboration, and education.

Washington

The Washington Nanotechnology Initiative was created in 2004. The University of Washington had already received over $200 million in nanotechnology-related research awards. Washington State University and the Pacific Northwest National Laboratories Environmental Molecular Sciences Laboratory were also among the earliest institutions nationally funded for pioneering research. In 2003, the Washington Technology Center, Pacific Northwest National Laboratories, Avogadro Partners LLC, and scientists from the state's research universities came together to assess how to best take advantage of the developing nanotechnology opportunity. Seed financing for a formal assessment came through an Economic Development Initiative (EDI) grant from the department of Housing and Urban Development (HUD) in FY 2004. The result was the Washington Nanotechnology Initiative (WNI). The WNI Action Agenda includes:

- Establish new programs in each of Washington's key nano-affected industries;

- Recruit high profile technologists to research and commercial organizations;

- Recruit a facilitator to develop a collaborative, interactive, statewide nanotech community and assure recognition and visibility worldwide;

- Create applied development centers focused on nanotechnology processes, fabrication, product development, and support services;

- Develop and fund an integrated nanotechnology research agenda at Washington universities;

- Develop training programs to assure the state's workforce has the nanotechnology skills when needed.

Wisconsin

In 2004 Governor Jim Doyle called for creation of a new $375 million research institute called the Wisconsin Institute for Discovery at the University of

Wisconsin-Madison. The Institute was proposed to include specialists in biochemistry, nanotechnology, computer engineering, and bioinformatics. The public-private Institute is intended to enable researchers to exercise their independence to convert their discoveries into commercial ventures that will create jobs. The Governor said it will be built and financed over 10 years, with support from state and private funds totaling $375 million. The first phase of the project will use approximately $50 million already set aside for BioStar IV.

Earlier in 2004, Governor Doyle signed legislation to fuel the process of turning ideas into jobs by leveraging over $250 million of venture capital to help start-up companies grow. When announcing the Institute for Discovery, the Governor also directed the Department of Commerce to make those resources available to companies that emerge from the Institute for Discovery.

The university incorporated the proposed institute into its master plan issued in 2005.

CHAPTER NINE

Cardiovascular Disease in New Jersey: Review of Current Strategies and Opportunities

By
Mary Ellen Cook and Joel Cantor

Introduction

Cardiovascular disease (CVD), also known as heart and blood vessel disease, is the leading cause of death in the United States and in New Jersey. In 2003 alone, over 26,000 New Jerseyans died from heart disease and stroke combined (NJDHSS Center for Health Statistics, 2005). More than 70 million Americans suffer from heart disease, accounting for approximately one quarter of the entire US population. (US Department of Health and Human Services, 2005). Cardiovascular disease is broad-based and can affect individuals from many different backgrounds, ages, races, and lifestyles. Risk factors for cardiovascular disease are varied, but many are reducible.

In order to address reducible risks, the State of New Jersey employs a broad range of strategies focused on cardiovascular disease and preventive services. The State has implemented several interventions, pilot studies, and policy-related activities to improve overall cardiovascular health. State resources also fund governmental and non-governmental organizations to address cardiovascular disease as well as surveillance programs to ensure that consumers of cardiovascular health care are receiving the best possible medical intervention and preventive services. The State also publishes an annual Cardiac Surgery Report and Hospital Performance Report, providing consumers with extensive information on cardiovascular disease care in the State's hospitals.

- Commissioned by the New Jersey Department of Health and Senior Services, this report:
- Provides an overview of cardiovascular disease in the United States and New Jersey;
- Reviews New Jersey's current approach to addressing cardiovascular health;
- Identifies innovative strategies for addressing cardiovascular disease as employed by other states;
- Outlines options for strengthening New Jersey's approach.

For the purposes of this report, we use a broad definition of cardiovascular disease, unless otherwise noted. This definition includes peripheral vascular disease, stroke (both ischemic and hemorrhagic), hypertension, angina, myocardial infarction, and congestive heart failure.

Overview of Cardiovascular Disease

Cardiovascular disease can be broken down into two major categories: coronary artery disease and cerebrovascular disease. Characteristics of each of these are varied. Coronary artery disease occurs as the result of the restriction of blood flow through the arteries that supply the heart muscle. This can lead to angina, acute myocardial infarction (commonly referred to as heart attack), arrhythmias, congestive heart failure, and, ultimately, cardiac arrest. (American Heart Association, 2005). Cerebrovascular disease results from either occlusion or hemorrhage of an artery supplying an area of the brain, which can lead to stroke. Stroke is defined as a sudden impairment of the brain resulting from interruption of circulation to any of its parts. (US Department of Health and Human Services, 2003). Detected and treated promptly, some individuals can make a full recovery from these circulatory system conditions, but there is also the potential of impairment or even death as a result of cardiovascular disease.

There are many risk factors for cardiovascular disease. Gender plays a role in the incidence of cardiovascular disease with men having a greater risk of heart attack. Age is also related to cardiovascular disease; over 83% of people who die from cardiovascular disease are over the age of 65. (US Department of Health and Human Services, 2003). There are also large differences in rates of cardiovascular disease by other demographic characteristics. For example, African American males are more likely to suffer from cardiovascular disease then their white counterparts. However, it is not clear the extent to which cultural factors, genetics, discrimination, or other factors contribute to demographic disparities. In addition, socioeconomic status is linked with an individual's ability to access affordable, quality health care services, another factor that must be accounted for when analyzing race as a risk factor for cardiovascular disease.

Many major risk factors for cardiovascular disease can be addressed through lifestyle changes and/or medication. Potentially modifiable risk factors identified by the American Heart Association (AHA) are shown in Table 1. The risk factors associated with an increased susceptibility to stroke are similar to those for cardiovascular disease, including hypertension, tobacco use, high blood cholesterol, physical inactivity and obesity, diabetes, and excessive alcohol use. Risk factors specific to stroke, according to the American Stroke Association, are described in Table 2.

Table 1: Risk Factors Associated with Coronary Artery Disease

Risk Factor	Definition
Tobacco Use	The AHA notes that the use of tobacco products increases a person's likelihood of contracting some form of cardiovascular disease by two to four times that of nonsmokers. Often, sudden cardiac arrest is associated with smoking for individuals who suffer from heart disease.
High Blood Cholesterol	As an individual's blood cholesterol level increases, so does the risk of heart disease. This risk factor in combination with any of the others mentioned can greatly increase the likelihood of a heart attack.
Hypertension	Hypertension, also termed high blood pressure, causes the heart to work harder than necessary to pump blood through the body. During this process, the increased workload of the heart can cause the heart to become stiffer and thicker. (American Heart Association, 2005). Again, in combination with other risk factors, the risk of heart disease increases with the detection of high blood pressure.
Physical Inactivity	Physical inactivity is another contributor to heart disease that plagues the United States. Physical inactivity can lead an individual to be overweight or obese, or to suffer from hypertension and stress. Rigorous exercise decreases the risk of heart disease and works to eliminate other risk factors.
Obesity and Overweight	Excess weight increases an individual's risk of contracting heart disease. The National Health and Nutrition Examination Survey, administered between 1999 and 2000, found that more than 64% of all adults in the United States are either overweight or obese. (American Heart Association, 2005). The risk associated with weight gain increases when fat build-up is located in the middle portion of the body.
Diabetes Mellitus	Diabetes greatly increases an individual's risk of heart disease, even when blood sugar levels are kept under control.
Alcohol Consumption	Excessive alcohol consumption increases the risk of heart disease. However, 1.5 fluid ounces of 80-proof spirits per day for women and two per day for men have been associated with a lower risk of cardiovascular disease. (North American Association for the Study of Obesity, 2005). Although the American Heart Association recognizes that controlled alcohol use does lower the risk of cardiovascular disease, the AHA does not recommend that non-drinkers begin to drink or that current drinkers increase their alcohol intake.
Stress	Life stress can add greatly to an individual's risk for heart disease. Stress can lead to high blood pressure and contribute to other risk factors such as overeating or smoking. Stress is more likely to occur in combination with physical inactivity.

Table 2: Additional Risk Factors
Associated with Cerebrovascular Disease

Risk Factor	Definition
Carotid or Other Artery Disease	This disease affects the carotid arteries that supply blood to the brain. Individuals who suffer from this disease often have carotid arteries that become narrowed by fatty deposits, restricting blood flow to the brain and causing a stroke.
Atrial Fibrillation	This risk factor is associated with a pooling of blood in the heart due to an irregular beat. Consequently, the pooled blood can clot and potentially travel to the brain, causing a stroke.
Certain Blood Disorders	A high red blood cell count can lead to the formation of blood clots, increasing an individual's risk of having a stroke. Another blood disease, sickle cell anemia, is prevalent in African Americans. It causes an individual's red blood cells to stick to blood vessel walls, causing a clot to form resulting in stroke.
Transient Ischemic Attacks	Also known as "mini-strokes," a series of these mild strokes can be a predictor of a more serious episode in the future.
Other Types of Heart Disease	Individuals who suffer from other types of heart disease are more susceptible to stroke.

Morbidity and Mortality in the United States

In the United States, cardiovascular diseases account for over a quarter of the population's total deaths. Although, the number of deaths due to cardiovascular diseases has been following a downward trend nationally, heart disease and stroke are still the first and third (respectively) causes of death in the US. (American Heart Association, 2005). Many Americans are unaware, or choose to ignore, that the lifestyle decisions they make on a daily basis can contribute to cardiovascular disease, including overeating, inactivity, and smoking. Fortunately, individuals can be educated on these risk factors to change their behaviors and reduce the likelihood of disease developing or progressing. At times, however, other social factors exist that block some individuals from receiving this education, acting on their increased awareness of risks, and/or accessing care needed to prevent or control cardiovascular disease.

Disparities in Cardiovascular Disease

The 1979 Surgeon General released the report "Healthy People: National Health Promotion and Disease Prevention Objectives," which outlined a set of national "health targets," including an overall reduction in mortality for various age groups. Building on the health objectives of the 1979 report, "Healthy People 2000" was released in 1990 with national heath care goals for the country, including decreasing racial and ethnic health care disparities. The latest set of national health objectives, "Healthy People 2010," was released in 2000 by the US Department of Health and Human Services. This report focused on increasing "individuals" quality and years of healthy life and eliminating health disparities in the United States. (US Department of Health and Human Services, 2003).

According to the National Center for Health Statistics (NCHS), data from the National Health and Nutrition Examination Survey and the National Health Interview Survey show that black or African American men in the United States are more likely to die from diseases of the heart (371.1 men per 100,000) than men of any other race. The death rate for white men (294.1 men per 100,000) is followed by Hispanic/Latino men and then Native-American men (See Table 3). Asian or Pacific Islander men run the lowest risk of death from diseases of the heart, with 169.8 deaths per 100,000. The NCHS definition of diseases of the heart includes categories outlined by the World Health Organization's International Classification of Diseases and excludes cerebrovascular disease (see Table 3).

Similarly, the NCHS study revealed that black or African American women have a higher cardiovascular disease death rate than women of any other race or ethnicity (263.2 women per 100,000). The second highest cardiovascular death rate is for white women (192.1 women per 100,000), followed by Hispanic/Latino women, Native-American women, and, finally, Asian or Pacific Islander women (See Table 3).

Table 3: Diseases of the Heart's and Cerebrovascular Diseases's, Death Rates for all Ages per 100,000 Population, 2002*

	American Indian or Alaska Native	Asian or Pacific Islander	Black or African American	Hispanic or Latino	White
Diseases of the Heart, Women	123.6	108.1	263.2	149.7	192.1
Diseases of the Heart, Men	201.2	169.8	371.1	219.8	294.1
Cerebrovascular Diseases, Women	38.0	45.4	71.8	38.6	53.4
Cerebrovascular Diseases, Men	37.1	50.8	81.7	44.3	54.2

Source: National Center for Health Statistics. Health, United States, 2005. With Chartbook on Trends in the Health of Americans. Hyattsville, MD: 2005.

§ Diseases of the Heart are defined as World Health Organization International Classification of Diseases–10th Revision including I00–I02, Acute rheumatic fever, I05–I09, Chronic rheumatic heart diseases I11 hypertensive heart disease, I13, hypertensive heart and renal disease, I20–I25, Ischaemic heart disease, I260I28, Pulmonary heart disease and diseases of the pulmonary circulation, I30–I51, Other forms of heart disease.

¥ Cerebrovascular Disease underlying causes of death are defined by the International Classification of Diseases (ICD)–10th revision

*Rates per 100,000 are age-adjusted using the 2000 US standard population.

Black or African American men also have the highest death rate from cerebro-vascular diseases than any other race or ethnicity (81.7 men per 100,000), followed by white men (54.2 men per 100,000), Asian or Pacific Islander men (50.8 men per 100,000), Hispanic/Latino men (44.3 men per 100,000), and, finally, Native American or Native Alaskan men (37.1 men per 100,000). Similarly, Black or African American women are more likely to die of cerebrovascular disease (71.8 women per 100,000) than women from any other racial or ethnic group. White women have the second highest death rate from cerebrovascular diseases (53.4 women per 100,000), followed by Asian or Pacific Islander women, Hispanic/Latino women, and, finally, Native-American or Native Alaskan women (See Table 3).

The NCHS data also outline racial and ethnic disparities for selected cardio-vascular and cerebrovascular health indicators, including hypertension, obesity, and diabetes (Table 4). Although derived from the same document, it is important to note that the racial and ethnic categories vary between Table 3 and Table 4. According to these data, 28.2% of black or African American males suffer from hypertension, followed by Mexican men (of any race) at 21.5% and white men at 17.6%. A higher percentage of black or African American women suffer from hypertension (28.9%) than Mexican women (of any race) (21.2%) and white women (18.5%).

Table 4: Percent of Population Experiencing Disparities in Hypertension,
Obesity, and Diabetes by Race, Ethnicity, and Sex, United States, 20 Years and Over, Age Adjusted 1999–2002

Health Indicator	Black or African American, non-Hispanic	White, non-Hispanic	Mexican
Hypertension, Men*	28.8%	17.6%	21.5%
Hypertension, Women*	28.9%	18.5%	21.2%
Obese, Body Mass Index = 30 kg/m2, Men	27.8%	28.0%	27.8%
Obese, Body Mass Index = 30 kg/m2, Women	48.8%	30.7%	39.0%
Diagnosed with Diabetes (All sexes combined, including physician-diagnosed and undiagnosed)	14.8%	8.0%	13.6%

Source: National Center for Health Statistics. Health, United States, 2005. With Chartbook on Trends in the Health of Americans. Hyattsville, MD: 2005.
* Defined as a person having blood pressure greater than 140/90 mm Hg or reporting current antihypertensive therapy .

According to these data, a larger proportion of black or African American and Mexican women are also considered overweight or obese compared to their white counterparts. As illustrated in Table 4, 48.8% of all black or African American women and 38% of all Mexican women have a Body Mass Index of = 30 kg/m2. In comparison, only 30.7% of white women have a BMI of = 30 kg/m2. As described earlier, being obese or overweight greatly increases an individual's chance of suffering from cardiovascular disease. The information presented in Table 4 for those individuals who suffer from diabetes (both physician diagnosed and undiagnosed) combines both sexes. Black or African American men and women along with Mexican men and women have higher rates of diabetes (14.8%, 13.6%, respectively) when compared to their white counterparts (8%).

Additionally, socioeconomic factors play a role in an individual's ability to access health care services. More African Americans (24.7%) and Hispanics (21.9%) are living in poverty as opposed to white, non-Hispanic (10.8%) individuals. (DeNaves-Walt, Carmen, 2005). Based on data from the Centers for Disease Control and Prevention's (CDC's) 2005 National Health Interview Survey, a greater proportion of Hispanic individuals does not have health insurance (30.5%) when compared to black (17.4%) or white (10.2%) non-Hispanics. (Cohen, RA, 2005).

In sum, various risk factors, both reducible and unmodifiable, contribute to the prevalence of cardiovascular disease in the United States. Some risk factors, such as gender, race, and age, are not modifiable; however, the difference in CVD rates may be related to modifiable factors such as smoking, obesity, alcohol consumption, and access to care that is culturally competent. These risk factors are similar to those experienced in New Jersey, where cardiovascular disease prevalence mirrors that found nationally.

Cardiovascular Disease in New Jersey

Similar to the nation, cardiovascular disease is the leading cause of death in New Jersey. This portion of the white paper outlines state-specific patterns and trends in cardiovascular diseases. Overall, mortality due to cardiovascular disease has decreased in the State. The 2005 update of "Healthy New Jersey 2010" prospectively outlines the State's cardiovascular disease health objectives for the decade. This update includes targets and endpoints that differ from those presented in earlier versions of "Healthy New Jersey 2010" due to the adoption of the World Health Organization's ICD-10 codes and the utilization of the 2000 standard population for statistical age-adjustment.

Included in these objectives is a goal to reduce the age-adjusted death rate for coronary heart disease for African Americans and whites to 165.6 per 100,000 by 2010. A target and endpoint could not be established for Hispanic or Asian and Pacific Islander populations due to a small sample size and the data being statistically unreliable. The State also set a target to reduce the number of deaths due to cerebrovascular diseases to 38.6 per 100,000 people by 2010 for African Americans and whites. Achieving these goals depends not only on the state conducting surveillance of cardiovascular disease, promoting awareness of disease risk factors, and improving access to health care, but also on individuals leading healthier lives.

State Trends in Cardiovascular Mortality

New Jersey is home to over 8.5 million individuals. Encompassing over 7,400 square miles, New Jersey is the most densely populated state in the country, with 1,134 persons per square mile. (US Census, 2005). Like the US, cardiovascular disease and stroke are the first and third leading causes of death, respectively.

Table 5: Cardiovascular Disease-Related Death Rates in New Jerseyper 100,000, 1999-2003

	Heart Disease	Stroke	Total
1999	281.0	49.3	330.3
2000	281.4	51.2	332.5
2001	267.0	47.1	314.1
2002	262.5	46.8	309.3
2003	255.2	45.9	301.1

Source: New Jersey Department of Health and Senior Services, NJSHAD Query System

In New Jersey, the cardiovascular disease death rate for heart disease declined from 281.0 in 1999 to 255.2 persons per 100,000 by 2003 (see Table 5). The death rate for stroke also declined from 49.3 persons per 100,000 in 1999 to 45.9 persons per 100,000 by 2003. Both heart disease and stroke death rates increased between 1999 and 2000 but began a steady decline in 2001.

The largest decline shown in Table 5 is between the years 2000 and 2001, when the heart disease death rate decreased from 281.4 to 267.0 persons per 100,000. According to the New Jersey Center for Health Statistics' Health Data Fact Sheet, published in 2004, the reasons for this decline included reductions in the number of cardiovascular disease risk factors experienced by individuals as well as improvements in treatments for cardiovascular disease.

Racial and Ethnic Groups

New Jersey residents are highly diverse in terms of race and ethnicity. According to the 2000 US Census, the State's largest minority group is African American (13.6%), followed closely by Hispanics (13.3%). New Jersey is also home to many individuals of Asian descent, comprising 5.7% of the State's population. There are also many other ethnic groups, particularly groups consisting of recent immigrants, that add to the State's diversity. Similar to national trends, coronary artery disease and cerebrovascular disease in New Jersey are not experienced evenly among racial and ethnic subgroups (See Table 6).

Table 6: New Jersey Age-Adjusted Mortality Rates from Coronary Artery Disease and Cerebrovascular Disease per 100,000 Standard Population, 1999–2002

	White	Black	Hispanic*	Asian/Pacific Islander*
Heart Disease in 1999	215.0	218.9	126.2	91.4
Heart Disease in 2000	208.5	228.2	133.3	102.5
Heart Disease in 2001	194.0	221.2	128.6	87.9
Heart Disease in 2002	185.5	211.5	115.7	93.3
Cerebrovascular Disease in 1999	45.4	65.7	27.3	33.2
Cerebrovascular Disease in 2000	46.7	71.5	39.2	30.8
Cerebrovascular Disease in 2001	41.9	65.6	35.2	35.8
Cerebrovascular Disease in 2002	41.1	66.2	25.8	30.3

Source: New Jersey Department of Health and Senior Services. "Healthy New Jersey 2010, Update 2005." Trenton, NJ: June 2001. Available at http://www.state.nj.us/health/ chs/hnj.htm. Accessed July 2005.

*The number of Hispanic and Asian/Pacific Islander deaths is known to be understated.

As outlined in the 2005 update of "Healthy New Jersey 2010" (Table 6), African Americans were more likely to die from coronary artery heart disease and cerebrovascular diseases than their white counterparts between the years 1999 and 2002. While the rates for Hispanics and Asian/Pacific Islanders appear much lower, the data for these populations were known to understate the number of deaths. Therefore, these data cannot be relied upon for drawing concrete conclusions about the prevalence of coronary artery or cerebrovascular disease among these groups.

New Jersey Risk Factor Profile

Overall, the percentage of New Jersey residents with cardiovascular disease risk factors mirrors that of the nation. Table 7 provides prevalent statistics for selected cardiovascular risk factors among adults age 18 and older in New Jersey compared to the nation. As seen in Table 7, 18.8% of New Jersey adults used tobacco in 2004 as compared to 20.8% of adults nationally. Tobacco use is a significant risk factor for cardiovascular disease in New Jersey, and, according to a study of smokers in the State, "...half of respiratory disease deaths, over a quarter of all cancer deaths, and nearly 20 percent of CVD deaths in New Jersey in 1996-1998 were attributed to smoking cigarettes." (Baron, April 2001).

New Jersey's cholesterol check rates were slightly below the national average for individuals who had not had their cholesterol checked within 5 years (see Table 7). The most recent statistics retrieved from the Behavioral Risk Factor Surveillance System (BRFSS), a survey conducted by the NJDHSS and funded by the CDC, show that of those who had their blood cholesterol level checked in 2003, 34.5% were told by a doctor that they had high cholesterol levels. Lack of regular monitoring of blood pressure and cholesterol can contribute to the progression of cardiovascular disease.

Table 7: Prevalence of Cardiovascular Disease Risk Factors Among Adults(age 18 and older): New Jersey vs. United States, Various Years

	New Jersey	United States
Tobacco Use (2004)*	18.8%	20.8%
No Cholesterol Check within 5 Years, Data (2003)	18.8%	23.3%
No Blood Pressure Check Within 2 Years, Data (1999)	5.0%	5.4%
Physical Inactivity (2003)++	55.3%	52.8%
Obesity by Body Mass Index (2002)**	19.0%	22.1%
Alcohol Consumption (2004)~	4.5%	4.8%

Source: Centers for Disease Control and Prevention (CDC). Behavioral Risk Factor Surveillance System Survey Data. Atlanta, Georgia: U.S. Department of Health and Human Services, Centers for Disease Control and Prevention, 2005.
* Current Smoker
++ Adults with 30+ minutes of moderate physical activity five or more days per week, or vigorous physical activity for 20+ minutes three or more days per week.
** Body Mass Index (BMI) is 30.0 or more. BMI is defined as weight in kilograms divided by height in meters squared.
~ Heavy drinkers (adult men having more than two drinks per day and adult women having more than one drink per day).

In New Jersey, the prevalence of risk factors was also slightly below the national average for alcohol consumption in 2004 and obesity in 2002. As shown in Table 7, physical inactivity was the only risk factor that was greater in New Jersey than in the nation overall. In 2003, 55.3% of New Jersey citizens reported that they were physically inactive in comparison to 52.8% of individuals nationally. The data in Table 7 also reveals that in 1999, 5% of New Jerseyans and 5.4% of the national population had not had their blood pressure checked within two years. By 2003, according to a BRFSS report, 25.6% of New Jersey residents were told by a doctor, nurse, or other health professional that they had high blood pressure.

New Jersey State-Sponsored Cardiovascular Disease Programs

New Jersey has applied surveillance techniques, policy measures, and risk reduction interventions to address cardiovascular disease statewide. The NJDHSS works with the state legislature, advocacy groups, health care organizations, and individuals across the State to address cardiovascular disease risk factors that affect all New Jerseyans. NJDHSS addresses these risk factors at all levels of government and in the public and private sectors, playing an integral role in implementing efforts to address cardiovascular disease through dedicated resources and organizations, quality of care initiatives, risk reduction interventions, and policy-related activities.

Data and Surveillance

The NJDHSS conducts a number of surveillance programs to identify and track cardiovascular disease and underlying risk factors for the disease. The Center for Health Statistics (CHS) is an integral part of the State's surveillance and data tracking system. CHS "...collects, researches, analyzes, and disseminates New Jersey health data and information and serves as a resource to the Department in development of health data policy." (Center for Health Statistics, September 2005). Many of these data sets are available for public access through CHS's online reporting systems.

Several data systems managed by CHS track risk factors associated with cardiovascular disease, including the Behavioral Risk Factor Surveillance System. The BRFSS, partially funded by the CDC, is a long-standing, state-based surveillance program that uses a monthly telephone survey to monitor "major behavioral risk factors and chronic conditions associated with disability and death among adults." (Division of Adult and Community Health, CDC, 1995–2004). Cardiovascular disease risk factors are included in this survey as well as heart health statistics. The results from the BRFSS survey are used to monitor progress toward statewide public health objectives, such as those set forth in "Healthy New Jersey 2010."

CHS also provides the public with other forms of cardiovascular surveillance data, including:

- *The New Jersey State Health Assessment Data Query System* (NJ SHAD): This interactive query system provides individuals with customized maps and tables of New Jersey health data on a wide range of topics such as "the number of births to teenagers, the percentage of deaths due to HIV disease, the motor vehicle injury death rate, and the number of marriages [in New Jersey]." (Center for Health Statistics, October 2005). The NJ SHAD query system can also be used to determine the number of cardiovascular disease-related deaths in the State in any given year, broken down by a variety of risk factors.

- *The New Jersey Health Statistics Report Series*: These yearly reports summarize deaths, births, marriages, and population statistics for the State and its counties. Information is also available for selected municipalities. Together with NJ SHAD, users are able to customize tables and maps at the state, county, and municipal levels.

- *Healthy New Jersey 2010*: In response to the national "Healthy People 2010," "Healthy New Jersey 2010" outlines the State's health care goals for the current decade. Included in these goals are reductions in mortality due to cardiovascular disease and diabetes by the year 2010. Progress toward the "Healthy New Jersey 2010" goals was reported in 2005 using more current cardiovascular disease statistics.

- *Topics in Health Statistics*: This series of reports covers a variety of topics, including inpatient hospitalizations, sexual risk status and behavior, suicides, and estimates of healthy life expectancies. The topics that pertain to cardiovascular disease include cardiac arrest death statistics and trends, alcohol-attributable mortality, obesity and overweight studies, and smoking-attributable mortality.

The Center for State Health Statistics data systems provide vital information regarding the trends and patterns of cardiovascular disease and corresponding risk factors. This information is critical to monitoring cardiovascular disease in New Jersey.

In addition to this information, there are several mortality data systems and reports that address quality of care initiatives and diabetes surveillance reports as they pertain to cardiovascular disease risk factors. These will be discussed below.

The Office of Health Care Quality Assessment (HCQA) maintains patient-level data registries for each adult patient who undergoes a diagnostic or interventional cardiac catheterization or an open-heart surgery in New Jersey. HCQA also maintains patient-level data for all hospital inpatients diagnosed with congestive heart failure, acute myocardial infarction, and community-acquired pneumonia. Finally, HCQA maintains the New Jersey Discharge Data Collection system, which contains a copy of every hospital inpatient and emergency department admission, including patient-level demographic and clinical information. Data from these various databases, alone or in combinations, are used to assess compliance with hospital cardiac licensure standards, evaluate competing hospital certificate of need applications, and assess the quality of hospital care in specific areas (See Performance Assessment below).

Risk Reduction Interventions

The US Department of Health and Human Services (DHHS) provides states with funding to address many of the risk factors associated with cardiovascular disease. In New Jersey, this DHHS funding has been used to create programs that address individual tobacco use, diabetes prevention, and obesity and overweight risk factors for cardiovascular disease.

The New Jersey Comprehensive Tobacco Control Program is part of the Office of the State Epidemiologist and receives funding from a settlement agreement between 46 states and the tobacco industry. This program encourages individuals in New Jersey to quit smoking, offering resources for those struggling with tobacco addiction, including:

- NJ Quitnet (www.nj.quitnet.com): An online resource developed at Boston

University, NJ Quitnet provides 24-hour, on-line services that are tailored to meet an individual's needs. The site allows smokers to set a quit date and track their progress, and provides an opportunity for those quitting smoking to network with and lend support to one another.

- NJ Quitline (1-888-NJ-STOPS): Operated by the Mayo Foundation, this toll-free service provides trained counselors in 26 languages to help individuals quit smoking. The quitlines are open six days a week during and after business hours.

- NJ Quitcenters: These regional centers provide one-on-one and group counseling for those trying to quit smoking.

- Youth prevention activities: These activities include efforts by "REBEL" (Reaching Everyone by Exposing Lies), a group of teens statewide that educate their peers on the dangers of tobacco use. (Rutgers Center for State Health Policy, October 2006). In addition, the State sponsors "Not for Sale," a youth-driven anti-tobacco advertising campaign against Big Tobacco companies.

- Community prevention activities: The State partners with many local citizen groups and nonprofit organizations, including NJBreathes, an anti-tobacco coalition of over 40 statewide organizations working to reduce tobacco use in the State. NJGASP is another anti-tobacco organization that provides "technical support to municipalities to reduce tobacco use in the community." (NJDHSS, May 2006). In addition, the State works with the Communities Against Tobacco (CAT) coalition in all 21 counties. CAT strives to reduce tobacco use on the local level. The University of Medicine & Dentistry of New Jersey (UMDNJ) also offers a Tobacco Dependence Program to train health professionals on how to implement smoke-free environments in many settings.

In addition, the State legislature recently passed and implemented the Smoke-Free Air Act, banning indoor smoking in all indoor public places and work places across the State. It is estimated that, by reducing the number of smokers and amount of smoking, these resources have saved New Jerseyans over $54 million since October of 2000 in cigarette and health care costs associated with smoking. (New Jersey Quitnet, October 2005, http://nj.quitnet.com/).

In 2005, the NJDHSS published a diabetes surveillance report estimating that over 440,000 individuals statewide suffer from a form of diabetes, including over 176,000 individuals who have diabetes but have not been diagnosed. (Diabetes Prevention and Control Program, May 2005, http://nj.gov/health/fhs/diabpub.shtml). To address diabetes in the State, the New Jersey Diabetes Prevention and Control Program (DPCP) was established within the Department's Division of Family Health Services. The DPCP seeks to reduce the burden of diabetes in the State and to eliminate the disproportionate burden among population subgroups. Since 65% of people with diabetes die from heart attack or stroke, diabetes prevention and control efforts are integral to cardiovascular disease prevention and control efforts. Specific DPCP objectives focus on: 1) enhancing diabetes surveillance; 2) promoting primary prevention of diabetes; 3) improving disease management for those who already have diabetes (i.e. increasing rates of foot exams, eye exams, HbA1c testing, and immunizations among people with diabetes); 4) improving the diabetes public health infrastructure; and 5) eliminating racial/ethnic disparities. The DPCP engages in a broad range of activities, including:

- Publication of an extensive diabetes surveillance report that includes demographic, behavioral risk factor, morbidity, and mortality data relative to diabetes and associated complications, such as cardiovascular disease;

- Funding for the Diabetes Outreach and Education System, a community and professional diabetes education project that serves a five-county area of southern New Jersey (Ocean, Atlantic, Cape May, Cumberland, and Salem counties);

- Social marketing campaigns, such as distributing educational information via billboards, newsletters, email campaigns, and radio and newspaper public service announcements, that disseminate messages about the prevention of diabetes and its complications;

- Funding for the Commission for the Blind and Visually Impaired to conduct the Diabetic Eye Disease Detection Program, which provides eye screening services for low income, uninsured persons with diabetes;

- Support for local health department primary and secondary diabetes prevention activities;

- Support for efforts to improve the quality of diabetes care in Federally Qualified Health Centers and other venues;

- Support for the New Jersey Diabetes Council, an advisory Council to the Department. The Council is made up of 100 members and has a mission to "Improve the health and quality of life for the people of New Jersey by encouraging programs and policies that translate evidence-based research into prevention, detection, and treatment of prediabetes, diabetes, and related disorders." (Diabetes Prevention and Control Program, May 2005, http://nj.gov/health/fhs/diabpub.shtml);

- In conjunction with statewide partners, assessment of the State diabetes public health system and development of a strategic plan for addressing diabetes in New Jersey.

The NJDHSS Office of Minority and Multicultural Health (OMMH) addresses health care concerns of minority populations in New Jersey. The mission of this office is "to foster accessible and high-quality programs and policies that help all racial and ethnic minorities in New Jersey achieve optimal health, dignity and independence." (Office of Minority and Multicultural Health, http://nj.gov/health/commiss/omh/mission.shtml). OMMH has offered grant funding for community-based organizations to focus on cardiovascular disease-centered outreach in the community. Most recently, OMMH has awarded grants focused on diabetes prevention and control. The OMMH funded five minority, community-based organizations to conduct outreach, education, screenings, referrals, and follow-up focusing on diabetes, a health disparity area.

The Office of Women's Health (OWH) is involved in a risk reduction program that focuses on women and heart disease. OWH recently funded a 20-month initiative, "Take New Jersey Women to Heart," that included a campaign to "raise awareness and educate the general public as well as professionals about heart disease in women." (Office on Women's Health, http://www.state.nj.us/health/fhs/owh/cardiovascular_disease.shtml). In addition, the NJ Council on Physical Fitness and Sports, housed in the Division of Family Health Services, advocates for "health enhancing policies and legislation." (Division of Family Health Services, http://www.state.nj.us/health/fhs/documents/annual_report.pdf). Focused on overall health statewide, the Council addresses many risk factors associated with cardiovascular disease.

Emergency Cardiac Care

The Office of Emergency Medical Services (OEMS) oversees a statewide network of emergency services that are provided for all citizens of New Jersey. Emergency Medical services in New Jersey offer basic life support (BLS) and advanced life support (ALS) pre-hospital care for patients with signs and symptoms of cardiovascular disease. When a patient calls 9-1-1 for a medical problem or trauma, an ALS services ambulance is dispatched if a patient's symptoms meet certain criteria, including cardiac problems, respiratory distress, and/or a diabetic emergency. In 2004, New Jersey's ALS services responded to a total of 161,062 calls. Of these, a total of 44,697 were cardiac calls (including cardiac arrest). ALS service providers are equipped with 12-lead EKGs, allowing timely transmission of key information to hospital emergency departments for the diagnosis of heart attack or acute myocardial infarction, before arriving at the hospital. New Jersey is ahead of the rest of the country in requiring 12-lead EKGs on all ALS vehicles.

OEMS has also overseen three major distributions of free automated external defibrillators (AED) to emergency first responders. In 1999, a total of 156 AEDs were distributed statewide to police and fire departments, and 441 AEDs were given to volunteer first aid squads throughout the State in 2001. The most recent distribution effort was in 2004–2005, with over 1,500 defibrillators distributed to law enforcement agencies statewide, equipping every patrol unit in the NJ State

Police with an AED. Since police officers are often the first to arrive at a medical emergency site, cardiac patients receive the benefits of state-of-the-art rescue care prior to arrival at the hospital. By providing readily accessible treatment that can be safely provided by people immediately on the scene, a cardiac arrest patient's survival rate is increased. Prominently placed and easy to operate, these defibrillators "are phonebook-sized, battery-powered devices that evaluate a patient's heart rhythm, generate and deliver an electric charge to someone whose heart has stopped, and then re-evaluates the heart. The AEDs provide both voice and visual prompts that lead users through each rescue step. (NJ Department of Health and Senior Services, http://www.state.nj.us/health/news/p00807a.htm).

In 2001, the DHSS adopted certificate of need rules that permit hospitals with diagnostic cardiac catheterization laboratories to also offer primary, or emergency, angioplasty to patients having a heart attack. A growing body of research suggests that angioplasty when performed quickly is more effective than thrombolytic drugs and, therefore, the treatment of choice for heart attack patients. Thus, the Department adopted rule changes that increase access to this life-saving treatment. Primary angioplasty is now offered at community hospitals, in addition to the eighteen cardiac surgery centers in the State.

Quality of Care Monitoring and Reporting

New Jersey has launched several initiatives intended to improve the quality of care delivered to persons with cardiovascular disease. Published since 1997, the "Cardiac Surgery in New Jersey" report card for consumers calculates risk-adjusted coronary artery bypass graft surgery (CABG) mortality rates in New Jersey hospitals performing open-heart surgery. Generated by the Office of Health Care Quality Assessment (HCAQ), this report card indicates how each hospital's and individual surgeon's rates compare to the State average. This report has been associated with a more than 50% reduction, on a risk-adjusted basis, in mortality following CABG surgery between 1994 and 2003. (Department of Health and Senior Services, February 2006, http://www.state.nj.us/health/hcsa/documents/cardconsumer03.pdf).

Starting in 2004, HCQA has published annually the "New Jersey Hospital Performance Report." Since 2006, the report has provided consumers information on how often hospitals apply nationally-recognized best practices in treating patients with community-acquired pneumonia, heart attack, and congestive heart failure. Starting with the 2007 report, data has been published on the application of best practices for prevention of infection in surgical patients. The report provides five indicators of the adequacy of treatment for heart attack: 1) delivering aspirin on arrival at the hospital; 2) delivering aspirin at discharge from the hospital; 3) delivering a beta blocker on arrival at the hospital; 4) delivering a beta blocker on departure from the hospital; and 5) delivering an ACE inhibitor at discharge. (NJ Department of Health and Senior Services, September 2005, http://web.doh.state.nj.us/hpr/hpr2005.pdf).

These five treatments are known to significantly increase a heart attack patient's chances of survival and decrease the likelihood of another heart attack. The 2006 report added three other heart attack treatment indicators: 1) smoking cessation counseling for smokers; 2) length of time before performance of primary angioplasty; and 3) length of time before administration of thrombolytics. It also offered four measures for treatment of congestive heart failure: 1) use of ACE inhibitors; 2) assessment of left ventricular function; 3) smoking cessation counseling for smokers; and 4) appropriate discharge instructions. Although New Jersey ranked very low in studies of state performance on process of care indicators published early in the decade, by 2005 hospitals in NJ were outperforming hospitals in all other states on these process of care indicators. (New Jersey Department of Heath and Senior Services, March 13, 2006).

In 2005, the State released the latest version of the annual HMO Performance Report. Published since 1997, this document provides "information on the performance of New Jersey's managed health care plans, how well these plans deliver important health care services, and how members rate the services they receive. (New Jersey Department of Health and Senior Services, http://www.state.nj.us/cgi-bin/dhss/hmo/individual.pl?year=2004&page=introduction). The report identifies HMOs as better, the same, or worse than the statewide average on a number of indicators related to the care of patients with cardiovascular disease. Overall HMO performance has slowly but steadily improved since the first report was issued. While these performance reports have stimulated improvements in the care provided to New Jersey residents, much remains to be done.

Policy-Related Cardiovascular Activities

As mentioned above, NJDHSS continually reviews its certificate of need (CN) and licensure standards for hospital-based cardiovascular services to improve access to and quality of these services, and reduce mortality and disparities associated with cardiovascular disease. For well over a decade, the Department has benefited from the advice of the Cardiovascular Health Advisory Panel (CHAP), a group of cardiac surgeons, cardiologists, and other health care professionals, in formulating its CN and licensure standards and in developing the cardiac surgery performance report.

To expand access to cardiovascular care, the NJDHSS's Certificate of Need and Acute Care Licensing Office has used its CN authority to "link expansion of the number of cardiac surgery centers in New Jersey to demonstrated efforts to improve access to minorities." (New Jersey Department of Health and Senior Services, http://www.state.nj.us/health/csh). When considering competing applications, the Department gives preference to applicants more likely to enhance access to care for minority and medically underserved patients. This same consideration informed the Department's pilot expansion of low-risk diagnostic cardiac catheterization laboratories to community hospitals, and its subsequent policy of permitting widespread expansion of both full-risk diagnostic cardiac catheterization and primary angioplasty, referred to above. The demand for elective angioplasty in New Jersey has been growing steadily, from 16,976 cases in 1998 to 27,346 in 2004, largely as a result of the introduction of drug-eluting coronary artery stents, which have allowed lower risk catheterization procedures to substitute for a large proportion of higher risk CABG open-heart procedures. During this same period, open-heart surgeries have declined from 11,312 cases to 9,875. Because of this trend, and the widespread interest among both consumers and community hospitals in making elective angioplasty widely available, in 2005 the Department granted nine New Jersey hospitals approval to offer primary angioplasty as part of a three-year, multi-state, prospectively randomized study. This study, led by Johns Hopkins University researchers, is designed to determine whether elective angioplasty can be safely offered in hospitals that do not also offer cardiac surgery on-site.

In the area of cerebrovascular disease, the State enacted a law in 2004 designed to promote improvements in the treatment of stroke. The law articulated detailed standards for hospitals seeking designation as either a primary or comprehensive stroke treatment center. It also provided $3 million annually in grants to help hospitals meet these stringent standards. To date, a total of $6 million has been awarded to hospitals statewide seeking designation as a stroke treatment center. (Stroke Center Designation Grant, http://www.state.nj.us/health/hcsa/rfa_notice.pdf).

Obesity Prevention: Other State Agencies
Playing a Role in Cardiovascular Disease Control

In the past, New Jersey has had a higher rate of increase in obesity than the national average. BRFSS revealed that between 1991 and 2002, the percentage of NJ citizens considered obese rose from 9.9% of the population to 18.8% of the population. Further analysis of BRFSS data revealed that 59.6% of New Jerseyans were considered overweight or obese in 2004. A study published in 2001 by the Center for State Health Statistics noted that less well educated, minority males are disproportionately more likely to be overweight and obese in the State. The study concluded that, since eating and activity patterns are established in childhood, more emphasis on physical activity is needed at home by parents and in schools. (Boeslager, Georgette, July 2001).

The State has formed a Taskforce on Obesity to address obesity and overweight risk factors. This task force is made up of members appointed by the Governor, and includes individuals representing the food industry, medicine and public health fields, education, physical fitness, and recreation. The task force has been charged with creation of a statewide action plan with measurable goals to "study and evaluate, and develop recommendations relating to, specific actionable measures to support and enhance obesity prevention among the residents of this State, with particular attention to children and adolescents" (New Jersey State Legislature, http://www.njleg.state.nj.us/2002/bills/pl03/303_.htm). The action plan has been completed, and includes such topics as the promotion and dissemination of food guidelines, the monitoring of school children's body mass index, and the development of school and community-based programs for physical activity and fitness.

The Department of Agriculture has implemented a model school nutrition policy to promote healthy eating. The model policy asks that state Boards of Education recognize that "child and adolescent obesity has reached epidemic levels in the United States and that poor diet combined with the lack of physical activity negatively impacts on students' health, and their ability and motivation to learn." (NJ Dept. of Agriculture http://www.nj.gov/agriculture/divisions/fn/childadult/ school_model.html). To this end, the New Jersey Department of Agriculture asks that healthy lunch options be provided for students and physical activity be integrated into the school schedule.

The Department of Education requires that state public elementary and secondary schools adhere to a set of core curriculum standards in comprehensive health and physical education. Included in this curriculum is personal health, growth and development, nutrition, diseases and health conditions, safety, and social and environmental health. (New Jersey Department of Education, http://www.nj.gov/ njded/cccs/s2_chpe.htm#26). Fitness is also included as part of the curriculum, including physical activity, training, and achieving and assessing fitness, and teaching students how to maintain a healthy lifestyle to remain disease free.

National and Other State Cardiovascular Disease Control Strategies

While New Jersey has been active in cardiovascular disease surveillance, risk reduction, and care enhancement activities, it is beneficial to review innovative strategies addressing cardiovascular disease control nationwide, including other states' preventive measures. Analysis of these programs could assist New Jersey in efforts to reduce cardiovascular disease, because, despite all of the State's risk reduction efforts, gaps do still exist in primary and secondary cardiovascular disease prevention methods statewide.

Centers for Disease Control and Prevention: Innovative Strategies Overview

In many states, efforts to eliminate cardiovascular disease are partially, if not completely, funded by the CDC. The CDC has addressed cardiovascular disease by funding cardiovascular programs that are specific to each state's population needs, but the CDC stresses several areas where state cardiovascular programs should focus their attention: education, policy changes, system changes, and environmental changes. In the past, the CDC has funded programs that focus on four priorities to guide state cardiovascular planning:

- Increasing State Capacity: Planning, implementing, tracking, and ultimately sustaining interventions that address CVD as well as CVD risk factors;

- Conducting Surveillance: Monitoring CVD and related risk factors in the State and assessing existing state programs that target CVD;
- Supporting Promising Strategies: Identifying strategies that promote statewide heart healthy interventions;
- Promoting CV Health in Diverse Settings: Supporting efforts in health care facilities, worksites, schools, and other community settings.

In 1998, Congress approved funding for eight states to initiate a national, state-based heart disease and stroke prevention program. Today, 32 states and the District of Columbia receive CDC funding to operate prevention programs. Twenty-one states are funded as "capacity building" states, and 12 states are currently funded as "basic implementation" states, striving to enhance all capacity-building program activities through training and technical assistance. Starting with an overview of capacity building states, selected states highlighted below can serve as models for New Jersey.

Capacity-Building States: Connecticut, Ohio, and the District of Columbia

CDC-funded capacity-building states focus on several objectives to effectively address cardiovascular disease including:

- Facilitating collaboration among interested stakeholders from both the public and private sectors;
- Assessing the CVD burden statewide and creating strategies for primary and secondary heart disease and stroke prevention;
- Creating a plan for addressing cardiovascular disease based on heart-healthy policies;
- Changing physical and social environmental issues and eliminating disparities;
- Identifying culturally appropriate approaches to promote healthy lifestyles and focus on increasing awareness of CVD signs and symptoms. (State Programs Homepage, CDC, http://www.cdc.gov/dhdsp/state_program/index.htm).

Connecticut has received CDC funding since 2000, and has teamed with the local business and industry association to develop a survey to assess employers' attitudes toward policies and environmental issues affecting CVD risk factors. (State Program: Connecticut Capacity Building, http://www.cdc.gov/DHDSP/state_program/ct.htm). Connecticut is also using its funding to create Cardiovascular Health Pilot Projects to address CVD and stroke risk factors in various community settings. Ohio has used its CDC funding to develop a CVD profile paper outlining the burden of CVD in the state. In addition, Ohio used these funds to create a state plan as well as to identify priority populations that are vulnerable to cardiovascular disease. Since 2001, the District of Columbia has utilized its funding to coordinate a coalition that provides technical assistance and program support for addressing

CVD secondary prevention and risk factors. The District also coordinated a Chronic Disease Conference and developed a series of reports that contain mortality and risk factor data.

Basic Implementation States: New York, Florida, and Arkansas

Basic implementation states have relied on CDC funding to enhance and expand existing cardiovascular programs. Since 1998, New York State has used CDC funding to support several initiatives for its "Healthy Heart Program." Like Connecticut, New York has targeted worksites by developing "Heart Check," a survey tool to measure worksite support of healthy heart policies and environments. New York has funded county health departments, hospitals, and other nongovernmental organizations to perform training for worksites in need of change to promote heart health. (State Program New York, http://www.cdc.gov/DHDSP/state_program/ny.htm). New York also used CDC funding for mini-grants to faith communities that serve minority populations.

Since 2002, Florida has used dedicated cardiovascular disease and stroke prevention funding for a Cardiovascular Health Council to develop a statewide CVD plan and coordinate existing resources, at times partnering with existing cardiovascular-related programs to promote heart health. Florida has also used dedicated CVD monies to implement a public awareness campaign for women, specifically over the age of 65, about the signs, symptoms, and dangers of heart disease and stroke. (State Program Florida, http://www.cdc.gov/DHDSP/state_program/fl.htm).

Beginning in 2000, Arkansas has received CDC funding for basic implementation and most recently for a two-year demonstration project to survey and present information on state hypertension and cholesterol control. Arkansas has joined the CDC-funded Delta States Stroke Consortium comprised of 80 members from "the states of Alabama, Arkansas, Louisiana, Mississippi, and Tennessee, who have come together for the purpose of identifying and documenting opportunities for additional interventions that may reduce the burden of stroke in the central to west-central portion of the Southeastern United States." (Delta States Stroke Consortium, ttp://www.uabchp.org/page.asp?id=48). In addition, CDC funding has been used to support the distribution of clinical practice guidelines to over 3,600 health clinics statewide to promote evidence-based medicine and consistency in patient care.

Conclusions and Recommendations

New Jersey has been addressing cardiovascular disease statewide for a number of years through that include disease surveillance, risk factor identification and education, access to care improvement, and quality of care monitoring. As in other states, cardiovascular disease remains the number one cause of death in NJ, and continues to disproportionately affect African American men and women.

In a constrained resource environment it may be difficult to fund extensive new investments to address CVD. However, the State's ability to maximize the impact of existing and new resources that it invests to address cardiovascular disease could be strengthened by the following three recommendations:

- Create a centralized CVD control program: A variety of efforts to address cardiovascular disease are currently spread over several state offices and departments. Consolidating CVD information into one centralized location to create a control program would allow for more cross-program analysis and more refined priority setting and program evaluation. These steps could lead to better use of existing CVD resources, and establish priorities for new resources.
- Provide resources dedicated to addressing CVD statewide: New Jersey should seek funding to be used specifically to address CVD, conduct outreach, and eliminate racial disparities.
- Analyze the need for primary versus secondary CVD intervention to maximize the impact of outreach efforts: New Jersey should conduct a thorough analysis of existing CVD outreach efforts to determine what the focus of ongoing CVD efforts should be statewide.

Implementation of these recommendations should contribute to reductions in cardiovascular disease statewide. Additionally, more research should be conducted to determine the best way to distribute dedicated CVD funding. More in-depth state case studies would also provide New Jersey with a comprehensive look at national best practices for addressing cardiovascular disease.

Acknowledgements

This report was commissioned by the New Jersey Department of Health and Senior Services (DHSS). The authors gratefully acknowledge the assistance of DHSS staff, including Dr. Eddy Bresnitz, Deputy Commissioner, and State Epidemiologist Bonnie H. Wiseman of the Office of Public Health Services; Karen Halupke of the Office of Emergency Medical Services; Celeste Andriot-Wood, Elizabeth Solan, and Henry Sherel of the Division of Family Health Services; Gil Ongwenyi of the Office of Minority and Multicultural Health; and Marilyn Dahl, former Special Advisor to the Commissioner for Health Care Quality & Access. The report also benefited from the contributions of Sandra Howell-White, Jeff Abramo, Marlene Walsh, and Sabrina Chase from the Rutgers Center for State Health Policy.

References

American Heart Association. "Risk Factors and Coronary Heart Disease." Available at http://www.americanheart.org/presenter.jhtml?identifier=500. Accessed July 2005.

Baron, Maria L. Smoking-Attributable Mortality, New Jersey, 1996–1998. Topics in Health Statistics. Center for Health Statistics. New Jersey Department of Health and Senior Services. April 2001.

Boeselager, Georgette K. "Obesity and Overweight in New Jersey: Data from the New Jersey BRFSS." Topics in Health Statistics, Center for Health Statistics. July 2001.

Center for Health Statistics. "Frequently Asked Questions." Available at http://www.state.nj.us/health/chs/faqs.htm. Accessed September 2005.

Center for Health Statistics. "New Jersey State Health Assessment Data." Available at http://njshad.doh.state.nj.us/welcome.html. Accessed October 2005.

Cohen, RA and ME Martinez. Health insurance coverage: Estimates from the National Health Interview Survey, January–June 2005. Available at http://www.cdc.gove/nchs/nhis.htm. December 2005

DeNaves-Walt, Carmen, Bernadette D. Proctor, Cheryl Hill Lee. US Census Bureau, Current Population Reports, P60–229, Income, Poverty and Health Insurance Coverage in the United States: 2004, U.S. Government Printing Office, Washington, DC, 2005.

Diabetes Prevention and Control Program, New Jersey Department of Health and Senior Services. "The Burden of Diabetes In New Jersey: A Surveillance Report." May 2005. Available at: http://nj.gov/health/fhs/diabpub.shtml.

Division of Adult and Community Health, National Center for Chronic Disease Prevention and Health Promotion, Centers for Disease Control and Prevention, Behavioral Risk Factor Surveillance System Online Prevalence Data, 1995–2004.

Division of Family Health Services, NJ Department of Health and Senior Services. "Annual Report FY 2004 Family Health Services." Trenton, NJ: 2005. Available at http://www.state.nj.us/health/fhs/documents/annual_report.pdf. Accessed February 2006.

Jencks, Stephen, Edwin Huff, Timothy Cuerdon. "Change in the Quality of Care Delivered to Medicare Beneficiaries, 1998–1999 to 2000–2001." Journal of the American Medical Association. Volume 289, No. 3. January 15, 2003.

Jencks, Stephen, Timothy Cuerdon, Dale Burwen, Barbars Fleming, Peter Houck, Annette Kussmaul, Dvie Nilasena, Diana Ordin, David Arday. "Quality of Medical Care Delivered to Medicare Beneficiaries, A Profile at State and National Levels." Journal of the American Medical Association. Volume 284, No. 13. October 4, 2000.

New Jersey Department of Agriculture. "Model School Nutrition Policy." Available at http://www.nj.gov/agriculture/divisions/fn/childadult/school_model.html.

New Jersey Department of Education. "Comprehensive Health and Physical Education." Available at http://www.nj.gov/njded/cccs/s2_chpe.htm#26. Accessed May 2006 .

New Jersey Department of Health and Senior Services. "2004 NJ HMO Performance Report Card." Available at: http://www.state.nj.us/cgibin/dhss/hmo/individual.pl?year=2004&page=introduction. Accessed September 2005.

New Jersey Department of Health and Senior Services. "Cardiac Surgery in New Jersey 2003, A Consumer Report." February 2006. Available at http://www.state.nj.us/health/hcsa/documents/cardconsumer03.pdf.

New Jersey Department of Health and Senior Services. "Comprehensive Tobacco Control." Available at: http://www.state.nj.us/health/as/ctcp/partners.htm. Accessed May 2006.

New Jersey Department of Health and Senior Services. "Governor's Initiative Provides 156 Defibrillators to 146 Towns." Available at: http://www.state.nj.us/health/news/p00807a.htm. Accessed October 2005.

New Jersey Department of Health and Senior Services. "Guide to New Jersey Hospitals, Select Hospital Comparisons." Available at http://web.doh.state.nj.us/hpr/. Accessed July 2005.

New Jersey Department of Health and Senior Services. "Healthy New Jersey 2010." Trenton, NJ: June 2001. Available at http://www.state.nj.us/health/chs/hnj.htm. Accessed July 2005.

New Jersey Department of Health and Senior Services. "New Jersey 2005 Hospital Performance Report." September 2005. Available at http://web.doh.state.nj.us/hpr/hpr2005.pdf.

New Jersey Department of Health and Senior Services, News Release. "New Jersey First in Providing Patients High-Quality Hospital Care." March 13, 2006.

New Jersey Department of Health and Senior Services, Center for Health Statistics. "NJ State Health Assessment Data." Available at http://njshad.doh.state.nj.us/ death1119.html. Accessed July 2005.

New Jersey Quitnet. "Quit Smoking Stats." Available at http://nj.quitnet.com/. Accessed October 2005.

New Jersey State Legislature. "Chapter 303, An Act Establishing the New Jersey Obesity Prevention Task Force." Available at: http://www.njleg.state.nj.us/ 2002/bills/pl03/303_.htm. Accessed October 2005.

North American Association for the Study of Obesity. "Obesity Statistics." Available at http://www.naaso.org/statistics/. Accessed July 2005.

Office of Minority and Multicultural Health. "Connecting Diverse Communities." Available at: http://nj.gov/health/commiss/omh/mission.shtml. Accessed September 2005.

Office on Women's Health, Family Health Services, NJ Department of Health and Senior Services. "Women's Heart Foundation." Available at http:// www.state.nj.us/health/fhs/njowh.htm. Accessed February 2006.

State Program Connecticut, Centers for Disease Control. "State Program: Connecticut Capacity Building." Available at http://www.cdc.gov/DHDSP/ state_program/ct.htm. Accessed July 2006.

State Program Florida, Centers for Disease Control. "State Program Florida Basic Implementation." Available at http://www.cdc.gov/DHDSP/state_program/ fl.htm. Accessed February 2006.

State Program Homepage, Centers for Disease Control. "CDC Heart Disease and Stroke Prevention Program." Available at http://www.cdc.gov/dhdsp/state_ program/index.htm/. Accessed February 2006.

State Program New York, Centers for Disease Control. "State Program New York Basic Implementation." Available at http://www.cdc.gov/DHDSP/state_ program/ny.htm. Accessed February 2006.

Stroke Center Designation Grant, New Jersey Department of Health and Senior Services. "Request for Application Notice". Available at http://www.state.nj.us/ health/hcsa/rfa_notice.pdf. Accessed May 2006.

University of Alabama at Birmingham, UAB Center for the Study of Community Health. "Delta States Stroke Consortium." Available at http://www.uabchp.org/page.asp?id=48. Accessed July 2006.

US Census Bureau. "New Jersey QuickFacts." Available at http://quickfacts.census.gov/qfd/states/34000.html. Accessed July 2005.

US Department of Health and Human Services. A Public Action Plan to Prevent Heart Disease and Stroke. Atlanta, GA: US Department of Health and Human Services, Centers for Disease Control and Prevention; 2003.

US Department of Health and Human Services, Centers for Disease Control and Prevention, and Coordinating Center for Health Promotion. "Prevention Heart Disease and Stroke, Addressing the Nation's Leading Killers 2005." Washington, DC, 2005.

CHAPTER TEN

Societally-Connected Thinking Using a Systems Approach: An Educational and Societal Imperative

By

Donald B. Louria, MD

Our educational system is not teaching students how to think critically, and is not adequately preparing them for long-term commitment to solving major societal problems. It is, thereby, failing both young people and our society. I and my colleagues propose a change in our educational approach that could make a huge difference. We believe we should include, as an intrinsic part of the curriculum, attempts to instill in students what we have called societally-connected thinking, one form of critical thinking that blends interdisciplinary learning with systems thinking. This has not been an intrinsic component of the educational process; instead, for the last four decades, our educational efforts have, in large part, focused on incorporation of technological advances. As a consequence, we now have two whole generations of decision makers at local, state, national, or international levels, who, in the aggregate, are inadequately trained to solve or even ameliorate major problems that threaten the future of our society.

Unless we imbue our students at all educational levels with the need to think in a societally-connected way, we will continue to develop decision makers who are unable to cope with the increasing complexity of the world, and a public that is not committed to participate in seeking solutions to major problems. This problem could lead to a societal catastrophe.

There are three interrelated components of societally-connected thinking:

Mandatory Interdisciplinary Courses: At every educational level—junior high school, high school, college, graduate school—the curriculum should include mandatory, interdisciplinary courses that cover the current, major problems facing society at local, state, national, and international levels, as well as the critical problems we are likely to face in future years, decades, and centuries. The courses must be interdisciplinary, obligatory, and learning-focused.

Systems (Non-Linear) Thinking: Students must be taught to think about these problems in a manner that is comprehensive, integrated, and holistic, and that uses the principles of systems thinking. That is the bedrock of our proposal.

Systems thinking is a framework for identifying interrelationships and patterns, for seeing the whole rather than just the parts. It requires that we think in terms of systems that are composed of circles of influence with various feedback loops and leverage points to exert change, instead of the linear (straight line) approach that characterizes most of our thinking processes. It helps us remember that, while we must often reduce problems into component parts to solve them, we must also place the problems and solutions back into the context of their systems. Systems thinking as an educational approach to complex problems is not the same as teaching in interdisciplinary fashion. Interdisciplinary courses can be and usually are, taught without requiring systems thinking; in contrast, a systems approach requires thinking in interdisciplinary fashion.

I shall give two examples that illustrate the usefulness of and the need for systems approaches to important problems.

The first is the ever-growing threat of devastating epidemics due to emerging or reemerging infections (I am referring now only to naturally-occurring epidemics, not those intentionally initiated under the rubrics of biological warfare or bio-terrorism). Emerging and re-emerging infections are those that are entirely new (such as HIV/AIDS), become rampant in a new geographic area, or reappear in a given area after many years of quiescence (diphtheria in the former-Soviet republics is a good example). Of course, the recent SARS (Severe Acute Respiratory Syndrome) mini-epidemic and the feared, new Asian bird influenza virus are emerging infections.

The simpler approach to these potentially devastating epidemics is to conduct world-wide surveillance, hopefully detect the epidemic early, obtain proper patient specimens, analyze the specimens, determine the nature of the infecting organism, and then, hopefully, treat the cases and contain the spread. Immunization is a part of that reaction pattern. That approach is (immunization aside) picking up the pieces after the event has occurred. We must take the actions included in the simpler linear approach, but, if we are going to prevent a horde of HIV/AIDS-type epidemics in the coming decades and centuries, it will also require a systems approach, examining all the linked, societal variables that provide the milieu in which emerging and re-emerging infections arise and thrive, and then finding leverage points in the system that can modify the entire system, thereby reducing the risk (see Figure 1).

The two, superordinating, societal determinants are population growth and global warming; others include: massive urbanization with disease-promoting slums; increase in the number of people living in poverty; larger numbers of refugees; wars; an aging population; the search for energy; malnutrition; increased international travel; and certain human behaviors. The best way to look at this extraordinarily important issue is as a gigantic system with interconnected, critical variables whose greater or lesser control or amelioration will lead to an output of more or less ferocious epidemics of emerging infections. Thus, in this case, both the simpler linear and the more complex systems approaches are required.

The second example relates to the medical recommendation to include fish in the diet. The scientific evidence now clearly shows that increasing dietary intake of omega-3 fatty acids, which are found, in large part, in oily fish, substantially reduces the risk of sudden death from severe abnormalities in heart rhythm that occur most often during a heart attack, but may occur in the absence of a heart attack. The evidence is so clear that adequate intake of omega-3 fatty acids saves lives that the current medical questions are now the following:

- What kinds of fish provide good amounts of omega-3 fatty acids?
- How often should they be eaten to achieve the maximum benefit?
- Instead of fish, can the available fish oil supplements be substituted?
- If fish oil supplements are used, what is the optimum dosage?

Thus, the linear approach is: omega 3 fatty acids prevent severe heart arrhythmias $\rightarrow$ oily fish have good content of omega 3 fatty acids $\Rightarrow$ eat more oily fish.

Is that all there is to it — scientific evidence and derivative, health-promoting recommendations? The answer is, absolutely not. In point of fact, the dietary recommendation that everybody include oily fish in the diet one or two times a week must be put into a systems thinking paradigm (see Figure 2). The derivative issues are:

- What is the impact on the dwindling fish populations if this recommendation is followed in the United States? In the world?
- What is the impact of this recommendation on the ecology of the oceans?
- If an increasing percentage of the oily fish originates from fish farms, what is the impact of these farms on the environment?
- What is fed to the fish on fish farms? If it is, in part, some sort of fish product, will this, in point of fact, accentuate the problem of profound reduction in the numbers of certain fish species?
- What are the sources of the omega-3 fatty acids in the commercially available fish oil supplements? If they are natural sources, will their use have potentially, major effects on the numbers of certain fish species in the oceans worldwide?

Then, of course, there are issues about the costs to the consumer of these oily fish, the percentages of the total dietary budget that will be required, and the possible adverse effects for less affluent people in regard to the purchase and utilization of other essential nutrients. The questions raised represent the start of a systems approach to what, on the surface, would appear to be an evidence-based scientific and health recommendation. But, thus far, nobody appears to have considered the necessity for placing the dietary recommendation in a systems thinking context. Indeed, to my knowledge, this is the first time anyone has suggested that a recommendation for increasing the dietary intake of oily fish is not just a medical and health promotion issue, but also a societal issue requiring a systems approach.

<u>Commitment to Problem Solving</u>: Our educational system must conscientiously and deliberately seek to instill in students a long-term, part-time, or even

full-time, commitment to addressing major societal problems and a commitment to lifelong learning. Active individual participation in problem solving can be at local, state, national, or international levels.

In decades past, we taught civics, making the assumption it would engender commitment; it infrequently did. Currently, some schools require participation in community projects, but this, too, is not likely to result in lifetime dedication to solving or ameliorating critical societal problems, unless the concept of commitment is vigorously nurtured throughout students' educational experience.

Attempts at instilling commitment must be accompanied by specific involvements that are rewarding enough to persuade students that they can indeed make a difference.

Implementing Educational Change

Once students understand and accept the tenets of systems thinking, they have the flexibility to adjust to the specific problems at hand, recognizing that some can be approached in a simpler, linear fashion, whereas others require a broader systems focus.

These changes in our education system will not cost a lot of money, but will require a change in the way most educators think.

Every high school student in the junior year (eleventh grade) could have a school-year-long course titled "The World Ecosystem." In this huge system, almost everything is related to everything else. This one course, taught by transdisciplinary teams building on teachings in earlier school years, could expose students to the major problems facing the global society and to complex interrelationships, and show them that multiple perspectives improve problem definition and analysis. Additionally, it will teach them to think like futurists and to utilize a systems approach. That is essential.

Educational modification is the vision; the three interrelated components are the goals within that vision. Once the educational establishment and the general public accept the vision and its goals, there are many and varied strategies and tactics that can be used by individual teachers, schools, institutions, and communities to achieve them. The proposed changes are intended for every level of the educational system, from junior high to graduate schools. Additionally, each person will have to decide for himself or herself which of the large number of societal problems deserve to be designated as important enough to merit that individual's attention and commitment.

The future of our society, indeed, if that society has a future, may well depend on how we teach our students to think about the major problems facing their society. Winston S. Churchill once said, "What is the use of living if it be not to make this muddled world a better place for those who will live in it after we are gone?" If we are going to follow that piece of Churchillian wisdom, we will almost certainly have to modify our educational system in accord with the three interconnected recommendations herein outlined.

References

1. Louria, DB, HF Didsbury, Jr., and F Ellerbusch: Societally-connected thinking using a systems approach: An educational and societal imperative. Reprinted (with a changed title) from 21st Century Opportunities and Challenges: World Future Society. Bethesda, MD, HF Didsbury, Jr, ed. 2003. Pgs 99–112.

2. Louria, DB: A systems approach to population growth and global warming. The Jersey Sierran. April–June 2005.

CHAPTER ELEVEN

CONstruction: Criminal Offender Neighborhood Stabilization Through Restoration of Urban Communities and Training In Occupational Necessities

By
Mike Presutti

This program proposal, herein described, combines an occupational training program with an urban renewal effort designed to rehabilitate criminal offenders and the physical communities where they often live. CONstruction works at many levels and creates the often-illusive "win-win-win" scenario. It offsets the per-inmate cost of incarceration; it trains, challenges, and encourages criminal offenders to become responsible citizens; and it provides asset appreciation of real property, which currently disproportionately drains the municipal resources of police, sanitation, and fire services. Ideally, at its core, CONstruction is a stabilization plan that can thwart the malignancy of crime and urban decay, and breed future development and revitalization in our inner city communities.

The occupational training portion of this program is derived from successful educational models for criminal rehabilitation and adult occupational training modules and my own experience teaching through the Sheriff's Office of Morris County and Morris County Vocational and Technical School in Denville throughout the mid-1990s.

Throughout our country, our inner cities are plagued with deteriorating infrastructure and crime. The following program aims to confront both of these scourges with the same mechanism.

It is my hope that the effort before you makes sense, eventually bears fruit, and contributes to the betterment of our inner cities and the people who dwell within them.

Executive Summary

The cost of incarceration is high and yields very little, real demonstrative change in behavior.

Our inner cities have within them decaying buildings, and neighborhoods. M, many of these buildings are owned by the municipalities and are abandoned or blighted. These buildings are breeding grounds for crime, vagrancy, and fires, and dumping grounds for unsanitary debris. Beside their tangible drain on their respective communities, these cancerous sections tend to depress both the minds of those who live there and the value of real property. Hopelessness is the common disposition of many who live in these neighborhoods, and urban flight only spreads the decay to adjacent streets and neighborhoods.

In very simple terms, CONstruction is a training program that purchases decayed and run-down city blocks or sections thereof, puts fences around these areas, and rehabilitates the properties using convicted criminal offenders who want to change themselves and their communities. It is a work program that is granted in lieu of a prison or jail term with the understanding that failure to perform in the program or attempt to better one's self, will result in a maximum adjudicated term in prison. The products of this endeavor are restored city blocks and a source of pride and purpose for young criminal offenders and their communities. In essence, it can be said that CONstruction breathes new life into people and property.

Ideally, the typical CONstruction project includes a mix of different types of buildings, which will assure a varied training program and culminate in a diversely zoned and restored neighborhood block. The diversity of buildings may include: varying scales of residential units, restaurant spaces, retail spaces, artisan shops, theaters, and open public spaces. All of these plans will be coordinated with the respective municipalities and professionally planned.

The financing of this project will be through private real estate investment trusts and corporate and individual philanthropy. Unlike typical charitable/philanthropic contributors, the "donor/investors" involved with CONstruction will receive back appreciated assets, with which they can do as they please because they retain ownership. This is a program devised for a proactive government able to use private interests directly for public good in an efficient *bottom-line* manner.

CONstruction Trainers

Even the best training program is doomed to fail if the trainers who promulgate the program are not the right people for the job. The right people to train young criminal offenders are often not industrial arts teachers from vocational schools, who ordinarily teach children. This program will utilize construction tradespeople and construction managers, who know real-world construction and often relate better to young criminal offenders than do school teachers. It has been my experience that construction workers and managers often come from similar socioeconomic backgrounds as do many criminal offenders, and hence relate to the "street" side of our world better than college-educated vocational teachers. The construction industry is unique in that most of the learning and training actually takes place on the job while doing the tasks with someone more experienced. You simply cannot teach adults, especially troubled adults, within only a classroom environment. On the job training in construction, supplemented by classroom work, is ideal for a quick and pedagogical structure.

Trainers in the CONstruction program will work alongside students, eat with them and send them out for coffee and donuts at breaks. The very same personal interactions that take place on a construction site will take place on the CONstruction jobsites. This personal interaction is necessary to help perpetuate camaraderie and teamwork among students and instructors, and will aid in positive role modeling. Our instructors will be special people, who are personally and professionally dedicated to the core CONstruction purposes. The jobsite will look and feel like any other construction site in town. The instruction will be a mix of hands-on manual work performed directly on the site's buildings, and "classroom" work performed in mobile trailers located within the construction site itself.

There are other advantages to such a hands-on pedagogical approach to construction using construction workers and construction managers. First, the student learns and becomes familiar with the construction jobsite just as it would appear in the real world. The student will learn everything, from the proper mechanics of a certain task to the job site's chain of command, by working in a real-life atmosphere with real expectations. This "embedded" position will provide as realistic a situation as possible for the student, because there will be budgets and ddeadlines. This is a proven "real bullets overhead" approach to learning optimally achieved using real-world construction people.

CONstruction trainers will receive training in how to teach and train adult criminal offender students, with an emphasis on adult motivation. We will seek to have the state university provide such services and abide by similar teaching modules as those adult training courses taught at the Region II OSHA Educational Center at The University of Medicine and Dentistry of New Jersey-School of Public Health.

The screening process for trainers will be instrumental to CONstruction success. We will look for people who share a genuine ambition for the program. They will have to be well-rounded experts in construction techniques, practices, methods, and protocol derived from hands-on experience. They will need to be able to "talk" the language of construction and the language of their audience, in a manner that will be persuasive. This nexus is vital, because trainers who talk condescendingly to their students will ultimately not be good facilitators of the program's content and purpose. Likewise, trainers who "spoon-feed" students without challenging them are likely to elongate the learning process and create a false sense of reality about the business of construction.

Inspiration and Source of Pride

The CONstruction project will take place in the same neighborhoods in which many of the offenders lived. Its presence will be a shinning light for renewal and a source of pride, not shame, as the project develops. CONstruction, at its core, is an urban renewal project. Little kids looking through the fence will see role models developing in front of their eyes: people who decided to change course and take a difficult path to better themselves, and, through that change, better us all. The people working on the CONstruction site will want to be there of their own volition. The ethos of all connected with CONstruction will not be one of "work camp." CONstruction will not have a chain-gang mentality—it will perpetuate a team spirit and seek a sense of community, all bent on renewal, renovation, and hard work. Through these efforts, CONstruction will promote community citizenship and teamwork, all essential tools for a successful career and a fruitful life. If budgets and circumstances allow, two separate CONstruction projects can take place simultaneously with a friendly rivalry between the two sites to simulate the competitive spirit in real business.

Besides the technical training, CONstruction will teach offenders the principles behind a good work ethic and even entrepreneurialism. The basic reason why I chose the construction industry as the ideal industry to create such a rehabilitation model is the relatively high percentage of self-employed people among the construction trades (see Department of Labor occupation overviews and outlooks). Our hope is that graduates of this program will eventually go into their neighborhoods and aid in their rejuvenation by becoming entrepreneurs. They will learn about the underlying costs of certain jobs, how to work on a project schedule, how to work safely, and how work with other workers, contractors, construction professionals, and the like.

Guest Instructors

The program will regularly have guest lecturers talk about their personal paths to success. Ideally, these people will be the self-made success types who came from similar backgrounds as the students; their contributions will provide both education and inspiration. Hopefully, these lecturers will instill hope within the students and help them believe they, too, can pull themselves up and achieve a better lot in life. It should be mentioned here that a "success" does not have to be a millionaire businessperson, but rather an ordinary person married and successfully raising a family. These guests may also provide an avenue for potential employment.

A Construction and Education Site Only

Although all of the students on the CONstruction site will be in probation or parole programs, no direct correctional or police activity will take place unless it is directly attributed to a new investigation or incident. The treatment of all student/ workers on a CONstruction site will be as employees only; to repeat, CONstruction will not perpetuate a chain-gang image, it will be with pride and dignity that these students work and learn. If the Department of Corrections mandates that officers will be needed to be present, they will be dressed in plain clothes appropriate to the site, and their numbers will be kept at a minimum, commensurate with the population. This presence will be only for security and not authority. The authority on a construction site is maintained by line managers and supervisors who will have autonomy on the sites. Any testing (urine, breathalyzer, blood tests) will take place outside of the CONstruction site.

Specific Training Goals

The following is the actual trade syllabus that CONstruction will follow. This syllabus will vary in size and scope according to site-specific conditions.

OSHA — 10 and 30 hour training
OSHA courses on scaffolding, trenching, cranes
Blueprint Reading
Welding/Cutting/Brazing
General Environmental Control
Medical and First Aid [CPR, AED]
Material Safety Data Sheets (MSDS) Workshops

Electric	Plumbing
Rough Carpentry	Drywall Hanging and Finishing
Concrete/Masonry	Finish Carpentry
Painting	Roofing
Heating and Air Conditioning	Carpentry
Cabinet Making	Advanced Electrical
Construction Project Coordination	Management

The set syllabus will be based on a host of different job-specific criteria, such as the type of renovation or construction, weather conditions, project site coordination, and availability of materials. The site supervisor will meet with workers every morning and coordinate a construction plan for that day's work, which will include the integration of classroom and work site. There will be several "tool box" talks during the day, and "downtime" will be spent in impromptu field training sessions. In time, learning and work will become indistinguishable.

Sample Syllabus (First Week Instruction)

• Student Introduction to CONstruction: Students are briefed on the program. Instructors explain to students the "ground rules" of the work site and what the program will expect from them.

- Construction Site Safety OSHA 10 hour: Before any workers enter a construction site, they must become familiar with the safety issues at the site. The OSHA 10 hour class is an ideal module for safety and will be the first construction-related learning module. In time, the instructor will provide the more extensive OSHA 30 hour training module. Students will go through a new worker initiation process.

- Job Site Hierarchy: The students will learn the authority structure for the people with whom they will be working. Trainers will discuss the tasks and authority of various people on the job site. They will include the trainers themselves, supervisors, support staff personnel, professional engineers, architects, surveyors, building department officials etc.

- Basic Introduction to Blueprint Reading. Elevations, plans, section drawings, and schedules will be taught at a very basic level. For example:

What does this drawing look like?
What room in a house would you find this drawing?

- Basic Construction Terminology: The trainers will introduce the construction site to students as if they were going into another country where, in order to get around and live, they would have to learn the language. CONstruction has its own language. The terminology taught here will include job site tools, equipment, and trade-specific peripherals.

- Basic Building Terminology: The trainers will display various components of a typical building such as studs, joists, rafters, slabs, and footings, and try to have the class distinguish among them. Later, the trainer will walk the site and point out some of the building components.

- Tour of Site: Students will learn the site and its structure. They will learn the names of various buildings (A,B,C etc). They will learn where bathrooms, offices, tool bins, and trailers classrooms are located, and, gain general site familiarity.

Entrance into the CONstruction Program

Upon conviction of a non-sexual, non-violent crime or after a period of time deemed appropriate by the court, a convicted person who demonstrates remorse and promise will be afforded an opportunity to enter into the CONstruction program. This will be a conditional sentence bound by court order.

The participants in the program will live on their own resources, however they will also receive New Jersey State welfare subsidies or the equivalent. They will know before going into the program that it will not be easy. They will have to work hard to learn, and will be informed that any problem can result in being sent back to prison or jail for the maximum sentence under law. In many ways, the risk is all theirs (the offenders), and the direction of the remainder of their lives may hang on such a decision.

Staying in the CONstruction Program

Continued participation in the CONstruction program will be based on New Jersey's existing Intensive Supervision Program. The New Jersey Judiciary operates what is known as the Intensive Supervision Program, or ISP, which has proved successful in rehabilitating serious offenders. Under ISP, offenders who are sentenced to state prison may apply to a panel of judges for release into this special monitoring and supervision program. To be eligible, applicants must demonstrate the willingness and ability to adhere to the program's strict guidelines.

Clients who apply to the Intensive Supervision Programs (ISP) through the Administrative Office of the Courts can obtain representation through the NJ Office of the Public Defender (NJOPD) for those hearings. ISP programs provide alternative, intermediate forms of community-based correctional supervision, allowing some offenders to serve sentences outside the traditional prison settings.

Those people convicted of a homicide, robbery, or sex offense, or sentenced on a first-degree offense, are not eligible for ISP. However, most other offenders may apply. The most common forms of community-based supervision involve Department of Corrections officers maintaining both telephone and personal contact with offenders. In some instances, electronic monitoring devices are required to be worn. We recognize that the State may assign an appropriate number of officers directly to the work site.

The program focuses on helping participants change their lives, so that they may avoid the influences that have contributed to their past problems. Drug, alcohol, and gambling counseling, curfews, community service, and employment requirements are among the guidelines that participants must follow to remain in the program.

All ISP participants are required to:

- Maintain full time employment in CONstruction;
- Maintain a diary and notebook of work-elated notes;
- Maintain a budget log;
- Submit to urine monitoring;
- Undergo extensive contact with probation/parole officers outside of CONstruction;
- Adhere to a restrictive curfew;
- Undergo rigorous surveillance.

Why the Construction Industry—Easy Entry and Outsource-proof

Traditionally, construction has had little or no barriers to entry. Construction is one of the few industries that does not require a high school degree or equivalent, and construction avails a worker the possibility of advancement and entrepreneurialism, regardless of education. Many "uneducated," successful tradespeople earn more than their "educated" counterparts. It is not uncommon for a master plumber or electrician, after less than a decade of experience, to earn in excess of $100,000 per year. There are few barriers.

With a growing population and the continued obsolescence and deterioration of real property, there will be, well into the future, a need for skilled construction tradespeople for both residential and commercial construction trade work.

The trend in America is for less educated labor to be outsourced to foreign countries; however, construction is one industry in which outsourcing of labor is, literally, impossible. Therefore, into the future, many occupations, which require much more education than construction, may actually shrink in size due to outsourcing, while construction work is forecast by the Department of Labor (DOL) to grow, because of the need for on-site service, constant renovation and general maintenance requirements of exiting structures, and a growing population.

Funding

Funding for CONstruction projects will come from public and private channels. Corporate sponsorships and in-kind donations from tool companies and material suppliers are anticipated and will be pursued. Incarcerating a convicted person costs the Department of Corrections tens of thousands of dollars per year. The costs to the State will be considerably less, because private, for-profit mechanisms will drive the program, and will, ideally, yield viable real property appreciation, albeit marginal. The fences that surround the projects will have sponsor placards to advertise their community involvement, and many avenues of tremendous media exposure will be sought. A reality television show has already been discussed and will be pursued further if this program comes to fruition. Such exposure would not only help fund this pilot concept, but would also promulgate its duplication throughout our country and perhaps beyond. Fundraisers, concerts, and the like will be an ongoing stream of revenue and heighten the societal impacts of the program.

Occupations

The construction occupations chosen for CONstruction were selected based on certain criteria. We had to make sure that the occupation would exist far enough into the future to provide someone with a lifelong opportunity to make a viable, thriving living. Our hope was also that each occupation would product a good-paying career with room to advance and the opportunity for self-employment. It is through self-employment that new jobs are created and individuals are allowed to pursue their dreams. The following is a breakdown of various occupations, including those for which CONstruction will train its participant students. The following information is based on numbers provided by the Department of Labor. Our own numbers tend to yield higher figures, because the northeast region of the country has historically higher wages and more plentiful construction. New Jersey is the most densely populated state in the country, so, statistically, these numbers are actually skewed lower than what we can anticipate for our State.

Fastest growing occupations and occupations projected to have the largest numerical increases in employment between 2002 and 2012, by level of education or training		
Education or training level	Fastest growing occupations	Occupations having the largest numerical job growth
First professional degree		
	Pharmacists	Lawyers
	Veterinarians	Physicians and surgeons
	Chiropractors	Pharmacists
	Physicians and surgeons	Clergy
	Optometrists	Veterinarians
Doctoral degree		
	Postsecondary teachers	Postsecondary teachers
	Computer and information scientists, research	Clinical, counseling, and school psychologists
	Medical scientists, except epidemiologists	Medical scientists, except Epidemiologists
	Clinical, counseling, and school psychologists	Computer and information scientists, research
	Biochemists and biophysicists	Biochemists and biophysicists
Master's degree		
	Physical therapists	Physical therapists
	Mental health and substance abuse social workers	Rehabilitation counselors
	Rehabilitation counselors	Educational, vocational, and school counselors
	Survey researchers	Mental health and substance abuse social workers
	Epidemiologists	Market research analysts
Bachelor's or higher degree, plus work experience		
	Computer and information systems managers	General and operations Managers
	Education administrators, preschool and childcare center/program	Management analysts
	Sales managers	Financial managers

	Management analysts	Sales managers
	Medical and health services managers	Computer and information systems managers
Bachelor's degree		
	Network systems and data communications analysts	Elementary school teachers, except special education
	Physician assistants	Accountants and auditors
	Computer software engineers, applications	Computer systems analysts
	Computer software engineers, systems software	Secondary school teachers, except special and vocational education
	Database administrators	Computer software engineers, applications
Associate degree		
	Medical records and health information technicians	Registered nurses
	Physical therapist assistants	Computer support specialists
	Veterinary technologists and technicians	Medical records and health information technicians
	Dental hygienists	Dental hygienists
	Occupational therapist assistants	Paralegals and legal Assistants
Postsecondary vocational award		
	Fitness trainers and aerobics instructors	Preschool teachers, except special education
	Preschool teachers, except special education	Licensed practical and licensed vocational nurses
	Respiratory therapy technicians	Automotive service technicians and mechanics
	Emergency medical technicians and paramedics	Hairdressers, hairstylists, and cosmetologists
	Security and fire alarm systems installers	Fitness trainers and aerobics instructors
Work experience in a related occupation		
	Self-enrichment education teachers	First-line supervisors/managers of retail sales workers
	Emergency management specialists	First-line supervisors/managers of food preparation and serving Workers
	Private detectives and investigators	First-line supervisors/managers of office and administrative support workers
	First-line supervisors/managers of protective service workers, except police, fire, and corrections	First-line supervisors/managers of construction trades and extraction workers
	Detectives and criminal investigators	Self-enrichment education Teachers

Long-term on-the-job training		
	Heating, air-conditioning, and refrigeration mechanics and installers	Electricians
	Audio and video equipment technicians	Police and sheriff's patrol officers
	Tile and marble setters	Carpenters
	Police and sheriff's patrol officers	Cooks, restaurant
	Electricians	Plumbers, pipe fitters, and steamfitters
Moderate-term on-the-job training		
	Medical assistants	Customer service representatives
	Social and human service assistants	Truck drivers, heavy and tractor-trailer
	Hazardous materials removal workers	Sales representatives, wholesale and manufacturing, except technical and scientific products
	Dental assistants	Medical assistants
	Residential advisors	Maintenance and repair workers, general
Short-term on-the-job training		
	Home health aides	Retail salespersons
	Physical therapist aides	Combined food preparation and serving workers, including fast food
	Occupational therapist aides	Cashiers, except gaming
	Personal and home care aides	Janitors and cleaners, except maids and housekeeping cleaners
	Security guards	Waiters and waitresses

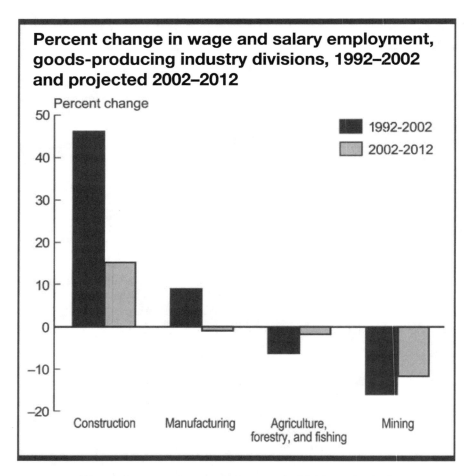

Percent change in wage and salary employment, goods-producing industry divisions, 1992–2002 and projected 2002–2012

Changing employment between 2002 and 2012

Grow much faster than average = increases of increase 36 % or more
Grow faster than average = increase 21% to 35 %
Grow about as fast as average = increase 10% to 20 %
Grow more slowly than average = increase 3% to 9 %
Little or no growth = increase 0% to 2 %
Decline = decrease 1 % or more

Brick Masons, Block Masons, and Stonemasons

Significant Points of Interest

- Job prospects are expected to be excellent;
- Most entrants learn informally on the job, but apprenticeship programs provide the most thorough training;
- The work is usually outdoors and involves lifting heavy materials and working on scaffolds;
- More than 1 out of 4 are self-employed.

Brick masons, block masons, and stonemasons held 165,000 jobs in 2002. The vast majority were brick masons. Workers in these crafts are employed primarily by building, specialty trade, or general contractors. Brick masons, block masons, and stonemasons work throughout the country, but, like the general population, are concentrated in metropolitan areas.

More than 1 out of 4 brick masons, block masons, and stonemasons are self-employed. Many of the self-employed specialize in contracting to work on small jobs, such as patios, walkways, and fireplaces.

Job opportunities for brick masons, block masons, and stonemasons are expected to be excellent through 2012. Many openings will result from the need to replace workers who retire, transfer to other occupations, or leave these trades for other reasons. There may be fewer applicants than needed because many potential workers prefer to work under less strenuous, more comfortable conditions.

Employment of brick masons, block masons, and stonemasons is expected to increase about as fast as the average for all occupations over the 2002-12 period, as population and business growth create a need for new houses, industrial facilities, schools, hospitals, offices, and other structures. Also stimulating demand will be the need to restore a growing stock of old masonry buildings, as well as the increasing use of brick and stone for decorative work on building fronts and in lobbies and foyers. Brick exteriors should remain very popular, reflecting a growing preference for durable exterior materials requiring little maintenance.

Employment of brick masons, block masons, and stonemasons, like that of many other construction workers, is sensitive to changes in the economy. When the level of construction activity falls, workers in these trades can experience periods of unemployment.

The median hourly wage for brick masons and block masons in 2002 was $20.11. The middle 50% earned between $15.36 and $25.32. The lowest 10% earned less than $11.55, and the highest 10 % earned more than $30.66. Median hourly earnings in the industries employing the largest number of brick masons in 2002 are shown below:

Nonresidential building construction	$22.12
Foundation, structure, and building exterior contractors	$20.26

The median hourly wage for stonemasons in 2002 was \$16.36. The middle 50% earned between \$12.06 and \$20.76. The lowest 10% earned less than \$9.43, and the highest 10% earned more than \$26.59.

Earnings for workers in these trades can be reduced on occasion because poor weather and downturns in construction activity limit the time they can work. Apprentices or helpers usually start at about 50% of the wage rate paid to experienced workers. Pay increases as apprentices gain experience and learn new skills.

Some brick masons, block masons, and stonemasons are members of the International Union of Bricklayers and Allied Crafts workers.

Rough and Finish Carpenters

Significant Points of Interest

- About 30% of all carpenters—the largest construction trade in 2002— were self-employed.
- Job opportunities should be excellent.
- Carpenters with all-round skills will have the best opportunities for steady work.

Carpenters, who make up the largest building trades occupation, held about 1.2 million jobs in 2002. One-third worked for general building contractors, and one-fifth worked for special trade contractors. Most of the rest of the wage and salary workers worked for manufacturing firms, government agencies, retail establishments, and a wide variety of other industries. About 30% of all carpenters were self-employed.

Carpenters are employed throughout the country in almost every community.

Job opportunities for carpenters are expected to be excellent over the 2002-12 period, largely due to the numerous openings arising each year as experienced carpenters leave this large occupation. Contributing to this favorable job market is the fact that many potential workers prefer work that is less strenuous and has more comfortable working conditions. Because there are no strict training requirements for entry, many people with limited skills take jobs as carpenters, but eventually leave the occupation because they dislike the work or cannot find steady employment.

Employment of carpenters is expected to grow about as fast as the average for all occupations through 2012. Construction activity should increase in response to demand for new housing and commercial and industrial plants and the need to renovate and modernize existing structures. The demand for larger homes with more amenities and for second homes will continue to rise, especially as the baby boomers reach their peak earning years and can afford to spend more on housing. At the same time, the demand for manufactured housing, starter homes, and rental apartments also is expected to increase as the number of immigrants grows and as the relatively small baby bust generation, which followed the baby boom generation, is replaced by echo boomers (the children of the baby boomers) in the young adult age groups.

However, some of the demand for carpenters will be offset by expected productivity gains resulting from the increasing use of prefabricated components, such as perching doors and windows and prefabricated wall panels and stairs, which can be installed very quickly. Prefabricated walls, partitions, and stairs are lifted into place in one operation; beams—and, in some cases, entire roof assemblies—are lifted into place using a crane. As prefabricated components become more standardized, builders will use them more often. In addition, improved adhesives will reduce the time needed to join materials, and lightweight, cordless, and pneumatic tools—such as nailers and drills—all make carpenters more efficient.

Carpenters can experience periods of unemployment because of the short-term nature of many construction projects and the cyclical nature of the construction industry. Building activity depends on many factors—interest rates, availability of mortgage funds, the season, government spending, and business investment—most of which vary with the state of the economy. During economic downturns, the number of job openings for carpenters declines. New and improved tools, equipment, techniques, and materials require vastly increased carpenter versatility. Therefore, carpenters with all-round skills will have better opportunities for steady work than carpenters who can do only a few, relatively simple, routine tasks.

Job opportunities for carpenters also vary by geographic area. Construction activity parallels the movement of people and businesses and reflects differences in local economic conditions. Therefore, the number of job opportunities and apprenticeship opportunities in a given year may vary widely from area to area.

In 2002, the median hourly wage for carpenters was $16.44. The middle 50 % earned between $12.59 and $21.91. The lowest 10% earned less than $9.95, and the highest 10% earned more than $27.97. Median hourly earnings in the industries employing the largest numbers of carpenters in 2002 are shown below:

Non residential building construction	$18.31
Building finishing contractors	$17.30
Residential building construction	$16.02
Foundation, structure, and building exterior contractors	$16.01
Employment services	$12.58

Earnings can be reduced on occasion, because carpenters lose work time in bad weather and during recessions when jobs are unavailable. Some carpenters are members of the United Brotherhood of Carpenters and Joiners of America.

Carpet, Floor, and Tile Installers and Finishers

Significant Points of Interest

- Forty-three percent of all carpet, floor, and tile installers and finishers are self-employed, compared with 19% of all construction trades workers.

- Most workers learn on the job.

- Carpet installers, the largest specialty, should have the best job opportunities.

- The employment of carpet, floor, and tile installers and finishers is less sensitive to fluctuations in construction activity than that of other construction trades workers.

Carpet, floor, and tile installers and finishers held about 164,000 jobs in 2002. Forty-three percent of all carpet, floor, and tile installers and finishers were self-employed, compared with 19% of all construction trades workers. The following tabulation shows 2002 wage and salary employment by specialty:

Carpet installers	82,000
Tile and marble setters	33,000
Floor layers, except carpet, wood, and hard tiles	31,000
Floor sanders and finishers	17,000

Many carpet installers worked for flooring contractors or floor covering retailers. Most salaried tile setters were employed by tile setting contractors, who work mainly on nonresidential construction projects, such as schools, hospitals, and office buildings. Most self-employed tile setters work on residential projects.

Although carpet, floor, and tile installers and finishers are employed throughout the nation, they tend to be concentrated in populated areas where there are high levels of construction activity.

Employment of carpet, floor, and tile installers and finishers is expected to grow about as fast as the average for all occupations through the year 2012, reflecting the continued need to renovate and refurbish existing structures. However, employment of one specialty—floor sanders and finishers—is projected to grow more slowly than average due to the increasing use of refinished hardwood and similar flooring. Carpet installers, the largest specialty, should have the best job opportunities.

Carpet as a floor covering continues to be popular, and its use is expected to grow in structures such as schools, offices, hospitals, and industrial plants. Employment of carpet installers also is expected to grow because wall-to-wall carpeting is a necessity in the many houses built with plywood, rather than hardwood, floors.

Similarly, offices, hotels, and stores often cover concrete floors with wall-to-wall carpet, which must be periodically replaced.

Demand for tile and marble setters will stem from population and business growth, which should result in more construction of shopping malls, hospitals, schools, restaurants, and other structures in which tile is used extensively. Tile is expected to continue to increase in popularity as a building material and to be used more, particularly in the growing number of more expensive homes, leading to faster than average growth for tile and marble setters. Demand for floor layers and sanders and finishers will expand as a result of growth in construction activity, particularly related to residential homes and commercial buildings, and as some people decide to replace their plywood floors with hardwood floors. Job opportunities for tile and marble setters and for floor layers and sanders, relatively small specialties, will not be as plentiful as those for carpet installers.

The employment of carpet, floor, and tile installers and finishers is less sensitive to changes in construction activity than that of most other construction occupations, because much of the work involves replacing carpet and other flooring in existing buildings. As a result, these workers tend to be sheltered from the business fluctuations that often occur in new construction activity.

In 2002, the median hourly wage for carpet installers was $15.67. The middle 50% earned between $11.39 and $21.03. The lowest 10% earned less than $8.90, and the top 10% earned more than $27.15. In 2002, the median hourly wage of carpet installers working for building finishing contractors was $16.09, and in home furnishings stores, $14.64.

Carpet installers are paid either on an hourly basis or by the number of yards of carpet installed. The rates vary widely depending on the geographic location and whether the installer is affiliated with a union.

The median hourly wage for floor layers was $16.15 in 2002. The middle 50% earned between $11.42 and $20.81. The lowest 10% earned less than $8.58, and the top 10% earned more than $26.87.

The median hourly wage for floor sanders and finishers was $13.22 in 2002. The middle 50% earned between $10.38 and $16.97. The lowest 10% earned less than $8.96, and the top 10% earned more than $22.51.

The median hour wage for tile and marble setters was $17.20 in 2002. The middle 50% earned between $12.96 and $22.39. The lowest 10% earned less than $10.21, and the top 10% earned more than $28.22. Earnings of tile and marble setters also vary greatly by geographic location and by union membership status.

Apprentices and other trainees usually start out earning about half of what an experienced worker earns, although their wage rate increases as they advance through the training program.

Some carpet, floor, and tile installers and finishers belong to the United Brotherhood of Carpenters and Joiners of America. Some tile setters belong to the International Union of Bricklayers and Allied Craftsmen, while some carpet installers belong to the International Brotherhood of Painters and Allied Trades.

Cement Masons, Concrete Finishers, Segmental Pavers, and Terrazzo Workers

Significant Points of Interest

- Job opportunities are expected to be favorable.

- Most learn on the job, either through formal 3-year or 4-year apprenticeship programs or by working as helpers. Like workers in many other construction trades, these workers may experience reduced earnings and layoffs during downturns in construction activity.

- Cement masons often work overtime with premium pay, because, once concrete has been placed, the job must be completed.

Cement masons, concrete finishers, segmental pavers, and terrazzo workers held about 190,000 jobs in 2002; segmental pavers and terrazzo workers accounted for only a small portion of the total. Most cement masons and concrete finishers worked for concrete contractors or for general contractors on projects such as highways, bridges, shopping malls, or large buildings such as factories, schools, and hospitals. A small number were employed by firms that manufacture concrete products. Most segmental pavers and terrazzo workers worked for special trade contractors, who install decorative floors and wall panels.

Only about 1 out of 20 cement masons, concrete finishers, segmental pavers, and terrazzo workers was self-employed, a smaller proportion than in other building trades. Most self-employed masons specialized in small jobs, such as driveways, sidewalks, and patios.

Opportunities for cement masons, concrete finishers, segmental pavers, and terrazzo workers are expected to be favorable as the demand meets the supply of workers trained in this craft. In addition, many potential workers may prefer work that is less strenuous and has more comfortable working conditions.

Employment of cement masons, concrete finishers, segmental pavers, and terrazzo workers is expected to grow about as fast as the average for all occupations through 2012. These workers will be needed to build highways, bridges, subways, factories, office buildings, hotels, shopping centers, schools, hospitals, and other structures. In addition, the increasing use of concrete as a building material will add to the demand. More cement masons also will be needed to repair and renovate existing highways, bridges, and other structures. In addition to opportunities for job growth, other openings will become available as experienced workers transfer to other occupations or leave the labor force.

Employment of cement masons, concrete finishers, segmental pavers, and terrazzo workers, like that of many other construction workers, is sensitive to the fluctuations of the economy. Workers in these trades may experience periods of unemployment when the overall level of construction falls. On the other hand, shortages of these workers may occur in some areas during peak periods of building activity.

In 2002, the median hourly wage for cement masons and concrete finishers was $14.74. The middle 50% earned between $11.52 and $20.02. The top 10% earned over $26.02, and the bottom 10% earned less than $9.31.

In 2002, the median hourly wage for terrazzo workers and finishers was $13.42. The middle 50% earned between $10.46 and $17.72. The top 10% earned over $23.70, and the bottom 10% earned less than $8.94.

Like those of other construction trades workers, earnings of cement masons, concrete finishers, segmental pavers, and terrazzo workers may be reduced on occasion, because poor weather and downturns in construction activity limit the amount of time they can work. Cement masons often work overtime with premium pay, because once concrete has been placed, the job must be completed.

Many cement masons, concrete finishers, segmental pavers, and terrazzo workers belong to the Operative Plasterers' and Cement Masons' International Association of the United States and Canada, or to the International Union of Bricklayers and Allied Craft Workers. Some terrazzo workers belong to the United Brotherhood of Carpenters and Joiners of the United States. Nonunion workers generally have lower wage rates than do union workers. Apprentices usually start at 50% to 60% of the rate paid to experienced workers.

Construction Laborers

Significant Points of interest

• Job opportunities should be good.

• The work can be physically demanding and sometimes dangerous.

• Most construction laborers learn through informal on-the-job training, but formal apprenticeship programs provide more thorough preparation.

• As in many other construction occupations, employment opportunities are affected by the cyclical nature of the construction industry and can vary greatly by the State and locality.

Construction laborers held about 938,000 jobs in 2002. They worked throughout the country, but, like the general population, were concentrated in metropolitan areas. Almost all construction laborers work in the construction in-dustry, and almost one-third work for special trade contractors. About 14% were self-employed in 2002.

Job opportunities for construction laborers are expected to be good due to the numerous openings arising each year as laborers leave the occupation. In addition, many potential workers are not attracted to the occupation because they prefer work that is less strenuous and has more comfortable working conditions. Oppor-tunities will be best for workers who are willing to relocate to different worksites.

Employment of construction laborers is expected to grow about as fast as the average for all occupations through the year 2012. New jobs will arise from a continuing emphasis on environmental remediation and on rebuilding infrastructure—roads, airports, bridges, tunnels, and communications facilities, for example. However, employment growth will be adversely affected by automation as some jobs are replaced by new machines and equipment that improve productivity and quality.

Employment of construction laborers, like that of many other construction workers, can be variable or intermittent due to the limited duration of construction projects and the cyclical nature of the construction industry. Employment opportunities can vary greatly by State and locality. During economic downturns, job openings for construction laborers decrease as the level of construction activity declines.

The median hourly wage for construction laborers in 2002 were $11.90. The middle 50% earned between $9.33 and $17.06. The lowest 10% earned less than $7.58, and the highest 10% earned more than $23.36. Median hourly earnings in the industries employing the largest number of construction laborers in 2002 were as follows:

Highway, street, and bridge construction	$14.48
Nonresidential building construction	$12.97
Other specialty trade contractors	$12.35
Foundation, structure, and building exterior contractors	$11.89
Residential building construction	$11.42

Earnings for construction laborers can be reduced by poor weather or by downturns in construction activity, which sometimes result in layoffs.

Apprentices or helpers usually start at about 50% of the wage rate paid to experienced workers. Pay increases as apprentices gain experience and learn new skills. Some laborers belong to the Laborers' International Union of North America.

Drywall Installers, Ceiling Tile Installers, and Tapers

Significant Points of Interest

- Most workers learn the trade on the job, either by working as helpers or through a formal apprenticeship.

- Job prospects are expected to be good.

- Inclement weather seldom interrupts work, but workers may be idled when downturns in the economy slow new construction activity.

Drywall installers, ceiling tile installers, and tapers held about 176,000 jobs in 2002. Most worked for contractors specializing in drywall and ceiling tile installation; others worked for contractors doing many kinds of construction. About 33,000 were self-employed independent contractors.

Most installers and tapers are employed in populous areas. In other areas, where there may not be enough work to keep a drywall or ceiling tile installer employed full time, carpenters and painters usually do the work.

Job opportunities for drywall installers, ceiling tile installers, and tapers are expected to be good. Many potential workers are not attracted to this occupation because they prefer work that is less strenuous and has more comfortable working conditions. Experienced workers will have especially favorable opportunities.

Employment is expected to grow about as fast as the average for all occupations over the 2002-12 period, reflecting increases in the numbers of new construction and remodeling projects. In addition to jobs involving traditional interior work, drywall employment opportunities will come from installation of insulated exterior wall systems, which are becoming increasingly popular.

Besides those resulting from job growth, many jobs will open up each year because of the need to replace workers who transfer to other occupations or leave the labor force. Some drywall installers, ceiling tile installers, and tapers with limited skills leave the occupation when they find that they dislike the work or fail to find steady employment.

Despite the growing use of exterior panels, most drywall installation and finishing is done indoors. Therefore, drywall workers lose less work time because of inclement weather than do some other construction workers. Nevertheless, they may be unemployed between construction projects and during downturns in construction activity.

In 2002, the median wage for drywall and ceiling tile installers was $16.21. The middle 50% earned between $12.43 and $21.50. The lowest 10% earned less than $9.76, and the highest 10% earned more than $28.03. The median hourly earnings in the industries employing the largest numbers of drywall and ceiling tile installers in 2002 were:

Building finishing contractors	$16.50
Nonresidential building construction	$14.66

In 2002, the median hourly wage for tapers was $18.75. The middle 50% earned between $14.57 and $24.68. The lowest 10% earned less than $11.07, and the highest 10% earned more than $29.32.

Trainees usually started at about half the rate paid to experienced workers and received wage increases as they became more highly skilled. Some contractors pay these workers according to the number of panels they install or finish per day; others pay an hourly rate. A 40-hour week is standard, but the workweek may sometimes be longer. Workers who are paid hourly rates receive premium pay for overtime.

Electricians

Significant Points of Interest

- Job opportunities are expected to be good.

- Most electricians acquire their skills by completing an apprenticeship program lasting 3 to 5 years.

- More than one-quarter of wage and salary electricians work in industries other than construction.

Electricians held about 659,000 jobs in 2002. More than one-quarter of wage and salary workers were employed in the construction industry, while the remainder worked as maintenance electricians employed outside the construction industry. In addition, about one in 10 electricians was self-employed.

Because of the widespread need for electrical services, jobs for electricians are found in all parts of the country. Job opportunities for electricians are expected to be good. Numerous openings will arise each year as experienced electricians leave the occupation. In addition, many potential workers may choose not to enter training programs because they prefer work that is less strenuous and has more comfortable working conditions.

Employment of electricians is expected to grow about as fast as the average for all occupations through the year 2012. As the population and economy grow, more electricians will be needed to install and maintain electrical devices and wiring in homes, factories, offices, and other structures. New technologies also are expected to continue to stimulate the demand for these workers. For example, buildings will be rewired during construction to accommodate use of computers and telecommunications equipment. More factories will be using robots and automated manufacturing systems. Additional jobs will be created by rehabilitation and retrofitting of existing structures.

In addition to jobs created by increased demand for electrical work, many openings will occur each year as electricians transfer to other occupations, retire, or leave the labor force for other reasons. Because the training for this occupation is long and difficult and the earnings are relatively high, a smaller proportion of electricians than of other craft workers leave the occupation each year. The number of retirements is expected to rise, however, as more electricians reach retirement age.

Employment of construction electricians, like that of many other construction workers, is sensitive to changes in the economy. This impact results from the limited duration of construction projects and the cyclical nature of the construction industry. During economic downturns, job openings for electricians are reduced as the level of construction activity declines. Apprenticeship opportunities also are less plentiful during these periods.

Although employment of maintenance electricians is steadier than that of construction electricians, those working in the automotive and other manufacturing industries that are sensitive to cyclical swings in the economy may be laid off during recessions. Also, efforts to reduce operating costs and increase productivity through the increased use of outsourcing for electrical services may limit opportunities for maintenance electricians in many industries. However, this concern should be partially offset by increased job opportunities for electricians in electrical contracting firms.

Job opportunities for electricians also vary by area. Employment opportunities follow the movement of people and businesses among states and local areas, and reflect differences in local economic conditions. The number of job opportunities in a given year may fluctuate widely from area to area.

In 2002, the median hourly wage for electricians was $19.90. The middle 50% earned between $14.95 and $26.50. The lowest 10% earned less than $11.81, and the highest 10% earned more than $33.21. Median hourly earnings in the industries employing the largest numbers of electricians in 2002 are shown below:

Motor vehicle parts manufacturing	$28.72
Local government	$21.15
Building equipment	$19.54
Nonresidential building contractors	$19.36
Employment services	$15.46

Depending on experience, apprentices usually start at between 40% and 50% of the rate paid to fully trained electricians. As apprentices become more skilled, they receive periodic increases throughout the course of their training. Many employers also provide training opportunities for experienced electricians to improve their skills.

Many construction electricians are members of the International Brotherhood of Electrical Workers. Among unions organizing maintenance electricians are the International Brotherhood of Electrical Workers; the International Union of Electronic, Electrical, Salaried, Machine, and Furniture Workers; the International Association of Machinists and Aerospace Workers; the International Union, United Automobile, Aircraft and Agricultural Implement Workers of America; and the United Steelworkers of America.

Hazardous Materials Removal and Safety Workers

Significant Points of interest

- Working conditions can be hazardous, and the use of protective clothing and equipment is often required.

- Formal education beyond high school is not required, but a training program leading to a Federal license is mandatory.

- Good job opportunities are expected.

Hazardous materials removal workers held about 38,000 jobs in 2002. About seven in 10 were employed in waste management and remediation services. About 6% were employed by specialty trade contractors, primarily in asbestos abatement and lead abatement. A small number worked at nuclear and electric plants as decommissioning and decontamination workers and radiation safety and decontamination technicians.

Job opportunities are expected to be good for hazardous materials removal workers. The occupation is characterized by a relatively high rate of turnover, resulting in a number of job openings each year stemming from experienced workers leaving the occupation. In addition, many potential workers are not attracted to this occupation, because they may prefer work that is less strenuous and has safer working conditions. Experienced workers will have especially favorable opportunities, particularly in the private sector, as more state and local governments contract out hazardous materials removal work to private companies.

Employment of hazardous materials removal workers is expected to grow about as fast as the average for all occupations through the year 2012, reflecting increasing concern for a safe and clean environment. Special-trade contractors will have strong demand for the largest segment of these workers, namely, asbestos abatement and lead abatement workers; lead abatement should offer particularly good opportunities. Mold remediation is an especially fast-growing segment at the present time, but it is unclear whether its rapid growth will continue: until a few years ago, mold remediation was not considered a significant problem, and, perhaps a few years from now, less attention will be paid to it, again.

Employment of decontamination technicians, radiation safety technicians, and decommissioning and decontamination workers is expected to grow in response to increased pressure for safer and cleaner nuclear and electric generator facilities. In addition, the number of closed facilities that need decommissioning may continue to grow, due to Federal legislation. These workers also are less affected by economic fluctuations, because the facilities in which they work must operate, regardless of the state of the economy.

The median hourly wage for hazardous materials removal workers was $15.61 in 2002. The middle 50% earned between $12.37 and $22.18 per hour. The lowest 10% earned less than $10.29 per hour, and the highest 10% earned more than $26.60 per hour. The median hourly wage for remediation and other waste management services, the largest industry employing hazardous materials removal workers in 2002, was $14.92 for the same year.

According to the limited data available, treatment, storage, and disposal workers usually earn slightly more than asbestos abatement and lead abatement workers. Decontamination and decommissioning workers and radiation protection technicians, though constituting the smallest group, tend to earn the highest wages.

Insulation Workers

Significant Points of Interest

- Workers must follow strict safety guidelines to protect themselves from the dangers of insulating irritants.

- Most insulation workers learn their work informally on the job; others complete formal apprenticeship programs.

- Job opportunities in the occupation are expected to be excellent.

Insulation workers held about 53,000 jobs in 2002. The construction industry employed four out of five workers; most worked for building finishing contractors. Small numbers of insulation workers held jobs in the Federal Government, in wholesale trade, and in shipbuilding and other manufacturing industries that have extensive installations for power, heating, and cooling. Most worked in urban areas. In less populated areas, carpenters, heating and air-conditioning installers, or drywall installers may do insulation work.

Job opportunities are expected to be excellent for insulation workers. Because there are no strict training requirements for entry, many people with limited skills work as insulation workers for a short time and then move on to other types of work, creating many job openings. In addition, many potential workers may prefer work that is less strenuous and that has more comfortable working conditions. Other opportunities will arise from the need to replace workers who leave the labor force.

In addition to openings that result from replacement needs, new jobs for insulation workers will grow about as fast as the average for all occupations through the year 2012, due to growth in residential and nonresidential construction. Demand for insulation workers will be spurred by continuing concerns about the efficient use of energy to heat and cool buildings, resulting in increased demand for these workers in the construction of new residential, industrial, and commercial buildings. In addition, renovation and efforts to improve insulation in existing structures will increase demand.

Insulation workers in the construction industry may experience periods of unemployment because of the short duration of many construction projects and the cyclical nature of construction activity. Workers employed in industrial plants generally have more stable employment, because maintenance and repair must be done on a continuing basis. Most insulation is applied after buildings are enclosed, so weather conditions have less effect on the employment of insulation workers than on that of some other construction occupations.

In 2002, the median hourly wage for insulation workers was $13.91. The middle 50% earned between $10.58 and $18.36. The lowest 10% earned less than $8.45, and the highest 10% earned more than $26.29. Median hourly earnings in the industries employing the largest numbers of insulation workers in 2002 are shown in the following tabulation:

Building equipment contractors $15.30
Building finishing contractors $12.97

Union workers tend to earn more than nonunion workers. Apprentices start at about one-half of the journey worker's wage. Insulation workers doing commercial and industrial work earn substantially more than those working in residential construction, which does not require as much skill.

Painters and Paperhangers

Significant Points of Interest

- Largely due to worker turnover, employment prospects should be good.

- Most workers learn informally on the job as helpers; however, training authorities recommend completion of an apprenticeship program.

- Two in five painters and paperhangers are self-employed, compared with one in five of all construction trades workers.

Painters and paperhangers held about 468,000 jobs in 2002; most were painters. Around 42% of painters and paperhangers work for contractors engaged in new construction, repair, restoration, or remodeling work. In addition, organizations that own or manage large buildings—such as apartment complexes—employ maintenance painters, as do some schools, hospitals, factories, and government agencies.

Self-employed, independent painting contractors accounted for two in five of all painters and paperhangers, significantly greater than the one in five of construction trades workers in general.

Job prospects should be good, as thousands of painters and paperhangers transfer to other occupations or leave the labor force each year. Because there are no strict training requirements for entry, many people with limited skills work as painters or paperhangers for a short time and then move on to other types of work. Many fewer openings will arise for paperhangers because the number of these jobs is comparatively small.

In addition to the need to replace experienced workers, new jobs will be created. Employment of painters and paperhangers is expected to grow about as fast as the average for all occupations through the year 2012, reflecting increases in the level of new construction and in the stock of buildings and other structures that require maintenance and renovation. Painting is very labor-intensive and not susceptible to technological changes that might make workers more productive and, thus, restrict employment growth.

Jobseekers considering these occupations should expect some periods of unemployment, especially until they gain experience. Many construction projects are of short duration, and construction activity is cyclical and seasonal in nature. Remodeling, restoration, and maintenance projects, however, often provide many jobs for painters and paperhangers even when new construction activity declines. The most versatile painters and skilled paperhangers generally are best able to keep working steadily during downturns in the economy.

In 2002, the median hourly wage for painters, construction and maintenance, was $13.98. The middle 50% earned between $11.08 and $18.00. The lowest 10% earned less than $9.10, and the highest 10% earned more than $23.90. Median hourly earnings in the industries employing the largest numbers of painters in 2002 are shown below:

Allocable government	$17.46
Residential building construction	$14.01
Building finishing contractors	$14.00
All categories of real estate	$11.62
Employment services	$10.21

In 2002, the median wage for paperhangers was $15.22. The middle 50% earned between $11.52 and $20.38. The lowest 10% earned less than $9.04, and the highest 10% earned more than $25.64.

Earnings for painters may be reduced on occasion because of bad weather and the short-term nature of many construction jobs. Hourly wage rates for apprentices usually start at 40% to 50% of the rate for experienced workers, and increase periodically. Some painters and paperhangers are members of the International Brotherhood of Painters and Allied Trades. Some maintenance painters are members of other unions.

Plumbers, Pipe fitters, and Steamfitters

Significant Points of Interest

- Job opportunities should be excellent because not enough people are seeking training.

- Most workers learn the trade through four or five of formal apprenticeship training.

- Plumbers, pipe fitters, and steamfitters make up one of the largest and highest paying construction occupations.

Pipe layers, plumbers, pipe fitters, and steamfitters constitute one of the largest construction occupations, holding about 550,000 jobs in 2002. About seven in 10 worked for plumbing, heating, and air-conditioning contractors engaged in new construction, repair, modernization, or maintenance work. Others did maintenance work for a variety of industrial, commercial, and government employers. For example, pipe fitters were employed as maintenance personnel in the petroleum and chemical industries, in which manufacturing operations require the moving of liquids and gases through pipes. About one of every 10 pipe layers, plumbers, pipe fitters, and steamfitters was self-employed. One in three pipe layers, plumbers, pipe fitters, and steamfitters belongs to a union.

Jobs for pipe layers, plumbers, pipe fitters, and steamfitters are distributed across the country in about the same proportion as the general population. Job opportunities are expected to be excellent, as demand for skilled pipe layers, plumbers, pipe fitters, and steamfitters is expected to outpace the supply of workers trained in this craft. Many potential workers may prefer work that is less strenuous and has more comfortable working conditions.

Employment of pipe layers, plumbers, pipe fitters, and steamfitters is expected to grow about as fast as the average for all occupations through the year 2012. Demand for plumbers will stem from building renovation, including the increasing installation of sprinkler systems, repair and maintenance of existing residential systems, and maintenance activities for places having extensive systems of pipes, such as power plants, water and wastewater treatment plants, pipelines, office buildings, and factories. The enforcement of laws pertaining to the certification requirements of workers on jobsites will create additional opportunities and demand for skilled workers. However, the number of new jobs will be limited by the growing use of plastic pipe and fittings, which are much easier to install and repair than other types, and by increasingly efficient sprinkler systems. In addition to new positions resulting from employment growth, many jobs will become available each year because of the need to replace experienced workers who retire or leave the occupation for other reasons.

Traditionally, many organizations with extensive pipe systems have employed their own plumbers or pipe fitters to maintain equipment and keep systems running smoothly. But, to reduce labor costs, many of these firms no longer employ full-time, in-house plumbers or pipe fitters. Instead, when they need plumbers, they rely on workers provided under service contracts by plumbing and pipefitting contractors.

Construction projects provide only temporary employment. So, when a project ends, pipe layers, plumbers, pipe fitters, and steamfitters working on the project may experience bouts of unemployment. Because construction activity varies from area to area, job openings, as well as apprenticeship opportunities, fluctuate with local economic conditions. However, employment of pipe layers, plumbers, pipe fitters, and steamfitters generally is less sensitive to changes in economic conditions than is employment of some other construction trades. Even when construction activity declines, maintenance, rehabilitation, and replacement of existing piping systems, as well as the increasing installation of fire sprinkler systems, provide many jobs for pipe layers, plumbers, pipe fitters, and steamfitters.

Plumbers, pipe fitters, and steamfitters are among the highest paid construction occupations. In 2002, the median hourly wage for pipe layers was $13.70. The middle 50% earned between $10.96 and $18.43. The lowest 10% earned less than

$9.20, and the highest 10% earned more than $24.31. Also in 2002, the median hourly wage for plumbers, pipe fitters, and steamfitters was $19.31. The middle 50% earned between $14.68 and $25.87. The lowest 10% earned less than $11.23, and the highest 10% earned more than $32.27. Median hourly earnings in the industries employing the largest numbers of plumbers, pipe fitters, and steamfitters in 2002 are shown below.

Nonresidential building construction	$19.65
Building equipment contractors	$19.52
Utility system construction	$17.81
Ship and boat building	$16.62
Local government	$16.21

Apprentices usually begin at about 50% of the wage rate paid to experienced pipe layers, plumbers, pipe fitters, and steamfitters. Wages increase periodically as skills improve. After an initial waiting period, apprentices receive the same benefits as experienced pipe layers, plumbers, pipe fitters, and steamfitters.

Many pipe layers, plumbers, pipe fitters, and steamfitters are members of the United Association of Journeymen and Apprentices of the Plumbing and Pipefitting Industry of the United States and Canada.

Plasterers and Stucco Masons

Significant Points of Interest

- Plastering is physically demanding.

- Plastering is learned on the job, either through a formal apprenticeship program or by working as a helper.

- Job opportunities are expected to be good, particularly in the South and Southwest.

Plasterers and stucco masons held about 59,000 jobs in 2002. Most plasterers and stucco masons work on new construction sites, particularly where special architectural and lighting effects are required. Some repair and renovate older buildings. Many plasterers and stucco masons are employed in Florida, California, and the Southwest, where exterior stucco with decorative finishes is very popular.

Most plasterers and stucco masons work for independent contractors. About one out of every 10 plasterers and stucco masons is self-employed.

Job opportunities for plasterers and stucco masons are expected to be good through 2012. Many potential workers may choose not to enter this occupation, because they prefer work that is less strenuous and has more comfortable working conditions. The best employment opportunities should continue to be in Florida,

California, and the Southwest, where exterior plaster and decorative finishes are expected to remain popular.

Employment of plasterers and stucco masons is expected to grow about as fast as the average for all occupations through the year 2012. Jobs will become available as plasterers and stucco masons transfer to other occupations or leave the labor force.

In past years, employment of plasterers declined as more builders switched to drywall construction. This decline has halted, however, and employment of plasterers is expected to continue growing as a result of the appreciation for the durability and attractiveness that toweled finishes provide. Thin-coat plastering—or veneering—in particular, is gaining wide acceptance as more builders recognize its ease of application, durability, quality of finish, and sound-proofing and fire-retarding qualities, although the increased use of fire sprinklers will reduce the demand for fire-resistant plaster work. Prefabricated wall systems and new polymer-based or polymer-modified acrylic exterior insulating finishes also are gaining popularity, particularly in the South and Southwest regions of the country. This trend is not only because of their durability, attractiveness, and insulating properties, but also because of their relatively low cost. In addition, plasterers will be needed to renovate plasterwork in old structures and to create special architectural effects, such as curved surfaces, which are not practical with drywall materials.

Most plasterers and stucco masons work in construction, where prospects fluctuate from year to year due to changing economic conditions. Bad weather affects plastering less than other construction trades, because most work is indoors. On exterior surfacing jobs, however, plasterers and stucco masons may lose time, because plastering materials cannot be applied under wet or freezing conditions.

In 2002, the median hourly wage for plasterers and stucco masons was $15.91. The middle 50% earned between $12.33 and $20.67. The lowest 10% earned less than $9.94, and the top 10% earned more than $26.81.

The median hourly wage in the largest industries employing plasterers and stucco masons in 2002 was $15.99 in building finishing contractors, and $14.94 in foundation, structure, and building exterior contractors.

Apprentice wage rates start at about half the rate paid to experienced plasterers and stucco masons. Annual earnings for plasterers and stucco masons and apprentices can be less than the hourly rate would indicate, because poor weather and periodic declines in construction activity can limit work hours.

Roofers

Significant Points of Interest

- Most roofers acquire their skills informally on the job; some roofers train through three-year apprenticeship programs.

- Jobs for roofers should be plentiful, because the work is hot, strenuous, and dirty, resulting in higher job turnover than in most construction trades.

- Demand for roofers is less susceptible to downturns in the economy than demand for other construction trades, because most roofing work consists of repair and reproofing.

Roofers held about 166,000 jobs in 2002. Almost all wage and salary roofers worked for roofing contractors. About one out of every three roofers was self-employed. Many self-employed roofers specialized in residential work.

Jobs for roofers should be plentiful through the year 2012, primarily because of the need to replace workers who transfer to other occupations or leave the labor force. Turnover is higher than in most construction trades—roofing work is hot, strenuous, and dirty, and a significant number of workers treat roofing as a temporary job until something better comes along. Some roofers leave the occupation to go into other construction trades.

Employment of roofers is expected to grow about as fast as the average for all occupations through the year 2012. Roofs deteriorate faster and are more susceptible to weather damage than most other parts of buildings, and periodically need to be repaired or replaced. Roofing has a much higher proportion of repair and replacement work than most other construction occupations. As a result, demand for roofers is less susceptible to downturns in the economy than demand for other construction trades. In addition to repair and reproofing work on the growing stock of buildings, new construction of industrial, commercial, and residential buildings will add to the demand for roofers. Jobs should be easiest to find during spring and summer when most roofing is done.

In 2002, the median hourly wage for roofers was $14.51. The middle 50% earned between $11.23 and $19.56. The lowest 10% earned less than $9.15, and the highest 10% earned more than $25.35. The median hourly wage for roofers in the foundation, structure, and building exterior contractors industry was $14.57 in 2002.

Apprentices usually start at about 40% to 50% of the rate paid to experienced roofers and receive periodic raises as they acquire the skills of the trade. Earnings for roofers are reduced on occasion, because poor weather often limits the time they can work.

Some roofers are members of the United Union of Roofers, Waterproofers and Allied Workers.

Sheet Metal Workers

Significant Points of Interest

- Nearly two-thirds of the jobs are found in the construction industry; about one quarter are in manufacturing.

- Apprenticeship programs lasting four or five years are considered the best training.

- Job opportunities in construction should be good.

Sheet metal workers held about 205,000 jobs in 2002. Nearly two-thirds of all sheet metal workers were found in the construction industry. Of those employed in construction, almost half worked for plumbing, heating, and air-conditioning contractors; most of the rest worked for roofing and sheet metal contractors. Some worked for other special trade contractors and for general contractors engaged in residential and commercial building. One-quarter of all sheet metal workers work outside of construction, and are found in manufacturing industries, such as the fabricated metal products, machinery, and aerospace products and parts industries. Some work for the Federal Government. Compared with workers in most construction craft occupations, relatively few sheet metal workers are self-employed.

Job opportunities are expected to be good for sheet metal workers in the construction industry and in construction-related sheet metal fabrication, reflecting both employment growth and openings arising each year as experienced sheet metal workers leave the occupation. In addition, many potential workers may prefer work that is less strenuous and that has more comfortable working conditions, thus limiting the number of applicants for sheet metal jobs. Opportunities should be particularly good for individuals who acquire apprenticeship training. Job prospects in manufacturing will not be as good, because construction is expected to grow faster than the manufacturing industries that employ sheet metal workers. Because some sheet metal manufacturing is labor-intensive, manufacturers sometimes move production to lower wage areas or countries.

Employment of sheet metal workers in construction is expected to grow about as fast as the average for all occupations through 2012, reflecting growth in the demand for sheet metal installations as more industrial, commercial, and residential structures are built. The need to install energy-efficient air-conditioning, heating, and ventilation systems in the increasing stock of old buildings and to perform other types of renovation and maintenance work also should boost employment. In addition, the popularity of decorative sheet metal products and increased architectural restoration are expected to add to the demand for sheet metal workers. On the other hand, slower-than-average job growth is projected for sheet metal workers in manufacturing.

Sheet metal workers in construction may experience periods of unemployment, particularly when construction projects end and economic conditions dampen construction activity. Nevertheless, employment of sheet metal workers is less sensitive to declines in new construction than is the employment of some other construction workers, such as carpenters. Maintenance of existing equipment—which is less affected by economic fluctuations than is new construction—makes up a large part of the work done by sheet metal workers. Installation of new air-conditioning and heating systems in existing buildings continues during construction slumps, as individuals and businesses adopt more energy-efficient equipment to cut utility bills. In addition, a large proportion of sheet metal installation and maintenance is done indoors, so sheet metal workers usually lose less work time due to bad weather, than other construction workers do.

In 2002, the median hourly wage for sheet metal workers was $16.62. The middle 50% earned between $12.15 and $23.03. The lowest 10% of all sheet metal workers earned less than $9.50, and the highest 10% earned more than $29.53. The median hourly earnings in the largest industries employing sheet metal workers in 2002 are shown below:

Federal Government	$19.73
Building equipment contractors	$17.47
Building finishing contractors	$16.77
Foundation, structure, and building exterior contractors	$15.48
Architectural and structural metals manufacturing	$14.60

Apprentices normally start at about 40% to 50% of the rate paid to experienced workers. As apprentices acquire more skills throughout the course of their training, they receive periodic increases until their pay approaches that of experienced workers. In addition, union workers in some areas receive supplemental wages from the union when they are on layoff or shortened workweeks.

Structural and Reinforcing Iron and Metal Workers

Significant Points of Interest

- Most employers recommend a three- or four-year apprenticeship.

- During economic downturns, workers can experience high rates of unemployment.

- The danger of injuries due to falls is high; those who work at great heights do not work in wet, icy, or extremely windy conditions.

Structural and reinforcing iron and metal workers held about 107,000 jobs in 2002. Around four out of five worked in construction, with nearly half working for foundation, structure, and building exterior contractors. Most of the remaining ironworkers worked for contractors specializing in the construction of homes; factories; commercial buildings; religious structures; schools; bridges and tunnels; and water, sewer, communications, and power lines.

Structural and reinforcing iron and metal workers are employed in all parts of the country, but most work in metropolitan areas, where the bulk of commercial and industrial construction takes place.

Employment of structural and reinforcing iron and metal workers is expected to grow about as fast as the average for all occupations through the year 2012, largely on the basis of continued growth in industrial and commercial construction. The rehabilitation, maintenance, and replacement of a growing number of older buildings, factories, power plants, highways, and bridges are expected to create employment opportunities. In addition to new jobs that arise, other job openings will result from the need to replace experienced ironworkers who transfer to other occupations or leave the labor force.

The number of job openings fluctuates from year to year with economic conditions and the level of construction activity. During economic downturns, ironworkers can experience high rates of unemployment. Similarly, job opportunities for ironworkers may vary widely by geographic area. Job openings for ironworkers usually are more abundant during the spring and summer months, when the level of construction activity increases.

In 2002, the median hourly wage for structural iron and steel workers in all industries was $19.55. The middle 50% earned between $14.45 and $26.00. The lowest 10% earned less than $10.81, and the highest 10% earned more than $31.81. In 2002, the median wage for reinforcing iron and rebar workers in all industries were $17.66. The middle 50% earned between $12.72 and $25.74. The lowest 10% earned less than $10.07, and the highest 10% earned more than $31.40.

The median hourly wage for structural iron and steel workers in 2002 in foundation, structure, and building exterior contractors was $21.35 and, in nonresidential building construction, $16.98. Reinforcing iron and rebar workers earned median hourly earnings of $18.46 in foundation, structure, and building exterior contractors in 2002.

Many workers in this trade are members of the International Association of Bridge, Structural, Ornamental, and Reinforcing Iron Workers. According to the union, average hourly earnings, including benefits, for structural and reinforcing metal workers who belonged to a union and worked full time were 34% higher than the hourly earnings of nonunion workers. Structural and reinforcing iron and metal workers in New York, Boston, San Francisco, Chicago, Los Angeles, Philadelphia, and other large cities received the highest wages.

Apprentices generally start at about 50% to 60% of the rate paid to experienced journey workers. Throughout the course of the apprenticeship program, as they acquire the skills of the trade, they receive periodic increases until their pay approaches that of experienced workers.

Earnings for ironworkers may be reduced on occasion, because work can be limited by bad weather, the short-term nature of construction jobs, and economic downturns.

Appendix

Existing Outreach Infrastructure

There are currently several community-based programs in Brooklyn, New York, using the CONstruction model, for occupational outreach. The following describes a group that is working with many, formerly incarcerated individuals and other economically depressed workers. I used a private example because it is ideal for making our communities better places to live and work. Ultimately, private money fuels commerce.

The New York City Site Safety Manager's Apprentice/Mentor Program
A Private Venture by: Homeland Safety Consultants, Inc.

General Program Description:

The New York City Site Safety Manager's Apprentice Program is a mentor construction program for Homeland Safety Consultants (HSC), Inc. Through a mix of classroom training and field training, the apprentice program supplies on-the-job training and supplemental classroom construction and safety education. The apprentices come from economically depressed areas, and our mentors come from the field; they are seasoned site safety managers from HSC.

For decades, minorities have been under-represented in the construction industry, especially within the ranks of managerial construction positions. This private program seeks to educate and train minority apprentices to become licensed New York City site safety managers, thereby increasing their representation in well paying managerial positions. This program also seeks to assist and encourage minority entrepreneurs within the construction industry.

Within a period of 18 to 24 months, each apprentice achieves all the necessary experience and training requirements to sit for the NYC Site Safety Manager's certification test. Upon passing this test, each apprentice receives his or her NYC Site Safety Manager's license. The curriculum for this apprentice program includes a comprehensive mix of on-the-job training and safety and construction classroom education. The contracting client is only responsible for field-related expenditures. The curriculum contained within this program seeks to develop apprentices beyond the minimal educational and training requisites for their subsequent licenses. We have set this standard to produce extremely viable safety managers for the construction industry.

Requirements for New York City
Site Safety Manager's License:

- Upon completion of the apprenticeship program, all apprentices meet the following New York City Department of Building (NYCDOB) requirements for examination candidate eligibility:
- Completion of an 18-month, on-the-job-training program under a certified NYC Site Safety Manager;
- Completion of NYCDOB's 40-hour Site Safety Manager's Course.

Classroom Construction and Safety Training:

Throughout the apprenticeship, each apprentice receives classroom training based on construction industry standards and codes for New York City, New York State, and the United States Department of Labor's Occupational Safety and Health Administration (OSHA). This comprehensive classroom training complements field training and reinforces fundamental standards in construction processes and occupational safety and hygiene.

Classroom training emphasis various OSHA and New York City courses, that HSC is approved and authorized to teach through NYCDOB and the Region II OSHA Educational Center located at The University of Medicine and Dentistry School of Public Health of New Jersey (UMDNJ-SPH), respectively. The mentor company, HSC, includes other classroom programs specifically developed to provide supplemental training beyond NYCDOB prerequisites. These additional programs are designed to create a working familiarity with construction building techniques and their applicable safety standards. The classroom work totals well over 200 hours, and includes the following courses:

- 15-Hour Construction Terminology
- 10-Hour OSHA Construction
- 15-Hour Blueprint Reading
- 30-Hour OSHA Construction
- 10-Hour Electrical Safety
- 10-Hours Fall Protection Safety
- 10-Hour Soils and Excavation Safety
- 5-Hour NYC Anti-corruption Compliance
- 10-Hour Pedestrian Safety and Flagger
- 5-Hour Construction Violence Prevention
- 32-Hour OSHA and New York City Scaffold Training
- 16-Hour OSHA 7600 Disaster Site Worker Construction
- 40-Hour OSHA Hazardous Waste Operations and Emergency Response
- 40-Hour NYC Department of Buildings Site Safety Managers

The following are some course descriptions:

10-HOUR OSHA Construction Outreach

This course introduces OSHA policies, procedures, and standards as well as construction safety and health principles. The course reviews the scope and application of the OSH Act and General Duty Clause, and examines areas that are most hazardous. Upon successful completion of the course, participants receive an OSHA construction safety and health 10-hour course completion card. Topics include:

- Introduction to OSHA and the General Duty Clause
- General Provisions, Recordkeeping
- Fall Protection, Scaffolding
- Personal Protective Equipment and Lifesaving Equipment
- Materials Handling, Storage, Use, and Disposal
- Mechanized and Construction Equipment
- Hand and Powered Tools
- Excavation
- Fire Protection
- Electrical
- Signs and Barricades

40-HOUR HAZWOPER Training

This class meets the requirements for Hazardous Waste Operations and Emergency Response, under 29 CFR 1910.120. Instruction includes lecture, video, demonstrations, games, workshops, and hands-on activities. Each student receives a student manual, NIOSH pocket guide, and DOT Emergency Response Guidebook. Quizzes are administered daily, and certificates are issued upon successful completion.

30-HOUR OSHA Construction Outreach

This program provides instruction on a variety of safety standards applicable to the construction industry, as required by OSHA. Topics include:
- Introduction to OSHA Standards – at least Two Hours
- Electrical, Subpart K – at least Two Hours
- Fall Protection, Subpart M – at least Two Hours
- Occupational Health and Environmental Controls
- Hazard Communication, Subpart D
- Health Hazards in Construction, Subpart D
- Personal Protective and Lifesaving Equipment, Subpart E
- Fire Protection and Prevention, Subpart F
- Materials Handling, Storage, Use, and Disposal, Subpart H
- Tools - Hand and Power, Subpart I

- Welding and Cutting, Subpart J
- Scaffolds, Subpart L
- Cranes, Derricks, Hoists, Elevators, and Conveyors,
- Motor Vehicles, Mechanized Equipment, and Marine
- Overhead Protection; and Signs, Signals, and Barricades,
- Concrete and Masonry Construction, Subpart Q
- Steel Erection, Subpart R
- Stairways and Ladders, Subpart X
- Confined Space Entry

CHAPTER TWELVE

A Closer Look
at the Haitian Learner

By
Lovie E. B. Lilly

Introduction

Several research studies have contributed to the knowledge about immigrant students and how they assimilate and acculturate into American society. As increasing numbers of immigrant families migrate to the United States, the focus on education implications and awareness warrants our immediate attention, because not only are immigrant families concerned with establishing themselves in the context of socioeconomic stability, but also, more importantly, they have expectations for the learning opportunities that await their children in this country. For public school educators, in particular, the level of preparedness that we institute is crucial, since schools are the "first ports of entry to American culture for these children." (Suarez-Orozco, 2000).

As foreign-born student enrollments continue to increase, it will be essential that those responsible for teaching and learning develop local policies and innovative practices, which provide equitable learning opportunities for these students. This responsibility will require educational leadership, resourcefulness, professional collaborations, and the recognition of these "new types of learners" and their families as members of educational communities. Moreover, educators must challenge themselves to consider the uniqueness of the culture that now presents itself in today's classrooms, as diverse populations prepare themselves for academic achievement and the promise of successful futures.

It is important to begin with a brief discussion of the terms "knowledge" and "learning," and explore how they might apply to specific student populations. The American Heritage Dictionary of the English Language (2000) defines "knowledge" as "the act, process, or experience of gaining information or skill. It can be gained through schooling or study. Learning can be defined as the sum or range of what has been perceived, discovered, or learned." Oftentimes educators use these definitions interchangeably. Schools are learning institutions and storehouses of knowledge, shared among educators and learners. The school, while standing as a symbol of scholarship, culture, and traditions, provides opportunities for students to develop intellectually and socially through curricula. Learning, as typified through diversity, is an extension of this knowledge. It acknowledges individual and cultural differences. Learning is the accumulation of knowledge, which, Bruner (1979) explains, should be cultivated within each person so that the individual, through his or her cultural identity, aptly personifies knowledge. This process begins in the cradle of one's cultural heritage (Bruner, 1979).

The Haitian Student at the Secondary Level

The immigrant population that is the focus of this educational discussion is of African descent. Prior to migration, Haitian students are members of a rich heritage that is deeply rooted in the traditions of the family, culture, and customs of that society. Some of these customs include language, oral traditions, religion, strong familial ties, and the strong sense of national identity. (Laguerre, 1998). As an ESL teacher noted, "The Haitians I am familiar with are loving, family oriented, and religious people." (Interview, ESL Teacher, 7/7/2004). When Haitian students enroll in American schools, they are ambassadors of a culture that needs to be more clearly understood in preparation for future learning experiences. As increased numbers of Haitian students assemble in American classrooms, it will be imperative that educators observe them carefully, listen to their voices, and examine their cultural pasts, because, wedged between two countries, are learners who bring their own individuality and seek to find membership in their new learning environment.

In the discussion that follows, Haitian students will be briefly described, followed by indicators that pertain to language, socialization, previous learning experiences, Haitian school documents, perceptions of the learner, and achievement patterns. This information is based upon my research observations and interactions with Haitian students and American educators during the past three years, in addition to research observations and discussions that were conducted in Port-au-Prince, Haiti in November 2004.

There are three aspects of the Haitian student that should concern educators. First, many Haitian students have not been formally educated since the primary years, or the educational process was interrupted due to changes in the family structure. This is particularly true for students who migrate from the rural areas. (Laguerre, 1998). In extreme cases, some Haitian students have never attended school; therefore, adjusting to school settings, particularly at the secondary level, is extremely difficult. Second, most of the students speak French and/or Haitian Creole, an indigenous language, which, until recently, had not been used as an instructional tool in Haiti. (Laguerre, 1998). Third, political tensions in Haiti have historically interrupted the schooling process, and, consequently, the educational system has not been successful in the management of an infrastructure that methodically educates children. Reform efforts are contingent upon political maneuvers and the Haitian economy. Finally, the processes of transitioning from one country to another and through various social networks are of concern. Klopner (1985) defines social adjustment as cultural relocation. In this sense, Haitian immigrant students are relocating their experiences, customs, language, and identities from one environment to another, while looking for educational settings where they can mature and achieve. In some instances, Haitian students have separated from family structures that once provided emotional support and familial care. The dreams of emigration and the anticipation of attending American public schools may well be threatened by the realities of immigration and students' roles as immigrants in new communities and learning environments. Linguistics and sociocultural differences, along with new issues regarding race, continue to distinguish them from native-born students, and isolate them from immediate interconnectedness with the school community.

Although Haitian students' previous learning experiences vary, language is the one common denominator that distinguishes them as learners in their new environments. English language learning is quite challenging for all Haitian immigrant students. "I know what I want to say, but I cannot find the words," one student told me. (Student interview, 5/28/2004) Language is the channel through which communication is received and transmitted. For Haitian immigrant students, this medium is part of a litany of cultural characteristics, which begins with the mother tongue called Haitian Creole. It is the framework of their cultural, linguistic existence. In 1979, Buchanan referred to Haitian Creole as "the dominant symbol of their enhanced self and group identity as Haitians and a symbol of the unity and equality among Haitian immigrant." The language is recognized as a cultural asset for the development of the community. Haitian students are generally observed using their own native language, as they develop their own communities within the context of schools. This enables them to practice "code-switching," weaving from Haitian Creole to English. In addition to the use of Haitian Creole, those students who attended private schools are educated in French, the language used, historically, as the instructional tool in Haitian educational practices. (Simmons, 1985, Rorro, 1988).

In areas of socialization, Haitian students form their own "familial structures," which support the sustained use of Haitian Creole, cultural exchanges, and other emotional needs. It is within the safety of this inner circle that Haitian students rehearse the use of the English language and exchange emotional support within the learning process. These patters of socialization are most observable in informal school settings. Occasionally, Haitian students can be observed interacting with African-Americans, Africans, Whites, Latinos, or Asians; however, patterns of socialization clearly reflect more unification among themselves.

Haitian immigrant students' previous learning experiences are, by and large, symbolic of the former educational context, that being private or public schooling. Historically, statistics have revealed that more private schools exist in Haiti than public schools. (Salome, 1984; Simmons, 1985; Rorro, 1990). It is important to note that the connotation of "private" in the Haitian context is not necessarily comparable to its meaning in the United States. There is a dichotomy between Haitian private and public schools. Private schools or "colleges" are generally managed and funded through religious or commercial organizations. Some are more afflu-ent, while others are poorly run, ill equipped, and staffed by teachers with mini-mal training. (Simmons, 1985). In contrast, the Haitian government funds public schools or "lycees." (Salmi, 2000; Rorro, 1990). The public schools in Haiti are run by the state and do not have the capacity to offer quality educational services similar to some of the better private schools. Some of the disparities include gen-eral funding, teacher qualifications, extreme overcrowding, curriculum, facilities, and textbooks. (Salmi, 2000).

Some Haitian school documents include data that is not always easily inter-preted by guidance professionals or administrators, making it difficult to transfer learning from one county to another. A US guidance counselor explained that, "When I get the material, it is translated by one of the French teachers because I do not understand the information. We need training on how to interpret materials from Haiti. It's always different. It's hard and sometimes we don't know what to do!" (Interview, Guidance Counselor, 5/28/2004). Moreover, educators are finding that both private school and public school records do not always reflect develop-mental experiences from the primary years to the secondary level. It is quite typical to find gaps in the learning cycles for Haitian students, and, in some cases, to find students who are over-age. In extreme circumstances, Haitian students enroll in schools with no records of previous schooling experiences, thereby challenging educators to begin the schooling process at the secondary level.

The skills that Haitian learners possess are quite diverse. Some are perceived as capable learners. They enter classroom environments with levels of prepared-ness, which demonstrate that they have had previous learning experiences in Haiti. Educators note these students have high expectations for achievement and success in the American schools. Other Haitian students are characterized as motivated, serious-minded learners, who are highly respectful of teachers' au-thority, demonstrate courteous behavior, and have a high regard for the learning environment. A science teacher noted that, "Education is a way out of poverty, therefore the Haitian students take it more seriously than others." (Interview, Science Teacher, 3/25/2004). Conversely, some Haitian students are not experi-enced, because there is little educational foundation, and they do not know what to expect in American schools. The assertion here is that if students have had previous schooling experiences in Haiti, especially in affluent, private school settings, the likelihood for acceleration in the American educational context is far greater in comparison to those who attended poorer schools, or who have not experienced schooling at all.

Academic performance trends vary among Haitian students, as seen in a group of students who currently attend a public high school in northern New Jersey. A few are performing at high levels, however the vast majority of the students are performing at below average levels mainly due to linguistic differences. Those students, who are enrolled in French classes, perform quite well. In one instance, a student who had attended a private school qualified for Advanced Placement (AP) French, and the student's final grade for the year was a "B." However, this result is not common among the majority of the learners.

Student performance was examined according to core content courses, which include math, language arts, social studies, and science. In the math program, students were enrolled in English as Second Language (ESL) classes or in mainstreamed classes, which included algebra and geometry. Overall, math proficiency averages in the ESL program were in the "D" range, while averages in the mainstreamed classes were in the "C+" range. A math teacher observed that, "Sometimes the Haitian students don't know how to talk about math! The vocabulary is missing for them and I don't know if they understand the material or not!" (Interview, Math Teacher, 3/24/2004). In language arts, the students received instruction under the ESL Program with average overall achievement in the "C+" range. One student did not receive credit because his English language proficiency was extremely limited, but in French he earned a "B," thereby suggesting that he is a learned student, who needs to develop skills in the new language. As an ESL teacher put it, "Language is the great divider!" (Interview, ESL Teacher, 3/29/2004).

Students were also enrolled in the ESL social studies class that provides instruction on local culture and government. The students are required to conduct research and to perform considerable amounts of writing tasks, in order to develop an English vocabulary. The overall composite score for this group was "C-." Finally, in the sheltered ESL biology class, the average composite score equaled "D+." The teacher of record reported that the students were completely foreign to laboratory lessons. Two students successfully passed physics with grades averaging in the "B" range, and one student took honors chemistry, completing the year with a "C" average. Unfortunately, the teacher said, "The language barrier is huge. It makes it difficult for them to understand questions that I am asking and to communicate the knowledge that they bring." (Interview, Science Teacher, 6/2/2004). There is sufficient evidence to suggest that Haitian students who migrate to the United States with formalized previous schooling experiences are performing at high levels and at faster rates, in comparison to those who have come from backgrounds with minimal schooling. "There is a major dividing line," said the ESL teacher. "Those who have had experiences are achieving, and the others are not. When there is a lack of developmental education and learning, there is little evidence of background knowledge." (Interview, ESL Teacher, 3/29/2004).

Conclusions

Educationally, there are several implications that are central to this discussion. In one sense, classroom teachers are challenged by the responsibilities of teaching Haitian learners. They know very little about them as students, or about the Haitian culture and its educational system. In addition, American teachers have perceptions of the country and its citizens, where illiteracy rates are among the highest in the western hemisphere. (Arthur, 2002). Now that Haitian students are living in our communities and learning in our schools, it is understandable that language similarities accomplish and support educational goals. Then again, linguistic differences and other types of cultural barriers that stand between teachers and learners thwart those goals.

If American learning institutions are going to educate foreign-born populations equitably, Suarez-Orozco (2000) reminds us "to adequately, fairly, and systematically" examine their abilities, strengths, and disabilities through assessments that will place students in appropriate academic programs. We must know where they come from; what their pasts reflect socially, politically, and educationally; and what knowledge they bring with them. Haitian students and their families will require support while adjusting to public secondary school environments. Older or over-age students are challenged by academic expectations and testing requirements at the secondary level, and by the difficulty of reconciling their social identity. Many Haitian students and their families will not have had previous experiences with large educational systems; therefore, American educators must continue to develop initiatives and practices that will welcome newcomers, such as the Haitians. While visiting Haiti in November 2004, I had opportunities to meet with educators from that country. When asked to make recommendations to American educators so that we could better serve their progeny, two Haitian principals/directors shared the following:

1. Understand them as Haitians. Know the culture. Know their traditions. Know their beliefs.
2. Know their culture, including all of the events that affect behavior and allow an individual to manifest his or her identity.

These recommendations and others like them are significant to this discussion. Yet, the question that still begs resolve is: *With what we know about the Haitian learner, how can school communities make better informed decisions for them as learners?*

References

American Heritage Dictionary of the English Language (2000). (4th Edition). Houghton Mifflin Company.

Arthur, C. (2002). *Haiti: a guide to the people, politics, and culture.* New York, NY: Interlink Books.

Bruner, J. (1979). *On knowing: essays for the left handed.* Cambridge, MA: Harvard University Press.

Hadjadj, D. (2000). *Education for all in Haiti over the last 20 years.* Kingston, Jamaica: Office of the UNESCO Representative in the Caribbean/Caribbean Monograph Series.

Klopner, M. (1985). *A composite profile of Haitian immigrants in the United States based on a community needs assessment.* Dissertation. New Brunswick, NJ: Rutgers University.

Laguerre, M. (1998). *Diasporic citizenship: Haitian Americans in Transnational America.* New York: St. Martin's Press.

Rorro, G. (1988). *Academic achievement of Haitian limited English proficient students in the New Jersey public schools.* Dissertation. New Brunswick: Rutgers University.

Rorro, G. (1990). *Haitian voices: considerations for the classroom teacher.* Trenton, NJ: New Jersey Department of Education.

Salmi, J. (2000). Equity and quality in private education: The Haitian paradox. *Compare: A Journal of Comparative Education*, 30(2), 163–178.

Salome, B. (19884). *Education and development: The case of Haiti.* Paris: OECD, pp. 26.

Simmons, R. (1985). *Haiti: a study of the educational system of Haiti and a guide to the academic placement of students in educational institutions of the United States.* Word Education Series.

Suarez-Orozco, C. (2000). Meeting the challenge: schooling immigrant youth. *NABE News*, November/December, 6–9, 35.

CHAPTER THIRTEEN

Postsecondary Education Patterns of Enrollment, Support and Accommodations among Students With Disabilities: A State-Wide Survey

By
Sal Pizzuro and Frank Rusch

Abstract

The generation of Americans that has the most at stake in the future of the country is the least engaged in the nation. A study was undertaken to examine postsecondary success among graduates of New Jersey's high school special education programs, and 327 members of the class of 2002 were queried regarding postsecondary employment, access to services from social service agencies, community activities, and living arrangements. The results of the study imply that more effective support is needed in order to enable students with disabilities to make a smooth transition from school to postsecondary or adult living.

Rusch, Keller, and Ganguly (2004) have suggested that during the twenty years in which "transition" has been addressed in the Individuals with Disabilities Education Act (IDEA), the postsecondary success rate of special education graduates has not improved. Public Law 98-199 reauthorized IDEA in 1983, and subsequent reauthorizations mandated specific transition services. The special education community needed to address outcomes in addition to employment to ensure that special education graduates obtained access to postsecondary education and related quality of life opportunities. In addition, it was vital that valid measures be established in order to ensure reliable scrutiny of postsecondary success among young adults with special needs. Soon after the passage of P.L. 98–199, Halpern (1985) suggested that the special education community might adjust its goals in creating an outcome model that allows adults with special needs to have a full quality of life. Later, Halpern (1995) suggested that we may have to adjust our definition of "success" in order to determine postsecondary outcomes. Such a definition, it has been pointed out, will require the establishment of valid measures of achievement. (Pizzuro, Baird, Fisher, Fogarty, Gonyo, Kreoll, Reilly, and Humphrey, 1996). According to Weiner (1995), expectations for postsecondary graduates should be no different than the goals that are set for the public at large. Indeed, the authors of this brief analysis concur that, although expectations should be no different, the enrollment and participation of individuals with special needs in postsecondary programs, services, and activities may be one thing, but actual graduation is quite another.

A statewide study was conducted in New Jersey in an attempt to obtain updated information related to postsecondary engagement among students with disabilities. Further, we sought to determine the extent to which students were employed. Specifically, we polled 327 former special education students to determine their rate and level of enrollment in postsecondary education, living arrangements at home or in alternative settings, access to services/accommodations, and involvement in recreational/community activities.

Findings

Participants represented approximately 100 New Jersey School Districts and Transition Coordinators. The respondents included students with disabilities within the "wild" category who were considered to be capable of engaging in independent living and competitive employment. All held high school diplomas that were non-distinctive from the diplomas that were granted to their non-disabled peers.

Among recent graduates, approximately 36% (N=117) are receiving services from agencies at the postsecondary level. Twenty-eight percent (N=91) of respondents indicated that they are either enrolled part-time (N=13) or full-time (N=78) in college; 14% indicated that they are enrolled in a technical school part-time (N=30) or full-time (N=16). Nearly 72% (N=235) of the respondents are living at home with their parents. Only 1.5% of the recent graduates are living independently. Fewer than 29% (N=94) of the respondents were receiving training on a full-time basis. Forty-eight percent (N=157) of the respondents receive services/accommodations from a social service agency, such as the Division of Vocational Rehabilitation, the Division of Developmental Disabilities, or a supported employment agency. The majority of respondents within this group (N=59) receive such services from a postsecondary school or training program, such as a community college, four-year baccalaureate granting institution, or vocational school.

Recommendations

It must be considered that the results suggest a more successful outcome than is representative of the general special education population. If so, a possible explanation is that respondents who are the products of more effective transition programs are more likely to participate in survey research than those individuals who receive lower quality services. For example, a strong relationship between high school special education programs and the Division of Vocational Rehabilitation (DVR) of the New Jersey Department of Labor may have created a setting that has helped to facilitate enrollment in formal postsecondary education, albeit at the community college or vocational school level. However, relatively few of the respondents were receiving training on a full-time basis. In addition, these young graduates do not appear to have achieved a significant level of independence, as noted by the fact that two-thirds of these individuals continued to live at home with their parents or guardians, and fewer than 2% were living independently.

The implications of the survey results strongly suggest that more effective support is needed in order to enable students with disabilities to make a smooth transition from school to postsecondary or adult living. This issue must be scrutinized with larger sample sizes from more diverse geographical regions of the country. The results of this study provide implications for future studies that examine independent living, employability, access to accommodations, and the level of community engagement among young adults with disabilities at the postsecondary level. It should be noted that, given the short period of time between graduation and the beginning of data collection, results should be considered only as possible inferences and suggestions for future studies. The findings reveal implications for future studies that will include larger sample sizes and be more longitudinal in nature. The current study limited participation to recent high school graduates. Future subjects should include students with special needs who "dropped out" before the completion of a high school program.

References

1. Halpern, A. (1985). "Transition: A look at the foundations. *Exceptional Children,* 53, 48–61.
2. Halpern, A., P. Yovanoff, B. Doran, and M. Benz. (1995). "Predicting postsecondary outcomes for school leavers with Disabilities." *Exceptional Children,* 62 (2), 151–164.
3. Hasazi, S. B., L. R. Gordon, and C. A. Roe. (1985). Factors associated with the employment of young adults with mental retardation. "Education and Training in Mental Retardation," 25, 52–61.
4. Rusch, F. R., K. Keller, R. Ganguly, and D. Braddock. (2004). *Underestimating our nation's investment in segregation: Integrated versus segregated employment.* University Park: The Pennsylvania State University.
5. Pizzuro, S., S. Baird, M. B. Fisher, C. Fogarty, M. Gonyo, G. Kreoll, A. S. Reilly, and L. A. Humphrey. (1996). "A proposed paradigm shift from the 'Opportunity to Learn' compliance mandate to a 'Results/Accountability' initiative." *The Learning Consultant Journal,* 15, 22–29.
6. Weiner, C. S. (1995). "Employers do not accept 85%." *Teaching Exceptional Children,* 2 (1), 10–14.

Appendix A

NJ Postsecondary Study
Total Possible
N = 327
Date of graduation from high school: 2002 for all 327

1. Circle all that apply to you:

a. College	Part-time = 13	Full-time =78
b. Technical School	Part-time = 30	Full-time =16
c. Training Program	Part-time = 0	Full-time = 0
d. On-the-job-training	Part-time = 6	Full-time = 0
e. Apprenticeship	Part-time = 0	Full-time = 0

Employed: Full-time = 27

Unemployed = 192

2. Circle the living situation that applies to you.

Living away at college/school = 87
Living independently and alone = 5
Sharing an apartment/house with roommates = 0
Living at home with parents/family = 235
Living in a supported living home = 0

3. Are you receiving services/accommodations for persons with disabilities?

Yes: 117   No: 210

4. If you answered yes to question 3, please circle all agencies that provide the services:

DVRS = 39
DDD = 33
Commission for the Blind = 0
UCP = 0
Access link (or other transportation services) =3
Supported employment agency = 6
WICK =3
SSI = 8
Support services/accommodations at school/training program = 59
Other = 6

6. Are you participating in recreational/community activities?

     Yes: 36   No: 29

7. If you answered yes to question 6, please list the activities:

     Soccer (2), volunteer firefighting (1), college recreational activities (20), church choir (1), college clubs (9), Spectrum for Living (1), college band (1), college track (1)

CHAPTER FOURTEEN

Hero Killing: Examining America's Infatuation With Creating and Destroying its Leaders

By
Richard A. Lee

I – Introduction

And the night comes again to the circle studded sky
The stars settle slowly, in loneliness they lie
'Till the universe explodes as a falling star is raised
Planets are paralyzed, mountains are amazed
But they all glow brighter from the brilliance of the blaze
With the speed of insanity, then he dies (Ochs).

In his song "Crucifixion," singer/songwriter Phil Ochs describes America's infatuation with creating – and then tearing down – its heroes and leaders. The song begins and ends with nearly identical verses, underscoring the cycle in which society creates and destroys its heroes and leaders, and then begins the process anew.

Ochs, a popular folksinger in the late 1960s and early 1970s, originally wrote the song about the assassination of John F. Kennedy. He later extended it to include the assassinations of Robert F. Kennedy and Martin Luther King Jr. and eventually to what he termed "hero killing" in general. If Ochs had not taken his own life at the age of 35, he may well have extended the message of "Crucifixion" to a new era of leaders that society created and destroyed while it reveled in every detail of the destruction.

In terms of fallen American leaders, Richard Nixon quickly comes to mind. Re-elected president by a landslide in 1972, he was forced to resign two years later for his role in the Watergate cover-up. More recently, New Jersey Governor James E. McGreevey provided another example. A rising young star in the Democratic Party, he became, in 2002, New Jersey's youngest governor and came to the statehouse filled with promise and a bright future. But after two and half years of bad press, low poll numbers, and constant controversy over his appointments and actions, McGreevey, who was married and the father of two daughters, announced that he was gay, had had a consensual relationship with a man, and was resigning from office.

In the 30 years between the Nixon and McGreevey resignations, America has created and destroyed many leaders and heroes. But these two men are the bookends that hold the others between them. They lived in different generations, they grew up on opposite sides of the country, and they belonged to different political parties. But there are striking similarities in their stories. And their personal stories help explain why America continues to destroy the heroes it creates.

In this paper, I use the work of several critical theorists to further explain the manner in which America treats its heroes. By examining the myth of the self-made man and how it drives individuals to construct false images under the mistaken guise that the public is looking for leaders who have achieved the American Dream, I will demonstrate how the careers of Richard Nixon and Jim McGreevey – like those of other modern-day leaders – followed a progression that has been in existence for hundreds of years: first, positions of leadership become unattractive so people choose outsiders as their rulers; then, the public starts selecting rulers against whom they have a grudge; and, eventually, society turns its rulers into scapegoats and blames them for all of its problems.

II – The American Dream

Given the inevitability of such a miserable fate, why would Richard Nixon, Jim McGreevey, or anyone else aspire to a leadership position? The answer lies in the myth of the American Dream. It is why people flock to movies like *Rocky* in which individuals with a modicum of talent and ambition rise to success from their working class roots. Like the wrestling fans Roland Barthes described in his book of essays, *Mythologies*, the populace knows that what it is watching is not real, but it wants to believe it anyway (pp. 18–19).

The American Dream carries a message that hard work makes it possible to achieve anything. For Nixon, it was the story of a common man who became President of the United States. For McGreevey, it was the opportunity to grow up in a working, middle class family and rise to governor of the State of New Jersey.

But in reality, a commitment to hard work does not even guarantee a decent standard of living, let alone a ticket to success. Almost one-third of the people listed on *Forbes* magazine's wealthiest list are born into it. At least another quarter of the *Forbes* list inherited businesses, land, or other assets that they built into successful enterprises. Other "self-made" men, such as Ross Perot, achieved success largely due to timing and government policies. The start of Perot's computer data processing business coincided with the federal government's creation of Medicare and Medicaid, which made data processing a premium. Likewise, taxpayer-funded research, market regulators, and intellectual property laws created the market that helped turned Internet entrepreneurs into billionaires (Collins, pp. 1–15).

Nevertheless, the myth of the American Dream continues. It is why those who want to become leaders go to great extent to fit the mold of the self-made person. They place great value in convincing the public that they are self-made, the products of the classic rags-to-riches story in which an individual born into humble surroundings rises to great power through hard work, intelligence, and a little luck. If they succeed, others can too. Barthes captured the essence of this argument in his essay on politicians' use of portraits in election campaigns: "A photograph is a mirror, what we are asked to read is the familiar, the known; it offers to the voter his own likeness, but clarified, exalted, superbly elevated into a type. This glorification is in fact the very definition of the photogenic: the voter is at once expressed and heroized, he is invited to elect himself" (pp. 91–92).

This helps explain why, during America's most recent presidential election, multimillionaires Dick Cheney and John Kerry each stressed their humble roots. In their acceptance speeches at their respective party's nominating convention, Cheney spoke of how his grandmother lived in a railroad car, while Kerry fondly recalled his days as a Cub Scout and his mother's role as den mother.

Similarly, Nixon and McGreevey constructed public images of themselves as self-made men that often belied reality. For example, Nixon had no interest in poker, but he played the card game regularly in the Army so he could be "one of the boys." (Wills, p. 72). Likewise, McGreevey rarely spoke of his degrees from Georgetown, Columbia, and Harvard, but he never missed an opportunity to tell people how he grew up in a working class family, the son of a Marine Corps drill instructor and a nurse.[1]

As Garry Wills wrote in his biography of Nixon, this assumption of "public folksiness" has become a convention of American politics (p. 144). "The choice constantly being forced on the American politician is to be a man of (Democratic presidential candidate Adlai) Stevenson's elegance, but unelected, or a man who hides his own intelligence and feeling in order to voice the sentiments of the crowd," Wills said (p. 149). Nixon and McGreevey chose the latter option.

Initially, the choice led to success, but ultimately it contributed to their downfalls because, as Wills wrote, the common man does not really want a common man for a leader. While Nixon and McGreevey generated popular support by "dumbing" themselves down, they also created resentment. "I think this explains the vague dislike for Nixon that many experience," Wills said (p. 147). "It is not caused by any one thing he has done or omitted, but by an oppressive moralism and air of apology."

Writing in 1970, Wills noted that this pattern was not unique to Richard Nixon, but had become "one of the permanent aspects of American politics" (p. 147). The image that Jim McGreevey chose to convey, like the convention rhetoric of Dick Cheney and John Kerry and the actions of countless politicians who rose to power after Richard Nixon, demonstrates the truth in Wills' observation.

III – The Rise to Power

In the green fields a turnin', a baby is born
His cries crease the wind and mingle with the morn
An assault upon the order, the changing of the guard
Chosen for a challenge that is hopelessly hard
And the only single sound is the sighing of the stars
But to the silence and distance they are sworn

So dance dance dance, teach us to be true
Come dance dance dance, 'cause we love you (Ochs)

Richard Nixon and Jim McGreevey followed similar paths to their leadership positions. Nixon earned degrees at Whittier College and Duke University Law School, and joined a law firm in his hometown of Whittier, California. He ran successfully for Congress in 1946, built a strong reputation for his efforts to fight Communism, and won election to the US Senate in 1950. Two years later, at the age of 39, he was elected vice president. He lost a close election for the presidency in 1960, but returned to win the nation's highest office in 1968.

McGreevey, with his Ivy League degrees in hand, began his career in modest public sectors jobs – as an assistant county prosecutor in Middlesex County, New Jersey, and later as a staff attorney for the New Jersey General Assembly, where he began to make the contacts and connections that would later form the foundation of his political career. At 28, he was appointed executive director of the New Jersey Parole Board. Two years later, he left the public sector to become an attorney and regional manager for Merck & Co. He entered politics in 1989, winning a hotly contested race for the State Assembly. Rather than seek reelection in 1991, he ran successfully for mayor of Woodbridge Township, where he had lived for over a decade. As a mayor (and later as a state senator), he built himself into a statewide figure and narrowly lost the New Jersey gubernatorial election in 1997. Like Nixon, he returned, winning the governorship four years later in 2001.

In describing the challenges he confronted in office, McGreevey frequently used a John F. Kennedy quote: "When we got into office, the thing that surprised me the most was that things were as bad as we'd been saying they were." Indeed, both he and Nixon were, as Ochs described, "chosen for a challenge that is hopelessly hard." Their challenges were not the obvious ones. For Nixon, it was not the challenge to unite a nation that was bitterly divided over the war in Vietnam. For McGreevey, it was not the unprecedented fiscal problems he inherited as he tried to restore confidence in state government. Instead, the greatest test they faced was to survive as leaders in a culture in which they were already doomed.

IV – The Fall from Power

Images of innocence charge him go on
But the decadence of destiny is looking for a pawn
To a nightmare of knowledge he opens up the gate
And a blinding revelation is laid upon his plate
That beneath the greatest love is a hurricane of hate
And God help the critic of the dawn.

So he stands on the sea and shouts to the shore,
But the louder that he screams the longer he's ignored
For the wine of oblivion is drunk to the dregs
And the merchants of the masses almost have to be begged
'Till the giant is aware, someone's pulling at his leg,
And someone is tapping at the door.

So dance dance dance, teach us to be true
Come dance dance dance, 'cause we love you (Ochs)

An explanation of the fate for which American heroes are destined can be found in Sigmund Freud's *Totem and Taboo*. Because of excessive restrictions placed on early royalty – such as when, where, and how long a king is allowed to stay in certain places – Freud contended that the honor of being a ruler ceased to be attractive: "There is no confidence that the ruler will use his tremendous power to the advantage of his subjects as well as for his own protection; he is therefore distrusted and surveillance over him is considered to be justified," he wrote (p. 65). As a result of these and other restrictions, societies sometimes had to force people – often outsiders – to become their leaders.

It is not difficult to view Nixon and McGreevey not only as outsiders, but also as individuals who were isolated within their own political parties. Political pow-erbrokers used Nixon and his strong conservative, anti-Communist ideology to balance the Republican presidential ticket in 1952 and heal the wounds of a party that had been shattered during the primary and the nomination process. But they were ready to drop him from the ticket when he became a potential liability. Even as vice president in the Eisenhower administration, Nixon was an outsider. There were parts of the White House he never saw until Lyndon Johnson gave him a tour during the 1968 presidential campaign. While President Dwight Eisenhower was making summit decisions, Nixon watched football games. Even when Nixon lobbied for a trip to Russia and then prepared extensively, he was undercut by the president – first by not even being told that negotiations were already under way to arrange for Soviet Premier Nikita Khrushchev to visit America, and then by Eisenhower's decision to publicly announce the Khrushchev visit while Nixon was still in Russia, sending a message to the world that the vice president's trip to the Soviet Union, like his role in the administration, was virtually meaningless. (Wills, pp. 124–126).

McGreevey became a statewide public figure with the support of New Jersey powerbrokers who used him when it was to their advantage to get what they wanted. However, their support was shallow. After nearly upsetting incumbent Governor Christine Whitman in 1997, McGreevey became the Democratic Party's presumptive candidate for 2001. But when it appeared that the governor's office was ripe for the party's taking, Democratic Senator Robert Torricelli, who was regarded as a close McGreevey ally, attempted a coup. With the gubernatorial election still more than a year away, Torricelli mounted an aggressive campaign to wrestle the support of New Jersey's Democratic powerbrokers and become the party's 2001 candidate. McGreevey, fighting for his political survival, beat back the challenge with a series of shrewd political maneuvers and his unparalleled around-the-clock work ethic. But the price he paid was great, as exemplified by the actions of Newark Mayor Sharpe James.

James was instrumental in providing McGreevey with the support he needed, and, when McGreevey became governor, he repaid the mayor's favor by pushing for state funding to build a sports arena in Newark. It was a project that had little public support outside of Newark, but James desperately needed it to win reelection in May. McGreevey announced his plan for state funding a few days before the election, and voters returned James to the mayor's office. But just one month later, the legislature balked at McGreevey's plan, infuriating James, who also was a state senator. With the end of New Jersey's fiscal year approaching, James then refused to vote for the Governor's budget and delayed adoption of the spending plan for a full day – creating the possibility of a shutdown of state government – until he received assurances that funds would be available for the arena.

Freud's commentary on the fickle manner in which earlier societies treated their rulers could easily have been written about Jim McGreevey and Richard Nixon: "His (the ruler's) life is only valuable so long as he discharges the duties of his position by ordering the course of nature for his people's benefit. So soon as he fails to do so, the care, the devotion, the religious homage which they had hitherto lavished on him cease and are changed into hatred and contempt; he is ignominiously dismissed and may be thankful if he escapes with his life. Worshipped as a god one day, he is killed as a criminal the next" (p. 60).

This was vividly illustrated by Jennifer Sands, a woman who asked McGreevey to write the forward for a book about coping with the loss of her husband, who died in the World Trade Center attacks. McGreevey agreed, and she was touched and appreciative. But when she read reports – all of which were attributed to anonymous sources – that McGreevey's resignation was tied to his decision to give a man with whom he had had an affair a state job as a homeland security advisor, she sang a different tune. "I don't want anyone to think, because his name appears on my book, that I in any way support him, his lifestyle or his deceit," she told the *Asbury Park Press* (Picard).

V – Fanning the Fires of Resentment

Then his message gathers meaning and it spreads across the land
The rewarding of his pain is the following of the man
But ignorance is everywhere and people have their way
Success is an enemy to the losers of the day
In the shadows of the churches, who knows what they pray
For blood is the language of the band.

The Spanish bulls are beaten; the crowd is soon beguiled,
The matador is beautiful, a symphony of style
Excitement is ecstatic, passion places bets
Gracefully he bows to ovations that he gets
But the hands that are applauding are slippery with sweat
And saliva is falling from their smiles

So dance dance dance, teach us to be true
Come dance dance dance, 'cause we love you (Ochs)

Not only are rulers outsiders, they frequently are individuals who are resented by society. "Their veneration, their very deification, is opposed in the unconscious by an intense hostile tendency," wrote Freud (p. 66). As an extreme example, he cited the savage Timmes of Sierra Leone, who "made it a rule to elect some man against whom they have a particular grudge" and routinely beat their elected king on the night before his coronation (p. 67).

America's leaders play right into this scenario. The "New Alignment for American Unity" that Nixon created for his 1968 presidential campaign was a coalition of people who supported the same principle for different motives. It included traditional Republicans, liberals, residents of the southern states, black militants, and a catchall group called the Silent Majority that allowed Nixon to claim he had the support of those who never vocalized an opinion. (Wills, pp. 68-69). "Nothing positive unites Nixon's five groups," wrote Wills (pp. 69-70). "Their common note is resentment of government, not only from different motives (as Nixon admits) but conflicting motives. Urged on, these resentments are bound to collide."

Similarly, McGreevey gained support by mobilizing people with strong opposition to various individuals, causes, and organizations. He held off Bob Torricelli's challenge not with fierce McGreevey loyalists, but with people who saw an advantage (usually personal) in keeping Torricelli out of the governor's office. A similar strategy helped McGreevey gain support of key county chairmen in 1997 to win the Democratic primary. Even his election as mayor of Woodbridge in 1991 was largely due to resentment (which he fanned) of the incumbent Democratic mayor, who was under indictment. "We ran as the unindicted Democrats," McGreevey would later joke when he recalled the campaign.

While resentment helps fuel the machines that bring individuals to power, it inevitably gets turned around and directed toward the leader. As Wills wrote, there is bound to be a collision among the different interests – something that Jim McGreevey discovered about the many constituencies that helped him get to the statehouse:

When the New Jersey State Council on the Arts named Amiri Baraka the State Poet Laureate, angry Jewish leaders demanded that McGreevey fire him, because he had written a controversial poem implying that Israel had advance knowledge of the September 11 terrorist attacks. Meanwhile, African American groups defended Baraka and urged the Governor to stick by him. Ironically, since the arts council had selected Baraka, McGreevey, as governor, had no power to remove him, just as he had had no role in his selection.

When McGreevey abandoned plans to nominate Zulima Farmer (a Hispanic) to the New Jersey Supreme Court because of revelations that she had a record of motor vehicle violations, missed court appearances, and unpaid fines, Hispanics were outraged and vowed revenge. Meanwhile, African American leaders made it clear they felt the governor was obligated to nominate a jurist of their race.

When a pro-Palestinian group planned a rally at Rutgers, The State University of New Jersey, Jewish leaders called upon McGreevey to cancel the event (even though he had no power to do so) while civil libertarians appealed to his sense of freedom of speech.

VI – Scapegoats

> *Then this overflow of life is crushed into a liar*
> *The gentle soul is ripped apart and tossed into the fire.*
> *First a smile of rejection at the nearness of the night*
> *Truth becomes a tragedy limping from the light*
> *All the heavens are horrified, they stagger from the sight*
> *As the cross is trembling with desire.*
>
> *They say they can't believe it, it's a sacrilegious shame*
> *Now, who would want to hurt such a hero of the game?*
> *But you know I predicted it; I knew he had to fall*
> *How did it happen? I hope his suffering was small.*
> *Tell me every detail, I've got to know it all,*
> *And do you have a picture of the pain?*
>
> *So dance dance dance, teach us to be true*
> *Come dance dance dance, 'cause we love you (Ochs)*

The public's resentment toward its leaders increases and evolves to a point in which the leaders become scapegoats who are blamed for all of society's ills. Nixon's downfall was the Watergate break-in and the subsequent cover-up, but he was blamed for many problems of the 1960s, including the war in Vietnam and the nation's faltering economy. Likewise, McGreevey was viewed as the cause of nearly all that was wrong in New Jersey. As Rene Girard wrote in *Violence and the Sacred*, in times of crisis, people spontaneously create a myth and a scapegoat such as Oedipus. "Oedipus is responsible for the ills that have befallen his people," Girard wrote. "He has become a prime example of the human scapegoat" (p. 77).

According to Girard, opposing groups resolve their differences by directing all of their anger toward the scapegoat, providing a means for the community to assign blame and free itself from responsibility. "Where only shortly before a thousand individual conflicts had raged unchecked between a thousand enemy brothers, there now reappears a true community, united in its hatred for one alone of its number," he explained. "All the rancors scattered at random among the divergent individuals, all the differing antagonisms now converge on an isolated and unique figure, the surrogate victim" (p. 79).

As the pattern continues, it becomes possible to blame the scapegoat even when there is no proof that the accusations are true. "The slightest hint, the most groundless accusation, can circulate with vertiginous speed and is transformed into irrefutable proof," Girard wrote. "The corporate sense of conviction snowballs, each member taking confidence from his neighbor by a rapid process of mimesis. The firm conviction of the group is based on no other evidence than the unshakable unanimity of its own logic" (p. 79).

Girard's theory is borne out by many of the accusations directed at McGreevey during his term as governor. That the McGreevey administration had its share of problems is indisputable, but as the governor's popularity decreased, Girard's words rang true as McGreevey became an easy target who was blamed for things that were not his fault:

- When Elizabeth Wong resigned as executive director of the New Jersey Higher Education Student Assistance Authority amid allegations of fiscal mismanagement, virtually every news outlet reported that Wong was the latest in a series of troubled McGreevey appointees. However, Wong actually was a holdover from the previous administration.

- In the wake of his resignation announcement, public anger grew over reports that McGreevey had placed an individual with whom he had a homosexual affair in charge of homeland security for the State, even though the identity of the individual was never confirmed by an on-the-record source, and his actual responsibilities for homeland security were far less than those reported and/or implied in media reports (Greenberg).

In stories chronicling McGreevey's downfall, several news organizations reported that he had used taxpayer money for a trip to Ireland, omitting the fact that he later reimbursed the state for the trip.

Even publications, as respected as *The New York Times*, were forced to issue corrections for stories that incorrectly said McGreevey was responsible for appointing controversial activist Amiri Baraka as Poet Laureate (an appointment made by the New Jersey State Council on the Arts), and that he had nominated

Zulima Farber for the Supreme Court and subsequently withdrawn the nomination when her motor vehicle problems came to light. (He actually never nominated her and had dropped her from consideration because of her driving record.)

Wills' narrative on the events that led to Nixon's "Checkers" speech also provides a vivid example of unfair accusations being leveled at a scapegoat. Nixon was nearly dropped from the Republican Party's 1952 presidential ticket when reports surfaced that a group of rich supporters was financing a secret fund that helped him live beyond his means. But the truth, as Wills explained, was that: "The fund was public, independently audited, earmarked for campaign expenses, and collected in small donations over two years by known Nixon campaign backers. It was neither illegal nor unethical. And the press soon discovered that the Democratic nominee, Adlai Stevenson, had similar funds, only larger in their amount and looser in their administration" (p. 95).

In the process of becoming scapegoats, leaders also lose credit for their accomplishments. Nixon will forever be remembered for Watergate, not for ending the war in Vietnam, eliminating the military draft, or opening relations with China. McGreevey is destined for a place in the history books as the nation's first openly gay governor, yet his term included major advances in education, the environment, and stem cell research.

VII – Conclusion

Time takes her toll and the memory fades
but his glory is broken, in the magic that he made.
Reality is ruined; it's the freeing from the fear
The drama is distorted, to what they want to hear
Swimming in their sorrow, in the twisting of a tear
As they wait for a new thrill parade.

The eyes of the rebel have been branded by the blind
To the safety of sterility, the threat has been refined
The child was created to the slaughterhouse he's led
So good to be alive when the eulogy is read
The climax of emotion, the worship of the dead
And the cycle of sacrifice unwinds.

So dance dance dance, teach us to be true
Come dance dance dance, 'cause we love you (Ochs)

Whether it is political leaders such as Richard Nixon and Jim McGreevey, celebrities such as Michael Jackson and Martha Stewart, or sports stars such as Pete Rose, America has a long and well-documented history of building up – and tearing down – its heroes. This is not a random cycle. It is a clear pattern in which American leaders accept the myth of the self-made person, fanning the fires of resentment that lead first to their downfalls and later to their becoming scapegoats for problems they did not create. It is a cycle that dates back to the world's earliest societies – and there is no sign of change on the way. Stories and images about the American Dream continue to fill the nation's newspapers and its airwaves, as well as its movie theaters and bookstores.

In spite of its propensity for building up and tearing down its leaders and heroes, America also is a nation of great redemption. Today, Bill Clinton is a popular and powerful individual, despite his extra-marital transgressions that led not only to embarrassing personal revelations, but also to his impeachment by the House of Representatives. Likewise, athletes, actors, and musicians have overcome drug use, criminal convictions, and assorted domestic problems to return to the tops of their respective fields.

In the years following his resignation, Richard Nixon worked hard to rehabilitate his public image. Although he ultimately earned respect as an elder statesman with great expertise and experience in foreign affairs, his legacy remained entwined with Watergate and his resignation. In his memoirs and in his interviews, Nixon failed to provide the type of apology Americans sought. Instead, he frequently wrote and spoke about how he felt persecuted by the media.

McGreevey, in an autobiography published two years after his resignation, could have chosen a similar approach. But rather than blame the media, he provides a detailed and graphic account of his struggles with his sexual identity as an explanation of the events that ultimately caused him to leave the governor's office less than three years into his first and only term.

Unfortunately, in a nation as large as ours, the majority of Americans can only form their opinions of public figures through media reports and second- and third-hand information. And the images they see often are impersonal. They saw Nixon, the president, and McGreevey, the governor, but not Nixon or McGreevey, the person.

A speechwriter who once worked for a member of the Kennedy family told me he came to view Kennedy jokes in a completely different light after he started the job. The jokes do not seem funny when you work day-in and day-out with someone who knows the Kennedys as uncles and cousins — not as the punch lines of tasteless jokes or the targets of bitter personal attacks.

As public figures, Richard Nixon and Jim McGreevey have been – and will continue to be – judged by their colleagues, the press, and the men and women they represented. But in the finite time we spend on this planet and with our nation becoming increasingly polarized, there are lessons to be learned from the personal stories of Richard Nixon, Jim McGreevey, and the many others who have risen to the top only to fall from power.

Clearly, all America's fallen heroes are not innocent victims. In many cases, it was their actions that contributed to and made possible their downfalls. To effect change, America will need different types of leaders – individuals with true honesty and integrity who gain society's trust and support because of who they are, not who they pretend to be. This new breed of leaders cannot emerge until all segments of society (the rulers and the ruled) begin to grasp the damage that has been caused by years and years of the "hero killing" cycle that Phil Ochs described in "Crucifixion."

> *And the night comes again to the circle studded sky*
> *The stars settle slowly, in loneliness they lie*
> *'Till the universe explodes as a falling star is raised*
> *Planets are paralyzed, mountains are amazed*
> *But they all glow brighter from the brilliance of the blaze*
> *With the speed of insanity, then he died (Ochs).*

Notes

[1] This information and much of what follows on the career of James E. McGreevey is based on personal conversations, observations, and recollections from the past 20 years. These occurred while I was a reporter covering his early civic and political activities (1984 to 1989), a staff member of the New Jersey General Assembly while he was a state assemblyman (1990 to 1992), Public Information Officer of Woodbridge Township when he was the community's mayor (1992 to 2002), and Deputy Director of Communications during his term as governor (2002 to 2004).

References

Barthes, Roland. *Mythologies*. New York: Hill and Wang, 1957.

Collins, Chuck and Mike Lapham and Scott Klinger. "I Didn't Do It Alone: Society's Contribution to Individual Wealth and Success." *Responsible Wealth: A Project of United for a Fair Economy*. August 2004. <http://www.responsiblewealth.org/press/2004/notalonereportfinal.pdf>.

"Corrections." *New York Times*. August 27, 2004, A2.

Freud, Sigmund. *Totem and Taboo*. New York: Dodd, Mead & Company, Inc., 1918.

Girard, Rene. *Violence and the Sacred*. Baltimore: Johns Hopkins University Press, 1977.

Greenberg, Eric. "Aide's security post disputed." *Forward*. October 4, 2004. <http://www.forward.com/main/article.php?ref=greenberg20040819119.>.

Ochs, Phil. "Crucifixion." Lyrics. *Pleasures of the Harbor.* A&M Records, 1967.

Picard, Joseph. "9/11 kin: Gov made a mistake." *Asbury Park Press.* September 10, 2003, A1.

Wills, Garry. *Nixon Agonistes. The Crisis of the Self-Made Man.* Boston: Houghton Mifflin Company, 1970.

CHAPTER FIFTEEN

Frank Sinatra and the Moods of America

By
Michael P. Riccards

For more than two generations of Americans, Frank Sinatra was a highly visible celebrity and artist--far outlasting any other entertainer in U.S. history. In a recent poll for the New Jersey Hall of Fame in 2007, he was one of the first nominees. This essay seeks to explain Sinatra's longevity as a performer and the reasons why he was so successful throughout a very tumultuous era. New York disc jockey William B. Williams judged that Sinatra was "the most imitated, most listened to, most recognized voice of the second half of the twentieth century."

His voice was transmitted to the Apollo 12 astronauts, and is on more than 200 recordings that remain in production after his death. What made his longevity all the more remarkable was that Sinatra continued to be an evolving artist throughout his career. He was not simply a celebrity, such as Elizabeth Taylor, who has not had a major film part for decades, but rather he remained a practicing performer in the public eye. The key to Sinatra's success was, in part, that he was not an original artist, patenting new styles or new artistic byways, except in the introduction of "concept albums." He was a derivative entertainer, who, in some cases, fine-tuned acceptable venues, and did so with a nearly flawless sense of the moods of America.

Public Music

Frank Sinatra said it best—he was heavily influenced by the early, popular crooner, Bing Crosby. He once observed, "Every time Bing sang, it was a duet, and you were the other singer." Crosby, in turn, was compared to the romantic Italian-American baritone, Russ Columbo, whose life was prematurely cut short in a tragic accident, and who was an inspiration to other singers, including the great tenor Mario Lanza.

As the young Sinatra performed in roadhouses, saloons, and clubs, he was surrounded by other balladeers, who stood in front of assorted bands. What is of interest is that Sinatra was seen, almost immediately, as possessing some special quality that separated him from his prospective competitors, except for Crosby. Sinatra quickly recognized that the crooner style was only of limited utility, and that it would take him only so far. In fact, Sinatra's later comrade-in-arms, Dean Martin, would better epitomize that warbling style.

When Sinatra moved from a New Jersey roadhouse called the Rustic Cabin, near New York City, he first joined the Harry James and then the Tommy Dorsey Bands. The big bands of the swing era brought music to the public in ways that had never occurred before. Previously, the major opportunities for people to listen to music were in churches and in band concerts, such as those in the John Philip Sousa tradition. The big bands were the descendants of those uplifting, public concerts in the park celebrating patriotism and the ease of summer days.

Sinatra was not content to be an appendage of bands; he was the star, center stage, almost immediately. He did not rest on his youthful successes, but insisted on learning the disguised techniques of trombone players, who seemed to be able to carry notes longer than one would expect—eight, ten, or even sixteen bars.

He exercised, swimming and building up his slight physique to develop stronger lung capacity. But Sinatra learned another lesson, when Tommy Dorsey showed him how he played the trombone and was able to suck in additional air, unnoticed. It was a trick that only a fine musician could master. It was surely harder for a singer to adopt such a technique, but Sinatra was young and bold enough to try it out. That ability, plus his remarkable sense of timing and syntax, explained the early Sinatra style.

The way he alternated pausing and extension gave Sinatra the ability to do more than simply sing a song. It gave him the opportunity to tell a story in music. Other singers with much stronger voices did well expressing the harmonies of early twentieth century music, whether it was the classic tones of Victor Herbert, the robust tunes of Irving Berlin, or the celebrated lyrics of Ira Gershwin and Cole Porter. Sinatra could take some of those favorites and merge them with seemingly familiar stories, usually telling tales of romance.

He and his counterparts also reworked melodies from previous years. The American people in the 1930s received most of their music via the radio, and they knew many of the easy melodies that were in the repertoires of Crosby, Gene Austin, Rudy Vallee, Ray Eberly, and, later, Perry Como, Tony Bennett, Dean Martin, Frankie Laine, and others. But Sinatra took those tunes and turned them into personal monuments of self-revelation. Once, someone observed that people made love to Sinatra's songs, and asked him what music he made love to? Sinatra responded, on one occasion, that it was to his own music also. On another occasion, he named Tony Bennett. From any other person, it would have sounded presumptuous, but, for Sinatra, it seemed personal and true.

In 1930, the legendary Rudy Vallee tossed away his megaphone, an instrument that Sinatra used briefly, for the more sensitive microphone. The microphone lent a sense of intimacy and articulation to popular singing, and helped replace the loud sounds of such vocalists as Al Jolson and Sophie Tucker. Soon the bass replaced the tuba, and the rhythm guitar, the banjo.

Sinatra was an ambitious and shrewd artist, who did some radio early on. He was a populist entertainer, who could make fun of Cole Porter's elegant lyrics while still embracing his songs. Sinatra came from a lower-middle-class, Italian-American family from Hoboken, New Jersey, a city he later characterized as a "sewer." However, he confessed, "When I was there, I just wanted to get the hell out. It took me a long time to realize how much of it I took with me." His mother was a Democratic Party ward leader, a part-time abortionist, and a strong-willed figure who often wearied her only child. He dreamt of the big city across the river, and insisted to his friends that he could do what Crosby did.

She and he were liberals in the 1930s, admirers of Franklin Delano Roosevelt, when it was easy to follow that path. Sinatra continued that liberal commitment, especially regarding race relations, all of his life. Entertainment, like athletics and crime, is a real equal opportunity profession, and Sinatra never wavered from his commitment to social justice. He had bitter fights with the media and a string of bad marriages, but Sinatra established a reputation as a man of great philanthropy. When one of his daughters remarked that a person "looked Jewish," Sinatra snapped back at her for using a stereotype. Thus, the skinny Hoboken kid became a sort of democratic everyman. Once he observed about his alleged ties to criminals, "If what you do is honest, and you make it, you're a hero. If what you do is crooked, and you make it, you're a bum. Me—I grabbed a song."

Although his own voice, even in the early years, was not strong or powerful or broad in its range, Sinatra was an avid fan of the great opera singers. Unbeknownst to most people, Sinatra was heavily influenced by the techniques and traditions of grand opera. He was, for example, an admirer of the power of Luciano Pavarotti and many other great singers of a more structured art form than he had ever practiced.

The young Sinatra appears in photos as a slight, wide-eyed artist with large ears, but, in his early years, he became a teenage heartthrob. Once again, the phenomenon was not new. Another Italian-American, Rudolph Valentino, had sent women swooning with his dashing good looks and the exotic story lines of his films. Sinatra was not exotic, but he did preside over, if not encourage, the growth of the hysteria called the bobby-soxers. There had been screaming females at concerts before, of course, and a dozen of the girls at his Paramount Theatre appearance on December 30, 1942, were supposedly hired to add to that effect. But the overwhelming reaction to his concerts began to take on a cult-like significance, unmatched until the appearance of Elvis Presley and the Beatles. Commentators called it a form of mass hysteria, but it was much more complicated.

The United States in the 1930s and early 1940s was a provincial, dreary nation preoccupied with the Great Depression and about to enter into another world war. Sinatra was an intense reprieve. He projected a mild form of eroticism for the girls back home or for those seeking to escape from the tired young men who had bedded and wedded them. Sinatra was able to verify that there was a world of romance, of love stories, a time when the young still believed in fantasy as a way of life and as an escape. The huge Hollywood dream factories flourished in such an environment, because the fierce competition of television was not around. Hollywood enticed Americans into the dark world of stilted, drawing room comedies with highly charged dialogues, into garish, flashing musicals where beautiful women dressed as silver dollars or statues of liberty, or into authentic social dramas lamenting the plight of the Okies or the presence of a corrupt political order.

Sinatra fit into the élan of those times, but the story that he told was becoming even more his own. Ronald Colman, Spencer Tracy, and Humphrey Bogart moved from one role to another, and, in the end, they did create public personae. Sinatra, almost immediately, became a celebrity with his own presence. And, remarkably, he did it not the easy way on the silver screen, but by holding a microphone and filling in the blank spaces of people's imaginations.

More than any other performer, Sinatra's development at this time was also aided by the new techniques of amplification and recording. He understood the need to touch, to reach, and to captivate his audience. It was said that he held a microphone as if he were courting a woman. "I discovered very early that my instrument wasn't my voice, it was the microphone," Sinatra insisted. "An audience is like a broad. If you're indifferent, endsville." He was not just a vocalist, but also a person who told a romantic story in music.

He married the girl next door, and still enjoyed the favors of other females. His marriage, a child, and a perforated eardrum saved him from military service during the war, and so, in 1943, Frank Sinatra firmed up his position as America's premier vocalist, eclipsing, for a while, even his one-time role model, Bing Crosby.

As the Depression and the war ended, prosperity set in. More people had radios, and many more began to invest in phonographs. In 1938, one-half of all radio broadcasts were popular music. In 1933, there were 25,000 jukeboxes in the United States, but, by 1939, there were 225,000, and, by 1942, the number jumped to 400,000. Car radios were introduced in 1923, and became standard equipment by 1934. Record sales dropped to $5.5 million during the Depression, but, by 1940, sales hit $48.4 million, and, five years later, sales jumped to $109 million. In 1940, Muzak had become a part of modern American life in many offices and factories. By the 1950s, there was an increased use of syncopation, high fidelity, and the long-playing record technology—all of which supported the presentation of Sinatra's work. Sinatra was now available upon request, available whenever America felt in the mood. Following Crosby, Sinatra began to appear in the movies—even dancing with the agile Gene Kelly. Unlike the heartthrobs of films in the past, Sinatra was a sex symbol, who was nonthreatening to women. He had neither the dark side of Errol Flynn nor the suave sensuality of Robert Taylor or Ronald Colman. He was not a good character actor like Tracy or, Bogart, but was a friendly and recognizable performer.

Thus, by the late 1940s and early 1950s, Sinatra was a pleasant diversion for Americans. He could command a scene, dance respectably well, and look pleasant. Above all, he could reach out to an audience in the most intimate ways. The screen, the radio, and the phonograph spread the fame of the former saloon singer. What propelled Sinatra so far, though, was his fierce ambition, his perfectionism and professionalism, and his ability to gauge with almost Geiger counter accuracy the moods of post-war America.

The Dark Nights

After the Great Depression and the brutalities of war, Americans turned to making money, raising children, and creating a comfortable, materialistic life. In the 1960s, social commentators would express their disgust at the hedonism and self-centeredness of that generation. But their judgment overlooks the enormous sacrifices made; later more balanced historians would praise that time as "the heroic generation" of America.

As America paid homage, in public, to the values of family life, increasing strains began to be obvious. Without seeking to emulate his fellow countrymen, Sinatra experienced the traumatic unraveling of his own marriage. He had fallen for the tempestuous Ava Gardner, whose film career was far outpacing his modest efforts. They married in 1951, and were divorced eleven months later. Sinatra co-authored and recorded a song, "I Am a Fool to Want You," perhaps as a response to that breakup. It was said that he made the record in one take, and then walked out of the studio and into the night. As for Ava Gardner, she astutely observed, "The ability to flirt with the entire audience is one of Frank's primary gifts as a performer." Nelson Riddle, his artistic companion, however, maintained, "It was Ava who taught him to sing a torch song. She taught him the hard way." Like his fellow Italian-American friend, Joe DiMaggio, he had fallen for another celebrity—women of such beauty that the gods seemed to drive both men to near madness.

During this period of postwar success and strains, Sinatra ruptured his vocal cords. The consummate artist, whose words seemed like velvet, was, literally, speechless. And most disappointing to him was the quick evaporation of his so-called friends. Sinatra, who prized personal loyalty, could, at times, be a difficult person, one who made enemies and friends easily. His quick temper, suspicion of the media, and prickly behavior took their toll. Between 1949 and 1952, he lost his long-term film contract with MGM, had his television show canceled, was shunned by Universal Studios, and was dropped by his agent. By the early 1950s, Frank Sinatra's career was seemingly over. He had peaked and now seemed ready to extinguish himself.

Ironically, it was Ava Gardner's intercession that helped him land a part in a movie that re-established the 38 year-old Frank Sinatra as a major performer. He emerged in the forefront in movies, not in music. The character he played, Angelo Maggio, in *From Here to Eternity,* was a street-savvy kid eventually consumed by the fast life. Sinatra candidly noted once that he regarded the story as somewhat autobiographical. "I might have been Maggio," he observed. He received a mere $8,000 for the part.

As Holden Caulfield showed in J. D. Salinger's novel, *Catcher in the Rye,* published in 1951, Americans would become preoccupied with the need to be authentic, and not to be "a phony." Even to his enemies, Frank Sinatra was never a phony. He explained in one interview, "When I sing, I believe, I'm honest." That film part won him an Academy Award, and Sinatra became, in entertainment circles, a man resurrected—epitomizing the ups and downs of corporate life and uncomfortable domesticity. The American people were also beginning to feel the anxieties that were impinging on Sinatra's life. When he said he had been "up and down" in one of his ballads, he did more than sing a song. Frank Sinatra was once again giving the nation a tune that rang true.

As he talked about the uncertainties of love, the lingering sting of passions, or the difficulty of creating lasting relationships once characterized by romance, he seemed to reach into the souls of his audience. Sinatra sang the song, told the story so well, because he had lived the life.

The Second Time Around

The new Sinatra began the 1950s with the need to make money, overcome his sense of personal vulnerability, and bond with other males in an increasingly adolescent environment. He went on to form his own record companies, to deal with production problems, and to appear in a series of rather undistinguished films. Those films established him as a respectable drawing card, but they did not become the body of work that would mark him in the way it did his friend and hero, Humphrey Bogart.

His record companies, though, provided him with income so that he would never feel as vulnerable as he did during his down periods. Equally important, it reaffirmed his control over his own work. A partnership with arranger Nelson Riddle, starting in 1953, led to a remarkable blossoming of Frank Sinatra's balladeer style. He took his legendary unpleasantness and turned it, in 1969, into a reaffirmation of doing things "My Way." The public loved the song, for it asserted the American appreciation of individual freedom in an increasingly bureaucratic world of frightening careerists.

Most of all, America's mood was somewhat upbeat with John F. Kennedy's election in 1960. Sinatra shared Kennedy's dreams, socialized with some of the same people, and accepted his liberal agenda. But that world was quickly over, and all that remained were memories and his adolescent "Rat Pack"— entertainers who seemed more interested in jabbing each other on stage than in reaching the audience. Why Sinatra, with his great sense of unity with his fans, did the Las Vegas routine is unclear. He was called the Chairman of the Board at that time, but he was simply bored.

The overall theme of the new Sinatra, which his friends and many critics commented on, was his personal loneliness. Journalist Pete Hamill concluded that Sinatra "understood loneliness better than any other person of his generation. I mean a certain kind of urban loneliness." The singer called himself a manic-depressive, living a life of "violent emotional contradictions. I have an overactive capacity for sadness, as well as elation." Even after four wives and with the intrusions of his mother until late into his life, Sinatra seemed to be the solitary man who was unable to sleep, drank too much, and remembered until dawn came. He explained, "I'm for whatever gets you through the night." His friends, Martin, Como, and Bennett, could still sing the songs, but Sinatra became the very epitome of what he vocalized.

Usually artists transform themselves into celebrities, and, as their style goes out of fashion, they do too. But Sinatra did not retire until age 79, and he was able to redefine his art form because he lived such an ambiguous life. America, which came to regard marriage often as a temporary arrangement, would understand; in a man's world," people that were bored with responsibilities could relate to the pugnacious, solitary artist. Like John Keats, he began to live his own poetry.

The late 1950s and 1960s also lent themselves to a new style of music that was alien to Sinatra, and he deeply resented it at first, calling rock and roll "a rancid-smelling aphrodisiac." Elvis Presley, Little Richard, and others took the pulsating rhythms of black music and married them with white country tunes. Presley was more consciously sexual and not just sensual. He did not court the microphone, he seemed to mate with it. The new generation's moods were different, although Sinatra continued to star in more films, produce more albums, and do a little television--the latter never his real medium.

In the 1960s and 1970s, Sinatra returned from retirement, performing regularly until 1979. He went back to the concert halls and the public arenas. His performances were almost sold out as he became an even greater celebrity. He was awarded and feted and treated as an American icon. As he aged, he continued to do what he once did best—sing. And he sang the favorites that two generations now knew. Remarkably, he arranged and sang in the early 1990s the *Duets* albums with such contemporary artists as Barbra Streisand, Jimmy Buffet, Carly Simon, Stevie Wonder, Gloria Estéfan, Liza Minnelli, and Bono of U2.

He stopped performing when the ravages of age began to become too obvious. At his last couple of concerts, the great stylist could not remember the words to songs he had once made famous.

Summary

Frank Sinatra's career was an extraordinary Horatio Alger story. In the past, much of America's music was the province of the wealthy classes who could afford tickets to public music events. Radio, the phonograph, films, and television democratized American culture. And, in each, Sinatra did not pioneer a presence, but he skillfully exploited it. In the last several years, he even took the songs of the 1990s and matched them with his own voice. It was a rather startling synthesis. It showed that he knew that the artists were doing what he had done, only much longer.

Sinatra had helped to redefine popular culture and was a consummate professional in his use of the new technologies of recording and distribution. He could perform on film, talk on television, and be successful as a businessman. He could socialize with presidents, mob figures, and agents. But when all of those associations were over and done with, Sinatra came away with an unfailing sense of the popular sentiment.

He not only caught the sentiment, he helped to shape it and give it form, to embolden and define it. He reminded us of the seasons of a man's life, of the excitement of first love, of the strange associations between nature and passions. The great romantic poets would have understood his themes, his pauses, and his hesitations. One of his songs concludes, "Since love is gone/can't pull myself together/ guess I'll hang my tears out to dry."

As America went through a tumultuous transformation to a national culture with an international role, Sinatra could celebrate the old times, the good times, the bittersweet times. In a sense, he was a vocalist of remembrance of things past.

Beyond all of that, Sinatra's real world was the music, passed on for as long as we wish. In that world that he created, we came to see the dark nights, the fleeting days, and the awful loneliness that are too often the plight of modern man. Thus, Sinatra was able to capture, throughout his long career, the moods of America, even before we knew we were experiencing them.

This essay is based on a paper given at a professional conference titled "Frank Sinatra: The Man, The Music, The Legend" at Hofstra University, November 12-14, 1998.

References

Boorstin, Daniel J. *The Image: A Guide to Pseudo-Events in America.* New York: Harper & Row, 1964.

Clarke, Donald. *All or Nothing at All: A Life of Frank Sinatra.* New York: Fromm International, 1997.

Friedwald, Will. *Sinatra! The Song Is You: A Singer's Art.* New York: Scribner, 1995.

Hamill, Pete, *Why Sinatra Matters.* Boston: Little, Brown, and Co., 1998.

Kelley, Kitty. *His Way: The Unauthorized Biography of Frank Sinatra.* New York: Bantam, 1986.

Lahr, John. "Sinatra's Song," *New Yorker,* November 3, 1997, p. 76+.

Lahr, John. *Sinatra: The Artist and the Man.* New York: Random House, 1997.

Sinatra, Nancy. *Frank Sinatra: An American Legend.* Santa Monica, California: General Publishing Group, 1995.

Taraborrelli, J. Randy. *Sinatra: Behind the Legend.* Secaucus, New Jersey: Carol Publishing Group, 1997.

Tosches, Nick. *Dino: Living High in the Dirty Business of Dreams.* New York: Dell, 1992.

Zehme, Bill. *The Way You Wear Your Hat: Frank Sinatra and the Lost Art of Livin'.* New York: Random House, 1997.